**David Fox and Roman Verhosek**

D1142436

# Micro Java
# Game
# Development

✦Addison-Wesley

Boston • San Francisco • New York • Toronto • Montreal
London • Munich • Paris • Madrid •
Capetown • Sydney • Tokyo • Singapore • Mexico City

## Micro Java Game Development

Many of the designations used by manufacturers and sellers to distinguish their products are claimed as trademarks. Where those designations appear in this book and Addison-Wesley was aware of a trademark claim, the designations have been printed in initial capital letters or in all capitals.

The author and publisher have taken care in the preparation of this book, but make no expressed or implied warranty of any kind and assume no responsibility for errors or omissions. No liability is assumed for incidental or consequential damages in connection with or arising out of the use of the information or programs contained herein.

The publisher offers discounts on this book when ordered in quantity for special sales.

For more information, please contact:
Pearson Education Corporate Sales Division
201 W. 103rd Street
Indianapolis, IN 46290
(800) 428-5331
corpsales@pearsoned.com

Visit AW on the Web: www.awl.com/cseng/

Copyright © 2002 by Pearson Education

All rights reserved. No part of this publication may be reproduced, stored in a retrieval system, or transmitted, in any form or by any means, electronic, mechanical, photocopying, recording, or otherwise, without the prior consent of the publisher. Printed in the United States of America. Published simultaneously in Canada.

ISBN **0-672-32342-7**

05   04   03   02       4   3   2   1

First printing, **April 2002**

## Trademarks

All terms mentioned in this book that are known to be trademarks or service marks have been appropriately capitalized. Addison-Wesley cannot attest to the accuracy of this information. Use of a term in this book should not be regarded as affecting the validity of any trademark or service mark.

## Warning and Disclaimer

Every effort has been made to make this book as complete and as accurate as possible, but no warranty or fitness is implied. The information provided is on an "as is" basis.

**Associate Publisher**
Rochelle J. Kronzek

**Acquisitions Editor**
Carol Ackerman

**Development Editor**
Bryan Morgan

**Managing Editor**
Matt Purcell

**Project Editor**
George E. Nedeff

**Copy Editor**
Seth Kerney

**Indexers**
Ginny Bess
Sharon Shock

**Proofreader**
Harvey Stanbrough

**Technical Editor**
Bryan Morgan

**Team Coordinator**
Denni Bannister

**Interior Designer**
Anne Jones

**Cover Designer**
Aren Howell

**Page Layout**
Michelle Mitchell

# Contents at a Glance

**1** Introduction (or Everything I Wanted to Know About Micro Java Gaming But Was Afraid to Ask)................................................1

**I** **Small Devices** **23**

**2** The Mobile World................................................25

**3** Big Games, Small Screens................................................49

**II** **Before, Between, and Beyond J2ME** **83**

**4** Wireless Standards: How Data Goes To and Fro................................85

**5** Let's Talk: Instant Wireless Messaging................................121

**6** Wireless in Asia: i-mode and cHTML................................135

**7** The Wireless Landscape................................................147

**III** **The Java 2 Micro Edition** **161**

**8** J2ME Overview................................................163

**9** Creating a MIDlet................................................175

**10** Making the Most of Limited Resources................................201

**11** Making the Most of It: Optimizations................................209

**12** Multithreaded Game Programming................................225

**IV** **Let the Games Begin!** **239**

**13** High-Level Graphical User Interfaces................................241

**14** Working with Graphics: Low-Level Graphical User Interfaces................259

**15** Entering the Land of Sprites................................................277

**16** Managing Your Sprites................................................295

**17** Sprite Movement................................................307

**18** J2ME Audio Basics................................................325

**19** Be Persistent: MIDP Data Storage................................329

**20** Connecting Out: Wireless Networking................................349

| V | **J2ME Extensions** | **393** |
|---|---|---|
| 21 | PersonalJava, Connected Device Configuration, and Other Micro Java Blends...................................................................................395 | |
| 22 | iAppli: Micro Java with a Twist...............................................................407 | |
| 23 | Siemens Game API...................................................................................429 | |
| | | |
| **VI** | **Micro Racer** | **451** |
| 24 | Micro Racer: Putting It All Together .......................................................453 | |
| | | |
| **VII** | **Appendixes** | **479** |
| A | Low-Level GUI Classes................................................................................481 | |
| B | MIDP 1.1 ....................................................................................................493 | |
| C | Siemens Game API....................................................................................499 | |
| D | The iAppli API...........................................................................................505 | |
| | Index ..........................................................................................................511 | |

# Table of Contents

**1**  **Introduction (or Everything I Wanted to Know About Micro Java Gaming But Was Afraid to Ask)**  **1**

A New Era of Gaming ...................................................................................1

   A Brief History of Games ......................................................................1

   Multiplayer Mania .................................................................................2

   Micro Devices, Micro Lifestyles ...........................................................3

   Enter Micro Java ...................................................................................3

This Book's Mission ....................................................................................4

   The Game Plan .....................................................................................4

A Bit About Game Design ...........................................................................7

   The Game Design Process .....................................................................8

   Preproduction .......................................................................................8

   Prototyping ..........................................................................................17

   Programming .......................................................................................18

   Playtesting ...........................................................................................19

Show Me the Money: Micro Game Business Models ..............................20

   The Business Outlook .........................................................................20

   Advertising and Sponsorships .............................................................20

   Content Deals ......................................................................................21

   Pay-For-Play or Subscription ..............................................................22

Summary ...................................................................................................22

**Part I**  **Small Devices**  **23**

**2**  **The Mobile World**  **25**

A New Era of Gaming .................................................................................25

   Micro Devices ......................................................................................25

   The Micro Revolution Begins ..............................................................26

High-End Java Devices: Set-Top Boxes, Phones, Consoles ......................28

   PersonalJava .......................................................................................28

   JavaTV .................................................................................................30

   JavaPhone ............................................................................................30

   PingTel xpressa Phone ........................................................................30

   Sharp NC-10 IP Phone .......................................................................31

Personal Digital Assistants (PDAs) ..................................................31
    J2ME PDA Profile ..........................................................31
    PalmOS ...............................................................................32
    Microsoft Windows CE ...................................................33
    Symbian EPOC .................................................................34
    Sharp Zaurus SL-5000 ...................................................35
    URL: http://developer.sharpsec.com/ ......................35
    Other Linux Handhelds ...............................................35
    Micro Java Virtual Machines .......................................35
Mobile Phones and Pagers ...........................................................38
    Casio CdmaOne C452CA .............................................38
    Ericsson R380 .................................................................39
    Fujitsu F503i ...................................................................39
    Hitachi CdmaOne C451H .............................................39
    LG Telecom p510 (i-Book) ..........................................39
    Other LG Telecom Phones ...........................................40
    Matsushita/Panasonic P503i ........................................40
    Matsushita/Panasonic P503iS ......................................40
    Matsushita/Panasonic FOMA P2101V .......................40
    Mitsubishi D503i and D503iS ......................................41
    Mitsubishi J-D05 .............................................................41
    Motorola i85s ..................................................................41
    Motorola i50sx ................................................................42
    Motorola Accompli 009 PIC ........................................42
    Motorola, Accompli 008/6288 ....................................43
    Other Motorola Phones ................................................44
    NEC N503i ......................................................................44
    NEC FOMA N2001 ........................................................44
    Nokia 9210 and 9290 Communicator ........................44
    RIM/iPaq Blackberry .....................................................45
    Samsung SCH-X130, SCH-X230, SCH-X350, and SCH-X350 ........46
    Sharp J-SH07 ..................................................................46
    Siemens SL45i (or 6688i) .............................................46
    Sony SO503i .....................................................................47
    Toshiba J-T06 .................................................................47
Low-End Java Devices: Smart Cards and Embedded Chips ....................47
    JavaCard ..........................................................................48
    EmbeddedJava ................................................................48
Summary ..........................................................................................48

**3   Big Games, Small Screens                                      49**

Your Competition ...................................................................49
    Things to Look For ........................................................50
    The Near Future ...........................................................50
WAP Games ......................................................................51
    Wireless Games ...........................................................51
    Jamdat ....................................................................55
    PicoFun ...................................................................56
    Handy Games ..............................................................57
    FunCaster.com .............................................................59
    Unplugged Games ..........................................................59
    nGame .....................................................................60
i-mode Games ....................................................................62
    Dwango's Turibaka Kibun ................................................62
SMS Games .......................................................................63
    Fisupeli ...................................................................63
    Blue Factory ..............................................................63
    BotFighters by It's Alive ................................................64
    Vizzavi Footie and Trivia .................................................65
J2ME MIDP Games ................................................................65
    Karl Hörnell's MIDPman ..................................................65
    HolyCowBoy's BlockBuster and HolyMoley .............................66
    Draw Poker ................................................................67
    Cocoasoft .................................................................67
    RomeBlack's Mobile Internet Maze Game .............................69
    Sky Arts' Cube Game ....................................................70
    Jshape's M-Type and MIDP Street Fighter ............................70
    Spruce Team ..............................................................71
    Red Team's Dope Wars ..................................................71
J2ME Palm Games ...............................................................72
    Torunda! ..................................................................72
    Karl Hörnell's Iceblox and PalmWarp ..................................73
    Hobbit's Let Me Alone ...................................................73
iAppli Games ....................................................................74
    Squiral Game ..............................................................75
    Dwango's Samurai Romanesque .........................................75
    Dwango's Challenge! The Hard-Boiled Way ............................76
    Sega .......................................................................78
    Namco .....................................................................78

Capcom .......................................................................................79
Bandai Networks .......................................................................79
Cybird's Mini Game Tengoku .................................................79
Hudson Soft .............................................................................81
What Are You Waiting For? ..........................................................81

**Part II     Before, Between, and Beyond J2ME                            83**

**4     Wireless Standards: How Data Goes To And Fro               85**

Wireless Networks .......................................................................85
First Generation (1G) ...............................................................86
Second Generation (2G) ..........................................................86
Second (and a Half) Generation (2.5G) ..................................87
Third Generation (3G) .............................................................87
The Wireless Application Protocol (WAP) ...................................88
The WAP Protocol Stack ..........................................................89
WAP Architecture .....................................................................89
The Wireless Markup Language (WML) ...................................91
WMLScript .............................................................................105
Server-Side WAP ........................................................................108
Server Configuration .............................................................108
WAP and Java .........................................................................109
Development Environment ....................................................113
Handheld Device Markup Language (HDML) ...........................115
HDML Syntax .........................................................................116
Displays ..................................................................................116
Activities .................................................................................116
Actions ...................................................................................117
Hyperlinks ..............................................................................118
Images ....................................................................................118
WAP 2.0 and xHTML Basic .......................................................118
Summary ....................................................................................119

**5     Let's Talk: Instant Wireless Messaging                      121**

Messaging And Gaming .............................................................122
Short Message Service (SMS) ....................................................122
SMS Specifics ..........................................................................123
Short Message Service Centers (SMSCs) ...............................125
Free SMS Service ....................................................................125

Actually Sending SMS Messages ............................................... 127

    SMS Tools .............................................................................. 128

SMS and J2ME ....................................................................... 128

    Sample Server Code ............................................................. 129

Multimedia Messaging Service (MMS) ................................... 130

    Multimedia Message Service Centers (MMSC) ..................... 131

    Crack a SMIL ....................................................................... 131

    Simple SMIL Example ......................................................... 132

    Enhanced Messaging Service (EMS) .................................... 133

Summary ................................................................................ 134

**6    Wireless in Asia: i-mode and cHTML        135**

Using i-mode ......................................................................... 135

Compact HTML (cHTML) ....................................................... 136

    Character Sets ...................................................................... 137

    Emoji .................................................................................... 137

    cHTML Structure ................................................................. 138

    Standard cHTML Tags ......................................................... 139

    Input Forms ......................................................................... 140

    The Anchor Tag ................................................................... 142

    Images .................................................................................. 143

    <MARQUEE> ........................................................................ 144

Development Tools ................................................................ 144

Testing and Emulators .......................................................... 144

Summary ................................................................................ 146

**7    The Wireless Landscape        147**

Bluetooth ............................................................................... 147

    Bluetooth Protocols ............................................................ 149

    Bluetooth and Java ............................................................. 149

    Other Short-Range Applications ......................................... 149

    Broadband's Promise .......................................................... 150

Mobile Positioning ................................................................ 150

    How It All Works ................................................................. 150

    Forums and Associations .................................................... 151

    Privacy ................................................................................. 152

    Positioning Technologies .................................................... 152

m-Commerce ......................................................................155
    Charging for Content ....................................................156
    Micro Java and Money ...................................................156
Voice and Telephony ..........................................................157
    VoiceXML ...................................................................157
    VoiceXML Software .......................................................158
    Wireless Telephony Application Interface (WTAI) .................158
Unified Messaging (UM) .....................................................158
Summary ..........................................................................159

**Part III    The Java 2 Micro Edition                                    161**

**8    J2ME Overview                                                      163**

The Trinity of Java Platforms ...............................................163
It's a Small World After All .................................................165
    Using Java on Small Devices ...........................................165
    J2ME Rocks! ...............................................................165
Profiles and Configurations ................................................166
    Major J2ME Configurations ............................................166
    J2ME Profiles ..............................................................167
    The Kilobyte Virtual Machine ..........................................169
    The Java Application Manager ..........................................169
    Packaging into a JAR File ...............................................169
Connected in a Limited Way: The CLDC ................................170
    Security ....................................................................170
    Pre-verifying ..............................................................171
The Mobile Profile ............................................................171
    MIDP in a Nutshell .......................................................172
    Earlier Profiles ............................................................172
Summary ..........................................................................173

**9    Creating a MIDlet                                                  175**

Command-Line MIDlet Development ....................................175
Development Environments .................................................177
    Wireless Toolkit ..........................................................178
Lifecycle of a MIDlet .........................................................181
Displaying Stuff ...............................................................183
    Working with Screens ....................................................184
    Forms .......................................................................185

Menus and Commands ....................................................188
Creating Help and About Alert Screens ..................................192
    The Alert Class ...............................................192
    Splash Screens ................................................195
Global Properties .......................................................197
    Getting Application Properties .................................197
    Getting System Properties .....................................198
    Creating a Global Cache Class .................................198
Summary ...............................................................199

**10    Making the Most of Limited Resources    201**

The Limitations .......................................................201
    Processor Paucity .............................................202
    Memory Madness ...............................................202
    Video Vex .....................................................203
    Processors of the Future ......................................203
Memory Limitations ...................................................203
    Working Memory ...............................................204
    Storage Memory ...............................................205
Displays ..............................................................206
Breaking Through the Limitations .....................................206
    Detecting the Minimum Speed ..................................206
    Frame Rate ....................................................206
    Multiple Display Support ......................................207
    Black and White World ........................................207
Summary ...............................................................207

**11    Making the Most of It: Optimizations    209**

A Limited World .......................................................209
Making Code Optimal ..................................................209
    Code Size Optimizations .......................................210
    Making code Faster ............................................210
    Decreasing Memory ............................................210
    Device Availability ...........................................211
    Network Performance ..........................................211
Code Size Reductions ..................................................211
    Obfuscators and Name-Shortening .............................212
    The Object-Oriented Dilemma ..................................213
    Image Size Reduction .........................................215

Speeding Up the Code ...................................................................216
    Dealing with the Garbage Collector ..........................................217
    The Constructorless Way ...........................................................217
    Static Methods ..........................................................................218
    The Fast-Draw ...........................................................................219
Using Less Memory ........................................................................220
    String Versus StringBuffer .........................................................220
    Arrays Versus Vector and Hashtable .........................................221
Power Consumption ........................................................................222
Summary ..........................................................................................222

**12    Multithreaded Game Programming**                                    **225**

Threads ............................................................................................225
Extending the Thread Object .........................................................227
Implementing the Runnable Interface ...........................................229
Thread Priorities ............................................................................230
Thread States .................................................................................231
Synchronizations and Deadlocks ...................................................231
wait() and notify() .........................................................................232
Timers .............................................................................................233
Making Threads Better ...................................................................235
Summary ..........................................................................................237

**Part IV    Let the Games Begin!**                                          **239**

**13    High-Level Graphical User Interfaces**                              **241**

The Screen Class .............................................................................241
Forms and Alerts .............................................................................242
Lists .................................................................................................242
    List Types ...................................................................................243
    Choices, Choices .......................................................................244
Text Boxes .......................................................................................247
Items ...............................................................................................248
    Item State Listening ..................................................................249
    Choices .......................................................................................249
    Dates ..........................................................................................250
    Progress Meters .........................................................................251

String Items ...................................................................254

Image Items ..................................................................254

Text Inputs ...................................................................255

Tickers ...............................................................................257

Additional Libraries ..........................................................257

Summary ............................................................................258

**14  Working with Graphics: Low-Level Graphical User Interfaces          259**

The Canvas Class ..............................................................259

Canvas Events ...............................................................261

Custom Commands .........................................................262

Creating a Game Key and Pointer Handler ....................262

Handling Touch Screens ................................................263

Painting on the Screen .......................................................264

Working with Colors .......................................................267

Stroke Types .................................................................267

Drawing Lines ...............................................................267

Drawing Rectangles .......................................................268

Drawing Rounded Rectangles ........................................269

Drawing Arcs .................................................................269

Fonts ............................................................................269

Drawing Strings .............................................................271

Drawing Images .................................................................271

The Image Class .............................................................272

Clipping ........................................................................273

Translating ....................................................................274

Double Buffering ...........................................................274

Summary ............................................................................275

**15  Entering the Land of Sprites          277**

Sprites ...............................................................................277

Sprite Properties ...........................................................278

Animating Frames .........................................................279

The Sprite Class ............................................................280

Image Files ........................................................................283

Loading Included Images ...............................................283

Loading Images Over the Network .................................283

Image Size Reduction ....................................................284

Drawing the Sprites .......................................................285

Collision Detection .................................................................286

    Basic Collision Detection .............................................286

Creating Child Sprites .........................................................287

    Building the Player Sprite ............................................287

    Opponents .....................................................................289

Image Transparency .............................................................289

    Drawing by Pixels .........................................................289

    Drawing a Sprite's Chunks ...........................................292

    Implementation of Image Transparency ......................292

Summary ..............................................................................293

**16   Managing Your Sprites                                    295**

Networked Game Components .............................................295

    Downloading Images ....................................................296

    Downloading Other Media Types .................................297

Advanced Collision Detection .............................................298

    Solution 1: Multiple Levels ..........................................298

    Solution 2: Multiple Areas ...........................................300

The Sprite Manager ............................................................301

    Drawing Optimizations ................................................303

    Enhancing Sprite Collision ...........................................304

Summary ..............................................................................305

**17   Sprite Movement                                          307**

Floating-Point in J2ME .......................................................307

    Cheating the System .....................................................308

Game Initialization .............................................................314

Movement ...........................................................................316

    The Movement Routine ...............................................317

Piecing It All Together ........................................................319

    Handling Collision Detection .......................................319

    Endgame: Losing or Winning ......................................320

    The Final Game Thread ...............................................321

Summary ..............................................................................323

**18   J2ME Audio Basics                                        325**

Sounds Are (Barely) Possible ..............................................325

Summary ..............................................................................327

**19    Be Persistent: MIDP Data Storage                                          329**

RecordStore Overview ........................................................................329

RecordStore in Practice .....................................................................331

    addRecord() ................................................................................331

    getRecord() ................................................................................332

    setRecord() ................................................................................332

    deleteRecord() ..........................................................................332

    getLastModified() ....................................................................332

    getNextRecordID() ....................................................................333

    getNumRecords() ........................................................................333

    getSize() ....................................................................................333

    getSizeAvailable() ..................................................................333

    deleteRecordStore() ................................................................333

    EnumerateRecords() ..................................................................333

    The Game's New Methods ..........................................................334

    Writing the Code ........................................................................335

More RecordStore Joy .......................................................................340

Summary ............................................................................................347

**20    Connecting Out: Wireless Networking                                      349**

J2ME Networking Overview ..............................................................349

MIDP Networking ..............................................................................352

    A Little Info About HTTP .........................................................352

    HTTP Example ...........................................................................354

    Working Around HTTP's Limitations .......................................356

Setting Up Your Game Server ...........................................................357

Data Format .......................................................................................358

    Doing Your Own Packing ..........................................................358

    XML .............................................................................................359

    Encoding with DataOutputStream and DataInputStream ............361

Making a Multiplayer Car Racing Game ...........................................361

    Design the System ......................................................................362

    Special Considerations ...............................................................363

    The Messages .............................................................................365

    Weaknesses .................................................................................365

    The Client Side ..........................................................................366

    The Server Side ..........................................................................380

    Playing the Game ......................................................................388

Summary ............................................................................................392

**Part V    J2ME Extensions**                                                     **393**

**21    PersonalJava, Connected Device Configuration, and Other Micro Java
       Blends                                                                     395**

Connected Device Configuration (CDC) ...............................................396

    J2ME Foundation Profile ...............................................397

    The Personal Profile ...............................................397

PersonalJava ...............................................397

    PersonalJava APIs ...............................................398

    Double Buffering ...............................................398

    Developer Tools ...............................................400

    MIDP Plug-In for PersonalJava ...............................................403

    PersonalJava Design Considerations ...............................................403

PDA Profile ...............................................404

Java Game Profile ...............................................404

The J2ME Multimedia Profile ...............................................405

Summary ...............................................406

**22    iAppli: Micro Java with a Twist                                           407**

The Architecture of It All ...............................................408

    Provisioning ...............................................409

    Priorities, Priorities ...............................................412

iAppli: Like MIDP, But Not Quite ...............................................412

    User Interface ...............................................413

    Networking and Input/Output ...............................................423

Developing iApplis ...............................................425

Summary ...............................................428

**23    Siemens Game API                                                          429**

Getting Set Up ...............................................429

    Compiling ...............................................430

    Running with the Emulator ...............................................430

    Running on the Actual Phone ...............................................431

    Download Your Applet Over the Air ...............................................431

The Game SDK Overview ...............................................432

Images and Sprites ...............................................432

    Creating an Extended Image ...............................................432

    Blitting ...............................................433

Graphic Objects ...............................................434

Sprites .................................................................435
    Creating and Masking a Sprite ....................................436
    Sample Code .................................................437
TiledBackground .................................................................438
    The Tiles ...................................................439
    The Tile Background ..............................................440
Flashing ...............................................................442
Good Vibrations ........................................................442
Music, Sweet Music .....................................................443
    Melodies ....................................................443
GSM Functions ..........................................................446
    Making a Call ................................................446
    Accessing the Phone Book .........................................447
    SMS Messages .................................................447
Input Output ...........................................................447
    Sending and Receiving Data .......................................447
    Saving and Loading Files .........................................448
Summary ...............................................................449

Part VI    Micro Racer                                                 451

24    Micro Racer: Putting It All Together                             453
The Bad News ...........................................................453
The Good News ..........................................................454
Putting Together the Pieces ............................................455
    Adding Weapons ...............................................456
    Better Enemies: Artificial Intelligence ..........................463
    Better Control ...............................................464
    Adding Power-Ups ..............................................466
    Tying In the Game with the Data Store ............................469
    Tying In the Offline Game with the Online Garage .................472
    Future Work ..................................................475
One Game Running Everywhere ............................................476
    The Magic of Interfaces .......................................476
Summary ...............................................................478

**Part VII    Appendixes**                                                      **479**

**A    Low-Level GUI Classes**                                                  **481**

Game Classes ........................................................................................481

javax.microedition.lcdui.AlertType .........................................483

javax.microedition.lcdui.Command .............................................483

javax.microedition.lcdui.Display .............................................483

javax.microedition.lcdui.Displayable .....................................484

javax.microedition.lcdui.Canvas ...............................................484

javax.microedition.lcdui.Screen ...............................................485

javax.microedition.lcdui.Alert .................................................485

javax.microedition.lcdui.Form ...................................................485

javax.microedition.lcdui.List ...................................................486

javax.microedition.lcdui.TextBox .............................................486

javax.microedition.lcdui.Font ...................................................487

javax.microedition.lcdui.Graphics ...........................................488

javax.microedition.lcdui.Image .................................................489

javax.microedition.lcdui.Item ...................................................489

javax.microedition.lcdui.ChoiceGroup .....................................490

javax.microedition.lcdui.DateField .........................................490

javax.microedition.lcdui.Gauge .................................................490

javax.microedition.lcdui.ImageItem .........................................491

javax.microedition.lcdui.StringItem .......................................491

javax.microedition.lcdui.TextField .........................................491

javax.microedition.lcdui.Ticker ...............................................492

**B    MIDP 1.1**                                                              **493**

Main Packages ....................................................................................493

java.io Class Hierarchy ...................................................................493

java.io Interface Hierarchy ...........................................................494

java.lang Class Hierarchy ...............................................................494

java.lang Interface Hierarchy .......................................................495

java.util Class Hierarchy ...............................................................495

java.util Interface Hierarchy .......................................................496

javax.microedition.io Class Hierarchy ......................................496

javax.microedition.io Interface Hierarchy ...............................496

javax.microedition.lcdui Class Hierarchy ................................497

javax.microedition.lcdui Interface Hierarchy .........................497

javax.microedition.midlet Class Hierarchy .............................497

`javax.microedition.rms` Class Hierarchy ...............................................497

`javax.microedition.rms` Interface Hierarchy .........................................498

**C   Siemens Game API                                                    499**

Game Classes ...............................................................................................499

    `com.siemens.mp.game.Light` .................................................................499

    `com.siemens.mp.game.MelodyComposer` .............................................499

    `com.siemens.mp.game.ExtendedImage` ...............................................500

    `com.siemens.mp.game.GraphicObject` .................................................500

    `com.siemens.mp.game.Sprite` ...............................................................500

    `com.siemens.mp.game.TiledBackground` .............................................501

    `com.siemens.mp.game.GraphicObjectManager` .................................501

    `com.siemens.mp.game.Melody` ...............................................................502

    `com.siemens.mp.game.Sound` .................................................................502

    `com.siemens.mp.game.Vibrator` ...........................................................502

Siemens GSM Classes ................................................................................502

    `com.siemens.mp.gsm.Call` .....................................................................502

    `com.siemens.mp.gsm.PhoneBook` .........................................................502

    `com.siemens.mp.gsm.SMS` .......................................................................503

Input/Output Classes ...............................................................................503

    `com.siemens.mp.io.Connection` ...........................................................503

    `com.siemens.mp.io.File` .......................................................................503

    `public interface ConnectionListener` .........................................504

**D   The iAppli API                                                      505**

Packages .....................................................................................................505

`com.nttdocomo.io` Interfaces ...............................................................505

`com.nttdocomo.io` Interfaces ...............................................................505

`com.nttdocomo.lang` ...............................................................................506

`com.nttdocomo.net` .................................................................................506

`com.nttdocomo.ui` ...................................................................................506

`com.nttdocomo.ui` Interfaces ...............................................................508

`com.nttdocomo.util` ...............................................................................508

`com.nttdocomo.util` Interfaces ...........................................................509

IApplication ...........................................................................................509

**Index                                                                    511**

# About the Author

**David Fox** works for Next Game, Inc., creating Web and wireless multiplayer games. Prior to that, his design and development credits include Michael Crichton's "Westworld 2000," Fox Interactive's "X-Files: Unauthorized Access," and PlayLink's real-time strategy "Citizen 01." He is the author of several best-selling books about Internet technologies, and his writing frequently appears in publications such as *Salon.com*, *Gamasutra*, and *Developer.com*. David has presented topics in Java gaming at Sun Microsytem's JavaOne conference for the past three years, and has been the winner of the Motorola-Nextel Developer Challenge for the past two years.

**Roman Verhovsek** is CEO and co-founder of Cocoasoft Ltd., where he is leading a team of J2ME developers. He holds a bachelor's degree in electrical engineering from the University of Ljubljana, and is working on his master's degree of computer science. Since early 1996, he has focused primarily on Java technologies, and for last two years in particular on Java-enabled small devices. In 2001 he held a lecture on J2ME game development at the JavaOne conference. In his other life, Roman enjoys cooking, mountaineering, jogging, and traveling with his girlfriend, Lina.

# Dedication

*To Charlotte,*

*This Future is Yours*

*—David*

*To Lina, the princess of my heart, and Dixie, the silly cat*

*—Roman*

# Acknowledgments

Writing a book is like a little saga—lots of comedy, some moments of tragedy, and a veritable revolving door of plot turns. The Pearson Technology Group folks are among the most professional and resourceful I've had the privilege of working with, and ultimately responsible for this saga's success. Thanks to Shelly Kronzek for launching things off, Carol Ackerman for fearlessly navigating through muddy and rocky waters, Bryan Morgan for truly excellent advice and insight, Seth Kerney for kicking things into fighting shape, and George Nedeff for actually caring. Andy Langton, as he is wont to do, lent a surefire hand when one was desperately needed. And apologies to Louise for typing myself into oblivion all those unexpected weekends—especially the sunny ones.

*—David*

# 1

# Introduction (or Everything I Wanted to Know About Micro Java Gaming But Was Afraid to Ask)

**IN THIS CHAPTER**

- A New Era of Gaming
- This Book's Mission
- A Bit About Game Design
- Show Me the Money: Micro Game Business Models

## A New Era of Gaming

Ah, games.

Games have almost a religious, ritual aspect to them. They allow people to enter together into a higher state of being, pushing skills to new limits and experiences to new heights. They allow ordinary people to experience extraordinary emotions—the emotions of the warrior, the king, the spy, and the lover—while remaining protected in a safe environment.

Now all this might sound like a bit of a heavy-handed way to describe *Frogger*, but it's fair to say that games transport us and amuse us in ways that no other form of entertainment can.

## A Brief History of Games

Games have been with humanity since the beginning. A 5000-year-old Mancala-like game board, carved from stone, was recently unearthed in the Sahara. The game of Go, popular in Oriental countries, has reportedly been around since 2000 B.C. Backgammon-like games such as Tabula and Nard are talked about in ancient Roman scripts, and even in the Bible. And Tarot decks, initially used to help predict the future, evolved into today's Bicycle playing cards.

A decade or two ago, the only games that people spent much time with were professional sports, board games like *Monopoly* and Chess, paper and dice games such as *Dungeons and Dragons*, and card games like Poker or Hearts. Some games were for heavy money, some were bone-jarringly competitive, but most were just about good clean fun.

With the advent of computers, games entered a new era. Games became one of the main reasons many people brought these strange beige boxes called computers into their homes. Whether battling through a simple graphical tennis game such as *Pong*, or a rich, text-only world such as *Zork*, these were wholly new types of games that could be played anytime against a most formidable opponent: a game designer who had programmed your computer, long ago, showing it how to defeat you.

The arcade wave of the '70s and '80s, led by hits such as *Pac-Man*, captured the hearts and ate the quarters of millions of youths. Console systems such as the Magnavox Odyssey, the Atari 2600, Mattel Intellivision, and ColecoVision brought the fun of the arcade to the players' own living rooms. Then, in 1985, a box known as the Nintendo Entertainment System blew people away with stunning graphics and intricate gameworlds, typified by such hits as *Super Mario Brothers*.

Computer gaming entered a whole new stratum of mass popularity and acceptance with bestsellers such as *Doom*, followed by *Quake*, and later *Tomb Raider*. Clearly, ultra-realistic 3D worlds were a hit. The more a game made a player feel as if she were actually inside another reality, the better.

Graphics became richer and richer as 3D cards and engines doubled in speed and performance with each passing year. Super Nintendo gave way to the Sony PlayStation, and currently the Nintendo GameCube faces off against the PlayStation 2, not to mention Microsoft's daunting new Xbox.

## Multiplayer Mania

A funny thing happened on the way to virtual reality-ville. In the late '90s and early 2000s, with games like *Ultima Online, Everquest,* and *Age of Empires II*, not to mention the spread of casual game Web sites such as Pogo, Yahoo Games, and Microsoft's MSN Gaming Zone, it became clear that what mattered to a whole slew of gamers wasn't only the richness of graphics or the detail of blood and gore—but the presence of other, real people. *Multiplayer gaming,* long popular with the geek crowd, had entered the mainstream.

In a way, games had come full circle. Once again, games were serving a social purpose, becoming a way for two or more people to enter new worlds and test new skills together, relating to each other in entirely new ways.

## Micro Devices, Micro Lifestyles

While multiplayer gaming continues to grow in popularity, another big paradigm shift is happening.

It's becoming harder and harder to find people who don't carry network-enabled embedded devices with them wherever they go. Whether it's a PDA such as a Palm device or iPaq, or a mobile phone such as those crafted by companies like Nokia or Motorola, people are getting used to connecting and communicating with each other anytime, anyplace, and anywhere.

Today, there are more than 600 million mobile-phone users worldwide. In the United States and Europe, mobile phone users generally tend to be affluent, educated, and they often have lots of time on their hands. The picture is different on different continents. In Africa, Asia, and South America the masses have flocked to mobile phones because land-line access and Internet service are too expensive.

According to the Yankee Group, people in the United States spend 50% more time commuting than in any other country. This is the perfect time to pull out a mobile phone and play some quick games.

Additionally, Datamonitor has researched people's game-playing behaviors in Asia, Europe, and the United States, and has concluded that most people like to play wireless games on evenings and weekends.

In the near future, we will likely see micro devices become even smaller and more specialized. Phones the size of earplugs, voice-activated assistants on wristwatches, and smart chips on credit cards are all becoming a reality.

This is a continuation of the paradigm shift that began in the 1970s, with microcomputers taking the power away from huge, monolithic mainframes. Clearly, millions of small devices working together yields much more distributed power than one big, central device.

Unsurprisingly, games are keeping up and even helping to lead this paradigm. While it might seem silly to try to achieve a rich, meaningful immersion on a tiny 100×100 pixel screen, there's one thing mobile phone games give you that even the best consoles can't provide: They're always with you, and can be played anywhere you go. This not only means that games can now be more convenient, but wholly new types of games can be designed that take advantage of new lifestyles.

## Enter Micro Java

The Java language, created by Sun Microsystems, is another example of a paradigm shift. As a language that had no pointers or complicated memory operations, was object-oriented, secure, and could run on most any browser or platform, application development suddenly opened up to the masses in a way that never seemed possible before. Java made it possible for millions of programmers to create quality applications in record time and quantities.

The Java 2 Micro Edition (J2ME), or Micro Java, as we'll call it in this book, is an attempt to take the best aspects of Java and pare them down for smaller devices such as mobile phones; set-top boxes that add interactivity to television, pagers, handheld organizers and personal data assistants (PDAs); as well as embedded chips that you find in devices such as refrigerators, microwaves, "smart" credit cards, and automobiles.

Most every major mobile phone and handheld device manufacturer immediately realized the potential of J2ME: If Java were to be placed on the gadget, hundreds of thousands of developers would immediately be able to create applications and add value. Furthermore, because it's Java, a program written for one device would be able to run on another device with little or no modifications. That certainly makes more sense than trying to force developers to learn a native language and API in order to create programs for your phone.

Seeing the opportunity for Java on the handset, almost every major mobile phone manufacturer joined with Sun to create something called the CLDC: The Connected, Limited Device Configuration, along with the MIDP: The Mobile Information Device Profile. In later chapters, we'll get into greater detail about what all these wacky acronyms really mean. But the point to remember here is that mobile phone manufacturers have embraced Java in a way that not even PC manufacturers and browser makers have. Java is clearly the future platform of choice for mobile devices, and an ideal platform for mobile games.

## This Book's Mission

We have attempted to write the most in-depth guide showing you how to craft the most cutting-edge Micro Java games possible.

Whether you are a professional game designer hoping to expand your knowledge of various platforms, a game programmer who wants to port a game to a smaller device, a Micro Java enthusiast looking for a more entertaining book about more entertaining apps, or just a micro gamer hoping to catch a glimpse of what goes on behind the scenes, this book is for you.

### The Game Plan

This book is divided into six sections:

#### Part I: Small Devices
The book begins with a tour of current Java-enabled devices, showing the full canvas upon which you'll be able to paint. These devices include powerful, full-featured computer systems, set-top television boxes, and tiny, smart credit cards.

Next, we'll look at the current state of micro gaming. We'll go on a whirlwind tour of some of the most popular and revolutionary games out there. Because most of these games are not written in Java, we'll try to distill the most successful element of these games so that you can take the best ideas and run with them.

### Part II: Before, Between, and Beyond J2ME

In many cases, handheld games will not be written in Java alone. Rather, games will be built atop older mobile phone technologies. In the second section of this book we'll look at the technologies that surround and support J2ME gaming, such as the Wireless Application Protocol (WAP) and Standard Messaging System (SMS). Furthermore, we'll cover specific enhancements to the current crop of phones from brands such as Nokia, Siemens, Motorola, Ericsson, and NTT DoCoMo, allowing you to take games to a new level no matter what your target platform happens to be.

For example, some carriers provide location-based information. This is an extremely exciting and relevant tie-in to gaming. This will allow people to literally use their mobile phones to hunt down or otherwise play with each other through the physical, bricks-and-mortar world.

### Part III: The Java 2 Micro Edition

This section dissects the J2ME in all its gory detail. You'll learn how to build J2ME applications, which tools to use, and key programming techniques.

Programming for handheld devices is often much different than coding for a full-blown desktop computer. However, it doesn't have to be more difficult.

### Part IV: Let the Games Begin!

This is where things start getting deep. We'll thoroughly cover the nooks and crannies of J2ME, along with in-depth discussions on graphics, sounds, animation, multiplayer networking, and other game-related topics.

Additionally, one of the most important things this book will show you are the limitations of Micro Java and, in certain cases, how to get around them.

Each section will include lots of source code, so that you can immediately begin compiling, tweaking, and testing things out.

### Part V: J2ME Extensions

J2ME is a cross-platform standard. Any program you write in J2ME should work, more or less, on any other mobile phone or handheld device. However, every device has its own specialties and intricacies.

This section will cover other forms, profiles, and configurations of J2ME. For example, you'll learn a little bit about coding for a set-top television box. In addition, we'll focus on two popular Application Programming Interfaces (APIs) from the world's largest handheld hardware platforms.

Finally, this section will show you the best ways to take game elements from one platform and port them to others.

### Part VI: Micro Racer

Every good thing must reach its end. But rather than just stuff you full of knowledge and then leave you alone in the vast, dry desert to figure everything out, this book includes the full code to a superior Micro Java game that we call Micro Racer. Check out Figure 1.1 for a sneak preview.

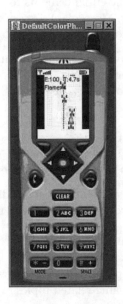

*FIGURE 1.1*   You will learn how to build this game.

Micro Racer is a fast moving, multiplayer experience. The game pushes the enveloper on Micro Java's graphical, sound, and networking abilities.

You begin the game with a simple racecar. You can race around all you want, picking up bonus points, avoiding crashes, and exploring new tracks.

Over time, however, your car will experience wear and tear and might even break down. You will need to log into The Garage to fix up your car.

At The Garage (see Figure 1.2), you'll be able to buy new parts, trade away old parts, and compare your score and standing. As you gain more and more money, you'll be able to soup up your car with turbo boosters, nitro packs, monster tires, spiked wheels, oil slicks, smoke screens, and other extras.

The people you trade with at The Garage are not artificial intelligences; rather, they are other actual players.

*FIGURE 1.2*    The Garage: Where you log online and trade car parts with other users.

Although Micro Racer is an advanced game, we believe you'll be able to do even better.

It is our hope that you will take this game, and the knowledge learned throughout this book, and go on to create bigger and better things.

## A Bit About Game Design

Before you can begin the fun/tedious/interminable process of actually typing Java code, compiling it, testing it, debugging it, and so on, you'll actually need to design the game you're interested in.

If you already have a game design written, or are working based on somebody else's game design, you can skip this section.

But if you're interested in a brief discussion of how the heck people think up new types of games, you've come to the right place.

Game design is always hard. Designing for a medium as new as mobile phones is even harder. But it is the best of worlds, as well as the worst of worlds. Although the devices you'll be designing for are limited compared to game consoles or PCs, they are also an entirely new phenomenon being used in entirely new ways.

If you can understand the way mobile phone users really think and act, you might be able to create a type of game that nobody has ever thought of before.

## The Game Design Process

Every game designer develops his or her game using a different process. Some people like to jump in and begin coding straight away; others like to create a monolithic 500-page design document outlining every last variable and button.

The type of process you use depends on the size and experience of the development team, as well as your personal philosophy on what makes a good game.

No matter what approach you choose, pretty much every game goes through the four P's:

1. Preproduction
2. Prototyping
3. Programming
4. Playtesting

## Preproduction

Preproduction usually involves generating a whole lot of paperwork.

Different game designers work in different ways. Some are technically minded, and like to jump right into the thick of things and create use-case diagrams, specifications, and so on.

Others are more artistically minded, and enjoy storyboarding the graphics, letting somebody else worry about how to make nitty-gritty interactions happen.

But pretty much everybody, at some point, needs to use regular pen and paper (or Microsoft Word) and just spell out the *story* of the game—the feel, the depth, the breadth, and the intent.

Taking the time to write clear design documents and storyboards during preproduction will pay off later during development. The more you can describe every bit of art, sound, and interaction, the easier it will be to put all these pieces together during the frantic phase of actual development.

The bigger your design team, the more helpful a solid design document will be in keeping everyone speaking the same language, understanding the same goals, and working on the same product.

## Answering Questions

Good design documents usually answer an implicit question. No matter how or when exactly you do it, every game designer will need to and answer the following questions:

- What is the game's genre?

- What are the limitations of the game?

- What is the game's central mission?

- What are the inputs, and what are the outputs?

- How will the game play out?

## Picking a Game Genre

There are literally millions of games in the world, and tens of thousands of computer games. But all these games can be broken down into genres.

A genre is more than a style of gameplay; it is also a mood. Different genres appeal to wholly different audiences. Clearly, a gory first-person shooter is expected to have a different interface, feel, sound effects, and speed than a long, drawn-out, and detailed military simulation game.

Genre will help define how the game looks, how it feels, how it plays, and who it is targeted to.

This section will briefly cover various genres, helping you to hone in on a gameplay experience.

## Copying, Stealing, and Cloning

A sad fact of life is that most games on the market are basically clones of other, more successful games.

When Java applets first came out, most of the games that people created were exact copies of old hits from the Apple II, Atari 2600, or Commodore 64 era. Often, the only thing that a programmer would change would be the name and a few graphics: *Pac-Man* might become something like *Pork Man*.

Likewise, it is tempting to take existing games and create Micro Java versions of them. Furthermore, there's nothing wrong with it. After all, classic games have been time-tested and proven to be popular with the masses.

### CAUTION

If you are creating games as a hobby, then there's no problem with taking your favorite arcade games and squeezing them into a mobile phone so that you, and others, can enjoy them portably.

However, if you are creating games commercially, not only is copying an existing game illegal, but you'll likely find that there won't be a big market for it. As much as people like to play their standard favorites, the world is thirsting for something new. History has shown us that the company or person that uses Micro Java to design a game genre that nobody has ever seen before will be the one that triumphs in the end.

All that being said, some of the best games ever created borrow familiar elements from one or more forgotten genres and breath new life into them. For example, real-time strategy games—games in which the player controls many discrete units, all at once—have existed for the past few decades. But it took Westwood Studios to create a game in the genre with a strong story, well-balanced play, and distinctive military units. The game was *Command and Conquer*, and it became an instant hit.

Because Micro Java game designers are stuck writing to such a limited platform, you are forced to think about unique game design itself, and not rely on fancy graphics and sounds to make sales. Some of the best games were black and white, 8-bit, and had less than 64K of memory. Try to analyze those games and understand what made them great. Using classic games for inspiration is not only acceptable, it is essential.

### What Types of Games Are Possible?

Ultimately, the most successful games will combine genres in entirely new ways. For example, the *Tomb Raider* series is so popular  because it blends action, adventure, puzzles—and the shapely Lara Croft.

The following list of genres is just a starting point to get you thinking. This list is in no way complete.

- Action Games—These are games that involve fast reflexes. The graphics are generally as realistic as possible, and the audio is usually rich and loud. The play is usually fast paced, and multiplayer versions are usually very responsive. The audience consists generally of adolescent males.

  Because of the speed, responsiveness, and powerful graphics, action games are probably the hardest genre to implement on mobile phones and other hand-held devices. This book will show you how to do it, anyway.

  Examples of such games include first-person shooters such as *Quake*, space games such as *Defender* or *Missile Command*, maze games such as *Pac-Man*, and paddle games such as *Pong*.

- Combat Games—These games usually involve two characters facing off against each other and trying to beat each other up. Often, the characters will have special powers. Winning the game requires that the player have quick reflexes as well as memorize all the possible "moves."

  Examples include *Virtua Fighter, Street Fighter,* and *Mortal Kombat*.

- Adventure Games—These are games that involve a quest of discovery through new worlds. These are usually structured similarly to a good movie or book, with a strong sense of story, character, plot, and locations.

  Originally, these games were wholly text-based, such as *Zork*; but more modern games such as *Monkey's Island* and *Riven* use advanced 3D graphics, strong artificial intelligence, and rich audio to flesh out the game worlds.

- Puzzle Games—These games require the player to use logic, and often involve the arrangement or matching of symbols. *Tetris* is the king of all puzzle games.

  The audience for puzzle games is usually made up of intelligent, crafty adults.

- Strategy Games—These games often involve lots of pieces, lots of possibilities, and rewards for thinking ahead.

  War games such as *Panzer General* are a popular type of strategy game in which you try to recreate a famous battle and pit various armies against each other. The audience for war games is very enthusiastic, but very small.

  Real-time strategy games such as *Command and Conquer* and *Warcraft* are much more popular with the masses. These games often involve more tactics than long-term strategy. Players must manage resources such as electricity and money while assembling specialized armies consisting of many different units. Quick reflexes are as important as long-term planning.

  Finally, classic two-player board games such as chess, Reversi, Connect Four, and checkers are strategy games. The audience for this type of classic turn-based game is truly mass market.

- Role Playing Games (RPG)—These games generally allow you to fill a role. Your character has certain attributes such as Strength and Wisdom, and these attributes can change over time as your character explores new dungeons and fights new monsters.

  Paper and dice games such as *Dungeons and Dragons* invented this genre. The typical audience for this type of game is similar to those who read science fiction—usually intelligent, male adolescents.

  With more graphical RPGs such as *Diablo III*, *Everquest*, and *Ultima Online,* the genre has moved online as the basis for a rich, social, active community.

- Simulation Games—These games allow the player to control a character, a machine, or system. Often, these games rely upon ultra-realistic graphics and control panels.

  The more specialized the simulation, the smaller the audience. A very detailed flight simulator may only appeal to real pilots. Real-life simulation games such as *SimCity* or *The Sims*, however, are widely popular with males and females, children and adults.

- Trivia Games—These games are tests of (often useless) knowledge. Trivia games can be played in a straightforward question-answer format, such as *Who Wants to Be A Millionaire?* or *You Don't Know Jack*, or by using a more sophisticated game board, as with *Trivial Pursuit*.

  Most game shows are based on trivia. The audience for trivia games is the mass market.

- Word Games—These games involve the creation of words, based on specific rules. The more words the player knows and is able to build, the better the player does. Examples of this genre are word builders such as *Scrabble* or word searches such as *Boggle*.

  Word games often appeal to an intelligent, middle-aged female audience.

- Card Games—Card games usually combine chance with skill. A player is dealt out a hand and must play out the hand, given a set of rules.

  A card game such as poker involves bluffing and betting, appealing to a much more hard-core gaming crowd than social trick games such as Hearts or Spades.

  Additionally, collectible card games such as *Pokemon* or *Magic: The Gathering* combine elements of the RPG, allowing players to collect decks of cards, battle the decks against other players, and combine cards to achieve unexpected results. This type of game usually appeals to adolescents or hard-core RPG gamers.

- Games of Chance—Any game based upon random result. Most casino games are games of chance, with a little skill thrown on top. Roulette, slot machines, or the card game War are the most basic games of chance.

  Games such as Backgammon involve chance, but also require a great amount of strategy.

- Sports Games—These games allow the player to experience physical sports such as football, basketball, wrestling, or skateboarding. The games usually have excellent graphics and highly realistic physics. These games usually appeal to the same fans that enjoy the sport itself.

  Some sports games are coaching or managing games, and allow the player to take a more strategic, top-down, and sideline approach to team building, player trading, or game-playing.

  A special subset of sports games worth singling out is racing games. These games usually involve very detailed roads and landscapes, very specialized user input, and very responsive physics.

- Toys—This is the rarest category of games, but also one of the most interesting. These games generally have no winner or loser, but allow the player to build or play with virtual pieces.

  Virtual pets, virtual mousetraps, virtual robots, digital musical instruments, and other educational and kids games often fall into this category.

### Know Thy Limits

The most important part of the game design process is to know the limitations of the medium. This book, especially Chapter 2, "The Mobile World," will help you to define exactly what your target platform can achieve.

### Designing Within Restrictions

In this book we're focusing on handheld devices such as mobile phones. A mobile phone typically has a tiny black and white screen, tiny bins of memory, ultra-slow screen refresh rates, turtle-like processor speed, and painfully limited sound.

So a game with instant trigger finger reactions, endless 3D dynamically shaded passageways, a massive multiplayer environment, and with a soundtrack by Green Day is *not* going to be possible on mobile phones. Not today, at least. There will definitely be a day—even relatively in the near future—when chipsets are fast enough and small screens are colorful enough for this to be possible.

In a way, designing a game for a mobile phone is a blast back to the olden days of game design, for platforms such as the Apple II and Commodore 64. You're now back in a world where every bit counts, only worse: You now have to fit it all on a postage-stamp size screen.

There is another drastic difference: One thing most J2ME-equipped mobile phones enable is easy interactivity with other mobile phones. For the first time, communication might become more important than gameplay.

### Designing Around Restrictions

It is useful to remember here that no matter how good a game's graphics are, the real action always occurs inside the player's head.

A game's graphics and other elements are only useful if they transport a player to a different *mindset*, and allow the player to experience a believable fantasy.

Your challenge, then, is to transport the player to a rich, believable, exciting, and emotional fantasy world while using minimal graphics and audio. Sound hard? Not really. Novelists and storytellers have been doing just that for centuries, using no graphics at all.

That is the first clue: Good writing in Micro Java games becomes more essential than ever.

A good Micro Java game designer is also about turning lemons into lemonade. Good designers can actually take new devices such as mobile phones and use them in ways that nobody has ever imagined or expected, but that are wholly intuitive and logical.

For instance, one of the most ingenious mobile phone games out there is a Japanese game called *Turibaka Kibun* (which means Crazy for Fishing), created by Dwango. To go fishing, you pick your bait, choose a fishing hole, and then literally extend the antenna of your phone and hold it out. Eventually your phone will vibrate, which means you have a fish on the line. If you get lucky, you'll be able to reel in a nice trout or bass.

While the game, shown in Figure 1.3, might sound a little strange to Western audiences, it is wildly popular in Japan. In fact, DoCoMo had to limit the number of fish one could catch each day because consumers were spending *too much* time and money with the game.

More information about this and other games can be found in Chapter 3, "Big Games, Small Screens."

Another example of a game-like event that could only happen in today's mobile phone era is a performance called Dialtones. This is a symphony concert performed entirely though the ringing of the audience's mobile phones! Visit `http://www.flong.com/telesymphony/` for more information and sample songs.

*FIGURE 1.3*   *Turibaka Kibun:* A game that would only be possible on a mobile phone.

### The Game's Mission
After you've decided what the genre will be, one of the first tasks of the game designer is to define the game's mission.

Most good games can be summed up using a simple sentence. The sentence should evoke an entire mood, and explain the central challenge of your game from the player's perspective.

For example, *Tomb Raider* can be summed up like this: You are a hot, sexy adventurer who must explore secret passageways within ancient tombs, collecting treasures while fighting off deadly creatures.

*Tetris* could be summed up this way: Different-shaped puzzle pieces are falling down a chute; you must rotate and arrange the shapes so that they land at the bottom forming complete rows.

Every design, artwork, and programming decision must then stem from this mission statement.

### Inputs and Outputs

A game, at its core, consists of user input, followed by some sort of output. You should try to list every type of input, and what the effect will be.

Some input occurs because the player does something. Other types of input occur just because the game state has reached a specific point.

Typical input and other events to keep track of and define include the following:

- The keyboard: Which keys on the handset will be used, when, and for what?

- The mouse or joystick: Most handheld devices do not have a mouse, but some do have a touch screen or stylus. How will this affect the input?

- Menus: What main and top menus will there be in your game?

- Buttons: What buttons will there be?

- Form widgets: How will elements such as pull-down menus, radio buttons, checkboxes, and text fields work together?

- Time: Will there be any countdown timers? How does time play a role in the game?

- Collisions: What happens when graphical elements collide?

Next, you should try to create a list of every element that will actually be in the game. These elements vary widely. Some will be visible on screen, and some will be hidden game state variables that your program will need to juggle:

- Graphical elements: What will the user see? These are usually 3D models or sprites.

- Sound effects: What audio effects should play, and when?

- Background music: What music will be playing?

- Background art: What will the environment look like, and how should it be rendered?

- Levels: Will the game have multiple levels? If so, what will differentiate them?

- Interface: In order for input to happen, there will need to be an interface. How will this interface look, roughly speaking? The interface also usually includes a readout of variables such as score, number of lives remaining, amount of ammunition, and so on. What information needs to be here?

- Artificial intelligence: Will there be any computer players? What will they look like?

- Global variables: Try to create a list of global variables that will change as the game is played. This includes the score, the round number, and so on.

Often, a design document will list each input and output element in a table and explain how different elements interact with each other. You should also try to explain the different classes and subclasses of elements, and how they all relate.

This document can often be used to define exactly how the program should be structured in an object-oriented manner. This will help the object-oriented Java programmer design the actual software. For example, a typical unit in your game may be a DeathMosquito. This DeathMosquito may be part of the FlyingUnit class, which may descend from the WarriorUnit class, which will be derived from the generic Unit class, which in turn may be a child of the Sprite class.

### Gameplay

The next step is to actually define the rules of the game. This is where you can begin to determine all the variables, graphical elements, and other gameplay elements.

Ultimately, you should be able to create a *game state*—a list of variables, or perhaps just an array of bytes, that defines the exact state of the game. Strip away the fancy graphics, graceful animations, streaming TCP/IP sockets, and eardrum-beating sound effects, and you'll notice that games—no matter their genre or complexity—amount to nothing more than a pile of bytes. Every player's move and every artificial intelligence decision eventually expresses itself as a change to this core game state data.

You should be able to stop the game at any time, restart it, plug in the game state, and be at the exact same place you left off.

Java makes it quite easy to keep an abstract notion of game state. Just create a class with all the data structures you need, tap in methods to access or change that data, and you're off and running. By designing state as an object, various parts of the state can quickly be accessed and altered.

Multiplayer games often keep the main copy of the state on the server side, with additional copies in each client. This permits the server to be the final judge of what the "game" actually is. The client, meanwhile, can contain just enough information to be responsive. In other words, the client should be able to tell whether a player's move is legal or illegal, but the server will actually register the move and make changes to the game state accordingly.

The other important piece of this picture is how the game is won, and exactly how to determine winners and losers. You should be able to analyze the game state variables and determine whether the game has reached the winning condition.

For multiplayer games, it is usually useful to draw a client-server diagram and show which messages will need to be sent over the network. This can help you create use-case scenarios to take care of any eventuality.

### Other Resources

There are many books, magazines, and Web sites that discuss game design. Some of the best resources can be found online:

- `http://www.gdse.com/`
- `http://www.gamasutra.com/`
- `http://www.gamedev.net/`

## Prototyping

The more original your game idea, the more important it is to prototype it. Until you and some friends are actually playing the game, you will never have any idea how successful your genius idea really is.

To prototype a game, one can commonly use a notepad, a few index cards, and some pencils. Each index card can be a game output element. You can position these relative to each other, or move them around accordingly.

Get a few friends together, explain the rules of the games, and "play it." You can act as the computer and game master, keeping track of the score and making sure everybody is playing correctly.

After a few minutes of play, it will become remarkably evident what the weaknesses and strengths of your game design are. Continue redesigning the game and retesting it, until your friends get sick of it or until you're happy with the results.

Additionally, you can easily prototype most games using Java Standard Edition (J2SE). This is another joy of Java—it is extremely easy to create a simple application that takes in command line input, processes some simple rules, and then spits out an output.

For example, if you are creating a new type of card game, you can have your Java prototype shuffle the cards, deal them out, accept valid moves, and keep track of who has what.

Eventually, if you only use text for input and output, it will be easy to transport the prototype in the Java 2 Micro Edition environment. The prototype can become the actual rules engine for your final game.

## Programming

This part of game development is similar to developing any other application. You've got a specification and you've got to carry it out, on time and on budget.

You've got to create your Java classes, possibly create a server, create any artwork or audio assets, and fold it all together.

Most games are basically an endless loop. Speaking in the most general terms, the loop works as follows:

1. Paint the screen.

2. Get any user input.

3. Make any game state changes.

4. Redraw the graphics or sounds accordingly.

Most games also have engines for each major multimedia aspect. The advantage of having a generalized engine is that it can be reused for future game products. Typical engines include some of the following:

- Graphics engines are a quick way of drawing the graphics. 3D games will have a special graphics *3D engine* that knows how to take three-dimensional X, Y, and Z coordinates and transform them onto a flat screen. Other games will have *sprite engines* that enable you to take many graphical components and animate them and move them around the screen relative to each other. Still other games will have *isometric engines* that draw 3D-looking graphics from a set perspective, actually using a series of two-dimensional overlays.

- Audio engines will play the soundtrack or other audio effects. Often, the engine will mix together different effects and be smart about fading music in or out depending on what is currently happening in the game.

- Artificial intelligence (AI) engines act as a separate player in the game. The AI player is able to compete in the game, often head-to-head against human players.

- Physics engines simulate real movement. Making a ball fall and then bounce appropriately takes a very complicated series of equations. A physics engine can provide this.

- Multiplayer engines will communicate with the network, often through a central server, and enable game sessions to speak with each other.

## Playtesting

After the entire game has been coded, debugged, and released, the development has just begun.

Because a game is not a cut-and-dry business application, there is usually no right or wrong. There is only fun and not fun. You may think your game is highly entertaining, but you're biased—you've been working on the sucker for the past few months. You also may not be representative of the market you're trying to appeal to.

Big game companies often hire focus groups to playtest their game. They also might release the game to a small group of beta testers. They'll try to get as much feedback as possible.

Many of the most popular games became huge successes because beta testers loved the game so much they worked hard trying to communicate small requests that would make the game even better. When the game company fulfilled these requests, beta testers felt a sense of ownership. They told all their friends to buy the game, and the news spread like wildfire.

The first playtester should be you. Be honest with yourself. What improvements can be made? What strategies are too hard, and why is it so easy to gain points if you know a certain trick?

Continue to tweak the game until you're absolutely certain there's nothing wrong with it. You should then have some friends of yours play your game. This will be more useful if your friends are avid gamers, and if they are game designers themselves. Watch them closely while they play, and ask them many open-ended questions about their experience. Notice when they get frustrated or bored. Notice when they get angry, or when they laugh.

In nearly every case, you will need to go back to redesign and reprogram your game. This might be as simple as changing a few values, adding a few power-ups, or removing a few restrictions. Or you might need to totally redo your graphics engine to make it animate more smoothly.

Often times, you'll need to drastically change your game design. And you will need to go through the entire prototyping and programming process again before you can be absolutely sure your new design idea works. Fun, huh?

As a rule of thumb, professional game companies often spend as much as a third of the game development cycle on playtesting and redesign.

## Show Me the Money: Micro Game Business Models

If you are a commercial game developer, then you are lucky indeed. You get to spend your days hacking, designing, and creating objects of joy and entertainment. You get to be a kid for a living.

But if you want to stay in business, you'll need to make money. Clearly, the business model you choose will differ depending on your end platform and upon your target audience.

Additionally, business models are strikingly different in the United States, Asia, and Europe. In Europe and Asia, for example, carriers such as NTT DoCoMo offer a profit split with content providers: The more a user chooses a particular piece of content, the more the content provider gets paid. This model is exciting, because it encourages thousands of developers to take their best shot at entertaining the masses.

To date, few North American carriers have been able to offer such a deal. Instead, most content providers must approach specific carriers and strike specific content deals. This makes it difficult for small developers to compete or earn any real revenues.

**NOTE**

United States carriers such as Cingular Wireless, Sprint PCS, and Nextel have expressed interest in creating profit-splitting services within the next year.

### The Business Outlook

Datamonitor predicts that the wireless gaming market in the United States will have grown to $3 billion in 2006, with 125 million players hungry for good new games.

### Advertising and Sponsorships

Advertising and sponsorships are probably the easiest business models to implement, but the most difficult in which to achieve solid revenues.

The idea is simple and well-known: Find a company that has a message, put that company's name, logo, or other creative elements within your game, and you've created a valuable vehicle for the company's message.

In fact, many companies have opted to create their own mobile phone games in order to deliver their brand to a cutting-edge audience.

Often, advertisements change from day to day. Ads appear below or to the side of game content. Alternatively, a full screen ad "interstitial" can be shown to the player before or after the game session.

Some of the best advertisements don't even seem like ads at all. For example, many racing games include logos "painted" on the racecars, and football games often include ad banners on the side of the stadium. This touch of realism actually makes the game better, while providing a permanent and well-seen home for a lucky advertiser.

The problem with micro devices, of course, is that there is not a lot of room for ads. Company logos are often small and washed out, and it is often hard to track the number of times a given ad is seen.

As screen resolutions improve, however, advertisements and sponsorships will likely become a smart choice. Top games will be able to charge hefty fees for ad placement. After all, if a mobile phone game really takes off, it has the potential to be experienced by more people, and more regularly, than any television, radio, or print ad campaign.

## Content Deals

Wireless service providers, cable companies, and other companies that provide the infrastructure for small devices have a lot to gain if a popular game comes along.

Because most mobile phone providers charge their users per minute, the longer a user is connected and playing a favorite game, the more minutes are being used up.

In addition, games could come with incentives. For example, if you pass a certain level in a game, you could get a coupon for 50 free minutes of mobile airtime. Players would work on the game for hundreds of minutes trying to earn a slight discount.

**WARNING**

Because some carriers charge a flat monthly fee for Internet use, these carriers desire games that *don't* stay connected and waste precious bandwidth!

But the point remains that carriers have invested more than $100 billion to create a faster, next-generation wireless infrastructure known as third-generation (3G). Current networks run 9.8 kilobits per second. A 3G network will run up to 50 kilobits per second—almost as fast as a computer's modem.

Clearly, carriers are counting on faster and richer applications, such as games, to attract new users and get a good return on their investment.

Currently, there are an estimated 16 million wireless game players in the United States alone. The ARC Group predicts that by 2006 there will be 280 million players. In Japan, NTT DoCoMo recently announced that 52% of wireless Internet revenues are due to games.

Several game companies have been able to strike content deals with major wireless carriers. If you have created a game that you believe will appeal to the masses, it's definitely worth talking with major carriers and figuring out a deal that makes sense for everyone.

### Pay-For-Play or Subscription

Charging players for a subscription to play a game is a clear path to revenues. For example, a player may be willing to pay $10 per month, $1 per game, or an additional 10 cents per minute.

However, most current users aren't willing to pay anything for mobile phone games. The main reason for this, of course, is that while there are many nice micro games out there, there are few that are so darn fun, so darn special, so darn enthralling, and so darn exciting that users would be willing to part with their cash.

This will change.

Bigger and more colorful screens, better audio capabilities, quicker network access times, and faster processors will allow for better games.

Additionally, carriers will begin to offer content providers more ways to bill users. Carriers and phone manufacturers are already beginning to create portals whereby users can use their credit cards to purchase and download Micro Java applications.

Someday soon, a company will create a micro game so good and so addictive that people will *have* to play it. Paying a buck or two per game will become second nature. The company that does this will make a fortune, and the world of micro gaming will be changed forever.

Perhaps that company will be yours.

## Summary

It is our hope that readers of this book will go on to do more than create an excellent crop of new games. We believe that given the paradigm shifts of always-on networking and in-pocket interactivity, the J2ME games of tomorrow have the potential to redefine the whole medium. In fact, given the pervasiveness of handheld devices and the potential for reaching a wider audience than ever before, a truly original game concept can revolutionize the world.

# PART I

# Small Devices

## IN THIS PART

**2** The Mobile World

**3** Big Games, Small Screens

# 2

# The Mobile World

**IN THIS CHAPTER**

- A New Era of Gaming
- High-End Java Devices: Set-Top Boxes, Phones, Consoles
- Personal Digital Assistants (PDAs)
- Mobile Phones and Pagers
- Low-End Java Devices: Smart Cards and Embedded Chips

## A New Era of Gaming

Get ready for a tour of the micro device world. This chapter will show you the attributes, limitations, and specifications behind the latest crop of gadgets capable of running Java 2 Micro Edition (J2ME). The list includes Personal Digital Assistants (PDAs), television set-top boxes, automotive navigation systems, home appliances, two-way pagers, credit cards, and mobile phones.

As you begin to think about developing games and other entertaining applications, this chapter will help you focus in on a target platform and give you some idea of your game design parameters.

> **NOTE**
>
> Keep in mind that new Java devices are constantly being introduced. While some of the devices listed here may amaze you, others will seem laughably out-of-date within the next year or so. An up-to-date list can be found on Sun's Web site: http://wireless.java.sun.com/device/.

### Micro Devices

While the definition of what exactly a *micro device* is may vary, J2ME focuses on everything from set-top boxes to tiny chips embedded in appliances—devices nearly as powerful as any desktop computer.

Although we will touch on all relevant J2ME platforms, this book focuses on mobile phones using the MIDP. This is for several reasons:

- It is expected that the vast majority of games written for J2ME will be for devices that are portable, have a screen for visual output, offer some amount of network access, and have a keypad for user input. In other words, a mobile phone. Although it is theoretically possible to create a game for a smart Java credit card—for example, a game wherein you guess the price of items before you purchase them—such situations will be rare.

- More advanced devices—such as set-top boxes that mix interactive content with TV video—will most definitely be popular platforms for many games. In fact, dedicated gaming consoles such as Sony's PlayStation 2 may actively support Java in the near future. However, games written for such appliances will likely use special graphics APIs and more advanced Java 2 Standard Edition (J2SE) libraries. At this time, there are few high-end devices focusing on J2ME.

Most cell phones use the MIDP profile of J2ME. However, bigger mobile phones with PDA functionality usually run the more advanced PersonalJava. Additionally, some phones—especially in Asia—run proprietary versions of Java. All of these standards will be discussed in Chapter 4, "Wireless Standards: How Data Goes To and Fro."

## The Micro Revolution Begins

When Sun Microsystems decided to create the Java 2 Micro Edition, many companies wanted to be a part of it. These companies all wanted to be able to add J2ME capabilities to their products.

Java holds many advantages:

- Most phones come with a set bundle of applications such as silly games, organization tools, and basic calculators. Mobile phone manufacturers realize that in order to stay competitive, phones will need to become expandable, and be able to support tons of different business and entertainment apps. Users will want to be able to download new software on-the-fly and erase old or irrelevant programs. A fully functional programming language such as Java makes that possible.

- It is estimated that 2.5 million developers around the world already know and love Java. Release a J2ME product and people can start developing for it right away, with little or no additional training.

- Lots of good stuff is already written in Java. There are already scads of cool Java applications and applets out there, making it easy to convert the best apps to a micro format.

- By supporting a de facto standard, hundreds of applications will be available for new devices the moment they hit the market. For example, if somebody creates a kick-butt shooter game in J2ME, then it will work on any current and future J2ME devices with few or no changes.

- Java has a well-defined security model. This means that manufacturers don't have to worry about a Melissa-like virus getting into a mobile phone's address book and automatically calling everybody up and sending them the virus.

- Instead of developing and maintaining a proprietary programming language across various devices, manufacturers would much rather license a stable, known language such as Java. The same language can now work across various processors and operating systems.

## Wide Support

Just some of the companies that are developing J2ME products and services include the following:

- Far EasTone
- Fujitsu
- Matsushita/Panasonic
- Mitsubishi
- Motorola
- NEC
- Nokia
- One 2 One
- Philips
- Research In Motion (RIM)
- Siemens
- SmarTone
- Sony
- Symbian
- Telefonica

Micro Java is rapidly taking hold all over the world.

## Asia

The first region of the world to adopt the Java 2 Micro Edition was Asia. In Japan especially, there has been massive acceptance and penetration of Java phones. According to Nikkei BP, there were 4.65 million J2ME phones in Japan in the first quarter of 2001—out of a total of 14.8 million mobile phones. That means that 31%

of phones in Japan will be Java phones. As handsets become more functional, it is expected that more than 40% of phones will support Java by the fourth quarter of 2001. Many different manufacturers—Matsushita/Panasonic, NEC Corp., Mitsubishi, Sony, and Fujitsu—are creating phones for Japan's NTT DoCoMo wireless service.

Other mobile network operators, such as Japan's J-PHONE GROUP, are unrolling third-generation wireless networks with Java-phones as the central component. In South Korea, LG Telecom introduced Java with their i-Book mobile phone.

### Europe

The European market was next to fall prey to the Java invasion. Many of the latest phones are being built atop the Symbian EPOC platform, which supports Java technology. Various companies will roll out anywhere from 40 to 60 million Java devices. Companies that have signed up to license the Symbian platform include Ericsson, Motorola, Nokia, Philips, and Psion.

In addition, manufacturers such as Siemens, Nokia, and Motorola released J2ME phones during the summer of 2001.

### North America

The first mobile phone to support J2ME was released in the spring of 2001 by Motorola. The i85s and i50sx phones, using the Nextel service and the Motorola iDen network, are predicted to be just the beginning of Motorola's new product line. The Motorola Accompli 008, released in July of 2001, is the first J2ME mobile phone for GSM networks. To understand more about GSM networks, check out Chapter 4.

Nokia has also recently announced that it will support Java technology in most of its future mobile terminals, with plans to sell more than 50 million Java handsets in 2002 and 100 million Java phones by the end of 2003. Nokia phones will support various flavors of Java, ranging from MIDP to PersonalJava and JavaPhone.

In addition, many North American wireless services already support Java, or are planning to support Java network traffic in the near future. These companies include Nextel, Cingular, and Sprint PCS.

## High-End Java Devices: Set-Top Boxes, Phones, Consoles

Most high-end devices run a special version of J2ME known as PersonalJava. In addition, many devices implement the JavaTV APIs.

Set-top box manufacturers that support J2ME include Motorola and Philips.

### PersonalJava

PersonalJava is an application environment for network-connected, resource-limited devices. Basically, it is a simplified, pared-down version of the Java 2 Standard

Edition that everybody knows and loves. The idea is to take the most popular features and libraries of Java and squeeze them into a smaller footprint.

Some features of the latest PersonalJava 3.0 include the following:

- Java Native Interface (JNI) 1.2 support

- Java Virtual Machine Debugging Interface (JVMDI) 1.2 support

- Java Virtual Machine Profiler Interface (JVMPI) 1.2 support

- The Truffle Graphical Toolkit—This allows for platform-independent, customized look and feel components. This includes the Touchable user interface, specially designed for touch screen devices. For example, Figure 2.1 shows a sample mail application designed using Truffle.

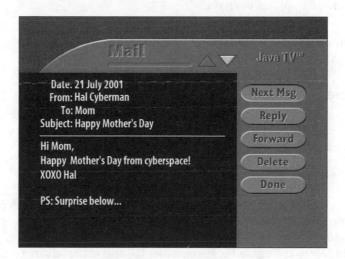

**FIGURE 2.1**    A visually appealing PersonalJava application.

The PersonalJava application environment is an additional set of libraries that sits atop the Connected Device Configuration (CDC) of J2ME. For more information about all this, see Chapter 8, "J2ME Overview."

More information, including a PersonalJava emulation environment and software for ensuring that your Java code is PersonalJava compatible, can be found at `http://www.javasoft.com/products/personaljava/`.

## JavaTV

JavaTV is an Application Program Interface (API) specifically designed for a digital television receiver. It sits atop PersonalJava and includes special functions for

- Streaming audio and video

- Accessing in-band and out-of-band data channels

- Changing channels

- On-screen graphical overlays

For more information on the Java TV API, visit `http://java.sun.com/products/javatv/`.

## JavaPhone

The JavaPhone 1.0 specifications are a set of routines with access to typical phone capabilities such as specific phone functionality, scheduling, contacts and phone books, power monitoring, and serial communications.

## PingTel xpressa Phone

This is not a mobile phone, but an actual digital desktop phone. All voice comes through over IP, allowing for amazing versatility and functionality. For example, the phone supports up to 1,024 simultaneous calls and can easily perform multi-party conferencing, forwarding, call logging, caller ID, and other advanced tasks.

The phone is entirely Java-based. It runs the PersonalJava environment, along with a host of other APIs to control calls and audio systems. It comes with its own xpress Window Toolkit (xWT) for user interface design, and supports Java Management Extensions (JMX), Java Naming and Directory Interface (JNDI), Java Database Connector (JDBC), Remote Method Invocation (RMI), Java Dynamic Management (JDMK), and Java Beans.

**Display Size:** 160×160

**URL:** `http://www.pingtel.com/homepage.php3`

### Sharp NC-10 IP Phone

This multimedia voice-over-IP phone is more than a cordless phone. It has fax, Web browsing, and e-mail services built in. All input occurs through the touch screen. It can also run Java applets.

**URL:** `http://www.sharp.co.jp/sc/eihon/nc10/text/sys.html`

# Personal Digital Assistants (PDAs)

Personal Digital Assistants commonly focus on storing a database of contacts with phone numbers, a calendar with schedules, a memo pad, and a to-do list. But PDAs such as the iPaq and Palm have become more than fads—after you start to rely on them, carrying them becomes almost as necessary as breathing.

In addition, most PDAs support third-party applications. This means that your PDA can have word processors, image drawing tools, and spreadsheets. One of the most popular categories of PDA apps is, of course, games.

## J2ME PDA Profile

There is currently a specification being written using the Java Community Process to extend and enhance the J2ME CLDC. The specification is called JSR-000030: The PDA Profile.

Companies working on the profile include Sun Microsystems, Palm Computing, Siemens, Motorola, Nokia, Sharp, and Sony. After this specification is complete, we can likely expect to see Java pre-installed on many more PDAs.

This profile will focus on handheld devices with the following attributes:

- No less than 512KB total memory (ROM and RAM combined) available for Java runtime and libraries, and no more than 16MB.

- Limited power (typically battery operated).

- User interfaces having at least a total resolution of at least 20,000 pixels, a pointing device, and character input.

The PDA profile adds a special display toolkit with special classes and objects for small screens. This will be subset of Standard Java's Abstract Window Toolkit (AWT). More information about the profile can be found at `http://jcp.org/jsr/detail/75.jsp`.

## PalmOS

Many handheld devices support the Palm Operating System (PalmOS). Palm Computing has a whole line of different devices—Palm V, the wireless Palm VII, Palm Vx, Palm m500, and Palm m505. There are also numerous modems available for Palms, made by companies such as Minstrel. Visit `http://www.palm.com/` for more details.

In addition, companies have licensed the PalmOS. Handspring, for example, created the Visor, the Prism, and the Visor Edge (shown in Figure 2.2). Handspring specializes in an expansion slot called the Springboard, which enables you to plug-in components such as digital cameras, global positioning systems (GPS), and more memory. Visit `http://www.handspring.com/` for more info.

*FIGURE 2.2*    The Handspring Visor Edge.

Sony also has a line of organizers using PalmOS. The Sony CLIE (pronounced klee-ay), for example, has a full color display, supports the Sony memory stick, and comes with a built-in MP3 player. Read more about the CLIE at `http://www.sonystyle.com/micros/clie/`.

Several new phones actually support the PalmOS. Handspring has a VisorPhone that clips into the Springboard slot on their Visor products, as shown in Figure 2.3. Kyocera has a device called the 6035 SmartPhone (previously known as the Qualcomm pdQ), with CDMA digital wireless access.

*FIGURE 2.3*    The VisorPhone.

## Microsoft Windows CE

Microsoft's handheld operating system, formerly known as PocketPC, looks and acts similarly to desktop versions of Windows such as Windows 95 and Windows NT. Many devices, ranging from micro-notebook computers to small cell phones, run atop the Windows CE environment. Windows CE supports micro versions of popular Windows software such as Pocket Outlook 2000, Pocket Internet Explorer, and Microsoft Money for PocketPC.

The Compaq iPaq series of handhelds is perhaps the most popular CE device, shown in Figure 2.4. Sleek, light, and with a beautiful back-lit color screen, it allows for 32MB of RAM and can support plug-in devices such as monitors, keyboards, and modems. It also has excellent sound quality and enables you to record voice memos or play MP3s. More details can be found at
`http://athome.compaq.com/showroom/static/iPAQ/handheld_jumppage.asp`.

*FIGURE 2.4*    The Compaq iPaq.

The range of Casio Cassiopeia series of handhelds have the capability to display more than 64,000 colors. Many use IBM's microdrive technology for additional storage and come with 32MB of RAM. More information can be found at
`http://www.casio.com/personalpcs/section.cfm?section=19`.

Hewlett Packard's Jornada series of handheld PCs and organizers also runs atop Windows CE. More info can be found at `http://www.hp.com/jornada/`.

### Siemens SIMpad SL4

This tablet-shaped computer, shown in Figure 2.5, offers organization tools and instant connection to the Internet. It is built atop Windows CE. To jump online, the pad need only point towards any infrared-capable mobile phone. It comes with 16MB of memory and can be expanded to 64MB. Most navigation occurs with your fingertip, touching the screen.

The SIMpad comes loaded with Insignia's Jeode KVM, allowing for full PersonalJava compatibility.

*FIGURE 2.5*    The SIMpad SL4.

More info can be found at `http://www.siemens.ie/News/simpad.htm`.

### Siemens SX45
This is a mobile phone with the capabilities of a full-blown Windows CE computer. Although Siemens plans to add Java functionary to the SX45, the current crop of devices will not have Java installed.

## Symbian EPOC

Symbian's EPOC operating system is a popular operating system that supports full-featured applications that fit on small devices.

Symbian OS Version 6.0 includes PersonalJava built in, and is the first commercial JavaPhone implementation on wireless devices. Future Symbian releases will support MIDP and CLDC, and be able to instantly run and deploy MIDlets.

Smartphones with Symbian will come with a MIDP and CLDC-capable KVM. Higher-end devices such as communicators and handheld computers will use a combination of PersonalJava and JavaPhone.

> **NOTE**
>
> Note that not every device with EPOC currently supports PersonalJava out of the box. Adding Java support is available, but up to the device manufacturer.

More information about Java's role at Symbian can be found at `http://www.symbian.com/technology/keytech-bigjava.html`.

### Psion netBook (Series 7)
This device, created by Psion Teklogix, is somewhere between a sub-notebook sized computer and a PDA. It is geared for the mobile workforce, and comes with full Java (J2SE) 1.1.4 support.

The netBook is very popular in Europe, and runs the Symbian EPOC platform along with the Psion Teklogix Java Platform.

**URL:** `http://www.psionteklogix.com/main/netbook.htm`

### Psion RevoPlus

This sleek pocket-sized EPOC device has 16MB of RAM, full WAP and HTML browsing, and full organizer personal functionality. The screen is touch sensitive, and you can write or select objects using a stylus. Check it out in Figure 2.6.

*FIGURE 2.6*    The Psion RevoPlus.

Although Java isn't pre-installed, you can install it with an included CD-ROM.

You can hold up an infrared-compatible mobile phone to instantly fire up the RevoPlus wireless functionality.

**Display Size:** 480×160 pixels

**URL:** http://www.psion.com/revoplus/

## Sharp Zaurus SL-5000

This device is really nifty! It has a full pop-out keyboard, CompactFlash expansion slots, a beautiful color screen, and a light, slim casing. Even better, it runs Linux as its operating system, and has the PersonalJava 1.2 environment pre-installed!

**Display Size:** 240×320

**URL:** http://developer.sharpsec.com/

## Other Linux Handhelds

Several other handhelds are coming out that run the Linux operating system.

For example, the Samsung Yopy, designed by a small company called GMate, has Linux at its core. More information can be found at http://www.yopy.com/. Any Linux device can be easily loaded with PersonalJava.

## Micro Java Virtual Machines

While most PDAs do not have Java pre-installed on them, it is almost always possible to get Java support. Some devices are even capable of running the full Java 2 Standard Edition. This section will show you some of the ways to fit a Java virtual machine (JVM) onto various devices.

### Javasoft's KVM for the Palm

You can download a full Software Development Kit (SDK) enabling you to develop Java applications on your desktop and then deploy them on your Palm.

**URL:** http://java.sun.com/products/cldc/

### Javasoft's MIDP for the PalmOS

Sun also offers a special version of MIDP for the PalmOS. You can download a binary release of the CLDC and MIDP libraries, along with a desktop utility that converts MIDlets into Palm's PRC files. In addition to all of MIDP's standard features, the library also includes some expanded PalmOS-only features:

- Palm preferences

- HotSync support

- MIDlet beaming support

**URL:** http://java.sun.com/products/midp/palmOS.html/

### Javasoft's PersonalJava for Windows CE

A binary version of the PersonalJava environment is available for Windows CE Version 2.11. A version for the latest Windows CE Version 3.0 or better is not available yet.

**URL:** http://java.sun.com/products/personaljava/

### IBM J9 VM

IBM's J9 Virtual Machine supports PalmOS, Windows CE, as well as pretty much every other major operating system out there. The Visual Age Micro Edition product enables developers to create CLDC as well as Connected Device Configuration (CDC) programs for J2ME.

**URL:** http://www.embedded.oti.com/learn/vaesvm.html

### Esmertec Jbed Micro Edition CDLC

Esmertec has created a small and fast JVM specially tailored to the Palm Operating System. Unlike many other JVMs, the JbedVM CLDC compiles Java bytecode to native code on the device itself, making execution times an order of magnitude faster than standard, interpreted JVMs.

**URL:** http://www.esmertec.com/p_jbed_cldc_long.html

### kAWT Extended KVM (xKVM)

Formerly known as the ColorKVM, this KVM version runs on color versions of the PalmOS 3.5 or better. This team has taken Sun's KVM 1.0.2 source code and added support for advanced Palm devices:

- Color and grayscale graphics, including 16-bit color for Handspring and other devices that support high resolutions.

- JogDial support for the Sony CLIE devices.

- HandEra 330s 240×320 QVGA high-resolution screen and support for minimizing and maximizing the silkscreen.

A special micro version of Standard Java's Abstract Window Toolkit can also be included in the KVM.

**URL:** http://www.kawt.de/

### Kadasystems Kada VM
This VM is a clean-room implementation of PersonalJava for the JVM. The VM comes packaged with the Kada APIs, which support PersonalJava 1.1.8 as well as java.sql and java.math for more advanced applications. The Kada APIs have a total footprint of 460KB.

There are two sizes of Kada VM you can download: The Kada Compact VM for simple AWT or network applications running on smaller devices; and the Kada Standard VM, which has support for database functionality.

Both versions of the KadaVM are available for PalmOS 3.5 or Windows CE.

**URL:** http://www.kadasystems.com/kada_vm.html

### MicroJBlend
Using the technology behind JBlend, which is a well-known and very quick embedded Java system, MicroJBlend is a KVM for Windows CE that supports the full J2ME MIDP specification. The latest version also supports NTT DoCoMo's i-Appli standard.

**URL:** http://www.jblend.com/en/overview/microJBlend.html

### Jeode EVM
The Jeode Embedded Virtual Machine (EVM) is a PersonalJava-compliant runtime environment available for many processors and devices, including the Windows CE 2.12 and 3.0. Jeode has created one of the fastest virtual machines out there.

A special iPaq version called JeodeRuntime is available, including plug-in support for Pocket Internet Explorer.

**URL:** http://www.insignia.com/products/default.asp

### NSIcom CrEme
CrEme is an augmented Java Virtual Machine, specially designed for Windows CE devices. The VM is easy-to-install and has a small footprint.

**URL:** http://www.nsicom.com/products/creme.asp

### HP chaiVM for Pocket PC

This virtual machine supports the full version of JDK 1.1.8 along with JNI. A version of Chai for the Jornada is freely available, and needs 16MB of memory to run.

A CLDC/MIDP version of chaiVM is expected out by the end of the year.

**URL:** http://www.hp.com/products1/embedded/products/platform/chaivm.html

### SAVAJE XE Operating System

This is a full-blown JVM for the StrongARM processor. It allows the full Java 2 Standard Edition with JDBC, Jini, RMI, and so on to run on the iPaq, the Psion netBook, and other such devices.

SavaJe XE has a 12MB footprint and requires a minimum hardware configuration of a 190MHz Intel StrongARM processor (SA1100/1110) with 32MB of RAM.

**URL:** http://www.savaje.com/products/savajexe.html

### Transvirtual Kaffe

Kaffe is a clean-room, open source implementation of the Java virtual machine and class libraries. Started by Tim Wilkinson and added to by dozens of contributors, Kaffe enables PersonalJava 3.0 programs to be run on nearly any platform or operating system. In addition to the full JDK 1.3 PersonalJava functions, Kaffe handles graphics, file management, and networking. A Windows CE version is available.

**URL:** http://www.kaffe.org/

## Mobile Phones and Pagers

Following are a list of known J2ME mobile phones and pagers. Each listing includes information about the phone's manufacturer, operating platform, and mobile network type.

Most phones will have links to Web sites where you can find more information about pricing and availability.

### Casio CdmaOne C452CA

This shock-resistant and water-resistant device runs the MIDP along with JBlend and EZPlus. It is available in Japan, utilizing the JDDI network.

**Wireless Network:** CDMA

**Display Size:** 120×133

**URL:** http://www.casio.co.jp/gzone/

### Ericsson R380

This is a PDA and phone. The screen is a huge, extremely roomy 360 pixels wide. The top of the phone flips open to reveal the screen as well as a full keyboard. Available in Europe and the United States.

**Platform:** Symbian EPOC

**Wireless Network:** GSM

**Display Size:** 360×120

**URL:** http://www.ericsson.com/WAP/products/r380.shtml

### Fujitsu F503i

This is Fujitsu's stab at the 503 line of phones. Like all DoCoMo phones, it runs using the J2ME/CLDC with special i-Appli class libraries.

**Wireless Network:** i-mode (PDC)

**Display Size:** 120×130/8 bits

**Limits:** 50 JAR files, with a maximum file size of 10KB

**URL:** http://pr.fujitsu.com/jp/news/2001/01/18-3.html

### Hitachi CdmaOne C451H

This device runs the MIDP along with JBlend and EZPlus. It is available in Japan, utilizing the KDDI network.

**Wireless Network:** CDMA

**Display Size:** 120×143 pixels/8 bits

**URL:** http://www.hitachi.co.jp/Prod/vims/mobilephone/

### LG Telecom p510 (i-Book)

LG Telecom's i-Book runs a special version of J2ME CLDC called Kittyhawk. Kittyhawk is similar to some of the older versions of MIDP. The phone is available only in South Korea.

**Wireless Network:** CDMA

**Display Size:** 128×128/4 grayscale

**Limits:** 10 JAR files, with a maximum file size of 60KB (45KB recommended).

**URL:** http://java.ez-i.co.kr

## Other LG Telecom Phones

LG Telecom's has several next generation phones running MIDP. These include the C-nain 200, CX-300L, Cyber-ez-X1. The other phones use the Kittyhawk Java profile, but the C-nain 2000 not only has a 4906-color screen, but runs pure MIDP.

**Wireless Network:** CDMA

**URL:** http://java.ez-i.co.kr

## Matsushita/Panasonic P503i

This is Matsushita's version of the 503 line of DoCoMo phones. It too uses the J2ME/CLDC, with special i-Appli class libraries.

The predecessor to this phone, the 503i, was the first Java phone to be released in the world. A glitch forced DoCoMo to recall more than 100,000 units.

**Wireless Network:** i-mode (PDC)

**Display Size:** 120×130/8 bits

**Limits:** 7 JAR files, with a maximum file size of 10KB

**URL:** http://www.mci.panasonic.co.jp/pcd/p503i/

## Matsushita/Panasonic P503iS

This beautiful DoCoMo phone folds up and has a slick color display. It too runs i-Appli.

**Wireless Network:** i-mode (PDC)

**Display Size:** 120×130/8 bits

**URL:** http://www.mci.panasonic.co.jp/pcd/p503is/

## Matsushita/Panasonic FOMA P2101V

This advanced phone actually has a video camera. Because it works with a third-generation mobile network, it is capable of real-time video conferencing! FOMA, by the way, stands for Freedom of Mobile Multimedia Access.The display is full, startling color. It is available only in Japan. It runs using NTT DoCoMo's i-Appli class library.

**Wireless Network:** 3G (W-CDMA)

**Display Size:** 176×220/18 bits

**URL:** http://foma.nttdocomo.co.jp/monitor/term/n-e-p2101v.html

## Mitsubishi D503i and D503iS

Mitsubishi weighs in with this 503 line of phone. It has a color display and runs on DoCoMo, using the J2ME/CLDC with special i-Appli class libraries.

**Wireless Network:** i-mode (PDC)

**Display Size:** 132×142/10 bits

**URL:** http://www.docomo-kansai.co.jp/text/mova/products/d503i/

## Mitsubishi J-D05

This advanced phone runs the full CLDC/MIDP using JBlend. It also includes J-PHONE-specific class libraries (JSCL). The phone not only has active-matrix color displays, but a large 1MB memory capacity and built-in digital camera. It is available only in Japan.

**Wireless Network:** i-mode (PDC)

**Display:** 12 bits

**URL:** http://www.j-phone-east.com/company/n/2001/010614_3.htm

## Motorola i85s

The Motorola i85s was the first J2ME/MIDP phone to be released in the United States, and has been available since March 2001. It is also available in Canada, Brazil, Israel, and the Middle East. The phone also features Nextel's popular two-way radio service. You see what it looks like in Figure 2.7.

*FIGURE 2.7*    Motorola's i85s: The first Java phone in the United States.

Currently, Nextel's Java service does not allow for network communications, so multiplayer games are not possible. Nextel plans to enable network access by the end of 2001, however.

Motorola also offers a service whereby MIDlets for the phone can be downloaded at www.motorola.com/idenupdate

**Wireless Network:** iDen

**Display Size:** 110×102/2 bits

**URL:** http://www.mot.com/LMPS/iDEN/products/i85s/i85s.html

## Motorola i50sx

The i50sx has all the features of the i85s phone such as voice activation and speaker phone, but is intended more for the consumer market than the business market. It has interchangeable, colored faceplates, seen in Figure 2.8.

*FIGURE 2.8*   Motorola's i50sx.

**Wireless Network:** iDen

**Display Size:** 110×102/2 bits

**URL:** http://www.mot.com/LMPS/iDEN/products/i50sx/i50sx.html

## Motorola Accompli 009 PIC

The Accompli 009 PIC is a cute little pager with a color display and a full tiny keyboard capable of running Java applications. See Figure 2.9.

*FIGURE 2.9*   Motorola's Accompli 009 PIC.

**Wireless Network:** GSM 900Mhz, GSM 1800Mhz, GSM 1900Mhz, GPRS

**Display Size:** 240×160 pixels

**URL:** http://commerce.motorola.com/consumer/QWhtml/a009.html

## Motorola, Accompli 008/6288

This advanced little device, shown in Figure 2.10, offers all the functionality of an organizer in the package of a phone. The screen is grayscale, but it includes a full date book, phone book, and even a dictionary. You can synchronize the phone with your computer to keep track of appointments and contacts.

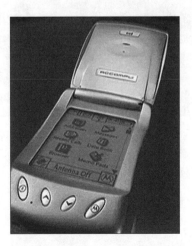

*FIGURE 2.10*   Motorola's Accompli 008.

Additionally, the Accompli 008 offers full on-screen keyboard and voice recognition. It also has handwriting recognition for Chinese as well as English, so you use a stylus to enter most of your information.

The phone is not currently available in North America. Currently the focus is in Europe and Hong Kong, where the phone has a Chinese-English dictionary installed.

**Wireless Network:** GSM 900Mhz, GSM 1800Mhz, GPRS

**Display Size:** 240×320 pixels total, 240×236 pixels usable display area

**URL:** `http://www.motorola.de/mobiltel/public/produkte/datenblaetter/accompli008/datenblatt.shtml`

### Other Motorola Phones

Other Motorola offerings include the i55sr (110×102 screen), the i80s (119×64/1 bit screen), and the i90c (111×110 screen). All of these phones run on the iDen network.

### NEC N503i

Every other Japanese manufacturer has created a 503 line of color phone, and NEC is no exception. Also like the others, it runs using the J2ME/CLDC with special i-Appli class libraries.

**Wireless Network:** i-mode (PDC)

**Display Size:** 120×130/10 bits

**URL:** `http://www.nec.co.jp/japanese/product/mobile/lineup/n503/`

### NEC FOMA N2001

This sleek, color display phone runs on third-generation mobile networks within Japan and supports J2ME/CLDC, along with NTT DoCoMo's i-Appli Java libraries. Like other FOMA phones, it has a video camera for true Dick Tracy-like video phoning.

**Wireless Network:** 3G (W-CDMA)

**Display:** 12 bits

**URL:** `http://www.nec.co.jp/japanese/product/mobile/n2001.html`

### Nokia 9210 and 9290 Communicator

This is another phone/organizer combination. The communicator folds open vertically, providing a full keyboard and a nice, large screen. The screen is full color and can play short video clips, and the high-speed network makes e-mail and other digital communications very efficient. Get a sneak peek of it in Figure 2.11.

*FIGURE 2.11*    Nokia's Communicator.

The phone has built-in fax, e-mail, and Web browsing. The 9290 version of the Communicator is intended for United States markets, and the 9210 version is already widely available in Europe.

The full PersonalJava 1.1.1 platform is built into the phone, and MIDP libraries can be added in on top of PersonalJava. The JavaPhone 1.0 API is also included.

**Platform:** Symbian EPOC

**Wireless Network:** GSM 900Mhz, GSM 1800Mhz. The 9290 supports GSM 1900Mhz

**Display Size**: 640×200/12 bits (463×168 available for Java MIDlets)

**URL for 9210:** http://www.nokia.com/phones/9210/

**URL for 9290:** http://www.nokia.com/phones/9290/

**Information About Java:**
http://forum.nokia.com/javaforum/main/1,6668,1_0_30,00.html

## RIM/iPaq Blackberry

The Blackberry, created by Research In Motion and licensed by Compaq, was one of the first devices to support the MIDP version of J2ME out of the box. Intended mostly for quick and easy wireless e-mail, the Blackberry has become a smash sensation in North America and abroad.

The screen size for various Blackberries ranges from pager-sized to Palm-sized.

**RIM URL:** http://www.rim.com/products/handhelds/index.shtml

**iPaq URL:** http://www.compaq.com/products/handhelds/blackberry/

More info about the Blackberry Java development can be found at http://developers.rim.net/tools/jde/index.shtml.

## Samsung SCH-X130, SCH-X230, SCH-X350, and SCH-X350

This group of phones run a special Java virtual machine called the XVM created by the Korean company XCE. The Java is MIDP compatible, with 256KB runtime memory and Korean Locale support (EUC-KR).

The SCH-X130 and SCH-X350 have displays of 128×128/2 bits. The SCH-X230 is 120×160/8 bits. And the SCH-X250 has a 120×160 screen with 8 bits of color.

The phone's focus is on top-notch sound capabilities. The phone uses 16 chord progressions instead of digital or mechanically produced sound. The phone will come with Top-40 hits as well as natural sound clips. There will also be a Palm Top Karaoke function. This will allow for excellent game background music and sound effects! The phone can also transfer data over CDMA 2000, which means rates can get as high as 144Kpbs.

**Wireless Network:** CDMA 2000

**Limits:** 90KB of application memory (including RMS databases), with 180K of runtime RAM

**URL:** http://www.samsung.com.au/samsung.asp?cat=11&obj=503

## Sharp J-SH07

The J-SH07, made for J-PHONE, runs the full CLDC/MIDP using JBlend. It also has the capability to run a set of J-PHONE-specific class libraries (JSCL).

The phone not only has a great color display, but can support 3D polygons. This means that 3D games are now totally feasible! Instead of transferring heavy bitmaps, graphics can be transported to the phone in fast vector format.

**Wireless Network:** i-mode (PDC)

**Display Size:** 120×160 pixels, 16 bits

**Limits:** Maximum JAR size is 30KB

**URL:** http://www.sharp.co.jp/products/jsh07/

## Siemens SL45i (or 6688i)

This phone not only supports J2ME with MIDP, but comes with additional Java class libraries enabling you to access special features such as the phone's vibrator, light, sound tones, melody composer, and better image manipulating. There is even an included game API! We will, of course, cover this API in great detail later in this book.

The phone comes with many games pre-loaded, including Bricks, Worm, Chess, Black Jack, and I-Skiing. Siemens has also made over-the-air provisioning of applications very easy and feasible. The phone also has a built-in MP3 player and a slot for MMC memory cards, with 32MB of standard memory. It even comes with a designer stereo headset, enabling you to activate some commands by voice.

**Wireless Network:** GSM 900Mhz, GSM 1800Mhz

**Display Size:** 101×80/1 bit

**Limits:** Maximum JAR size is 30KB

**URL:** http://www.siemens.com/page/1,3771,242906-1-999_5_0-0-pressIndex_20_bereichChoice_999,00.html

## Sony SO503i

Sony has created a 503 DoCoMo color phone, as well. It runs the CLDC with i-Appli DoCoMo classes.

**Wireless Network:** i-mode (PDC)

**Display Size:** 120×120/16 bits

**URL:** http://www.sony.co.jp/sd/products/Consumer/KEITAI/so503i/

## Toshiba J-T06

This advanced phone runs the full CLDC/MIDP using JBlend. It also includes J-PHONE-specific class libraries (JSCL). You can take snapshots with the built-in digital camera and send the picture, though One Touch Mail, to any other person. Pretty cool! The J-TO6 is available only in Japan.

**Wireless Network:** PDC

**Display:** 16 bits

**URL:** http://www.j-phone-east.com/company/n/2001/010614_2.htm

# Low-End Java Devices: Smart Cards and Embedded Chips

Although the game possibilities are somewhat limited, you may want to look into developing games for smart cards, embedded devices, medical instruments, smart chips in home appliances, and other small systems capable of running Java.

## JavaCard

Visa, American Express, Europay, and many other credit card companies around the world have put smart Java chips into their credit cards creating "smart cards."

Many embedded chips, and other small embedded devices, run via the JavaCard API. The JavaCard API is a secure, lightweight subset of J2ME classes intended for environments that have nearly no memory.

The reasons for adding Java to a credit card are plentiful. Typically, a credit card only has a magnetic strip with simple information such as the account number, expiration date, and cardholder's name. JavaCard enables much more advanced information to be stored on the card, such as vendor account information, personal profiles, frequent flier miles, or other incentive points. More information about JavaCard can be found at `http://java.sun.com/products/javacard/`.

## EmbeddedJava

Sun's EmbeddedJava technology is a way of taking a standard Java application environment and condensing it into small memory footprints. EmbeddedJava is different from the Java and PersonalJava platforms in that there are no core APIs that must be implemented. Rather, APIs can be configured depending on the target platform and the needs of the platform.

When using EmbeddedJava, you can grab any fields and methods from the core JDK 1.1.7 APIs (except java.applet) and leave behind the rest. Sun provides optimizing tools to create a scaled-down embedded environment. More information can be found at `http://java.sun.com/products/embeddedjava/`.

# Summary

Aren't some of these devices cool? And this is only the beginning... The rest of this book will show you how to actually program games that support all of these devices, and look their best on various types of screens. Want to know what you're up against? The next chapter will show you some actual wireless games currently out on the market.

# 3

# Big Games, Small Screens

## IN THIS CHAPTER

- Your Competition
- WAP Games
- i-mode Games
- SMS GAMES
- J2ME MIDP Games
- J2ME Palm Games
- iAppli Games
- What Are You Waiting For?

Over the next few pages, we'll look at some of the current micro games currently out on the market. Many of these games are popular blockbusters and come from top game companies such as Sega and Bandai, but you'll also notice that hobbyists and small independent teams have created some of the best examples out there.

This chapter covers a wide variety of games for various micro platforms:

- WAP games
- SMS games
- MIDP games
- J2ME Palm games
- iAppli games

## Your Competition

If you really want to design games that wow, it is highly recommended that you check out your competition. Playing and *studying* other games is a terrific way to get interface and gameplay ideas, learn what *doesn't* work, and become sure you're not doing something that has already been done.

Although many of these games are just tinier versions of games we've already seen, loved, and gotten addicted to, many of the most exciting products in this chapter are utterly original. You'll find games without graphics, games that rely on global positioning, and games that wouldn't work anywhere else but on a micro device.

The goodies in this chapter will show you that big-game concepts are indeed possible on the smallest of screens, and often with the smallest of budgets.

## Things to Look For

The reasons why the best games are fun to play are difficult to encapsulate. Finding gameplay features that work is especially important in the micro world, where there are so many limitations and so few examples of quality gaming.

Some qualities to look and aim for:

- Easy to learn—If the game is too complicated, most people won't take the time to hike up that learning curve. And there's almost no room for instructions on handheld device screens. So make things ultra-intuitive!

- Clarity of visuals—The graphics should be as large as possible. The screens are, as you know, very tiny, and most people like to hold the screens at chest level, about a foot away from their eyes.

- Simplicity of gameplay—The gameplay itself should use a few keys and be very clear and easy to understand.

- Quick game periods—Cell phone users often play games while waiting for meetings to begin, during quick subway commutes, or while sitting on the porcelain throne in the bathroom. Breaking your game into short, quick levels is usually a good idea.

- Interactivity—Playing against machines is cool. But if you can play the game against other humans, you've got some real competition! And you also have a built-in community, keeping people coming back to be with friends they have met.

## The Near Future

As new technologies come into play, Java micro games will become more powerful than ever. Some examples of these technologies are as follows:

- Color screens with better resolutions will make for bright, engaging graphics.

- Faster processors and video chips will provide better animation and even 3D graphics.

- Better audio capabilities will add the element of music and sound to games.

- Location-based technologies will give games the capability to know exactly where in the real world a player is standing. Games can be written engaging real players in the real world, using the phones only as a transparent tool to connect.

- Wireless connection technologies such as Bluetooth will give small devices short-range radio connectivity, enabling phones and other devices to connect to other phones, larger servers, or other peripherals—without using valuable and expensive wireless network services. This can allow for extremely quick multiplayer gaming, as long as both players are in the same vicinity. Likewise, third-generation networks will bring the power of broadband speeds to mobile devices.

## WAP Games

The Wireless Application Protocol (WAP), which is discussed in great detail in Chapter 4, "Wireless Standards:How Data Goes To and Fro," is a very simplistic game platform. All game traffic must be downloaded from the network and must be displayed in simple *cards*. The cards themselves are nothing more than small Web pages. You can basically display text, see simple black and white graphics, and enter basic data into a form. That's it! Worse yet, the downloading between each card is usually very slow, requiring a few seconds of patient foot-tapping.

Despite all these limitations, dozens of creative and daring individuals and companies have come out with an impressive array of WAP games.

### Wireless Games

**URL:** http://www.wirelessgames.com/

The Wireless Games Web site was created by a publisher of wireless games and other technologies called Digital Bridges (http://www.digitalbridges.com/). This British company is dedicated to creating and expanding the reach of WAP games.

Some of their offerings include the following:

**Sorcery**
Shown in Figure 3.1, this is a full-featured role-playing game. This game brings the worlds, characters, and play from the beloved Steve Jackson Sorcery game onto wireless phones.

The game is a typical fantasy adventure. You quest in search of the Crown of Kings, solving puzzles, fighting monsters, and building up your character.

*FIGURE 3.1*    Sorcery.

### Tanks

You play a tank commander, facing off against another tank. All you do is choose the direction you want to fire, select a velocity, and fire. Your opponent then gets a shot at you.

You can actually send your opponent messages as you shoot it out. A simple but engaging game.

### Fight KO

You are a trainer. You must take a virtual fighter and try to build the best boxer by juggling various attributes. You can then compete against other fighters, as shown in Figure 3.2.

The more your boxer fights, the more experienced he becomes. You can continually edit and save your character for future battles.

*FIGURE 3.2*   Fight KO.

### Code Breaker

In this simple game, you are a master safecracker trying to rob an entire town. You go from store to store, guessing codes and trying to get the loot. You have ten tries before the police show up.

### Mines

This is a WAP variation of the popular and addictive Mine Sweeper game that comes with all Microsoft Windows machines.

You must try to work your way to the center of a grid and grab the flag. But the going isn't easy—you must sniff out and avoid stepping on any mines.

### Casino Games

Wireless Games offers a suite of various games of chance, including

- High/Low
- Video Poker
- Blackjack (see Figure 3.3)
- Fruit Machine (Slots)

- Roulette

- Craps

*FIGURE 3.3*  Blackjack.

### Popular Classics

Additionally, there are a number of simple, popular classics offered:

- Hangman—Solve a hidden word puzzle or feel the pain.

- Fours—A "Connect-Four"-type game. Try to drop checkers into slots and get four in a row (see Figure 3.4).

- Tic Tac Toe—Everyone's favorite (and unwinnable) three-in-a-row game.

- Anagram—Try to unscramble phrases.

*FIGURE 3.4*  Fours.

### Wireless Pets

This is a simple virtual pet "game" created by The Games Kitchen, and borrowing from Bandai's popular Tamagotchi.

The idea is to take a baby pet and feed, care, and play with it. You must keep it happy and full, or it will get sick and possibly even die. Figure 3.5 shows a sample game session. Your pet "lives" in real time on the Wireless Games servers. You can log in and check on your pet at any time.

### Quiz Call and LMA Football Quiz

Trivia is one of the simplest and most sensible genres of wireless games. Trivia doesn't need a lot of fancy graphics or network speed—only a good database of tough questions. It's easy to quickly log in and challenge yourself to a few toughies at any time. Trivia is also something that is highly popular, given TV shows such as *Who Wants to Be a Millionaire?*

*FIGURE 3.5*    Wireless Pets.

Wireless Games offers two games:

- Quizcall—Answer five questions correctly and you can reach the ultimate Knock Out Round.

- LMA Football Quiz—How good is your knowledge of football (soccer, that is)? The highest scorers each day are posted for all to see.

### Top Trumps

This is a popular card-collecting game, licensed from Playaday.com. One player picks a statistic from the back of a selected card and issues a challenge to an opponent. If the opponent's card has a higher stat, then the opponent wins the card that you challenged with. Figure 3.6 shows a sample card.

*FIGURE 3.6*    Top Trumps.

### Wentworth Golf

This advanced game lets you play on a 3D simulation modeled after an actual golf course. You and your caddy must choose the best club based on the wind and course conditions, and then hit the ball in a given direction. Figure 3.7 shows a sample screen.

*FIGURE 3.7*    Wentworth Golf.

## Jamdat

**URL:** http://www.jamdat.com

Jamdat has become one of the most successful wireless game companies in the world. The following is a sampling of Jamdat's games:

### Gladiator

One of the most popular WAP games in the world is Gladiator. This game brought in more than 3.2 million extra minutes of airtime on the Sprint PCS service in the first three months after it launched in October 2000.

The rules are extremely simple: You are a gladiator challenging an opponent to head-to-head combat. You can choose which area of the body to strike at, what type of strike to deliver, and how to defend, as shown in Figure 3.8.

Your gladiator will grow stronger with each win. You can then take your new, stronger gladiator and challenge other players.

At its heart, Gladiator is no more than a multiplayer version of Rock-Paper-Scissors. However, clever graphics, engaging text, and a strong community base have turned the game into a sort of epic.

*FIGURE 3.8*   Gladiator.

Other games by Jamdat include

- Home Run Derby—A baseball game of pitcher versus batter. Two players face off. The pitcher chooses the type of pitch, and the batter chooses the type of hit. The result will range from a strike to a home run.

- Krazy Konondrum—A party game where you get to answer questions such as, "Would you rather be a doughnut or a pomegranate?" The game takes your answers and compiles them with other people's, generating a live survey or poll.

- Rock, Paper, Sizzer and Roshambofu—Jamdat has several versions of the original Rock-Paper-Scissors game. In Roshambofu, you play the game against an Ancient Master, as shown in Figure 3.9.

*FIGURE 3.9*    Roshambofu.

## PicoFun

**URL:** http://www.picofun.com/

This Swedish company has created a set of innovative offerings.

### Lifestylers
This clever game goes beyond the "Virtual Pet" genre, allowing you to act as a master to another human being. Players can pick their goals, depending on the personality type of their characters. You can then balance your character's various attributes and skills, as shown in Figure 3.10.

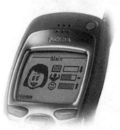

*FIGURE 3.10*    Lifestylers.

Your Lifestyler character lives, eats, sleeps, dates, and works—just like you. But there are all sorts of highly humorous and wacky situations and confrontations, where choices must be made. Choose how your character behaves, and the character will begin to fall into different lifestyle categories, including Casanova, Athlete, Couch Potato, Average Joe, Geek, and Clown.

### Picofun Football

Picofun Football, released in 2000, was one of the world's first multiplayer WAP games. This soccer simulation game allows you to manage your own team. You can pick from dozens of players to buy and sell. You must also pay good salaries and keep morale high. During fantasy games against other players, you can see detailed statistics.

### On the Green

On the Green is a highly detailed golf simulation game. There are numerous courses, each with different graphics, hazards, and scenery. With each hole, you can choose your club, angle of swing, and the power of the swing. As you play, you can progress up 13 skill levels.

### Wall Street Wizard

Wall Street Wizard is a fantasy stock market trading game. You can trade real shares with fake money. Every player starts with the same amount of money, and whomever's portfolio has the highest percentage gain at the end of each month is a winner.

### Fight Arena

This is a multiplayer battle where you can choose to play against another player or against a computer challenger. With each fight, your character's abilities will improve. To reach the number one ranking, you must successfully beat all computerized and human opponents.

## Handy Games

**URL:** http://www.handy-games.com/hg/index.php

This German company has created some of the goriest and sexiest WAP games out there. Quite an accomplishment on such a small, black-and-white screen....

### WAP Knights

This is another dungeon-exploring role-playing game. As illustrated in Figure 3.11, you must work your way through a maze fighting monsters and seeking treasure. You will eventually find keys to open doors to new levels. The graphics are particularly good for WAP, and they're rendered on-the-fly. You can also save the game at any time and continue at your leisure, which is a nice feature for the on-the-go game player.

*FIGURE 3.11*    WAP Knights.

### WAP Tanks

This is a turn-based tank battling game. You face off against the enemy in a 5×5 grid speckled with buildings. You can perform two actions each move, with the option to either move, fire, or repair your tank. This game can be played against other people or against the computer. You work your way up a high score list with each new battle.

### WAP Massacre

This is another fighting game, very similar to Jamdat's Gladiator. The gruesome graphics, however, are much more advanced, as shown in Figure 3.12.

*FIGURE 3.12*    WAP Massacre.

### WAP Interpol

You take on the role of an Interpol cop, chasing a criminal around the world. You must hunt from locale to locale, gaining clues and learning more about your suspect. When you think you've got the criminal identified, you can issue an arrest warrant.

### WAP Crates

This is a logic puzzle wherein you move various crates across a grid, trying to match a given pattern. You must carefully study the board and pick a strategy with each level.

### WAP Girlfriends

This game is another variation on the "Virtual Pet" genre. In this case, you're in a relationship with a "Virtual Girlfriend." You must keep up with your girlfriend's demands, choose different ways to make money for her, and be sure to pay attention to your girlfriend regularly. Figure 3.13 shows a sample screen. The game is a little sexist, of course, but if you're into that sort of thing, the juvenile humor of it all might be for you.

*FIGURE 3.13*  WAP Girlfriends.


## FunCaster.com

**URL:** http://www.funcaster.com/

FunCaster offers 30 different types of games, including casino, chance, mind, leisure, word, and kids games. Some of the more unusual offerings include

- Mermaid—A game of pure chance. You can choose from five different rocks. Choose a rock, then guess what type of marine lifeform lives beneath. You can double your score if a mermaid appears.

- Shapez—Guess the arrangement of four shapes, given six possible shapes, as seen in Figure 3.14. The play is similar to the classic Mastermind game.

*FIGURE 3.14*  Shapez.


## Unplugged Games

**URL:** http://www.ungames.com/

Unplugged Games creates back-end game technology as well as original wireless games. The founders of the company come from a strong game background and are focused on using small devices in innovative ways.

### Void Raider

Void Raider is a complex, rich game of intergalactic trade and war. You begin as the Ensign in command of a tiny starship, and must capture enemy merchant ships, selling the cargo at a profit. You can also hire yourself out as an escort, and protect friendly merchant ships from enemy raids. If you get good enough, you can even go on hunts for enemy privateers, kidnap them, and demand random.

You must manage your crew, your ship's engine, and your weapons. As you earn more money, you can upgrade your ship and hire better crews. You can eventually get promoted to Fleet Admiral.

### Rags 2 Riches

In this wacky game, you are a fashion designer trying to predict next season's trends. This is a rich guessing game with amusing writing and wacky situations.

### Word Trader

Word Trader is one of the most original WAP games out there. You are given a list of five words. Each word is associated with a different category, such as animals or cooking. You trade away the words you don't want to other players, and then get new words dealt to you at random. The idea is to build a list of five within the same category.

After you've made a match, you "claim" that category. The first player to claim six out of eight categories is the winner.

## nGame

**URL:** http://www.ngame.com/index.html

nGame features games that can be played across multiple platforms. Many of their games work on the Web, on interactive TV, and on mobile phones.

The company has dozens of WAP games, including nearly every classic casino game. They also have a great selection of originals:

### Alien Fish Exchange

Try to breed the most exotic aquatic life! You are given a few alien fish to start off with. Take care of your fish, feeding them and playing with them, to encourage them to mutate into new breeds. The game features dozens of different breeds, each with different attributes and behaviors.

The game is multiplayer and the world is persistent—you can log off the game at any time, and your fish continue to grow...or waste away. You can access your virtual aquarium from the Web, your cell phone (Figure 3.15) or your digital TV set (Figure 3.16).

*FIGURE 3.15*   Alien Fish Exchange on a cell phone.

*FIGURE 3.16*   Alien Fish Exchange on digital TV.

### Carrier Force

You command a fleet of eight ships—patrol boat, minesweeper, assault ship, submarine, destroyer, cruiser, battleship, or aircraft carrier. Select two of your ships to fight. If you use a powerful ship, you will always win—but you want to avoid sacrificing a powerful carrier against a lowly patrol boat. Points are gained for every enemy ship you defeat, as seen in Figure 3.17. The game can be played against human players or against the computer.

*FIGURE 3.17*   Carrier Force.

### Chop Suey Kung Fu

You choose a Kung Fu Master and then fight against an opponent. Each turn, both players pick from a selection of martial arts moves. More powerful moves are less likely to hit. As with most other nGame games, this game is playable against either humans or the computer.

### Data Clash

You are a hacker. Your job is to create various attack programs and do battle with other players across the network. You must also write your own defensive programs, because you can be attacked at any time.

The game is in a persistent world. Your programs can be attacked whether you are logged in or not. As you explore the network, you will also compete against dozens of other hackers. Your can maintain your programs by logging in via the Web, digital TV, or mobile phone.

There are 90 different offensive and defensive programs to choose from! Figure 3.18 shows a sample screen from the game.

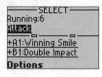

*FIGURE 3.18*    Data Clash.

# i-mode Games

The i-mode platform and phones have similar capabilities to WAP, but generally provide much faster service and have the potential to display color graphics. There are hundreds of different games, many of them similar to the games reviewed in the previous sections.

### Dwango's Turibaka Kibun

**URL:** http://www.dwango.com/

It's not often that a cell phone game becomes a sensation. And who would have thought that the game to take Japan by storm isn't about princesses, monsters, or soldiers, but about *fishing*?

As of early 2000, Dwango Kamone, the company's site for i-mode games, has accumulated more than 1.5 million users. Some of the most popular wireless games in the world can be found here.

Turibaka Kibun literally means "crazy for fishing" in Japanese. The idea couldn't be simpler. You choose a place to fish, select your bait, and then...wait. See Figure 3.19 for a sample screen shot.

*FIGURE 3.19*    Turibaka Kibun.

Eventually your phone will call you back. If your phone is on vibrate mode and you hold out the antenna, it'll even feel like a virtual fishing rod.

# SMS Games

The Simple Messaging System (SMS) is a simple way of sending instant text messages from cell phone to cell phone. The latest specifications enable graphics as well as text, along with more advanced interaction. See Chapter 4 for additional information on SMS.

There are many SMS games. All of them are equally simple: You send a special message to particular number, and you will get another message in return.

## Fisupeli

**URL:** http://www.fisupeli.com/

The Finnish company Sonera Zed, in conjunction with Small Planet Ltd., has created a game similar to Turibaka Kibun called Fisupeli. The game is available only in Finland.

To play, you simply send a text message FISU to the number 400. You will then get a text message back describing your fishing environment. Over time, you will get text message alerts containing one to three different types and sizes of fishes.

You can log into the accompanying Web site at any time to see your fishing history.

## Blue Factory

**URL:** http://www.bluefactory.com/

In addition to WAP games, Blue Factory specializes in games for SMS. Currently the games are focused on European carriers Europolitan-Vodafone, Telia, Mviva, Halebop, and Sonera Zed.

Their collection of games includes the following:

- Hunters & Collectors—This is an advanced multiplayer game that uses global positioning technology. The characters are cuddly but dangerous rabbits, beavers, and other fuzzy animals.

  The way it works is ingenious. Sign up and pick an animal to be your avatar. When two players are close to each other (based on their actual position in the real world) a duel is initiated. They will get an SMS message indicating that the battle is ready to begin.

  Each player sends an SMS message with the amount of ammunition they want to use and their choice of weapon. The results of the duel will be shown, as in Figure 3.20.

  Players can log into the Hunters & Collectors Web page to buy new weapons, check their stats, or look at the game map.

- Cool Vibes—Another dueling game using real positioning, this game is similar to Hunters & Collectors, but based in a psychedelic, tripped-out 60s world.

- Flirtylizer—Not exactly a game, but extremely cool! Sign up and you can flirt anonymously with anyone you choose. Using mobile positioning, the Flirtylizer will point out where your secret admirer is located.

- Get Nessie!—A game where you try to "fish" for the Loch Ness monster. It also includes dial-in elements with actual voices.

- Banana Battle—Estimate the distance to an opponent and then fling a banana at them. All game messages are exchanged via SMS.

- ExtremeQuiz, FootBallQuiz, SciFiQuiz, and CelebriQuiz—All variations on an SMS trivia game with questions about extreme sports, football, sci-fi, or celebrities.

*FIGURE 3.20*    Hunters and Collectors.

## BotFighters by It's Alive

**URLs:** http://www.itsalive.com/ and http://www.botfighters.com/

One of Sweden's most popular cell phone games is called BotFighters. Players create robots and can select elements like shield, weapon, eyes, and armor.

Using mobile positioning, you are notified when you are in the vicinity of another robot. You can issue SMS attack messages to the number 6688 to try to defeat other robots. Unlike other dueling games, BotFighters is literally about being quickest on the draw—whoever sends the attack message first will win. Damage depends on the weapon used and the amount of armor the target bot is wearing.

If you log into the BotFighters Web site, as shown in Figure 3.21, you can upgrade your robot and buy new weapons. More importantly, you can sign contracts to find and destroy other robots, and earn lots of virtual money in the process. You can retrieve information about the top assassins and view their actual known positions on a map of the city. This allows you to literally track down your target in the real world, getting close enough to their location to zap them.

It works like a virtual paintball game, and it has become somewhat of a craze in Stockholm. Some players have gone so far as to engage in car chases and ambushes. The game costs $5 to $10 a month on top of regular cell phone charges, depending on usage.

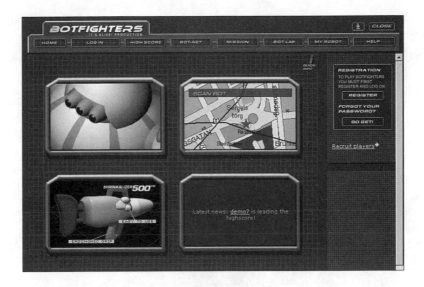

FIGURE 3.21    BotFighters.

### Vizzavi Footie and Trivia

URL: `http://www.vizzavi.co.uk/`

Sign up for one of these games—currently only available through the Vodaphone system—and you can star in your own game show. You can opt to answer football (soccer) trivia or general trivia questions. The questions arrive via SMS, and you must send an SMS answer back. The faster you answer them, the more points you'll get. After each weekly competition, a list of the top ranking players will be sent to all opponents.

## J2ME MIDP Games

This book will focus highly on the Mobile Information Device Profile (MIDP) of J2ME, because it acts as the backbone for all small, mobile devices. Although the official release of MIDP is in its early stages, many companies and hobbyists have managed to put out an impressive line of games. Clearly, the speed in which games can be designed, programmed, and deployed is a result of the widespread use of Java and programmers' expertise in using it.

### Karl Hörnell's MIDP-Man

**URL:** `http://www.javaonthebrain.com/java/midpman`

An independent programmer named Karl Hörnell has put out some of the most impressive MIDP games, for both the Palm OS and cell phones. A cute and effective Pac-Man clone named MIDP-Man and shown in Figure 3.22, pushes MIDP's limits.

*FIGURE 3.22*   MIDP-Man.

## HolyCowBoy's BlockBuster and HolyMoley

**URL for BlockBuster:** `http://holycow.tripod.co.jp/cooldownboy/blockbuster.htm`

**URL for HolyMoley:** `http://holycow.tripod.co.jp/cooldownboy/holymoley.htm`

BlockBuster, created by a Japanese programmer who calls himself HolyCowBoy, is a takeoff of Breakout or Arkanoid. Move the paddle back and forth in order to catch the bouncing ball. The ball will break apart blocks, sometimes releasing valuable pills that make your paddle bigger or cause the ball to move more slowly. Figure 3.23 shows the game in action.

Holy Moley is a "whack-a-mole game" that ingeniously lets you use your phone's numeric keypad to quickly whack moles that pop out of holes. You'll need quick reflexes! And be careful not to whack a flower. The game has six different stages. Figure 3.24 illustrates all the mole-whacking fun.

*FIGURE 3.23*    BlockBuster.

*FIGURE 3.24*    Holy Moley.

## Draw Poker

**URL:** http://www.rr.iij4u.or.jp/%7Ekoichi/index.html

This is a simple but full-featured draw poker game created by another Japanese programmer named Koichi. A screen sample is shown in Figure 3.25.

*FIGURE 3.25*    Draw Poker.

## Cocoasoft

**URL:** http://www.cocoasoft.com/index.html

Some of the most advanced MIDP games out there were written by none other than Roman Verhovsek—CEO of Cocoasoft and coauthor of this book.

### Axion

Axion is a quick-moving arcade game. You fly your ship through different landscapes, avoiding a wide variety of bad guys—each of which exhibits a different difficulty and behavior.

As you progress through the levels, you will pick up different weapons and types of missiles, as shown in Figure 3.26.

**FIGURE 3.26**   Axion.

The game will connect to a server and keep track of the top 100 players. Slightly different versions of the games are available for different phones. If your phone supports sound or vibrations, so does the game—your phone vibrates with each explosion!

### i-Skiing

i-Skiing, shown in Figure 3.27, is a simple downhill slalom competition. Move your skier back and forth between the flags, racing against the clock. You will assessed a time penalty if you miss flags. There are also a number of different slopes to try.

**FIGURE 3.27**   i-Skiing.

Different versions of the game work on MIDP, iAppli, Personal Java, and KittyHawk (LG Electronics' i-Book phone). Multiplayer features will be provided in the near future.

### Jerry the Cat: Indiana Jerrys

Indiana Jerrys is a complete side-scrolling platform game, similar to Super Mario Brothers or Manic Miner. You must move through different levels, avoiding bad dogs. Different levels have elevators and other moving platforms, as well as power-ups and goodies that can earn you a higher score. Figure 3.28 depicts Jerry in action.

**FIGURE 3.28**    Jerry the Cat.

Additionally, the game is multiplayer, with the capability for people across the world to compete in the same levels.

## RomeBlack's Mobile Internet Maze Game

**URL:** http://www.romeblack.com/Wireless/playing.html

The game takes the simple Rock-Paper-Scissors idea and adds a new twist: You log in with your cell phone and join up to five other players in a maze. You take the role of either a rock, a piece of paper, or a pair of scissors, as seen in Figure 3.29.

You then chase opponents around the maze, while being chased by them. Rock will beat scissors, scissors will always beat paper, and paper will beat rock. Whoever is caught loses that round of the game.

Both a Palm and MIDP version of the game are available.

**FIGURE 3.29**    Internet Maze Game.

## Sky Arts' Cube Game

**URL:** `http://www.skyarts.com/`

The Sky Arts site features several different puzzle games for MIDP, along with a reversi and poker game.

In the Cube game, various colored cubes will fall from the top of a grid. If four or more of the same colored squares are positioned in a horizontal or vertical line, then they will disappear from the grid as shown in Figure 3.30. Any cubes higher up will fall, causing chain reactions. If you wait too long, then the cubes in the grid will grow until there is no more room, and you will lose the game. The other cube games provide variations on this theme.

**FIGURE 3.30**    Cube game.

## Jshape's M-Type and MIDP Street Fighter

**URL for M-Type:** `http://www.jshape.com/mtype/index.html`

**URL for Street Fighter:** `http://www.jshape.com/msf/index.html`

M-Type is a Micro Edition version of the popular 80s arcade game called R-Type. You simply move your ship around, avoiding fireballs from bad guys and trying to beat the big boss at the end of each level. This game boasts some of the most impressive graphics to ever reach the small screen, as shown in Figure 3.31.

**FIGURE 3.31**    M-Type.

MIDP Street Fighter is a takeoff of one of the most popular arcade fighting games of all time. Although the game is not quite as advanced as the arcade version, it allows you to pit two martial arts characters against each other, as in Figure 3.32.

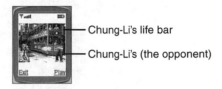

Chung-Li's life bar

Chung-Li's (the opponent)

*FIGURE 3.32*　　Street Fighter.

## Spruce Team

**URL:** http://www.spruce.jp/freemidlets/

The Spruce Team in Japan has created an entire suite of famous arcade games:

- Spruce Invaders—A smaller version of Space Invaders.
- Spruce Tennis—A simple paddle and ball game.
- Spruce Blocks—A Tetris clone.
- Spruce Shooter—A simple fly-and-shoot game.
- Spruce Matchup—A simple concentration memory game.
- Spruce Driver—A racing game, similar to the game that we will be creating together during the course of this book. See Figure 3.33 for a screen shot.

*FIGURE 3.33*　　Spruce Driver.

## Red Team's Dope Wars

**URL:** http://www.redteam.co.uk/dopewars/

Meanwhile, the Red Team in Great Britain has created a MIDP version of the popular text game Dope Wars, seen in Figure 3.34. Travel between Afghanistan, Colombia, and other international locales buying and selling illegal narcotics. Avoid CIA agents and use false-bottomed suitcases and ceramic handguns.

**FIGURE 3.34**    Dope Wars.

Most of the action happens as text messages, but this simple and funny trading game is still fast-paced and, well, addictive.

## J2ME Palm Games

The exact specification for J2ME on Palms and other PDAs is still being worked out. But early release versions of the Kilobyte virtual machine (KVM) and a reduced set of J2ME classes were made available to the public as far back as two years ago.

---

**NOTE**

Any MIDP game or other application can run just fine on the Palm, as long as the MIDP libraries are installed. See Chapter 2, "The Mobile World," for a full list of platforms and devices that support MIDP.

---

The following sections offer a sampling of some of the work that people have done with these early samples.

### Torunda!

**URL:** http://www.aa.alpha-net.ne.jp/kataho/to/index.html

This simple game, created by a Japanese programmer name Kataho, allows you to control a fairy-like character. You move around the screen collecting gems, trying to avoid random flashes of lightning, as seen in Figure 3.35.

The full source code is available at Kataho's Web site, as well as a level editor that lets you design your own game maps.

*FIGURE 3.35*    Torunda!

## Karl Hörnell's Iceblox and PalmWarp

**URL for IceBlox:** http://www.javaonthebrain.com/java/palmblox/

**URL for Warp:** http://www.javaonthebrain.com/java/palmwarp/

These are examples of fast-action arcade games. In Iceblox (Figure 3.36), you control a penguin that must smash through or slide strategically-placed blocks, avoiding or crushing bad guys.

*FIGURE 3.36*    IceBlox.

In PalmWarp, shown in Figure 3.37, you fly a space ship through 3D-looking levels. The goal is simple—move up and down shooting bad guys and avoiding their attacks. There are all sorts of cool-looking characters in this game, such as buzzsaws, tanks, and bazooka birds.

## Hobbit's Let Me Alone

**URL:** http://www.puzzle.gr.jp/hobbit/index.html.en

Yet another Japanese game programmer called Hobbit has created a slew of numerical puzzle games for J2ME. One of the most interesting is called Let Me Alone, shown in Figure 3.38. The goal is to fill blocks in a grid so that the same number doesn't appear more than once in a given row or column.

*FIGURE 3.37*   PalmWarp.

*FIGURE 3.38*   Let Me Alone.

## iAppli Games

NTT DoCoMo's specialized version of Micro Java is called iAppli. We'll learn all about it in Chapter 22, "iAppli: Micro Java with a Twist."

There are many versions in DoCoMo's 503-line of phones supporting iAppli, and it is a very popular service in Japan. In general, iAppli is much more suitable for games than the basic MIDP classes, with support for great sound, full color, and better graphics and animation.

Many of the top game companies in Japan have created iAppli product lines. And other big players such as the Disney Internet Group International (DIG) have become content providers for i-mode.

As a whole, iAppli provides a great glimpse of Micro Java's near-term future: As a powerful platform for professional-quality pocket games.

## Squiral Game

**URL:** http://www.ai.mit.edu/people/hqm/imode/squiral/index.html

This game, created by Henry Minsky, is a quick-moving Tron clone. Check it out in Figure 3.39.

*FIGURE 3.39*    Squiral.

## Dwango's Samurai Romanesque

**URL:** http://www.dwango.co.jp/kamone/samurai/

Samurai Romanesque is of the most advanced role-playing games ever created, not to mention one of the most advanced mobile games ever. You play the role of a samurai in the Era of Warlords (1468 to 1600), trying to rise from foot soldier to general.

The game costs 300 yen per month (about $3), and allows players to join a massively multiplayer world. Up to 500,000 players can exist on the same server simultaneously, able to meet, fight, trade, gossip, and chat with each other.

You can use your mobile phone offline to train your samurai in the art of the sword, and then log in to the gameworld to do real-time battle. This allows you to have some fun with the game without paying packet fees, or if you are in an underground area with bad network coverage.

The game has some unusual, fascinating details. For example, you age one year per day of each session. The weather in the gameworld is determined using real-time Japanese weather information. If it is raining outside, it will also be raining in the gameworld—making travel and swordplay difficult.

You can live to be about 40 years old. During your life you can opt to become a ruler, or you can serve a master. As time goes by, your hair might recede and you will earn battle scars. Meeting, courting, and flirting with women takes several days and careful acting. Eventually, you might marry and birth a child. The child will actually inherit some of your character's traits. After a game session ends, your character dies, but you can control your child as the next generation of samurai.

The game includes several hundred towns, each of which is full of teahouses, shops, and inns. As you walk through a town, as shown in Figure 3.40, the graphics scroll from side to side. Your goal is to reach castles, where you are given missions or the opportunity to join armies.

**FIGURE 3.40**   Walking through a town in Samurai Romanesque.

Traveling between towns occurs in real time, though you can hire horses or rickshaws to get there faster. If you like, you can log off during transit. However, other players can attack you at any time!

Every so often, huge epic battles between competing warlords occur, as shown in Figure 3.41. You can fight for a given lord and be rewarded for bravery if you emerge victorious.

**FIGURE 3.41**   Battling in Samurai Romanesque.

## Dwango's Challenge! The Hard-Boiled Way

Dwango also provides a multiplayer game-matching service for iAppli called Challenge! The Hard-Boiled Way. Because the service uses a dedicated server, all game moves are transferred at high speeds and reflected on players' phones almost instantly.

In addition, the server uses *pseudo push* to cut down on packet fees. Data is only sent over the network, from server to phone, when necessary. If somebody's mobile connection is interrupted, their game state will be stored until they reconnect.

The service allows you meet, chat with, and face off against remote human opponents. Players' ratings are stored, and players can be automatically matched up based on ability.

The service offers six different games:

- The Billionaire—A popular card game. A pack of cards is distributed between up to four participants. Each player is marked with a rank, ranging from billionaire to pauper. The poor must give their best cards to the billionaire. The discarding then begins with the lowest numbered card. The player who gets rid of all cards first is the winner. Figure 3.42 shows this game in action.

- Reverse—A Reversi or Othello clone, where players take turns placing either black or white checkers on the board, trying to surround and then flip the opponent's pieces.

- Chess—The strategic game of kings, shown in Figure 3.43.

- Gobang—A simpler variation of the popular game Go, where players place pebbles on a grid in an attempt to line up five pieces in a row.

- Pincer Checkers—A variation of the popular Shogi game, where two players try to surround each other's pieces.

- Military Checkers—A unique checkers game using military artwork.

*FIGURE 3.42*  Billionaire.

*FIGURE 3.43*    Chess.

## Sega

Sega has created a version of its popular Sonic the Hedgehog side-scroller game for i-mode. You must collect rings while avoiding enemies. Figure 3.44 depicts a sample screen. Sega also plans to create a cell phone version of its popular Out Run game.

*FIGURE 3.44*    Sonic the Hedgehog.

## Namco

The creators of the popular fighting game Tekken have created a low-latency version for i-mode. In Tekken Command Battle, shown in Figure 3.45, players can face off and choose to attack, parry, or throw. A word then appears. Whoever types in the word faster and more accurately will cause more damage.

*FIGURE 3.45*    Tekken Command Battle.

In addition, Namco is releasing some of its classic titles for i-mode on its EZweb service. Expect to be able to play classics such as Pac-Man and Galaxian.

## Capcom

Capcom plans to extend its Biohazard game franchise with a micro i-mode game called Biohazard iSurvivor. In this role-playing game, you move around Raccoon City fighting zombies and improving your character's abilities. Players will also be able to team up with others to complete their quest.

## Bandai Networks

The company that created the Tamagotchi virtual pet is focusing heavily on iAppli Java games. Descriptions of some planned releases include the following:

- A gambling game where players can place odds on the outcome of different types of future events. Players will be able to check out odds, and even buy and sell properties, trying to become king of the town.

- A game in which you correspond by e-mail with virtual girls. The more responsive you are, the more intimate your relationships will get.

- Mystic Grapple—A virtual trading card game where you command sorcerers and summon monsters, trying to collect the best deck of cards.

- A golf simulation game.

- Mah Jong—Travel around Japan and compete in different mah jong tournaments.

## Cybird's Mini Game Tengoku

**URL:** http://www.cybird.co.jp/english/

Cybrid has created a service called Mini Game Tengoku (Game Paradise), available to i-mode users for 315 yen (about 3 dollars) per month. The service will include 14 different games:

- GliderAction—Lift your glider to the right or left and try to ride the currents to land softly on the landing pad. You must avoid hazards such as crows and UFOs, and earn extra points by grabbing jewels that dangle from balloons.

- Seed no Bohken (The Adventures of Seed)—Control Seed as he moves around a maze, avoiding monsters. Similar to Pac-Man.

- Seed no Meikyu Tanken (The Labyrinth Adventures of Seed)—A similar game, where Seed runs through a labyrinth using seeds as weapons—he can plant them, causing trees to quickly grow and block enemy monsters.

- TypeCannon—This educational game, shown in Figure 3.46, tests your math skills. An equation will flash across the screen, and you must type in the correct number solution to hit the target with your cannonballs.

- Takoyaki King—You must quickly grill takoyaki (octopus dumplings) for your demanding customers, and sell them all. If you serve them too raw or too burnt, you will lose customers.

- Snake—This game, shown in Figure 3.47, is a much more graphically advanced version of the black and white Snake game found on many Nokia phones. Move around the screen eating eggs, growing longer with each egg you eat. You must avoid crashing into walls…or your own tail!

- Businessman—Keep customers happy by selling them good products while making high profits. A simple business simulation game.

- Ohajiki Daisenso (The Great War of Ohajiki)—A marbles-like game where you pick a direction, choose a force, and then fire balls around the board, trying to knock your opponent's balls off.

- Reversi—The classic black and white checkers game.

- Gomoku Narabe (Go)—Another classic game.

- Poker—A quick draw poker game.

- Hikkoshi Meijin (The King of Moving)—Organize objects within a room, trying to clear away enough space for your little red sofa.

- CannonBubble—Change the angle and force of your cannon, shooting bubbles in the sky. Try to arrange three bubbles of the same color to make them pop.

- CubeBuster—A concentration game where you must flip cards and try to find matches.

*FIGURE 3.46*   TypeCannon.

*FIGURE 3.47*   Snake.

### Hudson Soft

**URL:** `http://www.hudson.co.jp/eng/index.html`

Hudson Soft also provides an arcade site called "webbeeHudson" that allows i-mode users to play micro versions of classic Hudson Soft games. Here are some samples:

- Miracle GP—A car racing game.

- Miracle Quest—A role-playing game, shown in Figure 3.48, involving more than 200 different scenarios.

- Miracle Detective—A criminal-pursuit game.

- Miracle Golf—Participate in weekly golf tournaments. You can practice offline or compete online against others. Figure 3.49 offers a glimpse.

**FIGURE 3.48**   Miracle Quest.

**FIGURE 3.49**   Miracle Golf.

## What Are You Waiting For?

It took Nintendo about ten years to sell a hundred million Game Boys. In the year 2001 alone, it is expected that nearly *four hundred* million mobile phones will be sold.

There's a big, big market out there for mobile games, maybe even bigger than the market for PC or console games. So time's a' wastin'!

In the next chapter we'll cover popular mobile phone standards that can serve as a basis for your games.

# PART II

# Before, Between, and Beyond J2ME

## IN THIS PART

4  Wireless Standards: How Data Goes To and Fro

5  Let's Talk: Instant Wireless Messaging

6  Wireless in Asia: i-mode and cHTML

7  The Wireless Landscape

# 4

# Wireless Standards: How Data Goes To And Fro

**IN THIS CHAPTER**

- Wireless Networks
- The Wireless Application Protocol (WAP)
- Server-Side WAP
- Handheld Device Markup Language (HDML)
- WAP 2.0 and xHTML Basic

Micro Java is a pretty advanced beast. However, J2ME would not have been possible without older mobile technologies. J2ME is built atop and within other standards that relegate such things as network communication, voice communication, data transfer, and text display.

These standards are often used in creating Micro Java games. For example, a multiplayer game will often involve players being matched up and chatting in a sort of lobby. This lobby may not be written in Java at all, but rather in a simpler text protocol such as WAP. Other games may want to send out standard mobile messages, or even call up special voice numbers.

The standards we will look at in this chapter include the following:

- The Wireless Application Protocol (WAP)
- The Handheld Device Markup Language (HDML)
- WAP 2.0 and the Extensible HyperText Markup Language (xHTML)

In Chapter 5, "Let's Talk: Instant Wireless Messaging," and Chapter 6, "Wireless in Asia: i-mode and cHTML," we'll go on to discuss other major standards, such as SMS Instant Messages and Japan's popular i-mode service.

## Wireless Networks

It would be overkill, in a book about Micro Java games, to delve into too much detail about all the various types of wireless networks currently available. However, when designing micro games, it is essential to know not only your target hardware platform, but also the makeup of the networks you plan to support.

Multiplayer game developers, in particular, must understand a little about the networks that their games run upon in order to design servers that can accommodate them.

## First Generation (1G)

When people talk about the first generation of wireless networks, they are usually referring to the analog voice-centric systems of the 1980's.

The most popular types of these networks include Advanced Mobile Phone Services (AMPS) and NMT.

Although the wireless world could never have gotten off the ground without analog technology, these were very primitive systems relative to today's standards, limited in both functionality and capacity.

## Second Generation (2G)

Second generation networks are digital and circuit-switched. In a circuit-switched network, Phone A will find a free physical path to Phone B. This path then becomes dedicated to these phones, and is kept free from outside interference for the duration of the phones' connection.

Because all data that goes across the network is compressed into bits and bytes, the networks can support better voice quality without static, deal with a higher capacity of callers, require less power, and offer global roaming.

More importantly, the data sent over 2G networks does not have to be voice at all. Short messages or other electronic data—such as game moves—are perfectly valid.

While the data rates of 2G networks are usually good enough to support voice communications, full back-and-forth Internet access is still extremely slow (on the order of 9.6Kbps).

Briefly, here's a description of the major wireless 2G wireless networks around the world:

- Code Division Multiple Access (CDMA)—This technology uses digital encoding and special routines to divide a given chunk of the radio spectrum into different slots. This technique allows many people to share the same radio channel. Existing CDMA systems can handle data speeds from 9.6Kbps to 14.4Kbps. In the United States, Sprint PCS and Verizon Wireless run on CDMA networks.

- Time Division Multiple Access (TDMA)—This was the first digital standard in the United States, beginning in 1993. TDMA divides a radio channel into time slots, each of which is a fraction of a second long, and allocates different phone calls within each slot. In the United States, Cingular is the largest TDMA carrier.

- Global System for Mobile Communications (GSM)—This is the first digital standard developed in Europe, and a variant of TDMA. Different versions of this operate anywhere from the 900MHz to 1.9GHz frequency radio bands. GSM allows mobile phone users to roam across different networks, so that the same phone can work in more than 170 different countries. The data speeds can reach 9.6Kbps. In the Unites States, VoiceStream Wireless is one of the biggest GSM carriers.

- Personal Digital Cellular (PDC)—A Japanese standard based on TDMA. PDC operates in the 800Mhz and 1500MHz bands.

- Integrated Digital Enhanced Network (iDEN)—This network, created by Motorola in 1994, works on the 800MHz, 900Mhz, and 1.5GHz bands. It is based on TDMA and allows for more walkie-talkie–like functionality, such as dispatching, as well as paging, data, and fax. In the United States, Nextel is the largest iDEN carrier.

## Second (and a Half) Generation (2.5G)

GSM technologies have been enhanced to create an expanded set of standards called the General Packet Radio Services (GPRS), specially designed to work with the Internet and multimedia services such as music and video. This network is optimized for data speeds ranging from 114Kbps to 170Kbps, and will support roaming.

The biggest difference with this new packet-switched system is that cell phones are always online and connected. Users are typically charged depending on how much data is actually shipped back and forth. The system also allows voice calls to be made simultaneously to data transfer.

Because the network is packet-switched, a physical connection is not held and dedicated between two phones. Rather, network packets are routed as quickly as possible across logical paths. This also allows the same data to easily and efficiently be shared among many users at the same time.

The idea with GPRS is to take standard GSM service and transition it into third generation systems such as UMTS (see the next section). In fact, GPRS is sometimes referred to as GSM-IP, since it is a more robust version of GSM based on Internet Protocols (IPs).

## Third Generation (3G)

We are now entering the era of 3G. Third generation systems are intended to serve high-speed Internet data, complex teleconferencing, flicker-free video, and CD-quality music. Data speeds are designed to range from 144Kbps to 2Mbps (megabits per second).

Some of the major standards supporting 3G networks include the following:

- Wideband Code Division Multiple Access (W-CDMA)—W-CDMA is mostly used in Japan. NTT DoCoMo's brand name for 3G services is Freedom of Mobile Multimedia Access (FOMA).

- Universal Mobile Telecoms Network (UMTS)—A standard deployed throughout Europe.

- International Mobile Telecommunications 2000 (IMT 2000) —A global standard created by the International Telecommunication Union.

- Code Division Multiple Access 2000 (CDMA 2000)—This is a radio transmission technology bringing narrowband CDMA into the third generation.

## The Wireless Application Protocol (WAP)

**URL:** http://www.wapforum.org

The Wireless Application Protocol (WAP) is a set of standards based on the Internet Protocols (IP) and the Extensible Markup Language (XML). WAP is an open and global standard for wireless applications. WAP was designed to operate seamlessly over CMDA, CDPD, and all other major wireless network types.

WAP's primary technology—the Wireless Markup Language (WML)—is based on HDML and was developed by Unwired Planet (which became Phone.com and is now Openwave), Motorola, Nokia, and Ericsson. These companies and others have formed an open organization devoted to WAP called the WAP Forum.

WAP content is accessed using standard Uniform Resource Locators (URLs), just as Web pages are. Pages written in WML have the .WML extension, just as most HTML pages end with .HTML.

---

**NOTE**

Most modern mobile phones support some version of WAP. Many phones come preloaded with the Openwave (Phone.com) Mobile Browser.

---

The following section is not intended to be a full WAP primer. Rather, it will provide a brief overview of most WML tags and attributes, allowing you to create simple WAP structures in which to support your Micro Java games.

## The WAP Protocol Stack

The protocols that make up WAP are based strongly on the Internet Protocols. The Web protocol stack includes old favorites such as HTML, HTTP, SSL, UDP/IP, and TCP/IP. This is a very robust and efficient suite of protocols, to be sure. However, the Web stack itself is quite large, and provides more functionality than most mobile phones need.

Because of this, a special WAP protocol stack was created. The stack includes, in order

- An application layer—The actual application used to display things to the user. This uses the Wireless Application Environment (WAE) displaying pages written with WML.

- A session layer—How connections are made. This layer uses the Wireless Session Protocol (WSP).

- A transaction layer—How data is divided. This layer uses the Wireless Transaction Protocol (WTP).

- A security layer—Encrypts the data. This layer uses Wireless Transport Layer Security (WTLS).

- A datagram layer—How the data is packaged and sent across the network. This is done using the Wireless Datagram Protocol (WDP). The WDP can use different bearers, such as CDPD, SMS, and so on.

Wireless carriers and cell phone manufacturers need to worry about implementing all these protocols properly. Lowly game developers need only focus on writing the actual applications using WML and WMLScript.

## WAP Architecture

A WAP browser works very similarly to a Web browser, and a WAP server works similarly to a Web server. As in the Web world, the client requests a page from a server. The server then responds with the page data. There is no continual connection. If the server has more data to send to the client, then another client request must first be made.

In the world of WAP, a phone is known as a *user agent*. In fact, most WAP pages come to the phone from a standard Web server, directed through a special server called a *WAP gateway*.

Figure 4.1 shows the typical WAP architecture.

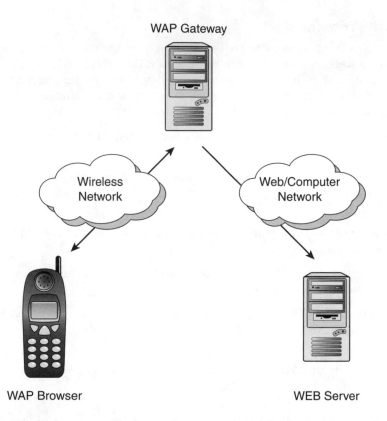

*FIGURE 4.1*    The WAP architecture.

Gateway machines are typically housed and maintained by wireless service providers. The process works as follows:

1. A mobile phone user asks for a specific URL.

2. The request is sent over a proprietary wireless network, using WAP protocols, to a gateway machine.

3. The gateway translates the request to HTTP and sends it to a standard Web server.

4. The Web server will grab or dynamically generate the content (usually a WML document) and send this response back to the gateway.

5. The gateway encodes the WML and WMLScript into byte code and sends it to the phone.

6. The phone processes the byte code and displays the first card to the user.

This process, shown in Figure 4.2, allows a Sprint PCS game player and a Verizon Wireless user to communicate via a central Web server even though they are using different wireless networks.

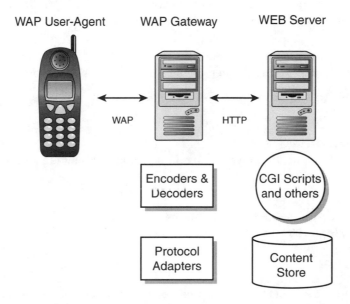

**FIGURE 4.2**   The WAP process.

## The Wireless Markup Language (WML)

The Wireless Markup Language is very similar, in concept, to the Hyper Text Markup Language (HTML) used to create most Web pages. Obviously, a rich HTML Web site with snazzy animations, tons of colors, and fantastic music won't look quite so snazzy on a postage-stamp-sized black and white screen. WML was built to address the typical mobile phone's limitations:

- The screen is 20 or fewer characters across, and only three to six lines tall. As such, WML needs only very basic text formatting and layout abilities.

- Most phones have only a small amount of memory and rudimentary processor power. As such, the object model of how WMLScript can dynamically access a WML deck is vastly simplified.

- Typically, a phone only has only a numeric keypad. As such, all of WML's input methods are basic edit fields and option selections. Nothing that might rely on mouse or keyboard input is supported.

- Data transfer rates are extremely slow, which means latency is extremely high. As such, WML applications are not sent as separate pages requiring many separate requests and responses, but as one big deck separated into individual cards.

- Bandwidth, or the amount of data that can be uploaded or downloaded per second, is extremely limited. WML and WMLScript are usually compressed into tight runnable byte code, which means that a heavy WML file doesn't need to be parsed on the phone, but rather on the gateway server.

WML is currently released as version 1.3. However, most phones only support WML 1.1. The WML tags in this chapter should work with WAP 1.1 browsers and up.

There is also an almost-complete WAP 2.0 specification, which we will discuss later in this chapter.

### WML Basics

Every WML file must begin with a standard prologue, including an XML header and a document definition tag:

```
<?xml version="1.0"?>
<!DOCTYPE wml PUBLIC "-//WAPFORUM//DTD WML 1.1//EN"
    "http://www.wapforum.org/DTD/wml_1.1.xml">
```

---

**WARNING**

Since WML is based on XML, it is case sensitive—every tag and attribute should be in lowercase. Also, tags cannot be nested incorrectly. For example, the following line is illegal and will generate errors:

```
<p><b>Hello!</p></b>
```

---

The rest of the code must be surrounded by <WML> and </WML>.

### A Game of Cards and Decks

In the world of the desktop Internet browser, there are Web sites and Web pages. On a mobile phone, there are decks and cards.

A *card* is a screen that a user sees and can interact with. There can only be one card visible at a time. There is no notion of various windows that can be moved around, minimized, or maximized. Each card is surrounded by the tags:

```
<CARD id="id" title"title">
```

and

```
</CARD>
```

The `id` attribute refers to the name of the card. This name must be a single word with no spaces or wacky characters. Every card in a deck must have a different `id` name.

The `title` attribute is a short description of the card, and is usually displayed at the top of the mobile phone's screen. Each card must have at least one paragraph in it, as designated by the tags <P> and </P>.

---

**NOTE**

Some WAP phones do not show the card title at all, so don't rely on it being there.

---

A *deck* is a set of cards. When your mobile phone downloads a WML file, it is getting an entire deck. The first card in the deck is activated. Later cards can then be activated using their `id` as the user selects various menu or other options.

A deck must begin with

```
<DECK>
```

and end with

```
</DECK>
```

So, taking all these rules together, the world's simplest WML file might look like this:

```
<?xml version="1.0"?>
<!DOCTYPE wml PUBLIC "-//WAPFORUM//DTD WML 1.1//EN"
    "http://www.wapforum.org/DTD/wml_1.1.xml">
<wml>
<card id="main" title="Welcome!">
<p>
Wow! This is one of the world's most simple WML files!
</p>
</card>
<card id="second" title="Second Page">
<p>
Wow! The second card!
</p>
</card>
</wml>
```

On a phone, the above file would appear as in Figure 4.3. Note that the menu command line is automatically inserted as part of the WAP browser.

*FIGURE 4.3*    A simple WML file.

### Anchors Away

You can use anchors to go from one card to another, or to actually load a new deck from the server. Anchor text or images will be hypertext, and will usually appear underlined. Players will be allowed to select this hypertext using the up/down/left/right keys on their mobile phones.

The <anchor> tag contains inner tags:

- <go href="deck.wml#card">Click Here</go>—Loads a new WML deck and brings up a specific card. If you omit the # symbol in the href attribute, then the first card in the given deck will be brought up.

  Likewise, if you omit the deck name completely and only use the # symbol, then you can jump to a card within the currently active deck.

  The <go> tag is similar to the <A> hyperlink tag in HTML. It allows you to send a request to the server, asking for a specific URL.

  Note that the <go> tag can also contain a special tag called <postfield> that allows you to post parameters to the Web server:

  ```
  <postfield name="myparameter" value="myvalue"/>
  ```

- `<prev/>`—Goes to the previously loaded WML card.

- `<refresh>`*Click Here*`</refresh>`—Reloads the current card.

- `<noop/>`—No operation. This does nothing at all. This is usually done to show a command that is currently disabled.

So, to switch to a new card in a deck

```
<anchor>
  Select here to bring up a new card
  from the current deck
  <go href="#card2"/>
</anchor>
```

To switch to a new deck entirely

```
<anchor>
  Select here to bring up a new deck
  <go href="test.wml"/>
</anchor>
```

Most requests will return a new WML document. The WML document can be static, or created dynamically by a CGI script, Java servlet, JSP, ASP, or other server-side technology.

For example, a request to a Java servlet might look like this:

```
<go href="myservlet.jsp?c=getNewWMLPage"/>
```

The `<refresh/>` tag allows you to change certain variables and then reload the same or a different card:

```
<anchor>
  Select here to refresh variable x
  <go href="test.wml"/>
  <refresh>
   <setvar name="x" value="30"/>
  </refresh>
</anchor>
```

Note that you can also use the `<a>` tag, similar to HTML, which is the same as using the `<anchor>` and `<go>` combination:

```
<a href="#newcard">Select here to bring up a new card.</a>
```

Or

```
<a href="deck.wml">Select here to bring up a new deck.</a>
```

### Text Formatting Tags

Since a mobile phone doesn't have a lot of room or a wide variety of colors and fonts, only a few tags are actually supported in WML.

The most popular tags for formatting text include the following:

- `<br/>`—Used to add a line break. Because this tag stands alone and has no closing tag, it must contain a slash.

- `<p>`*My Paragraph*`</p>`—Separates chunks of text into paragraphs.

- `<strong>`*I am mighty*`</strong>`—Used to make text stronger (usually the same as making text bold).

- `<em>`*Emphasize me, baby!*`</em>`—Used to emphasize text (usually the same as italicizing).

- `<b>`*I am bold*`</b>`—Used to make text bold.

- `<i>`*I am italic*`</i>`—Used to make text italicized.

- `<u>`*I am underlined*`</u>`—Used to underline text.

- `<small>`*Wee little me*`</small>`—Makes text smaller.

- `<large>`*Big bad me*`</large>`—Makes text larger.

So the following code might appear as in Figure 4.4:

```
<?xml version="1.0"?>
<!DOCTYPE wml PUBLIC "-//WAPFORUM//DTD WML 1.1//EN"
"http://www.wapforum.org/DTD/wml_1.1.xml">
<wml>
<card title="Sample Formatting">
<p>
Hello<br/>
<b>I'm bold</b><br/>
<i>I'm italic</i><br/>
<u>I'm underlined</u><br/>
<big>I'm big</big><br/>
<small>I'm small</small>
</p>
</card>
</wml>
```

**FIGURE 4.4**   Some formatted text.

Be aware that some phones do not support many of these tags. For example, an older WAP browser may only allow paragraph breaks and line breaks, but no bolding, italicizing, or underlining.

---

**NOTE**

You can add a comment to a WML file using the same comment tags that work in HTML:

`<!—A funny little comment—>`

---

**Tables**

Although using tables is discouraged because there's usually not enough room for them, standard table tags are supported similarly to HTML.

You surround your table with

`<table columns=5 rows=5>`

and

`</table>`

You can create rows and columns using the following tags:

- `<tr>`*Row*`</tr>`—Surrounds a given row of text.

- `<td>`*Column*`</td>`—Creates a given column.

The following code creates a small two-by-two column table:

```
<table columns="3">
<tr>
<td>Top Left</td>
<td>Top Right</td>
</tr>
<tr>
<td>Bottom Left</td>
<td>Bottom Right</td>
</tr>
</table>
```

For example:

| | |
|---|---|
| Top Left | Top Right |
| Bottom Left | Bottom Right |

### User Input Tags

The user input controls will look different on every phone you use. You can use many of the same input elements that you'll find in an HTML form.

**Input Fields**   Typically, a user input field is an empty box in which a person can type in a number, word, or phrase. Because typing on a cell phone is usually an arduous task, many phones will bring up a special screen when an input field is selected.

You can create a standard input field named "test" as follows:

```
<input name="test"/>
```

An input field possesses several attributes:

- name—The name of the field, which will become a variable name you can access later or send to the server.

- emptyok—Set to true if the text field can be left blank. By default this is set to false.

- maxlength—The maximum length of characters that a user can enter.

- size—The width of the field, indicated in number of characters.

- title—Sets a title for the input field. This will be displayed on some phones when the user is inside this field.

- `type`—Sets the type of input field. By default this is `text`, but you might also have a `password` type of field. In password fields, anything the user enters usually appears as an asterisk, for added security.

- `value`—Sets the default value for this input field.

- `format`—The type of data that can be entered in the field. The default is `*M`. The types are as follows:

A—Uppercase alphabetic characters

a—Lowercase alphabetic characters

N—Numeric characters

X—Uppercase characters of any type

x—Lowercase characters of any type

M—All characters

Precede any of the these types with an asterisk to indicate that any number of characters can be entered.

Precede any of the these types with a specific number from 1 to 9 to specify that the user must enter a specific amount of the given character type.

So, to create a 10 character-wide input field that must be numeric and can contain only 10 characters, you would use the following:

```
<input name="test" size="10" maxlength="10" format="*N"/>
```

**Option Groups**    You can create a pull-down option list by surrounding the list with the <optgroup> and </optgroup> tags, and surrounding each individual option using the <option> and </option> tags:

```
<optgroup title="A Test">
 <option value ="first">First Option</option>
 <option value ="second">Second Option</option>
</optgroup>
```

Each option tag can take several attributes, such as:

- `value`—Sets the value for the option that will be dumped into the variable, should the option be selected.

- `onpick`—This attribute takes a URL or anchor card name as a parameter. If the given option is selected, then the given URL is requested.

**Check Boxes and Radio Buttons**    To create check boxes, you can use the `<select multiple="true">` tag. Check boxes are a list of options preceded by boxes, and any number of the boxes can be selected or unselected.

Set the `multiple` attribute to `false` to create radio buttons. Radio buttons show the user several options. Only one of the options can be selected. If a new option is selected, then any previous selections are automatically unselected.

Other attributes for the `<select>` tag include:

- `name`—Name of the variable that will hold any selected value.

- `value`—Set the default value of the variable to be set.

- `iname`—Name of the initial variable that will hold the initial value.

- `ivalue`—Sets the initial value for the option that will be dumped into the variable, indicated by the option group's name.

So, the following would be used to create a simple list of radio buttons:

```
<select multiple="false" name="mychoices">
  <option value="choice1">First Choice</option>
  <option value="choice2">Second Choice</option>
  <option value="choice3">Third Choice</option>
</select>
```

This might appear as shown in Figure 4.5.

*FIGURE 4.5*    A group of radio buttons.

**Field Sets**   Finally, you can visibly group the buttons together into a sort of set. To do so, simply surround elements inside your user input forms with

```
<fieldset title="My Title">
```

and

```
</fieldset>
```

This can help group check boxes or radio buttons.

**Example**   So, taking all this together, you can make a form as in Figure 4.6 using the following WML file:

```
<?xml version="1.0"?>
<!DOCTYPE wml PUBLIC "-//WAPFORUM//DTD WML 1.1//EN"
"http://www.wapforum.org/DTD/wml_1.1.xml">
<wml>
<card title="My Input Form">
<p>
Name: <input name="Name" size="10"/><br/>

<fieldset title="A Field">
<select multiple="true">
<option value="a">A</option>
<option value="b">B</option>
</select>
</fieldset>
</p>
</card>
</wml>
```

**The `<do>` Tag**   The `<do>` tag lets the user perform some sort of global command or other task on the current card. The command will usually appear in the soft-key menus at the bottom of the mobile phone's display. Most phones allow for two soft keys. If you create more than two `<do>` options, then one of the soft-key commands will usually become Menu, which will lead to a special menu of additional choices. The label attribute is the label for the command that will be shown to the user.

The name attribute creates a variable name for the element.

*FIGURE 4.6*   Some user input fields.

The type attribute lets you choose what sort of command you wish to create. Various browsers will display these commands in different ways. Usually, up to two commands can be shown on the screen, mapped to the mobile phone's two command buttons. Other phones may display the commands in a nested menu, or along with a special icon.

The following are some valid <do> command types:

- accept—Acknowledgement of a message or event.

- prev—Navigate back to a previous deck.

- help—Help about this card.

- reset—Reset the WAP browser.

- options—A selection from a list of options.

- delete—Delete an item or choice.

- unknown—A special type, not one of the preceding types.

To perform an action, simply surround it with the <do> and </do> tags. To jump to a card in the current deck named card2, you could use

```
<do type="accept" label="OK!">
  <go href="#card2"/>
</do>
```

The following command will add a back command to the current card, allowing you to go to the previously loaded card:

```
<do type="prev" label="Back">
  <prev/>
</do>
```

**Variables**   WML files are capable of keeping track of and changing simple variables. This lets your WML application keep information between cards.
To explicitly set the variable i to 10, use the <setvar> tag:

```
<setvar name="i" value="10"/>
```

Whenever you create an input element, the results are stored as variables. Simply use the name of the element preceded by a dollar sign. You can surround the variable name by parentheses to separate it from any other text.

So, to create a small application that asks the user for their name and then displays it, you could use the following code:

```
<?xml version="1.0"?>
<!DOCTYPE wml PUBLIC "-//WAPFORUM//DTD WML 1.1//EN"
"http://www.wapforum.org/DTD/wml_1.1.xml">

<wml>
 <card id="input">
<input name="myname" size="10"/>
<select input="Name:">
</select>
<do type="accept" label="OK!">
  <go href="#result"/>
</do>
</card>

<card id="result">
<p>Your name is: $(myname)</p>
</card>
</wml>
```

The name is input in the first card (with the id of input). Then the card with the id result is called, as soon as the OK! button is pressed. The result is then displayed.

### Images

As with HTML, WML does support an <img> tag:

```
<img src="me.wbmp"/ alt="Me">
```

The resultant image might appear as in Figure 4.7.

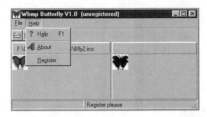

*FIGURE 4.7*    A beautiful WAP image.

The src attribute points to an image in the WBMP format. This format is a special, tiny black-and-white bitmap created to fit snugly on wireless devices.

---

**NOTE**

The WAP 2.0 specification proposes the use of color images.

---

The alt attribute lets you substitute a word or phrase instead of an image, for phones or WAP browsers that do not support images.

There are several tools and plug-ins available at the following Web sites that allow you to convert GIF or BMP images to the WBMP format:

- WBmpCreator—http://www.wbmpcreator.com

- MobImage—http://www.pyweb.com/tools/

- Gif2Wbmp—http://www.towap.net/download/
  index.php?cmd=gif2wbmp&langue=2

- Wbmp Butterfly—http://inin-wap.avalon.hr/zdravko/wbmpfly.htm

### Timers

When using WAP, the connection between a mobile phone and the server does not remain persistent between requests. If the server needs to send an update to the client, it has no way to do so until the client explicitly requests a new deck.

Many games and other time-sensitive applications will need to constantly poll the server, asking for any new updates. This can be done using a simple WML timer.

Set the `ontimer` attribute of the `<card>` tag to point to the WML page you wish to update. You can then use the `<timer value="10"/>` tag to create the countdown, setting the value in tenths of a second.

To refresh the WML document every three seconds, simply use the following:

```
<card ontimer="test.wml">
<timer value="30"/>
<p>Some Message</p>
</card>
```

## WMLScript

If you've followed along so far, you've noticed that WML has very limited interactivity on the client side. Really, all you can do is display simple text and images, collect a little information via user input forms, and send it all to the server to process.

Just as HTML has JavaScript (based on the ECMAScript standard), some WML browsers support a special client-side scripting language called WMLScript. WMLScript is a much simpler subset of ECMAScript. In addition, WMLScript is compiled into bytecode by the WAP gateway before being sent down to the phone.

> **WARNING**
>
> Many WAP Browsers do not support WMLScript. Be sure to research your target platform before relying on any client-side scripting. Check out the excellent table at `http://www.allnetdevices.com/faq/useragents.php3` to determine what version of WAP your target device supports.

WMLScript is used, for the most part, to verify user input before wasting precious time sending it to the server. For example, if you ask your game player for his age, a simple WMLScript can be sure the input is indeed a number, isn't negative, and isn't over 200. If the results aren't valid, a dialog box can pop up telling the player to enter a new number.

In addition, some versions of WMLScript allow you to access special features of the user agent, such as the following:

- Dialog boxes to alert the user of something or to request input
- Make phone calls
- Access the SIM card

- Access or change the address book

- Configure the phone preferences

### Accessing WML Script

WMLScript files are stored separately from WML files. They usually have the `.wmls` extension.

You can access a WMLScript file's WML the same way you would request any other document:

```
<go href="test.wmls"/>
```

You can access specific external functions within WMLScript using the hash symbol. This allows you to pass in variables. For example, the following file requests a variable called `myvar` and then passes it to the `process()` function within a WMLScript file:

```
<?xml version="1.0"?>
<!DOCTYPE wml PUBLIC "-//WAPFORUM//DTD WML 1.1//EN"
"http://www.wapforum.org/DTD/wml_1.1.xml">
<wml>
<card id="Input" title="Request Variable">
<do type="options" label="Go">
<go href="test.wmls#process('myvar')"/>
</do>
<p>
Type something here:
<input type="text" name="myvar"/>
</p>
</card>
</wml>
```

### WMLScript Example

You can make a simple guessing game entirely on the client side using WMLScript. For example, you can create a dialog box that asks the user for a random number.

A function will pick a random number and compare it the user's guess, and show a card indicating whether the user was correct.

The following is the code for `GuessNumber.wml`:

```
<?xml version="1.0"?>
<!DOCTYPE wml PUBLIC "-//WAPFORUM//DTD WML 1.1//EN"
```

```
"http://www.WAPforum.org/DTD/wml_1.1.xml">
<wml>

<card id="guess">
   <p>
   Guessing a Random Number...
   </p>
   <do type="accept">
      <go href="RandomGuess.wmls#guessrandom()" />
   </do>
</card>

<card id="right">
<p>
 You were right!
 Number was $(randresult)<br/>
</p>
</card>

<card id="wrong">
<p>
 Sorry. Wrong!
 Number was $(randresult)<br/>
</p>
</card>
</wml>
```

Here's the code for RandomGuess.wmls:

```
extern function guessrandom()
{
   // Request a number, 0 by default
   var thenum = 0;
   // Loop until a valid number is picked.
   do
   {
     var r = Dialogs.prompt("Pick a number between 1 and 10", "0");
     thenum = Lang.parseInt(r);
   }
   while (thenum < 1 || thenum > 10)

   var randnum = Lang.random(10)+1;
```

```
// set the randresult variable
WMLBrowser.setVar("randresult", randnum);

if (randnum == thenum)
  WMLBrowser.go("GuessNumber.wml#right");
else
  WMLBrowser.go("GuessNumber.wml#wrong");
};
```

The `guessrandom()` function is preceded by the `extern` modifier, meaning that it can be accessed by external WML or WMLScript documents.

Note that the variable `randnum` is a script variable, and can only be set and accessed within this WMLScript function.

The `randresult` variable, however, is set using WMLScript's `setVar()` method, meaning it will be an active browser variable—active and accessible as long as the player is visiting the current WAP site.

# Server-Side WAP

Most any Web server can serve out WML pages. You will, however, need to modify your server using the instructions given in this section.

## Server Configuration

Every response your Web server sends to a browser is tagged with a special header. One of the most important lines of the header tells the browser what the content-type of the document is. This content-type is expressed using a standard known as the *Multipurpose Internet Mail Extension (MIME)*.

The MIME type of HTML files, for example, is `text/html`. For WAP documents, you need to add several new MIME types to allow for WML files, WML script files, compiled WML files, and WBMP wireless bitmaps:

- `text/vnd.wap.wml`

- `application/vnd.wap.wmlc`

- `text/vnd.wap.wmlscript`

- `application/vnd.wap.wmlscriptc`

- `image/vnd.wap.wbmp`

Most Web servers make it easy to add new MIME types. Many servers have a `httpd.conf` file in which these types can be added.

## WAP and Java

Although some WAP pages will never change and can be written using a standard text editor or HTML authoring tool, most WAP games and game tools will involve lots of dynamic information such as game state, scores, number of users in a lobby, chat messages, and so on.

That means that the Web server will need to generate WML decks and cards on-the-fly. Server-side Java technologies, such as JavaServer Pages (JSPs) and Java Servlets, are a great way to pump out the necessary WML.

### A Servlet Game Lobby

For example, here's a simple servlet that can allow an unlimited number of players to chat with each other. This can lead up to a full-featured lobby where players can match up and then be joined together to play Java games.

The WAP need only call the servlet with one parameter:

`mymessage`

The servlet will take that message and return the last five lines of chat.

This is obviously a very simplified version of a game lobby. A real lobby would force users to log in with a password, keep track of the user's name, keep track of which chat lines each user has already seen, match players together, and kick off game sessions.

The `SimpleChatServlet.java` file looks like this, and is shown in Figure 4.8:

```java
import java.io.*;
import javax.servlet.*;
import javax.servlet.http.*;

public class SimpleChatServlet extends HttpServlet {

    // Store last five messages
    private static String message[] = new String[5];

    public void init() throws ServletException
    {
        // Set messages to blank for now
```

```
    for (int i=0; i < 5; i++)
      message[i] = "";
  }

  public void doGet(HttpServletRequest request,HttpServletResponse response)
    throws ServletException,IOException
  {
    // set content type as wap.wml
    response.setContentType("text/vnd.wap.wml");

    // create a print writer output
    PrintWriter out = response.getWriter();
    // get the latest message, if any
    String mymsg = request.getParameter("mymessage");

    // If the message isn't null, add it to the top of the queue
    if (mymsg != null)
    {
for (int i=4; i > 0; i—)
      {
          // Replace message with previous message
      message[i] = message[i-1];
        }
      message[0] = mymsg;
    }

    // write the data
    out.println("<?xml version=\"1.0\"?>");
    out.println("<!DOCTYPE wml PUBLIC \"-//WAPFORUM//DTD WML 1.1//EN\"");
    out.println(" \"http://www.wapforum.org/DTD/wml_1.1.xml\">");
    out.println("<wml>");
    out.println("<card title=\"Chatting\">");

    // Send any new messages back to this servlet
    out.println("<do type=\"accept\" label=\"Send\">");
    out.println(" <go href=\"/servlet/SimpleChatServlet\" method=\"get\">");
    out.println("   <postfield name=\"mymessage\" value=\"$mymsg\"/>");
    out.println(" </go>");
    out.println("</do>");

    out.println(" <p>");
```

```
        // print out the last five messages
        for (int i=0; i < 5; i++)
        {
    out.println(message[i]+"<br/>");
        }
        out.println("</p>");

        // Request a new chat message
        out.println("<p>");
        out.println("Chat: <input title=\"Enter Chat Message\" name=\"mymsg\"/>");
        out.println("<br/>");
        out.println("</p>");
        out.println("</card>");
        out.println("</wml>");
    }
}
```

*FIGURE 4.8*  A WAP chat application using a servlet.

Any WML card that requests this servlet will send its own chat message and retrieve the last five messages that have been sent. Effectively, this servlet will pump out a WML file that looks like the following:

```
<?xml version="1.0"?>
<!DOCTYPE wml PUBLIC "-//WAPFORUM//DTD WML 1.1//EN"
 "http://www.wapforum.org/DTD/wml_1.1.xml">
<wml>
```

```
<card title="Chatting">
<do type="accept" label="Send">
<go href="/servlet/SimpleChatServlet" method="get">
<postfield name="mymessage" value="$mymsg"/>
</go>
</do>
<p>
Message 1<br/>
Message 2<br/>
Message 3<br/>
Message 4<br/>
Message 5<br/>
</p>
<p>
Chat: <input title="Enter Chat Message" name="mymsg"/>
<br/>
</p>
</card>
</wml>
```

## Using JavaServer Pages (JSPs)

Similarly, JavaServer Pages (JSPs) can be used to dynamically create cards, using variables that can be created programmatically.

Here's a simple example:

```
<?xml version="1.0"?>
<!DOCTYPE wml PUBLIC "-//WAPFORUM//DTD WML 1.1//EN"
"http://www.wapforum.org/DTD/wml_1.1.xml">

<%
response.setContentType("text/vnd.wap.wml");
out.println("<wml>");
out.println("<card title=\"Today's Date\">");
out.println(" <p align=\"center\">");
out.println("Date: "+ new java.util.Date());
out.println(" </p>");
out.println("</card>");
out.println("</wml>");
%>
```

## Development Environment

To develop WAP applications, you can use a number of different environments. Every major cell phone manufacturer offers a software development kit that allows you to create and emulate their precise WAP environment.

More information can be found at these sites:

- PyWeb's Deck-It Previewer WAP Emulator—`http://www.pyweb.com/tools/`.

- Yospace SmartPhone Emulator—Shown in Figure 4.9, this tool lets you edit and view WAP content on many different types of handsets. You can download a trial version at `http://www.yospace.com/`.

- Ericsson WapIDE—`http://www.ericsson.com/mobilityworld/`

- Nokia's WAP Toolkit—Found at `http://www.nokia.com/wap`, Figures 4.10 and 4.11 show this toolkit in action.

- Motorola Mobile Application Developers Kit (MADK)—This kit works in conjunction with the Motorola Wireless IDE:

  `http://developers.motorola.com/developers/wireless/tools/`

- Openwave SDK (formerly Phone.Com's UP.SDK)—
  `http://www.openwave.com/products/developer_products/sdk/index.html`

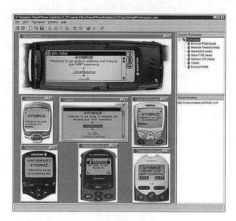

*FIGURE 4.9*   The Yospace SmartPhone Emulator.

**FIGURE 4.10**    The Nokia WAP Toolkit development environment.

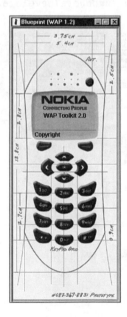

**FIGURE 4.11**    The Nokia WAP Toolkit WAP emulator.

# Handheld Device Markup Language (HDML)

**URL:** http://www.w3.org/TR/NOTE-Submission-HDML.html

HDML is a format extremely similar to WML. Like WAP's main presentation layer protocol, it is a simplified version of HTML specially designed to work well with mobile phones.

---

**NOTE**

HDML was developed by Unwired Planet (which became Phone.com and now is owned by Openwave) before WAP came about. Some of the older phones in the United States support HDML, but the language is rapidly being phased out in favor of the more robust WML. As such, we won't concentrate on it much in this book.

---

HDML is based strictly on existing Web standards and protocols. In addition to defining how a cell phone screen can be visually presented and laid out, HDML has elements defining the navigation between various screens.

Some differences between WML and HDML are the following:

- WML is based on XML. This means that people can use many popular XML authoring and parsing tools to create and deal with XML. For example, the eXtensible Style Sheet Language and associated Translations (XSL/XSLT) provide an easy way of taking the same content, putting it in XML, and popping it out as either HTML or WML.

- Since HDML is not based on XML, you can be a lot sloppier. You can use upper or lower case tags, nest tags, and you don't need to have a closing tag for every opening tag.

- HDML does not have a related DTD (Document Type Definition). That means you can't run an HDML document through a validator to make sure everything is in the proper format.

- HDML does not have any form of client-side scripting.

- HDML does not have timers.

- HDML does not have multiple-choice selection lists. However, HDML does allow you to add custom images to labels and choice groups, such as checkboxes and radio buttons.

- HDML has built-in bookmark functionality. Some WAP browsers offer bookmarks, but they are not part of the main specification.

- HDML offers nested activities—a convenient way of organizing your application's commands.

- HDML lets you set up mobile-originated pre-fetch of documents. This means you can pre-load your entire application and graphics. The user has a longer download time up front, but everything runs much more responsively afterwards.

- HDML offers key accelerators for links. That means that you can specify exactly which keys on the mobile phone's keypad will be associated with which action.

## HDML Syntax

All HDML files start with

```
<HDML VERSION=3.0>
```

The Version value, of course, depends on the version of HDML you are writing. The document ends with

```
</HDML>
```

## Displays

Just like WML, HDML documents contain many screens (decks) and each screen can be shown to the mobile phone user (as a card). In HDML, however, cards are called displays and indicated using the <DISPLAY> tag.

Each display can be given a NAME attribute.

## Activities

Every command that a user carries out is known as an activity. Each activity might have sub-activites. When you use the "GO" task under an <ACTION> tag, you are performing an activity.

For example, in a game lobby, the main activities might be to Join a Game or Chat. The Join a Game activity might have sub-activites such as Pick Game Name or Pick Opponents. Each step in an activity usually has its own HDML card.

You can use special attributes to indicate how the application behaves as the user navigates back and forth or cancels various tasks. You can even create sub-activities using the GOSUB attribute, to help group specific activities together under another activity.

## Actions

If you don't assign an activity to a key, then it will have a default activity assigned to it. For example

The <ACTION> tag is the way you can request user input. A special command will be shown to the user.

The TYPE attribute determines what type of action you're talking about. There are several action types:

- ACCEPT—A standard acknowledgement of a message or event. By default, this displays the previous card.

- HELP—By default, this shows a message that no help is currently available.

- PREV—By default, this action shows the previous card. If there is no previous card, the current activity is canceled.

- SOFT1—The first softkey is pressed.

- SOFT2—The second softkey is pressed.

- SEND—Something is being sent.

- DELETE—Usually used in text-entry fields. This action deletes the character to the left of the cursor.

Set the LABEL attribute to display a specific command to the user. What happens after the user selects that command depends on the value of the TASK and DEST attribute.

The most common TASK is GO, which means you want to jump to another document or card. DEST points to the desired destination. This can be another HDML file, or a card within the current document.

So, to go from card one to card two

```
<HDML VERSION="3.0">
 <DISPLAY>
  <ACTION LABEL="Hit Me" TYPE=ACCEPT TASK="GO" DEST="#card2">
    This is card one!
  </DISPLAY>
  <DISPLAY NAME="card2">
    And this is card two!
  </DISPLAY>
</HDML>
```

Other TASK values include the following:

- GO—Request a specific URL or card, along with the DEST attribute.

- GOSUB—Just like GO, this will request a specific URL. However, a new activity is pushed on the browser stack, which means the browser can keep track of where you're going and where you've come from. This makes it easy to cancel out or go backwards logically.

- PREV—Shows the previous card.

- RETURN—Return from a GOSUB nested activity to the previous activity.

- CANCEL—Cancels the current activity.

- CALL—Changes the phone to voice mode and actually dials the number specified by the NUMBER attribute.

- NOOP—Do nothing. A way to show a command but "disable" it.

### Hyperlinks

HDML allows you to create hyperlinks. However, there is no HREF attribute. Instead, you use DEST:

```
<A TASK="GO" DEST="test.hdml" LABEL="Hit Me" ACCESSKEY="1">
```

### Images

Finally, images can be dropped into HDML documents using the <IMG> tag:

```
<IMG SRC="myimage" ALT="Neat Image">
```

Most HDML browsers, such as UP.Link, support 1-bit images in the BMP format. Images that are too large for the display will be cropped, and images that aren't valid will not be shown at all.

## WAP 2.0 and xHTML Basic

**URL:** http://www.w3.org/TR/xhtml1/

The future of wireless markup languages appears to be xHTML Basic. All of the big wireless players are helping to craft the xHTML specification: Sun, Ericsson, Panasonic, Microsoft, Openwave (inventor of HDML and one of the main proponents of WAP), Access Co. (representing iMode's cHTML), and The World Wide Web Consortium (W3C).

The second version of WAP is based on xHTML. So what is it? The xHTML specification simply involves taking the whole kahuna of HTML version 4.01 and redefining it as a pure XML language. The beauty of xHTML is that today's Web browsers can instantly support and display it.

As with today's HTML, the content and layout of all the elements can be created in HTML, and the presentation look and feel can be specified using cascading style sheets (CSS).

What that means is that tomorrow's wireless languages will be an exact subset of major HTML and CSS tags and commands. This will make it much easier to define exactly how a mobile phone's content should look. Theoretically, phones will support slick interfaces, animation, pop-up menus, and lots and lots of color. It'll also make it really easy to create applications that work on both the Web and wireless browsers.

**NOTE**

WAP 2.0 and i-mode's cHTML (discussed in Chapter 6) seem to be converging into xHTML. Openwave, the leading provider of mobile phone browsers, has announced that it will be supporting xHTML in upcoming releases.

## Summary

In this chapter, we covered the gamut of wireless technologies that exist today, as well as those being used to build the 3G systems of tomorrow. In Chapter 5, we'll focus in on instant messaging, one of the most popular wireless data offerings.

# 5

# Let's Talk: Instant Wireless Messaging

**IN THIS CHAPTER**

- Messaging And Gaming
- Short Message Service (SMS)
- Actually Sending SMS Messages
- SMS and J2ME
- Multimedia Messaging Service (MMS)

This might sound obvious, but the thing that people find attractive about mobile phones isn't the innovative chipsets, advanced voice compression schemes, sophisticated data networks, sleek liquid crystal displays, or sexy plastic casing. It's the communication. The capability to reach other people and be reached, anywhere, anytime.

Text messaging picks up where voice communication leaves off. There are many times when a few thoughtful words are more efficient than a long conversation. In the desktop world, messaging programs such as Yahoo! Instant Messenger, America Online Instant Messenger (IM), and Microsoft Messenger have taken the Internet's populace, especially teenagers, by storm.

In case you've been living under a rock, all instant messenger programs work as follows: You create a list of buddies. When one of your buddies is online, you are notified. You can click on your buddy's name at any time and type a message to her. She can then type a message back.

In other words, instant messaging combines the articulate focus and assured delivery of e-mail with the immediacy of the telephone.

In the world of mobile phones, text messaging is an equally impressive and important phenomenon. Once again, the trend is being led by teens. Messages can be tapped into mobile phones and sent to and fro during classes, during work, or while on the run. You can receive a message while the phone is off, or while you are talking on the other line. Messaging fanatics have become perfectly adept at typing out complex sentences with tiny numeric keypads.

## Messaging And Gaming

Messaging will play a major role in gaming. Many of today's games (such as Electronic Art's *Majestic*) tap into instant messages as a way of communicating with the player. Tomorrow's handheld games will likely use messaging for many reasons:

- Friends can be notified when another friend is logged in and automatically be matched up to join the same game session.

- Teams of players can cooperate during a big multiplayer game.

- Competitors can tease, jab, brag, or cry to each other during games.

- Game status information such as top players, scores, hints, or other meta-game goodies can be sent as hourly, daily, or weekly updates.

- Messaging can be part of the game itself. For example, in a persistent world space-battle game you might be able to set up a space station with certain defenses. You can then set the captain of the station to notify you if it is being attacked. Log off the game and go about your business. A few hours or days later, while you're in the middle of an important business meeting, you might get a ring on your cell phone notifying you that your station's hull is receiving massive damage from a laser attack. You can then excuse yourself from the meeting and take care of more important business....

- Some carriers are allowing financial transactions through messaging, so players can pay for their game sessions this way.

## Short Message Service (SMS)

The world's foremost messaging standard is the Short Message Service (SMS), which is a simple format allowing for the transmission of alphanumeric messages. Almost every mobile service provider offers SMS messaging in one form or another.

If you think of e-mail as a letter, an SMS message is more like a postcard. With SMS, you can send a quick message to another person by using her phone number as the destination address.

SMS isn't as popular in the United States as it is in Europe and Asia. Whereas American mobile carriers make it difficult for their subscribers to message outside their networks, most European carriers have standardized messaging, enabling almost any mobile phone to send text messages to any other.

According to the GSM Association, more than 50 billion SMS text messages were sent over the world's GSM networks in the first three months of 2001, and the group forecasts that well over 200 billion global messages will be sent throughout the course of the year. In 1999, the average number of SMS messages was 1 billion per month. Now it's more than 16 billion, and heading toward 25 billion!

Different carriers charge different rates for SMS. Some carriers actually charge 10 cents to a dollar per message! Others offer a set number of prepaid SMS messages per month.

## SMS Specifics

**URL:** http://www.etsi.org/

SMS was created by the European Telecommunications Standards Institute (ETSI).

SMS messages are pure text. On GSM networks, a standard text message can be a maximum of 160 characters long. Each character is usually defined by a 7-bit alphabet similar to ASCII that includes major punctuation, accented letters, mathematic symbols, and numerals. Some other networks permit a maximum of 190 characters.

There are two formats in which you can send and receive SMS messages:

- Text mode
- PDU mode

Additionally, there are specialized versions of SMS that enable instant pop-up messages, as well as the capability to tack on multimedia and contact information. Some of these formats will be discussed later in this chapter.

### SMS Text Mode

SMS's Text mode is a preset and simplified encoding of the bit stream represented by the PDU mode. In other words, Text mode is the standard way in which English alphanumeric messages can be sent back and forth.

Most mobile phones support Text mode, and it acts as a kind of SMS lowest common denominator standard.

### Protocol Description Unit (PDU) Mode

Using the full PDU mode, *any* type of encoding can be created and implemented.

Using PDU mode adds a whole bunch of extra headers to the message, increasing the message size and telling the mobile phone exactly how to encode the alphabet the way the sender intended it.

Special SMS messages can be delivered from one carrier to another using PDU mode.

### Smart Messaging

**URL:** http://www.forum.nokia.com

Smart Messaging is an enhanced SMS format designed by Nokia. Many other phones support similar enhanced messages. These usually use a special 8-bit alphabet, with a maximum of 140 characters per message. These 8-bit characters are usually designated for digital data, not text. Data that can be sent over SMS depends on the carrier, but typical data formats enable the following:

- Simple black and white images.

- New operator logos. For example, if you change your phone service from Sprint to Nextel, then the Nextel logo can be sent down using SMS.

- "Musical notes" for new ring tones.

- Business cards and other contact information.

- Calendar and scheduling information.

- Over-the-air provisioning of WAP access, enabling a carrier to send bookmark lists, WAP homepage and server settings, and other WAP options.

- The WAP gateway can send the phone URLs using SMS. The phone is smart enough to grab the URL from the SMS message text and request the appropriate WML document.

### Unicode Messages

Additionally, 16-bit messages are enabled on many networks. This format can handle a maximum of only 70 characters per message.

The extended alphabet is used to support the Unicode (UCS2) format, capable of showing characters from alphabets such as Chinese, Japanese, Korean, Cyrillic, Hebrew, and Arabic.

More information about Unicode can be found at http://www.unicode.org/.

### Flash SMS

Many mobile phones support Flash SMS messages. These messages will literally flash up on the screen as soon as they arrive, without the need for the user to navigate through option menus. This provides more of a classic "instant messenger" feel.

Most Nokia, Siemens, Ericsson, and Motorola phones support this type of messaging. The user usually has the option to turn Flash SMS off if she finds it distracting.

To send a Flash SMS, the message data-coding scheme must be set to 16-bit Unicode with the message class 0, and the message should start with the character 0001. Thus, the message length itself can only be 69 Unicode characters.

## Short Message Service Centers (SMSCs)

All SMS messages are routed through a central server, known as a Short Message Service Center (SMSC). The SMSC is software that basically acts as a post office. It sits atop the operator's network and queues up messages, bills the sender, routes messages to phones, notifies the sender if the message can't be sent, and even sends return receipts when the messages are read.

The reason an SMSC is needed is that mobile phones are not always on. Users often switch their phones off, are out of the network coverage area, or run out of battery power. The SMSC stores each message and queues it up, trying to send it out as soon as possible. If the phone is unavailable, the SMSC will periodically keep trying. After the message is successfully sent, the SMSC deletes the message from its cache and continues on with other work.

Most operators permit you to tap into their SMSC using the Web or other open Internet connections. Every provider uses different protocols for their SMSC. For example, CMG uses a protocol called UCP/EMI, Logica uses SMPP, SEMA uses SMS2000, and Nokia uses CIMD.

---

**NOTE**

Game developers who plan on sending a lot of messages may need special permission or access from various carriers. Carriers are also sensitive about the type of information you send over their network, and want to avoid anything that can be construed as unwanted advertising, or *spam*.

---

Figure 5.1 shows the typical SMS architecture: Either a phone or Web server gateway machine can connect to a SMSC to send or receive SMS messages.

## Free SMS Service

The following are several SMS services you can use to send SMS messages from the Web:

- Free SMS around the world

    http://www.worldxs.net/sms.html

- GoZing

    http://www.gozing.com/

- MTNSMS

    http://www.mtnsms.com/

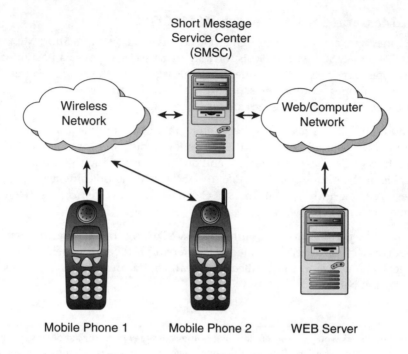

*FIGURE 5.1*    The SMS architecture.

There are also several services that enable you to use SMS to reach various Internet gateways. Many service providers have created their own portal, enabling you to send and synchronize your e-mail, schedule, or other contact information using SMS. For example

- Sprint PCS

    http://www.messaging.sprintpcs.com/sms/

- Nextel

    http://messaging.nextel.com/

- Airtouch (Verizon)

    http://www.app.airtouch.com/text_messaging/w.html

- Cingular

    http://www.mywirelesswindow.com/interactive_messaging

- AT&T Wireless

    http://www.mobile.att.net/mc/personal/pager_show.cgi

- Globtel

  `http://globtel.sknet.sk/`

- Eurotel

  `http://www2.eurotel.cz/sms`

Some carriers also allow you to use SMS to access the wider Internet. For example, one free server can be found at `http://www.excell.to/`. After you have registered, you can get the phone number of the gateway (which is in Italy) and actually send out an e-mail using SMS and the following format:

`EMAIL user@domain .subject.message body`

## Actually Sending SMS Messages

Desktops or servers can send SMS messages directly to a mobile phone by using the phone or SMCS software as a modem. Many mobile phones have cables enabling you to attach the phone to your computer's serial port.

If you are interested in creating your own SMS server, this can be a good way to tap into the wireless network and begin playing around.

To use SMS, send standard `AT` modem commands through the serial port and into the phone. For example

- `AT+CMGF=1`

  Changes the SMS sending mode to Text mode. Type `0` is used for PDU mode.

- `AT+CMGS="5551234567"`

  `<message>`

  `<Ctrl>+<Z>`

  This sequence dials the number (555-123-4567 in this case) and sends the message.

To test some of this stuff out, you can use the Hyper Terminal program that comes with Windows (3.1 or later).

Luckily, however, there are some ready-made SMS tools for you to tap into or interface with.

### SMS Tools

There are numerous SMS tools on the market, most of them geared toward carriers, large corporations, and other organizations that want to add SMS capabilities to their communications arsenal.

The following are some examples:

- SMS Gateway

  `http://www.winsms.com/`

  A utility that lets anyone send and receive text and binary SMS messages over GSM. The package also comes with a gateway that other Windows applications can communicate with using DDE, OLE, or the command line. If you want to create a huge game reliant on SMS, this package.is worth checking out.

- SMS-JDK

  `http://www.noctor.com/`

  This package, by Noctor Consulting, is a 100% Java interface to the SMS protocol. You can create Java applications that talk to the SMSC synchronously or asynchronously, with multithreading and custom call-backs. This means that several Java objects can communicate with one or more SMSCs at the same time. Additionally, applets can use a special SMS-JDK proxy to communicate with an SMSC.

- Kuulalaakeri

  `http://www.kuulalaakeri.com/`

  This is a Unix-based SMS gateway, based on the HTTP request method. You can tap into the API with any other program.

## SMS and J2ME

If you want to create a Micro Java game that uses wireless messaging, you can send out SMS messages using the followings steps:

1. Gain access to a SMSC that supports your subscribers. You might need to contact various wireless networks to arrange this. There are also companies that can act as a third party provider of SMS services for you.

2. Create or buy an SMS gateway server that lets you send commands to the SMSC over the Internet.

3. Create a database indicating different game players, what type of SMS service they use, and what their phone number is.

4. When you want to send a message to a user, have the gateway send the message to the appropriate SMSC, along with the number to dial.

5. The SMSC will ship off the desired message to the desired user.

If you want to receive SMS messages from game players, then the process is similar:

1. Create or hire an SMS out to a service that can handle the receipt of SMS messages. You will need to give out a telephone number that players can dial.

   Some game developers have struck deals with wireless providers and been given access to a short, special number. For example, to play Sonera Zed's Fisupeli fishing game, players can begin fishing merely by sending out a text message that says "FISU" to the special phone number 400.

2. When players send an SMS message to this number, the SMSC will decode the message and route it to your game server, along with the phone number or ID of the person who sent the message.

3. You can look up the player in your user database and adjust their game state as needed, and possibly send them out another SMS message as a response.

## Sample Server Code

Actually sending an SMS message, then, might work according to the following process.

You will need to have all the following pieces in place:

• The cell phone number of a player. Let's call the variable pNumber.

• The message to send, stored in a String variable called pMessage.

• Knowledge of which cell phone provider the player is using.

• Access to that cell phone provider's SMSC.

The access will usually be through a servlet with a command structure similar to

```
http://www.myprovider.com/sendsms?msg=Message&destination=
➥555-765-4321&callback
_number=555-123-4567 &priority=normal& date=4/15&time=10:30
```

To send a message to a specific provider, your Java code will look similar to the following:

```
String smsMsg = new String();
smsMsg = "msg=" + URLEncoder.encode(pMessage);
smsMsg = smsMsg + "&destination=" + URLEncoder.encode(pNumber);
smsMsg = smsMsg + "&callback_number=123456789";
smsMsg = smsMsg + "&priority=normal";

int date,month,hour,minute;
Calendar cal = Calendar.getInstance(TimeZone.getTimeZone("EST"));
date = cal.get(cal.DAY_OF_MONTH);
month = cal.get(cal.MONTH) + 1;
hour = cal.get(cal.HOUR);
minute = cal.get(cal.MINUTE) + 1;

smsMsg = smsMsg + "&date=" + URLEncoder.encode(month + "/" + date) ;
smsMsg = smsMsg + "&time=" + URLEncoder.encode(hour + ":" + minute) ;

URL cellUrl = new URL("http://www.myprovider.com/sendsms");
HttpURLConnection conn = (HttpURLConnection) cellUrl.openConnection();
conn.setRequestMethod("POST");
conn.setDoInput(true);
conn.setDoOutput(true);
conn.setUseCaches(false);
conn.setRequestProperty ("Content-Type", "application/x-www-form-urlencoded");

DataOutputStream ds = new DataOutputStream (conn.getOutputStream ());
ds.writeBytes (smsMsg);
ds.flush ();
ds.close ();
```

Note that you use the URLEncoder.encode() method to convert any strings into valid escape characters able to be sent over HTTP.

## Multimedia Messaging Service (MMS)

**URL:** http://www.wapforum.org

**URL:** http://www.3gpp.org/

Multimedia Messaging Service (MMS) is the next generation of wireless messaging. Focusing on entertainment applications, MMS is like a supercharged version of SMS with the capability to send e-mail, audio, video, and presentations. The MMS specification was created by the WAP Forum and the Third Generation Partnership Project (3GPP).

MMS uses a language called Synchronized Multimedia Integration Language (SMIL), which acts as a sort of script indicating exactly how and when multimedia should be displayed. This permits you to create small presentations and animations, not to mention rich game scenarios.

When a user gets an MMS message, a sort of slide show with audio and graphics begins playing right on their phone's screen. The user can generally choose to rewind and watch the slide show again, delete it, or store it for later viewing. Phones can only store a limited number of MMS messages before running out of room, so MMS messages usually expire after a few days.

> **NOTE**
>
> In general, MMS is intended only for carrier networks that can transfer data at a rate of 14.4Kbps or better.

## Multimedia Message Service Centers (MMSC)

Just as SMS has its SMSCs, MMS has MMSCs that act as a central post office to send and receive each message. An entire MMS is sent in the background, using WAP's Wireless Service Protocol (WSP) to "push" content down to the phone. As such, WAP 1.2 or better is needed to support MMS.

MMS messages might take a while to reach the phone. For example, if a message is 50 kilobytes long (400 kilobits), and is sent over a network that supports 10Kbps bandwidth, it will take 40 seconds to send the message down. However, MMS phones will not notify users of a new message until it has been entirely downloaded and is ready to play. This makes messages "seem" instant.

MMSC also features distribution lists, enabling a sender to compose one message for many recipients.

## Crack a SMIL

**URL:** http://www.w3.org/TR/REC-smil/

The Synchronized Multimedia Integration Language is, as its name implies, a language that enables you to synchronize the playback of multimedia content. The language can juggle music, voice, images, text, and even video. It shows exactly where visual elements are laid out on the screen, when to play audio elements, and how long everything is displayed before switching to a new "slide."

The language is based on XML, which is very similar to HTML, and was developed by major television, audio, new media, and video companies. The World Wide Web Consortium (W3C) standardized the final specification.

The content in SMIL messages is encapsulated using standard MIME types, with various phones capable of displaying and dealing with different formats of multimedia. Almost every MMS-capable phone will support these formats:

- Text
- JPEG
- GIF
- AMR Voice

Additionally, different carriers will permit different message lengths. Nokia, for example, is planning on permitting messages from 30 to 100 kilobytes in size.

## Simple SMIL Example

Using MMC and SMIL, then, you could create a game that shows a tiny image of your evil nemesis taunting you in a left-hand pane while text statistics about your army scroll by on the right. Meanwhile, scary music could play.

A SMIL file to achieve this might look something like this:

```
<smil >
 <head >
 <layout >
  <root-layout width="580" height="213" background-color="black"/>
  <!— Text region —>
  <region id="text" left="0" top="0" width="50" height="100"/>
  <!— Image region —>
  <region id="images" left="101" top="0" width="50" height="100"/>
 </layout>
 </head >
 <body>
 <par>
  <text src="message.txt" region="text_region" begin="1s" />
  <img src="badguy.gif" region="images_region" begin="1s" />
  <audio src="scary.au" clip-end="145s" />
  </par>
 </body>
</smil>
```

The preceding file only shows one sequence. You could easily use SMIL to set a duration for the sequence and then swap out graphical elements, add new text, and so on.

## Enhanced Messaging Service (EMS)

**URL:** http://www.3gpp.org/

Because networks and phones that can support MMS will take a while to hit the market, Alcatel, Ericsson, Motorola, and Siemens have developed an interim messaging standard called the Enhanced Messaging Service (EMS). The standard is defined by the Third Generation Partnership Project (3GPP).

EMS adds images, audio, melodies, and animations to SMS. Unlike MMS, which turns messages into a full-fledged slide show, EMS works more like a still picture. For instance, if you receive an EMS message, a special icon will indicate that an image, some music, or even a brief animation is attached. The EMS message can even combine types, so that a black and white graphic appears next to the message while a small clip of music plays in the background.

Features that EMS supports include the following:

- Text formatting—Text can be justified right, center, or left. And a large or small font can be used along with bold, italic, underlined, or strikethrough text.

- Black and white bitmap graphics—There are three supported graphic formats. Small (16×16 pixels), large (32×32 pixels), or custom. The maximum picture size is 96×64.

- Audio—You can compose simple melodies using 10 predefined sounds such as chimes, chords, ding, "ta da," claps, or a drum. You can also define and transmit your own 128-byte sounds.

- Animation—Two sizes of animation will be supported, (8×8 pixels) and large (16×16 pixels). Many phones will have predefined animations stored on the phone showing characters with emotions such as sad, happy, skeptical, flirty, and grieving. These animations can help punctuate text messages. Custom animations can also be sent over the air.

EMS-capable phones will begin shipping at the end of 2001 and are expected to be popular and widely used near the end of 2002.

## Summary

As you can see, messaging is simple to program. In fact, the key to dealing with messaging has to do more with setting up relationships with wireless carriers than hardcore programming or technical know-how.

Messaging provides an extremely compelling way to push content to game players, as well as a simple way of having players send information back to the game. Text and multimedia messaging will only continue to grow in popularity as it catches on with more and more people.

The next chapter will discuss the i-mode network, which has taken wireless Japan by storm. The Compact HTML language used to create content for i-mode will also be explained.

# 6

# Wireless in Asia: i-mode and cHTML

**IN THIS CHAPTER**

- Using i-mode
- Compact HTML (cHTML)
- Development Tools
- Testing and Emulators

There are tons of mobile phone users throughout the world, with the numbers growing rapidly. However, it seems that no place on Earth is as crazy for wireless computing as Japan. In fact, as of early 2001, 81% of the world's wireless Internet users could be found in Japan—we're talking about 20 million people!

There are many reasons for this success: dial-up Internet connectivity is expensive compared to mobile access; Japanese people spend an extremely large amount of time on public transportation; and Japanese culture meshes well with "cute" gadgets. But the foremost reason for the success of wireless computing is that Japan's leading wireless provider, NTT DoCoMo, made some smart choices and put together the right technologies and infrastructure to make mobile data access fun, easy, and well worth its price.

The network that serves all this up is called i-mode.

If you live in North America, i-mode is also coming to a phone near you: Last year, NTT DoCoMo bought 16% of AT&T Wireless, as well as pieces of wireless companies in the Netherlands, United Kingdom, Taiwan, and Hong Kong. In fact, the first American i-mode service is expected to roll out in Seattle at the end of 2001.

## Using i-mode

NTT DoCoMo has focused on making i-mode easy to use. If you opt to add i-mode service to your mobile phone, there will usually be a special button for i-mode features. When you press this button, a special menu with your favorite sites pops up, along with an index of 600 preferred i-mode partner sites.

i-mode service costs 300 yen (about $3) per month, and you are charged 0.3 yen for every 128-byte data packet. Unlike most American and European wireless services, you are not charged based on how long you are connected, but based on how much data you transfer. This is another big reason for i-mode's success: If you download a small adventure story and read it for 30 minutes, you are only charged a few pennies for the download size, not exorbitant fees for the 30 minutes.

> **NOTE**
>
> Many i-mode games are designed to have small packet sizes, with requests for new data as infrequently as possible.

In addition, most of i-mode's most popular sites charge a monthly access fee. Many game portals, for instance, charge an additional 300 yen per month. The charge is automatically tacked on to your wireless bill, and profits are split between NTT DoCoMo and the content provider.

> **NOTE**
>
> If you want to become an i-mode developer or find out more information about the business model, check out the English Web site at `http://www.nttdocomo.com/`

Many of today's i-mode handsets feature color screens. The latest i-mode phones now also support a version of Java called iAppli. For more information about this, check out Chapter 22, "iAppli: Micro Java with a Twist."

> **NOTE**
>
> Note that the maximum size for an i-mode page, including all cHTML markup and image, is 5KB. Anything larger than that will not be downloaded. NTT DoCoMo, in fact, recommends you limit your pages to 2KB.

## Compact HTML (cHTML)

**URL:** `http://www.w3.org/TR/1998/NOTE-compactHTML-19980209/`

Just as WAP has WML, the markup language used to create i-mode sites is cHTML. cHTML is nothing more than a subset of HTML versions 2.0, 3.2, and 4.0. The language also has a few special extras, such as tags that enable the user to dial a voice phone connection. There are also a special set of characters called emoji that enable you to drop in small graphic icons based on emotions, communication, transportation, and home life.

The simplicity of cHTML is also its power. Developers can use the dozens of Web authoring tools and services out on the market to build cHTML. In addition, a valid cHTML page is, by definition, valid HTML, and thus can be run or tested in any Web browser—although certain tags are specific to i-mode and will not show up properly. Furthermore, i-mode users can access any Web page in the world and see a simplified but complete version of it on their mobile phone screens.

---

**WARNING**

In practice, if you try to browse a Web page that hasn't been formatted for the small screen using cHTML, the page might be bigger than your handset's display size or memory, and only a portion of it will be shown.

---

Unlike WML 1.1, cHTML supports color, precise text and graphic placements, and other features more typical of complex, rich Web pages than the typical dinky wireless data applications.

cHTML was created by Access Co., Ltd. The World Wide Web Consortium (W3C) standardized the language in 1998. NTT DoCoMo phones currently run three versions of cHTML, each more sophisticated than the previous one.

## Character Sets

Because i-mode is currently only available in Japan, if you want to create an i-mode game you would do well to write all text in Japanese. The name of the encoding standard used with i-mode is Shift-JIS.

English characters, using the Western Encoding standard (ISO-8859-1), are also supported.

## Emoji

**URL:** http://www.nttdocomo.co.jp/english/p_s/i/tag/emoji/

One of i-mode's most often used features are small graphical icons known as *emoji*, or "picture characters." In all, there are 196 different icons, each the size of a text character, which can be dropped anywhere in a cHTML page.

Because the full set of emoji are stored on each i-mode phone, no graphical download is necessary. To create an emoji using cHTML, just use the &# escape characters along with the decimal code, followed by a semicolon. For example:

```
&#63647;
```

Emoji are associated with the following:

- Weather
- Zodiac signs
- News and sports
- Mood
- Flirtation
- Emotions
- Transportation and travel
- Finance and credit cards
- Math
- Places
- People

Several emoji can be seen in Figure 6.1.

*FIGURE 6.1*   A few emoji.

A full list of emoji can be found at NTT DoCoMo's Web site.

## cHTML Structure

A cHTML file looks exactly like an HTML file. It begins with <HTML>, ends with
</HTML>, and has a <HEAD> section and a <BODY> section:

```
<HTML>
<HEAD>
```

```
<TITLE>My Page</TITLE>
</HEAD>
<BODY BGCOLOR="#000000">
</BODY>
</HTML>
```

**NOTE**

The BGCOLOR background color attribute, of course, is only relevant on color phones. Black and white phones will ignore any color settings.

If you like, you can use <META> tags to let search engines and other Web-sniffing software know that the document is cHTML. The description should be fewer than 10 characters long:

```
<META name="CHTML" content="yes"><META name="description" content="Neat Page">
```

Although using <META> tags is recommended, it is not required.

## Standard cHTML Tags

Table 6.1 includes a list and short description of the common tags and tag attributes that i-mode's version of cHTML supports. For an in-depth description of these tags, it is suggested that you pick up a separate book about HTML or cHTML.

*TABLE 6.1*   Image Format Support

| Tag | Function |
| --- | --- |
| <! — —> | A comment. |
| &XXX; | Designates an escape character. For example, &amp; creates an ampersand. |
| <BASE href=http://www.base.com/> | A base URL. All paths used in the file will be relative to this URL. |
| <BLINK> | Blinks text. |
| <BLOCKQUOTE> | Puts text in a special quote block, surrounded by quotation marks. |
| <BR> | A line break. |
| <CENTER> | Centers blocks of text, images, or tables. |
| <DL>, <DD>, <DT> | Creates a definition list. |
| <DIR> or <MENU> along with <LI> | Creates a list of menus or directories. |
| <DIV align="left"> | Aligns a block of text to the left, center, or right. |
| <FONT color="#000000"> | Changes the color of a given piece of text. |
| <HR> | Creates a horizontal rule (a line). |

*TABLE 6.1*    continued

| Tag | Function |
| --- | --- |
| <UL> or <OL> along with <LI> | Creates an ordered or unordered list. |
| <OBJECT> | Adds a Java applet or other object to the page. See Chapter 22 for more information. |
| <P> | Creates a paragraph text block. |
| <PLAINTEXT> | Displays text exactly as typed, including all white space or other characters. |
| <PRE> | Displays text in preformatted font, including line feeds and white space. |

## Input Forms

cHTML enables you to create forms in exactly the same way you would with HTML.

Use the <FORM> and </FORM> tags to indicate a form, and use the method attribute to get or post the form to a servlet or other server-side CGI script. An additional attribute called utn enables you to designate the user's identification.

### The <INPUT> Tag

You can then use the <INPUT> tag to create various input widgets, using the name attribute to name each field. For example

- <INPUT type="text" name="myfield" size="10">—Creates a text field that is 10 characters wide. This is the default type. If you don't include a type attribute, then the input widget will be a text field.

- <INPUT type="password" name="mypass" value="hello">—Creates a password field with the initial value of "hello".

- <INPUT type="checkbox" name="box1" checked>—Creates a true/false checkbox that is checked by default.

- <INPUT type="radio" name="radiogrp">—Creates a radio button.

- <INPUT type="hidden" name="secret" value="secretval">—Creates a hidden field, enabling you to pass back variables to the server without the user being aware of it.

- <INPUT type="submit" value="Hit Me">—A submit button. When this is pressed, the form names and values will be passed to the server, as indicated in the <FORM> tag's method attribute.

- <INPUT type="clear" value="Reset Form">—A clear button. When this is pressed, all text fields are emptied.

### Special Form Attributes

An additional parameter you can add to most types of `<INPUT>` tags is `accesskey`. This useful option lets you associate a numeric key on the phone's pad with the input element. When this key is pressed, the given input widget will automatically be selected. You can set this value from 0 to 9.

For example, if you want to make it easy for a user to quickly access an input field to enter their name, you can write

```
Name: <INPUT name="Myname" accesskey="1">
```

Additionally, the `istyle` attribute lets you set the default character input mode. Supported in cHTML version 2, this attribute can help users quickly fill in forms. Values include

- 1—Full-space kana (Japanese letters)
- 2—Half-space kana (Japanese letters)
- 3—Alphabetic
- 4—Numeric

For example, if you have an input field for a phone number, you can set the default to numerals:

```
<INPUT istyle="4">
```

Password-type fields are automatically set to use the numeric style.

### The `<SELECT>` Tag

You can easily create a selection list using the `<SELECT>` tag. For example

```
<SELECT name="mylist" size="3" multiple>
<OPTION selected value="1">First Value</OPTION>
<OPTION selected value="2">Second Value</OPTION>
<OPTION selected value="3">Third Value</OPTION>
</SELECT>
```

The `size` attribute indicates the maximum number of rows long the list should be. The `multiple` attribute permits the user to select more than one option.

### The `<TEXTAREA>` Tag

Finally, the `<TEXTAREA>` tag is available for you to use. For example, to create a text box that is 2 rows high and 15 characters wide:

```
<TEXTAREA name="mytext" rows="2" cols="15">
```

Like other input widgets, it can be given an `accesskey` or `istyle` attribute.

## The Anchor Tag

One of the most important tags is the `<A>` anchor tag, which permits you to jump back and forth between different documents, or within the same page. To create an anchor, you use the `name` attribute

```
<A name="here">
```

And then to jump to the anchor

```
<A href="#here">
```

You can also jump directly to another cHTML page by designating the URL:

```
<A href="http://www.anotherpage.com/>
```

### Extended Anchor Tag Functions

There are also some specific commands that HTML doesn't support. The `<A>` tag can handle the `accesskey` attribute. For example, you can set it up so that if the user hits the 3 key, she will automatically be taken to the Neato.com cHTML site:

```
<A accesskey="3" href="http://www.neato.com/">Hit 3 To Go To Neato</A>
```

But wait, there's more! You can actually permit a user to dial the phone from a cHTML page:

```
<A href="tel:5551212">Call Mr. Suzuki</A>
```

You can also add a record to the mobile phone's stored telephone book:

```
<A telbook="Suzuki" kana="i" e-mail="friend@nowhere.com">Add Suzuki to the Phone
Book</A>
```

Additionally, you can also ship off an e-mail to a specific address with a given subject and body:

```
<A href="mailto:test@test.com" subject="My Subject" body="This is an e-mail
[ic:ccc] from i-mode.">Send an E-mail!</A>
```

More info about these tags can be found on NTT DoCoMo's Web site at `http://www.nttdocomo.co.jp/english/p_s/i/tag/`.

## Images

You can use GIF- and JPG-formatted images in your cHTML pages. Note, however, that the image size needs to be smaller than your target screen—usually that means the image will be 100×100 pixels or fewer.

Using a GIF with cHTML is the same as using one in HTML:

```
<img src="myimage.gif" alt="Alternate Text">
```

You can also use the `align` attribute to align nearby text with the image (set to `top`, `middle`, or `bottom`).

Additionally, you can set the `width`, `height`, and `hspace` for horizontal space to the left and right of the image, or `vspace` to add buffer space above and below the image.

Although many i-mode handsets only support black and white screens, a growing number feature 256-color screens. Many of today's i-mode handsets are also capable of displaying animated GIF 89a images.

Table 6.2 shows which types of images are supported by various cHTML versions.

*TABLE 6.2*   Image Format Support

| Format | 3.0 | 2.0 | 1.0 |
| --- | --- | --- | --- |
| Non-interlaced GIF | Supported | Supported | Supported |
| Interlaced GIF | Supported | Supported | Converted to non-interlaced GIF |
| Transparent GIF | Supported | Supported by color phones | Converted to non-interlaced GIF |
| Animated GIF 89a | Supported | Supported | Converted to non-interlaced GIF |
| JPEG | Only supported by some phones | Not supported | Not supported |

There are some limitations and guidelines for animated GIFs:

- The maximum length is five frames.
- The maximum size is 94x72 pixels. In fact, the 94x72 limit is a good rule of thumb for *all* images, and will be guaranteed to appear on every handset.
- The animation can only be played up to 16 times.
- Only four animated GIFs can be used in the same document.

Always remember to keep the document beneath the 5KB file size maximum!

<MARQUEE>

Another neat tag that cHTML supports is <MARQUEE>, which allows you to add hori-zontally-scrolling tickers to the cell phone screen. The marquee is one line high and as wide as the screen allows.

The <MARQUEE> tag takes the following attributes:

- behavior—You can set this to scroll to have text stop at the edge of the screen, slide to make text slide offscreen, or alternate to have it scroll back and forth.

- direction—Set this to left or right to indicate which direction you want the text to scroll.

- loop—Indicate how many different times you want the text to scroll. The maximum value is 16.

## Development Tools

There are a number of different cHTML- and i-mode-specific development tools that enable you to quickly craft and test your i-mode site.

Here are a few to check out:

- WapProfit i-mode Editor

  **URL:** http://www.wapprofit.com/products/imodedownload.html

  A Windows editor specifically geared to i-mode. You can easily create quick menus and emulate your site on a typical handset.

- i-JADE

  **URL:** http://www.zentek.com/i-JADE/

  Another complete i-mode development environment.

## Testing and Emulators

After you've completed your i-mode site, you might want to be sure it looks good on a number of different handsets.

Because cHTML is ultra-similar to HTML, you can actually test out much of your site using Internet Explorer or Netscape. However, this is only a good way of ensuring that all links are working properly. You won't be able to get a real idea of what your page will look like on an actual phone. Also, i-mode-specific tags and emoji will not work.

Unfortunately, most i-mode emulators are currently in Japanese. The reasons for this are obvious: The vast majority of i-mode users are Japanese, and in Japan it is very easy to use an actual i-mode phone to test your cHTML pages. Additionally, i-mode has an extremely wide variety of handsets. It is difficult to see exactly what users experience without using a real i-mode handset.

There are a number of emulators available, however, to give you a general sense of how things will really shape up. Unless you speak the language, you might have to play around a bit before understanding how everything works.

- i-Tool

  **URL:** `http://www.asahi-net.or.jp/~tz2s-nsmr/soft/itool/i-tool.htm`

  Shown in Figure 6.2, this is a full-featured i-mode Emulator that simulates D501i/F501i, P501i, and N501i phones

- C.media's Compact NetFront

  **URL:** `http://www.o modia.com/mail/formmail.html`

- Ezos

  **URL:** `http://www.ezos.com/`

  A three-in-one cHTML, WAP, and XHTML browser.

- i-browser

  **URL:** `http://www.charlietai.com/imode/`

  A Windows i-mode browser.

- i monde

  **URL:** `http://www.monde.to/imode/`

  An online i-mode browser.

- The Pixo Internet Microbrowser

  **URL:** `http://www.pixo.com/`

  A browser that supports both standard HTML and cHTML.

- X9 i-Mimic

  **URL:** `http://www.x-9.com/mimic/`

  A full i-mode emulator. The emulator is Web-based and tells you the document size, image size, and total size. It will even estimate the page download time and packet charge.

*FIGURE 6.2*    An i-mode emulator.

Additionally, there are third-party testing companies who will test your i-mode or iAppli pages on tons of actual i-mode handsets. For example, check out NooperLabs at `http://nooper.co.jp/labs/`.

## Summary

As you can see, i-mode and cHTML provide developers with a pretty powerful and easy-to-write method for bringing content to wireless phones.

As i-mode becomes more widespread, you can expect to see it evolve and possibly even merge with WAP to provide a powerful framework in which to place your Micro Java games.

Just as Java applets sit in HTML Web pages, your games can be surrounded by and supported by these cHTML pages. Chapter 22 has more information about how to make this happen.

# 7

# The Wireless Landscape

**IN THIS CHAPTER**

• Bluetooth

• Mobile Positioning

• m-Commerce

• Voice and Telephony

• Unified Messaging (UM)

• A Look at the Future

Using mobile phones to gab with friends is mighty cool—and convenient. Wireless telephony is so easy and routine these days that most of us take for granted the fact that we can carry worldwide communications gizmos in our hip pockets. But there are other uses for wireless devices—stuff that has the potential to make the cool even cooler. These enhancements are the stuff of science fiction, with vast implications for gaming and entertainment. Some of these enhancements are available today, some coming soon.

While the standards and protocols used in the wireless world are in constant flux, there are several that look like they're here to stay. These include the following:

- Bluetooth—A short-range wireless protocol that can turn the world into a vast high-speed data network.

- Mobile positioning—A set of technologies that can pinpoint exactly where in the physical world somebody is located.

- Mobile commerce (m-commerce)—Various technologies that make charging or transferring money quick and easy.

- Voice activation—Mixing voice with data in voice portals, or using one's voice as a navigation interface.

## Bluetooth

**URL:** `http://www.bluetooth.com/`

The colorfully-named Bluetooth is simply a standard for transmitting data using short-range radio waves and low power. The radius that Bluetooth can operate within is about 33 feet (10 meters). Radio waves can pierce most walls, and there's no requirement for two devices to be within line-of-sight of each other.

There are millions of possible uses for Bluetooth:

- Computers, PDAs, mobile phones, and other devices can constantly be talking to each other, synching address books and e-mail addresses. There's no need to place devices in cradles or point infrared ports in the right direction.

- Business folk can walk around a convention center and automatically collect a phoneful of business cards and even product brochures.

- A digital video or still camera can take photos or movies, sending them to the nearest mobile phone. The phone can then slowly transfer the images to a remote server.

- A laptop or mobile phone can zap documents to a nearby printer without any cables or hook-ups.

- A person can bounce between different offices around the world and instantly use her mobile phone, laptop, or PDA to tap into the company's network, accessing data and services.

- Stores can create incentives that "flash" advertisements or coupons to people's cell phones as they walk past.

- A phone can become a *Personal Trusted Device (PTD)*, which is kind of like a wireless extension of you and your wallet. You can use your mobile phone to gain access to your home, office, or top-secret cryogenic research laboratory. You can also use your phone to make purchases without swiping a credit card or signing a slip.

- A bunch of people in the same vicinity can play a high-speed multiplayer game, with quick reaction times and trigger-finger reflexes.

A Bluetooth device sends data in the 2.4GHz band, at a data rate of about 1MB per second. Compare that to today's second-generation wireless networks, which are lucky if they can reach 14.4 kilobytes per second. Even when third generation networks become prominent, local network technologies similar to Bluetooth will always be faster than cell-based communications.

Nokia, Ericsson, Motorola, and most other mobile device manufactures have begun releasing Bluetooth-enabled devices. Development kits for these devices are usually available on the manufacturer's Web sites.

**NOTE**

Bluetooth's name, by the way, comes from a 10th century Viking king named Harald Bluetooth. The protocol is named after him partially because he has a weird name, but also because he was a big believer in bringing different nations together. He helped unite Denmark and Norway.

## Bluetooth Protocols

The current Bluetooth specification is *huge* and very complicated. However, there are three major protocols defined; knowing about them might help you understand Bluetooth's various uses. The three protocols are as follows:

- RFCOMM—Allows basic stream connection between two devices.

- OBEX—Object-oriented exchanges. Establishes a standard way for hierarchical files, contacts, or calendar information to be synchronized and transferred.

- Service Discovery Protocol—A sniffing service that lets Bluetooth devices find one another and register various services.

## Bluetooth and Java

**URL:** http://jcp.org/jsr/detail/82.jsp

WAP or J2ME data can easily ride over a Bluetooth transmission stream. For example, a WAP browser should be able to grab a WML page or image from a nearby server using Bluetooth instead of HTTP.

There is currently a specification in the works to create a standard set of Java APIs for Bluetooth. The hope is to create an API based on the Generic Connection Framework defined in the CLDC. We will discuss the Connection Framework in later chapters.

## Other Short-Range Applications

There are a number of other protocols and methods of having a mobile phone communicate with nearby devices. Many phones already have infrared ports, capable of beaming data to laptops, Palms, and so on. An infrared beam's range, however, can reach only a few feet at most. And infrared ports must be in direct line-of-sight.

The i-mode service, for instance, has run trials of a service called Cmode. According to an NTT DoCoMo press release, the 'C' stands for "Coca-Cola, culture, and communication." Cmode permits the phone to act as a payment and control device. Point your phone at a Coke machine, hit a special code, and a can of your chosen drink pops out. The charge for your soft drink will show up on next month's mobile bill. You can also earn incentive points with every purchase, which can be cashed in for free drinks or other prizes.

Additionally, some vending machines are already able to send wireless messages to vendors when they are empty or in need of repair.

Other uses for short-range communications include the capability to control your home's lights, doors, or heating. One could even unlock one's car using a cell phone.

### Broadband's Promise

In the gaming world, companies are looking at short-range transmissions to give small devices the power of powerful game servers. For example, complex game software rendering or physics routines can run on a strong processor, and the results can be streamed down to the handset.

Eventually, wireless Local Area Network (W-LAN) and other solutions will permit data to be transferred to and from wireless phones at true broadband speeds.

## Mobile Positioning

One of the most useful, most exciting, and spookiest wireless enhancements is mobile positioning. Because many people carry mobile phones with them all the time, it can be said that a person *is* their phone. And a phone's location pinpoints exactly where a person is, and where they've been.

Although positioning has a lot of potential for abuse, with the right privacy controls it can become a wonderful thing. Not only can positioning save lives by helping police cruisers, ambulances, and fire trucks find the source of an emergency call, but there are countless business, entertainment, and game-specific applications.

Positioning, in fact, has the potential to mix the palpable joys of humans meeting each other in real life with the fantastic and organizational elements of a digital medium. With exact mobile positioning, games can begin to play people, rather than vice versa.

### How It All Works

This field of mobile technology is known as *Location Based Services (LBS)*. There are several components to any location system:

- Geographic Information Systems (GIS)—This is the map itself, along with tools that can bring map data down to the handset. Various systems can handle road maps (with streets, buildings, landmarks, gas stations, restaurants, bars, and so on) as well as topographical maps (mountains, rivers, forests, and so on).

- Location Management—This piece of software acts as a translator between the positioning equipment and the network servers that help use the location coordinates in a useful way.

Some of the major categories of Location Based Services include the following:

- Tracking—Entire fleets of trucks, boats, soldiers, or gamers can be tracked. Users can also subscribe to various m-commerce applications that track the user's whereabouts throughout a city and notify a person when he walks near a store that is offering a sale on a product that the person desires.

- Emergency—When a user dials an emergency number, the authorities will know exactly from where the call has been issued. The Federal Communications Commission (FCC) has asked all United States wireless carriers to provide accurate location information when users dial 911.

- Billing—By knowing where you are, your phone can figure out the cheapest or fastest carrier based on your area and use that network for all its traffic.

- Location Based Information—The most useful for games. By knowing a user's location, all sorts of funky things can happen within the game universe. Other typical applications include city guides, which can figure out where you are and show you the closest movie theaters, restaurants, or clubs.

## Forums and Associations

Ericsson, Motorola, and Nokia founded the Location Interoperability Forum (LIF) to create a standard way of developing location-based services on networks and handsets across the world. More information can be found at `http://www.locationfo-rum.org/`.

Another association called the Wireless Location Industry Association (WLIA) has also been formed. The association was formed to provide hardware, software, and services related to positioning. More info can be found at `http://www.wliaonline.com/`.

Additionally, the 3rd Generation Partnership Program (3GPP) is also working to standardize positioning systems for GPRS and WCDMA networks.

Ultimately, there are and will be many standards and many ways of positioning. Although it's useful to understand these technologies, most manufacturers will release a simple API enabling developers to easily locate and track users using basic commands.

It's already possible to develop positioning applications using existing APIs. For example, Ericsson's Mobile Positioning System (MPS) is a toolkit that provides such an API. The libraries are available in a number of languages, including Java. As a developer, you just need to write your application according to the API. The positioning will work no matter whether the user is on GSM, TDMA, or UMTS networks.

More information about Ericsson's MPS is available at
`http://www.ericsson.com/mps/`.

## Privacy

Every provider will handle privacy in different ways. In general, though, most mobile positioning services will offer several layers of security:

- Only accepted and legitimate service providers can log on to the positioning system's servers.

- In order to request a specific user's location, the user must have explicitly given the service provider permission to do so.

- Mobile subscribers can turn off the capability to be located altogether, whenever desired.

## Positioning Technologies

There are many different types of positioning. Different technologies provide various degrees of accuracy, standardization, time it takes to refresh a new position, latency to retrieve position details, and widespread acceptance.

The two main categories are as follows:

- Network-based solutions—This solution relies on using existing wireless networks, triangulating the signal that reaches the various cell towers serving a particular mobile phone. This can usually pinpoint the closest tower or antenna. The big advantage here is that special software and hardware isn't needed within each handset. See Figure 7.1 for an illustration. Some of these solutions include TDOA and AOA.

- Terminal- or handset-based solutions—This set of solutions tries to figure out exactly where a mobile phone is in the real world by calculating the direction and intensity of the signal that is coming down to the phone. See Figure 7.2 for an illustration. GPS is the most well-known terminal-based solution. Terminal-based solutions are usually the most accurate. The big disadvantage, however, is that the terminal usually must have special chips or other equipment built in.

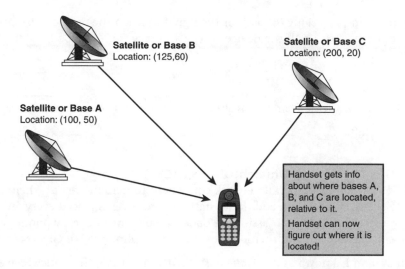

**FIGURE 7.1** Network-based positioning.

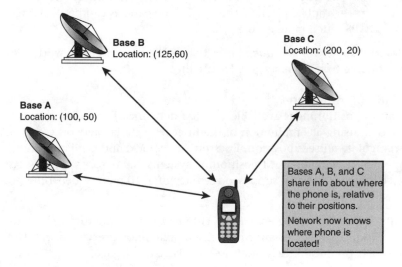

**FIGURE 7.2** Terminal-based positioning.

### Global Positioning System (GPS)

The most popular form of positioning is the Global Positioning System (GPS), often used by sailors, hikers, and truckers. A GPS device can receive a repeating signal from three or four satellites around the globe. By knowing which satellites the signals are coming from, and how long it takes for the signal to reach the device, it is possible to figure out where on earth the device is. The accuracy is pretty good, ranging from 5 to 40 meters.

> **NOTE**
>
> Note that the raw satellite information is often sent to the wireless network for the heavy processing.

### Assisted GPS (A-GPS) and Differential GPS (DGPS)

*Assisted GPS (A-GPS)* uses special network equipment to help figure out where the mobile device is. Basically, an additional static GPS receiver is placed every few hundred miles. This receiver's "assistance data" can be sent to nearby phones every so often, complementing information received by the phone's own GPS receiver.

A similar system is known as *differential GPS (DGPS)*. In DGPS, the static receiver *knows* exactly where it is, and thus can grab info from various satellites, measuring any timing discrepancies. The static receiver gives this error information to the roving receiver (the mobile phone). This way, discrepancies can be accounted for. This makes DGPS much more accurate.

Hybrid solutions like this are much faster than GPS alone, and can work even when a phone is unable to reach enough GPS satellites.

### GSM Location Positioning

GSM Location Positioning is available on GSM networks. The technology is very similar to GPS, using a combination of the Internet, cellular networks, and GPS satellites to triangulate a user's position. Ericsson, SnapTrack, and CellPoint are some of the companies working on GSM positioning systems. SnapTrack's Wireless Assisted GPS service has tested with a supposed accuracy of 5–10 meters, depending on how densely packed an area is.

Unlike GPS, GSM positioning enables users to be found while they're in dense cities, buildings, parking garages, or anywhere else mobile phone service works. Users can even keep their phones in their briefcases, pockets, or luggage.

### Time Difference of Arrival

The *Time Difference of Arrival (TDOA)* method involves special software or equipment to be installed on every transmission tower on a cellular network. Basically, each cellular tower times how long it takes for the signals from a mobile phone to reach it. By calculating how far a handset is from various towers, and by knowing the GPS location of each tower, the rough position of a handset can be determined. At least three base stations need to be able to receive signals from the phone in order for this method to work.

### Angle of Arrival

The *Angle of Arrival (AOA)* method is similar to TDOA, except it analyzes the angle of each signal instead of the time. Because the angle of a handset's signal is known, the network can figure out which direction the signal is coming from. When combined with TDOA, relatively precise positions are possible.

### Enhanced Observed Time Differential

*Enhanced Observed Time Differential (E-OTD)* is similar to TDOA, but in reverse. Rather than the network timing each signal, the handset does the timing and calculates where in the world it is relative to surrounding towers.

New phones will need to be designed to handle E-OTD, but by putting the power of positioning in the phone many privacy concerns can be handled. The accuracy is expected to be within about 125 meters.

### Radio Propagation

This clever method maps the *radio frequency (RF)* characteristics across an entire area. By analyzing a given handset's RF signal, it is possible to roughly estimate the device's position.

## m-Commerce

Mobile electronic commerce, also known as *m-commerce*, is an emerging and wide-ranging field. Commerce plays many roles in the wireless world. Just some of the angles include charging for telecommunications services, collecting money, and using mobile phones to tap into other stores, or banks.

Phone service plans break down into two wide categories:

- Prepaid—Before any call is made or wireless service is used, the user's account is checked and the appropriate amount is deducted as the phone is being used. Users who prepay can be thought of as customers, and users might often jump from one prepaid service or application to another.

- Postpaid—The mobile carrier keeps a detailed record of every call made or packet of data that passes through the handset. A detailed invoice is sent to the user at the end of each month. Postpaid users can be thought of as subscribers, because much of their data is known by the provider of the given content or service.

There are many intricate steps involved, including a call detail record (CDR), a rating engine to figure out how much each call should cost, and a routing routine to figure out which plan a user is using.

Packet networks such as GPRS must not only keep track of each minute of voice use, but also measure the amount of data being sent and received. There might also be additional charges for premium services or content.

Things get even more complicated as a user roams from one network to another. Carriers must settle accounts with each other, and exchange CDR data. Generally, third-party clearinghouses will help keep track of all this.

From a game developer's perspective, much of this shouldn't matter. A good game is a good game is a good game. But some games that have high numbers of data packets exchanged, or games that take a long time to play might cost the user more money than she is willing to spend. It is important for any game designer to understand the target business model and gear the game's life cycle and data transfer accordingly.

## Charging for Content

Today, most e-commerce companies that support wireless data charge for services or content the same way they do over the Web—by collecting credit card information. While typing in a credit card number isn't that hard to do on the Web, it becomes much more difficult and time-consuming to do over a mobile phone.

Some m-commerce interfaces are quick and easy, but they still require lots of additional work from the user's perspective. For example, Amazon.com has a nifty WAP interface that only requires a click or two to buy books, as long as you've previously set up your account and credit card number online.

NTT DoCoMo and many other carriers see the power in avoiding credit cards. Their goal is to become like mini-banks themselves and automatically and easily charge fees for content or services with the click of one button. These companies will then send a bill to the user.

## Micro Java and Money

Additionally, most mobile carriers now offer a profit sharing program for Micro Java developers. In the United States for example, Motorola and Nextel offer a comprehensive developer partnership. You can list your application on the iDEN Update Web site at `http://commerce.motorola.com/nextel/main/`, and charge any amount you want. Nextel and Motorola will split the proceeds with you.

The process works as follows:

1. You join the Motorola and Nextel developer program. Visit `http://developer.nextel.com/` for more information.

2. You create your game or entertainment MIDlet, and test it as much as possible using emulators and your own Motorola phone.

3. Nextel puts your application through a comprehensive review and testing process, to be sure it causes no harm to the phone.

4. If all goes well, your app gets added to the iDEN Update site and users around the world can begin to access it. Users may plug their phones into their computers and use their credit card to pay for additional applications. Additionally, Nextel now enables users to quickly and easily download Java apps over-the-air. The charge for apps will conveniently appear on the player's next bill.

Most other wireless carriers will likely support similar commerce models.

## Voice and Telephony

One thing about mobile phones will probably never change: They will likely never become more like computers than like telephones. People still love the ease of talking into a device and quickly communicating with others. In industrialized nations, telephones are an integral part of most people's lives. They require almost no interface, no special skills, and little effort—a person need only remember her receiver's phone number.

As such, voice-recognition, voice-to-text, and text-to-voice technologies are being heavily researched. There are already many voice portal companies that can take your voice commands and read you your e-mail, tell you the details on one of your phone book entries, or let you know what appointments you have in today's calendar.

### VoiceXML

**URL:** `http://www.voicexml.org/`

VoiceXML is a language that helps content providers create trees of voice menus that can be triggered as users say certain words or phrases. The language is controlled by the VoiceXML forum and is based on Extensible Markup Language (XML).

A VoiceXML system basically acts according to the following procedure:

1. A user calls a VoiceXML server. A default VoiceXML page is loaded. This page has certain commands. Typically, a menu of typical options is read to the user.

2. The server will then wait for a response. The user speaks her mind.

3. The server translates the request and retrieves a relevant VoiceXML page. The page can be stored on any Web server across the world. The page might contain another menu of options, or might be a dynamically-created chunk of text that can then be read to the user.

### VoiceXML Software

There are a number of digitized speech applications and libraries that already use VoiceXML. Some examples

- VoiceClient—An e-mail solution that uses VoiceXML to read out mail messages. You can plug in any text-to-speech engine you desire. More information can be found at `http://www.voiceclient.com/`.

- Voice Genie—A VoiceXML browser and server. Learn more at `http://www.voicegenie.com/`.

### Wireless Telephony Application Interface (WTAI)

**URL:** `http://www.wapforum.org/what/technical.htm`

The WTAI set of tools will enable a WAP developer to add all sorts of telephony features to a WML page. Many of the latest WAP implementations support WTAI.

For example, you could create a WML link that enables users to

- Dial a number and make a call directly from the browser

- Add to or edit the device's phone book

- Automatically send dial tones during a voice call

In the near future, it is reasonable to expect that the WTAI telephony functions will be available on many J2ME implementations. This will enable Java developers to use functions. For example, to make a call

```
WTACall call = WTAPublic.makeCall("5551234");
```

or to add a name to a phone book

```
WTAPublic.addPBEntry("5551234", "Harry Bigby");
```

## Unified Messaging (UM)

The notion of unified messaging is quite simple: People should be able to use any device to access and receive voice calls, voice-mails, video calls, faxes, e-mails, or any other type of communications. Instead of different accounts, phone numbers, and machines, the promise of unified messaging is to have all communications in synch and retrievable from computers, television sets, or mobile phones.

For example, a user could set up a UM system to issue forth an SMS message whenever a new e-mail is received. The UM system might then use text-to-speech technology to read the e-mail to the user over her handset.

Location-based services could help automatically determine where a user is and gear his messaging preferences automatically. For example, if a person is in a meeting room, then the system could be smart enough to hold all calls and route them to voice-mail.

In the world of games, UM offers a similar promise. A big game could have interfaces from set-top game consoles, voice activation over mobile phones, or data viewing through J2ME.

## Summary

Clearly, mobile phones are on the way to becoming as powerful as today's desktop PCs. The next generation of mobile devices already resembles some of today's top PDAs. Many companies looking to develop for tomorrow's mobile handsets are focusing on PalmOS devices and PocketPC computers, such as the Compaq iPaq. For example, the Norwegian company Fathammer is creating some software called X-Forge. This software is a tiny but complete 3D library that will enable game developers to render rich, beautiful, 3D worlds on mobile devices.

Micro Java will help code achieve portability between tomorrow's wide range of devices. A basic Java game that works on today's simple handsets can easily be expanded with better multimedia and network access for future devices.

You've been patient enough! In then next section, we will finally begin to look at how to make games using J2ME.

# PART III

# The Java 2 Micro Edition

## IN THIS PART

**8** J2ME Overview

**9** Creating a MIDlet

**10** Making the Most of Limited Resources

**11** Making the Most of It: Optimizations

**12** Multithreaded Game Programming

# 8

# J2ME Overview

**IN THIS CHAPTER**

- The Trinity of Java Platforms
- It's a Small World After All
- Profiles and Configurations
- Connected in a Limited Way: The CLDC
- The Mobile Profile

Let's warp back to 1995, the year when Java first came out. Mobile phones were rare, brick-like gizmos, and the Internet was just emerging outside the realm of university and government geeks.

A lot has happened since then. The Web business grew, expanded beyond all reason, exploded, then established itself as a stable mass medium. And mobile phones swept the world, especially throughout Europe and Asia, where phones are owned by two-thirds of the population. It is now expected that the total number of wireless subscribers will exceed one billion by the end of 2002, and the majority of these new appliances will be connected to the Internet.

So how does Java fit into in all this?

## The Trinity of Java Platforms

In the beginning, there was only one edition of Java. Despite setbacks—such as the rumor that the Indonesian island of Java sued Sun Microsystems—Java took off. Java was lucky enough to have caught the Web wave, and soon become a favored language among Internet developers.

Java grew to be a big sucker—far too massive to fit on small devices. There was clearly a need for a new breed of Java, one that fit and made the most of limited devices. In 1999, Sun Microsystems finally decided to split Java efforts into three directions. Each of these platforms would be targeted at different types of devices, as shown in Figure 8.1.

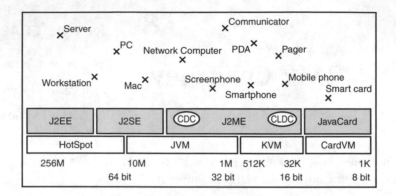

**FIGURE 8.1**   The Java virtual machine landscape.

The three platforms are

- Java 2 Platform, Standard Edition (J2SE)—For personal computers and workstations, and used mostly in the office or home. (http://java.sun.com/j2se/)

- Java 2 Platform, Enterprise Edition (J2EE)—For servers and middleware stations, and usually used in secured corporate areas. (http://java.sun.com/j2ee/)

- Java 2 Micro Edition (J2ME)—For small devices like mobile phones, pagers, PDAs, and communicators; as well as home devices such as microwaves and refrigerators, which are less powerful than personal computers. (http://java.sun.com/j2me/)

When developers talk about programming with Java, they are usually referring to J2SE, which is the basic Java standard. Java applets and Java applications run using J2SE, and it forms the core of J2EE and J2SE.

J2SE contains a fast virtual machine with a just-in-time (JIT) compiler, developer tools, and a set of libraries vital for the development of applications.

Unlike J2SE, J2EE represents a middleware container (an add-on to J2SE) that supports JSPs, Java Servlets, Enterprise JavaBeans (EJBs) and other J2EE APIs. It is meant for enterprise, multi-tier applications, where companies invest in expensive servers. With J2EE, developers prefer to focus on business logic instead of server implementation in order to speed up the development cycle and to make applications more robust.

But the platform we're focusing on in this book is J2ME. As micro appliances become increasingly important in our business lives, they also become potential platforms for heavy entertainment, games, and other types of fun. J2ME makes game development on such devices a reality.

And best of all, once you write a game that works on one type of J2ME device, it can easily be modified to work on them all.

# It's a Small World After All

In the past, micro devices came with their features hardcoded. Modern devices, however, support customization through the downloading of new services and applications from the Internet. Most major manufacturers have chosen J2ME as the standard for developing and deploying these new services.

## Using Java on Small Devices

There have been several attempts to bring Java technology down to the small devices. These efforts include Jump (`http://hewgill.com/pilot/jump/`) and Waba (`http://www.wabasoft.com`).

Jump is a Java language *front-end*—that is, it allows you to write programs in Java, but doesn't compile programs into Java classes. Rather, Java code is interpreted into assembly code and compiled natively. This is nice and fast, but it isn't really Java, and lacks Java's portability.

Waba, on the other hand, has its own virtual machine. However, it takes a few liberties with its capabilities and doesn't meet Sun's exact Java standard.

## J2ME Rocks!

The Java 2 Micro Edition (J2ME) was created by Sun, and fits in perfectly with other Java technologies. The language is focused specifically on the consumer and embedded market.

The main benefits of pure J2ME are as follows:

- Cross-platform compatibility—An application that uses 100% pure J2ME APIs can easily run on the wide range of devices of different models and from different vendors. This is perhaps the most compelling argument for using Java. Theoretically, an application written for a Motorola cell phone can also run on a Nokia, or even a Palm. The same code could be compiled and run as an applet in a Web browser, as an application on a million-dollar server machine, in your car's dashboard, or—eventually—in a Java-powered neural link to your own brain!

- Dynamic content—Applications on devices never go out of date. Just download a new one to meet new needs.

- Strong security—Security has always been one of Java's biggest concerns. Applications written in J2ME cannot access the device's hardware or other resources, making it nearly impossible to create viruses, Trojan horses, or other malicious programs.

- Large developer community—There are a few million Java developers already available worldwide on developer's portals, mailing lists, and discussion boards.

## Profiles and Configurations

Although different consumer devices such as mobile phones, pagers, and set-top boxes have many things in common, they also differ in form, function, and features. To address this diversity, J2ME attempts to be modular and easily customizable.

In order to support the kind of flexibility demanded by the embedded marketplace, the J2ME architecture is designed to be modular and scalable. This modularity and scalability is defined by the technology as three layers of software built upon the operating system of the device, as shown in Figure 8.2.

- Java virtual machine (JVM) layer

- Configuration layer

- Profile layer

The JVM layer is an implementation of a Java virtual machine customized for a particular device's operating system and supports a particular J2ME configuration.

The configuration layer defines the minimum set of Java virtual machine features and Java class libraries available on a particular category of appliances. This is usually a subset of J2SE.

The profile layer defines the minimum set of APIs available on a particular family of devices, such as mobile phones or PDAs. Applications are written for a particular profile, and are thus portable to any device that supports that profile. A device can support multiple profiles.

### Major J2ME Configurations

A *J2ME configuration* defines a minimum platform for each category of devices, each with similar requirements for total memory availability and processing power. A configuration defines various items that a hardware manufacturer or developer can expect to be available:

- Java programming language features

- Java virtual machine features

- Basic Java class libraries and APIs

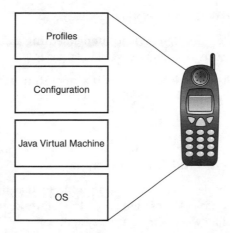

*FIGURE 8.2*   JVM layers.

At a high level, J2ME currently targets two categories of devices, each with its own configuration. These configurations were hammered out by companies such as Sun, 3COM, Bull, Ericsson, Matsushita, Mitsubishi, Motorola, Nokia, NTT DoCoMo, and Siemens:

- Connected Device Configuration (CDC)—This configuration is for shared and fixed connected information devices. Typical representatives of this category are TV set-top boxes, Internet TVs, and Internet-enabled screenphones. These devices have a large range of user interface capabilities, and memory availability between 2 and 16 megabytes. They usually use high-bandwidth network connections, mostly using TCP/IP. More info can be found at `http://java.sun.com/products/cdc/`.

- Connected, Limited Device Configuration (CLDC)—This configuration is for mobile-connected information devices. Mobile phones, pagers, and PDAs are examples of devices in this category. They have a very simple user interface with limited displays, a minimum memory size starting from 64 kilobytes, and low bandwidth network connection—often with unstable connectivity. Network communications are often not based on the TCP/IP protocol suite. Visit `http://java.sun.com/products/cldc/` for additional information.

## J2ME Profiles

A *J2ME profile* is a layer on top of the configuration. It addresses the specific demands of a certain device family. Its goal is to keep interoperability within a certain device family by defining a standard Java platform for that market.

Profiles can serve two distinct portability requirements:

- A profile provides complete APIs for implementing applications for a specific kind of device, such as a microwave, TV, or pager.

- A profile can also be created to support a significant group of applications that might be run on several categories of devices—for example, home banking or gaming applications.

It is possible for a single device to support several profiles. Some of them will be device-specific, and others will be application-specific.

Figure 8.3 shows a high-level view of how a profile such as the MIDP fits into a device. The lowest-level block represents the Mobile Information Device hardware itself. On top of this hardware is the native system software. This layer includes the operating system and libraries used by the device.

The next level is the CLDC or another configuration, which represents the K virtual machine and the associated libraries defined by the CLDC specification. This block provides the underlying Java with functionality upon which higher-level Java APIs are built.

There are two categories shown on top of the CLDC: MIDP APIs and OEM-specific APIs.

For example, Siemens has a special game API profile, which is discussed in Chapter 23, "Siemens Game API." Applications that use OEM-specific APIs might not be portable to the other MIDP devices.

Finally, the third-party applications—any games or other programs you write—sit atop all these APIs.

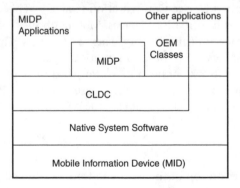

*FIGURE 8.3*    J2ME architecture overview.

## The Kilobyte Virtual Machine

The Kilobyte virtual machine (KVM) is a particular implementation of a Java virtual machine meeting the CLDC specification. As such, the KVM is a small and portable Java virtual machine, designed for small devices with limited resources. The main goal was to create the smallest possible virtual machine that would still maintain all the central aspects of the Java language, but would run on resource-limited devices with only a few hundred kilobytes of total memory.

It was designed to be

- Small, with a static memory footprint between 40 and 80 kilobytes

- Clean and portable

- Modular and customizable

- Complete and fast

The KVM is implemented in the C programming language; therefore, it can be easily ported to various platforms for which a C compiler is available. The virtual machine has been built around a bytecode interpreter with various flags and options to speed up the porting and improve the space optimization. It was already successfully ported to more than 25 devices, and it can be built with any ANSI-compliant C compiler.

## The Java Application Manager

The Java Application Manager (JAM) is a part of the KVM that serves as an interface between the operating system and the virtual machine. Like the KVM, the JAM is built-in to any J2ME-supporting device. The JAM works in the background, helping to launch your programs.

The JAM assumes that applications are available for downloading as JAR files by using networking or storage protocol. It reads the contents of the JAR file and its descriptor file from the Internet, and launches the KVM using the main class as a parameter. The JAM also handles each application's life cycle, installing, launching, and deleting Java apps.

## Packaging into a JAR File

Whenever a Java application intended for a CLDC device is distributed publicly, it must be formatted in a compressed Java archive (JAR) file. The next chapter will show you how to create JAR and other types of packages.

## Connected in a Limited Way: The CLDC

The entire CLDC implementation generally fits in fewer than 128 kilobytes. Its specification assumes that applications can be run in as little as 32 kilobytes of Java heap memory. Of course, this size is only theoretical. Most devices include not only the base CLDC classes, but tons of profile classes (such as MIDP) to handle user interface, networking, and other essential details.

The CLDC configuration addresses the following areas, using the following Java packages:

- `java.lang.*`—This represents the essential Java classes for working with the system and with different data types.

- `java.util.*`—This is the standard set of utility classes for working with collections and dates.

- `java.io.*`—Handles input and output.

- `javax.microedition.io.*`—A non-standard Java package that provides additional network functionality.

The Java virtual machine supporting CLDC is compatible with the original Java language specification by James Gosling, except for the following differences:

- No support for floating-point data types (no float and double)

- No support for finalization of class instances ( the method `Object.finalize()` does not exist)

- Limitation on error handling

- No support for Java Native Interface (JNI)

- No reflection features

- No support for thread groups or daemon threads

- No weak references

Floating-point support has been omitted primarily because of the majority of the CLDC target devices not having hardware support for floating point arithmetic. Other features were eliminated mostly because of strict memory limitations or potential security concerns in the absence of the full J2SE security model.

### Security

Security within the CLDC works as follows:

- Low-level virtual machine security is achieved by requiring downloaded Java classes to pass a classfile verification step.

- Applications are protected from each other by being run in a closed sandbox environment.

- Classes in protected system packages cannot be overridden by applications.

### Pre-verifying

The CLDC requires the capability of a Java virtual machine to identify and reject an invalid classfile. Because the standard classfile verification approach defined by J2SE is too memory-hungry for small appliances, the CLDC defines an alternative mechanism for verification.

In this alternative, each method in a downloaded Java classfile contains a stack map attribute. This attribute is newly defined in the CLDC. It is added to the standard classfile by a pre-verification tool that analyzes each method in the classfile. This step is typically performed on a server or desktop system before the classfile is downloaded to the device.

The presence of this attribute enables a CLDC-compliant Java virtual machine to verify Java classfiles much more quickly and with less VM code and RAM consumption, but with the same level of security as in J2SE.

We will go into more detail about how to pre-verify in Chapter 9, "Creating A MIDlet."

## The Mobile Profile

The first and, at the present, only available standard profiles on the market is the Mobile Information Device Profile (MIDP). This section covers some of the basics on MIDP, but for more detailed information, go to
http://java.sun.com/products/midp/.

The MIDP is designed to run on top of the CLDC. Devices that support the MIDP should have the following minimum set of characteristics:

- Display:

    Screen size of 96×54

    Display depth of 1 bit

    Aspect ratio of pixels approximately 1:1

- Input:

  One-handed keypad, or two-handed keyboard, or touch screen

- Memory:

  128 kilobytes of non-volatile memory for the MIDP components

  8 kilobytes of non-volatile memory for application-created persistence data

  32 kilobytes of volatile memory for Java runtime (for example, heap memory)

- Networking:

  Two-way, wireless, possibly intermittent, with limited bandwith

Most devices that implement the MIDP specification will be, at least initially, devices that exist on the market today, such as mobile phones and pagers.

## MIDP in a Nutshell

The MIDP has classes to handle the following:

- Application running

- User interface

- Persistent storage

- Networking

- Timers

## Earlier Profiles

MIDP was first released in September 2000. Before that, two Asian mobile operators announced their own non-standard profiles:

- Kittyhawk—Created by LG Telecom and Sun Microsystems. This has been replaced by MIDP.

- iAppli—Created by NTT DoCoMo. This is discussed fully in Chapter 22, "iAppli: MicroJava with a Twist."

The next MIDP specification, which also runs on Palm OS devices, will be announced in April 2002, and is being produced by the Mobile Information Device Profile Expert Group (MIDPEG), whose members include America Online, Ericsson, Motorola, Nokia, Palm, Sun Microsystems and others.

# Summary

J2ME is a platform that is slowly being accepted and deployed by most hardware manufacturers. In the near future, the majority of mobile phones, TV set-top boxes, pagers, and other micro devices will support J2ME.

Currently, CLDC is the only J2ME configuration available on the market, with two profiles laid on the top of it: MIDP and iAppli. Because the latter profile is used only by NTT DoCoMo, MIDP is the gold standard for small devices.

The next chapter will show you how to begin developing a MIDP application.

# 9

# Creating a MIDlet

**IN THIS CHAPTER**

- Command-Line MIDlet Development
- Development Environments
- Lifecycle of a MIDlet
- Displaying Stuff
- Menus and Commands
- Creating Help and About Alert Screens
- Global Properties

If you have any experience creating Java applications or applets, then programming in J2ME won't seem like such a stretch. The steps are basically the same:

1. Write your program and save it as a text file with the .java extension.

2. Compile it.

3. Pre-verify it.

4. Package it.

5. Test it.

6. Debug it.

7. Release it!

The only thing that should set off your mental alarm is step number 3—pre-verification. This might sound weird and complicated, but it's actually quite easy. The purpose of pre-verification is to go through your bytecode and set hints up so that the actual verification of bytecode on the micro device will happen much more quickly, saving you valuable startup time.

## Command-Line MIDlet Development

You don't really need any fancy tools to create a MIDlet. Simply install Java SDK 1.3 and the MIDlet libraries. Get the Java SDK 1.3 from http://java.sun.com/j2se/1.3/. Get the CLDC packages from http://www.sun.com/software/communitysource/j2me/cldc/download.html. And grab the MIDP libraries from http://java.sun.com/products/midp/.

Install everything into the same directory. To do so, create a directory similar to `mkdir j2me`. You should then unzip the `j2me_cldc-1_0-src-winsol.zip` file into the `C:\j2me\` directory. Then unzip `midp-1_0a-spec.zip` into the same directory.

You are now ready to write your MIDlet application. A bit later in this chapter, we will discuss what all these methods mean and how it all works. For now, just use a text editor to create the file `Hello.java`:

```java
import javax.microedition.midlet.*;
import javax.microedition.lcdui.*;

public class Hello extends MIDlet {
  private Display display;
  TextBox t = null;

  public Hello()
  {
    display = Display.getDisplay(this);
  }

  public void startApp()
  {
    t = new TextBox("Hello ", "Howdy!", 256, 0);
    display.setCurrent(t);
  }

  public void pauseApp() { }

  public void destroyApp(boolean unconditional) { }
}
```

Make sure the `Hello.java` program is in the `c:\j2me` directory.

You can now compile the program the same way you would compile any other Java application. Simply point to the appropriate MIDP and CLDC classes:

```
javac -bootclasspath c:\j2me\midp\classes Hello.java
```

This should create the `Hello.class` file. You can now pre-verify the class:

```
c:\j2me\cldc\preverify HelloMIDlet
```

This command will automatically create an "output" directory beneath the current directory and put the pre-verified class into this new directory. Move to the output directory as follows:

```
cd output
```

Then package your application into a JAR file. Whenever you build a MIDP application, you should place all pre-verified class files, images, and other resources into a JAR.

The command to package things up into a JAR named "HelloWorld" is thus:

```
jar cf HelloWorld.jar Hello.class
```

Every MIDlet package should also include a special JAD file. This simple text file is a description of what the JAR contains, what device it is intended for, and how much memory it takes up. Typically, a micro device will read the JAD file to determine how to download or otherwise deploy the JAR file.

So, create a file called HelloWorld.JAD with the following content:

```
MIDlet-1: HelloWorld, HelloWorld.png, HelloMIDlet
MIDlet-Jar-Size: 1178
MIDlet-Jar-URL: HelloWorld.jar
MIDlet-Name: HelloWorld
MIDlet-Vendor: Sun Microsystems
MIDlet-Version: 1.0
```

That's it! You can now load and run the HelloWorld.JAR and HelloWorld.JAD files onto any MIDP emulator or device!

## Development Environments

The procedure outlined in the previous section is kind of complicated, though, isn't it? Luckily, there are many development environments that do all the compiling, pre-verification, creation of JAR and JAD files, and other packaging for you. Metrowerk's Code Warrior has a J2ME plug-in, and Borland's JBuilder has a Handheld Express add-on. In addition, Nokia, Siemens, RIM, Zucotto, and Motorola all offer special SDKs and IDEs for J2ME development. Many of these vendor-specific IDEs are discussed in later chapters, but you can also get more information about each on the Web:

- RIM Blackberry IDE

  **URL:** http://developers.rim.net/tools/jde/index.shtml

- Zucotto WHITEboard

  **URL:** http://www.zucotto.com/whiteboard/

- Borland's JBuilder Mobile Set

  **URL:** http://www.borland.com/jbuilder/mobileset/

## Wireless Toolkit

Throughout this book, we will be focusing on a product called the J2ME Wireless Toolkit. You can download it from http://java.sun.com/products/j2mewtoolkit/.

The Wireless Toolkit, developed by Sun, is free of charge, complete, easy to use, and available for Windows, Linux, and Solaris. It also comes with a bunch of source code, including sample games such as Snake, Sokoban, a tile-sliding game, Pong, and Star Cruiser. It also includes a slew of emulators, shown in Figure 9.1, that enable you to test your applications on a black and white phone, a color phone, a pager, a Palm, or vendor-specific phones, such as the Motorola i85s.

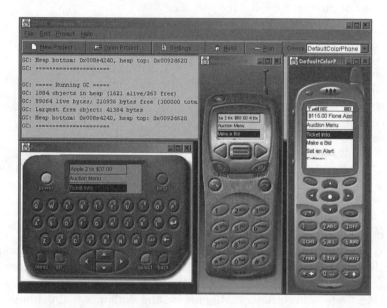

**FIGURE 9.1**    Sun's Wireless Toolkit. To run the Wireless Toolkit, you'll need Java itself (JDK 1.3 or better), which has all the engines and libraries necessary to compile code. If you don't already have the JDK, you can grab it at http://java.sun.com/j2se/1.3/. Be sure to install it per directions, with all the proper settings for classpaths and paths.

> **NOTE**
>
> The Java SDK must be installed *before* you install the Wireless Toolkit.

If you like, you can integrate the Wireless Toolkit with Sun's free Forte development environment. You can download Forte at http://www.sun.com/forte/ffj/.

The Wireless Toolkit can also be integrated into Borland's JBuilder.

## Developing a MIDlet with the Wireless Toolkit

Let's walk through the process of writing, compiling, testing, and packaging a MIDlet.

---

**NOTE**

The Wireless Toolkit is installed by default in the directory `C:\j2mewtk`. If you have chosen to install to a different directory, then modify all the following commands appropriately.

---

First off, you can run the Wireless Toolkit Preferences program to set up a proxy server, as well as the preferred heap size to emulate.

You can then run the Ktoolbar shortcut, which loads up a graphical menu with all your development options, as shown in Figure 9.1.

1. To create a new project, hit the New Project button. Give your project a simple name (with no spaces), and type in the name of the main MIDlet class. For example, if you are creating a Hello World application, use Project name "HelloWorld" and MIDlet Class name "Hello."

2. The settings dialog for the project will appear as in Figure 9.2. These are the properties that will eventually appear in the application's JAD file. You can modify the properties as you see fit. Underneath the MIDlets tab you can modify the display name of your MIDlet, the application's icon, and the application's main class file. Using an icon is optional.

   Note that any given JAR file might have several applications included within it. For example, you might want to package several games together into the same arcade.

   In any event, hit the OK button to save the settings. You can modify the settings at any time by hitting the Settings button.

3. A new directory will be created beneath the `C:\J2mewtk\apps` directory. In this case, we'll have a `C:\J2mewtk\apps\HelloWorld` directory. Beneath this directory will be four other directories: `bin`, `lib`, `res`, and `src`.

4. You can create your Java class or classes using any text editor or other development environment. Drop all the Java files into the `C:\J2mewtk\apps\HelloWorld\src` directory.

   For example, drop the `Hello.java` file (listed in the previous section) into this directory.

5. If your application uses any PNG images or other resources, drop those in the `C:\J2mewtk\apps\HelloWorld\res` directory.

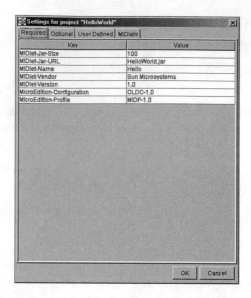

*FIGURE 9.2*    The settings dialog.

6. You can now compile, pre-verify, and package your application in one step. Just hit the Build button.

   If all goes well, the console will give you a Build Complete message. Otherwise, any errors will be shown. Go through your Java source files and correct any bugs.

7. You can test the program using the built-in emulator. Choose which device you want to emulate using the Device pull-down menu. You can choose DefaultGrayPhone for a phone with a black and white screen, DefaultColorPhone for a color screen, MinimumPhone for a the simplest possible MIDP device, Motorola i85s, Palm device, or RIM pager device.

   To run the emulator, hit the Run button. A list of all the MIDlets available for launching will appear. Select HelloWorld and then hit the Launch button. The application will run, as shown in Figure 9.3.

8. You can now actually build the JAR file. Select the top Project menu and choose the Package option. Look under the C:\J2mewtk\apps\HelloWorld\bin directory. You'll notice a HelloWorld.jar file and a HelloWorld.jad file.

   Actually installing the JAR and JAD files differs from device to device. Later chapters in this book cover how to deploy MIDlets on Siemens, NTT DoComo, and other devices.

*FIGURE 9.3*    The Hello World MIDlet.

## Lifecycle of a MIDlet

Why is a MIDlet called a MIDlet? Because it is a special type of applet that runs on MIDP-compliant devices. Cute, eh? Just as a standard Java applet extends the `java.applet.Applet` class, a MIDlet extends the `javax.microedition.MIDlet.MIDlet` class.

The `MIDlet` class contains all the goodies that the phone's application management system needs to tap into your application and start, pause, and end processes. The `javax.microedition.midlet.MIDlet` class has several abstract methods that you *must* define in your main class file:

- `public void startApp()`—This method is called the moment your MIDlet becomes active. While active, your MIDlet might run and access the phone's resources. The method is called when your program is first run, as well as when your program is released from the paused state.

- `public void pauseApp()`—Most MIDP devices permit the user to pause the current application. For example, if a player's phone rings, then she might choose to pause the game and answer the call. Whenever a pause event takes place, this method is called. While in the paused state, your MIDlet must release shared resources. This is also a good place to pause any game timers, and so on. This method will only be called when the MIDlet is in the active state. Some devices (such as the Siemens SL45i) never call this method; however, the method must always be included in your program.

- `public void destroyApp(boolean unconditional)`—When the user chooses to end the game, the phone will automatically call this method. At this point, your MIDlet will terminate and enter the destroyed state. In the destroyed state, the MIDlet should release all resources, stop all threads, and save any persistent state. This method can be called while the MIDlet is in either the paused or active state.

  The `unconditional` flag determines whether the program *must* quit, or whether it would just be *nice* if the program quits. If the flag is set to true, then the phone's user definitely wants out. The MIDlet must be sure to clean up all resources properly. However, some phones might try to quit the application after a given amount of idle time. In such a case, the `unconditional` flag will be set to false. The MIDlet can avoid entering the destroyed state by throwing a `MIDletStateChangeException`.

These states—active, paused, and destroyed—enable the handheld device's application management software to manage the activities of multiple MIDlets within the same runtime environment. It can select which MIDlets are active at a given time by starting and pausing them individually. The application management software maintains the state of the MIDlet and invokes methods on the MIDlet to change the states. The MIDlet implements these methods to update its internal activities and resource usage as directed by the application management software. The state change is not considered complete until the state change method has returned. It is intended that these methods return quickly. Listing 9.1 shows the structure of the world's simplest (and most useless) Java MIDlet:

*LISTING 9.1*   A Minimal MIDlet Implementation

```
import javax.microedition.midlet.*;

public class Game extends MIDlet
{
  public void startApp() {}
  public void pauseApp() {}
  public void destroyApp(boolean b) {}

  public void exit()
  {
    destroyApp(false);
    notifyDestroyed();
  }
}
```

The method exit() is added to provide a remote call to help terminate the application.

## Displaying Stuff

To draw something on the micro device screen, you need to access the display. To do so, you can use the javax.microedition.lcdui.Display class, which is statically included with every MIDlet.

Display represents the system's graphical display and input devices. It includes methods for retrieving properties of the device and for requesting that objects be displayed on the device.

There is exactly one instance of the Display class per MIDlet. To get a reference to the instance, call the getDisplay() method. The application may call the method anywhere in the code, at any time.

Any user interface objects that you can paint on the display must extend the Displayable class. Any Displayable object may have commands and listeners associated with it. The contents displayed and their interactions with the user are defined by subclasses. Basically, every screen that you'll want to show should be defined as a separate Displayable object.

A device can only show one Displayable object at a time. This object is referred to as the *current* Displayable object.

The Display class has the following important methods:

- isColor()—Returns true if the current device has a color screen, returns false otherwise.

- numColors()—Returns the number of colors or grayscales that can be represented on the device.

- getCurrent()—Returns the current Displayable object. The Displayable object returned might not actually be visible on the display if the MIDlet is running in the background, or if the Displayable object is currently obscured by a system screen. The value returned by getCurrent() might also be null if the setCurrent() method has not been called yet.

- setCurrent(Displayable nextDisplayable)—This is a key method that actually changes the current display. Simply pass in a new Displayable object. The change will typically not take effect immediately, but may be delayed so that it occurs between event delivery method calls. Because of this delay, a call to getCurrent() shortly after a call to setCurrent() is unlikely to return the value passed to setCurrent().

When a MIDlet application is first started, there is no current `Displayable` object. It is the responsibility of the application to ensure that a `Displayable` object is visible and can interact with the user at all times. Therefore, an application should always call `setCurrent()` as part of its initialization.

- `setCurrent(Alert alert, Displayable nextDisplayable)`—This is a version of `setCurrent()` specially suited for alerts. An alert is a special type of `Displayable` object that is intended to be shown and immediately dismissed. For example, a typical alert might be a dialog box that warns the player about some imminent problem.

  To use this method, set the alert as the current `Displayable` object and choose another screen as the `nextDisplayable`. As soon as the alert box is dismissed, the next `Displayable` screen will be shown.

## Working with Screens

The `javax.microedition.lcdui.Screen` class is the common superclass of all high-level user interface objects. The `Screen` itself is pretty simple. It simply allows you to add a title or scrolling ticker to the `Displayable` class.

Every screen that a user will see should be created as its own class. The display will automatically refresh whenever the contents of a screen are updated. For example, suppose a `List` object featuring a main game menu is currently being displayed. If the application inserts a new element at the beginning of the `List`, it is displayed immediately and the other elements will be rearranged appropriately. There is no need for the application to call another method to refresh the display.

---

**WARNING**

It is good programming practice to only change the contents of a screen when it is not visible (that is, while another `Displayable` is current). Changing the contents of the screen while it is visible may result in performance problems on some devices, and might also be confusing if the screen's content changes at the same moment when a user is interacting with it.

---

The following classes are subclasses of the `Screen` class:

- `Form`
- `Alert`
- `List`
- `TextBox`

All these classes inherit four methods from `Screen`:

- `getTitle()`—Gets the title of the `Screen`.

- `setTitle(String title)`—Sets the title of the `Screen`. If the `Screen` is physically visible, the visible effect should take place no later than immediately after the callback.

- `getTicker()`—Gets the scrolling ticker object used by the `Screen`.

- `setTicker(Ticker ticker)`—Sets a scrolling ticker to be used for this `Screen`, replacing any previous ticker. Several `Screen` objects within an application can share the same ticker. This is done by calling `setTicker()` on different screens with the same `Ticker` object.

## Forms

The `javax.microedition.lcdui.Form` class is the most commonly used child of `Screen`. It might contain an arbitrary mixture of items, such as images, text fields, date fields, gauges, and choice groups. In general, any subclass of the `Item` class can be contained within a `Form`.

Every mobile device will handle the layout, traversal, and scrolling of a form in a slightly different way.

The items contained in a `Form` are referred to by their indices, which are consecutive integers starting from zero. These items can be edited using the `append()`, `delete()`, `insert()`, and `set()` methods. More information about dealing with user interface items can be found in Chapter 13, "High-Level Approach."

Listing 9.2, for example, creates a start-up form and sets it as the current `Displayable`.

*LISTING 9.2*   Creating and Calling a Form

```
import javax.microedition.MIDlet.*;
import javax.microedition.lcdui.*;

public class Game extends MIDlet
{
  private Display display;

  public void startApp()
  {
    display = Display.getDisplay(this);
    StartForm form = new StartForm(this);
```

*LISTING 9.2*   Creating and Calling a Form

```
    display.setCurrent(form);
  }

  public void pauseApp() {}
  public void destroyApp(boolean b) {}

  public Display getDisplay()
  {
    return display;
  }

  public void exit()
  {
    destroyApp(false);
    notifyDestroyed();
  }
}
```

The code for the `StartForm` class can be seen in Listing 9.3.

*LISTING 9.3*   The `StartForm` Class

```
import javax.microedition.lcdui.*;

public class StartForm extends Form
{
  private Game game;

  public StartForm(Game game)
  {
    super("Micro Racer");
    this.game = game;
    StringItem item = new StringItem(
        "Welcome to Micro Racer!", null);
    append(item);
  }
}
```

The final product can be seen in Figure 9.4.

New forms must extend the `Form` class. The form's constructor must call the parent's constructor, which accepts the title as a parameter. To be able to access the MIDlet's `exit()` and other methods, a global variable pointing to the main `Game` class is provided.

`javax.microedition.lcdui.StringItem` is a user interface component to present different read-only text labels. More information about `StringItem` and other user interface components can be found in Chapter 13, "High-Level Graphical User Interfaces."

*FIGURE 9.4*    Game Intro screen.

Each `Form` has the following important methods:

- `append (Item item)`—Adds a user interface item into the `Form`.

- `append(String str)`—Adds a string to the `Form`.

- `append(Image img)`—Adds an image to the `Form`.

- `insert(int itemNum, Item item)`—Inserts an item into the `Form` just prior to the item number specified. The size of the `Form` grows by one. The `itemNum` parameter must be within the current range of actual items.

- `delete(int itemNum)`—Deletes the item at `itemNum`.

- `set(int itemNum, Item item)`—Sets the item referenced by `itemNum` to the specified item, replacing the previous item. The previous item is removed from the `Form`.

- `get(int itemNum)`—Gets the item at given position.

- `setItemStateListener(ItemStateListener listener)`—Sets the item state listener for the `Form`, replacing any previous listener. If the listener is null, it simply removes the previous listener. An item state listener enables your application to dynamically handle any changes to the form's items.

- `size()`—Returns the number of items in the `Form`.

Every Screen's subclass also implements the Displayable interface, which means you can use the isShown() method that returns true only if the Form is actually visible on the display. In order for a Displayable to be visible, all the following must be true:

- The MIDlet must be running in the foreground

- The Displayable must be the display's current screen

- The Displayable must not be obscured by a system screen

## Menus and Commands

Because the MIDP user interface is highly abstract, it does not dictate any concrete interaction techniques, such as soft buttons or menus. Even low-level interactions such as scrolling are hidden to the application.

Instead, MIDP defines the javax.microedition.lcdui.Command class. Whenever a user hits a button, menu, dial, touch-screen, or other supported input element, a particular command will be triggered.

Because every Screen's subclass implements the Displayable interface, every screen has access to a slew of command methods:

- addCommand(Command cmd)—Adds a command to the Displayable.

- removeCommand(Command cmd)—Removes a command from the Displayable.

- setCommandListener(CommandListener listener)—Sets a listener for Commands to this Displayable, replacing any previous CommandListener. A null reference is allowed, and has the effect of removing any existing listener.

Whenever the user hits a key (or does something else command-worthy), a command will be issued to any registered command listener. Every Command is made up of three elements:

- Label

- Command type

- Priority

A command label is a String that will be shown to let the user know what a command actually does. For example, most phones have two soft keys right beneath their display. A typical label might be set to "Quit." The word "quit" would then appear above the first soft key. When this key is pressed, the application will catch the command and exit smoothly.

Other times, a menu of various commands might be presented to the user, as shown in Figure 9.5. The user can use the phone's arrow keys to scroll to a particular command and select it.

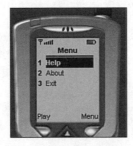

**FIGURE 9.5**   A sample menu of commands.

A command's type specifies the intent of the command. For example, if the application specifies that the command is of type BACK (to go back to the previously shown screen), then some devices will automatically associate all back commands with a given soft key. The defined command types are as follows:

- BACK—Returns the user to the previous screen.

- OK—A command that is a standard positive answer to a dialog.

- CANCEL—A command that is a standard negative answer to a dialog.

- EXIT—A command used for exiting from the application.

- HELP—A request for online help.

- ITEM—A command type relevant to a particular user interface item on the screen.

- SCREEN—An application-defined command that somehow pertains to the current screen.

- STOP—A command that will stop some currently running process or operation.

Finally, the command's priority value describes the importance of this command relative to other commands on the same screen. Priority values are integers, where a lower number indicates greater importance. The actual values are chosen by the application. A priority value of one indicates the most important command.

Typically, a mobile device will position a command on the screen based on its type and then order similar commands based on their priority. This usually means that the command with the highest priority is placed so that user can trigger it directly (using the soft keys), and that commands with lower priority are placed on an inner menu.

It is also possible for several commands to have the same priorities and types. If this occurs, each device will choose the order in which they are presented. Usually, the first command you create in your code will be given higher priority.

The `javax.microedition.lcdui.CommandListener` interface is used by applications to receive high-level events that are invoked by commands. The application must provide an implementation of a listener and must provide an instance of it on a screen in order to receive high-level events on that screen.

---

**WARNING**

The specification does not require the platform to create multiple threads for event delivery. Thus, if the listener method does not return, or the return is delayed, the system might be blocked. The `Listener` method should always return immediately.

---

Listing 9.4 shows a typical set of commands, along with a listener. The first command, Play, will appear in the bottom row of the screen, linked to the first soft key. The second soft key will be linked to an command named Menu (created automatically by the phone).

When the Menu soft key is hit, the remaining commands will appear in a menu, as shown in Figure 9.5.

*LISTING 9.4*    A Command Listener

```
import javax.microedition.lcdui.*;

public class StartForm extends Form
    implements CommandListener
{
  private Game game;
  private Command playCommand;
  private Command helpCommand;
  private Command aboutCommand;
  private Command exitCommand;

  public StartForm(Game game)
  {
    super("Micro Racer");
    this.game = game;
    StringItem item = new StringItem(
        "Welcome to Micro Racer!", null);
    append(item);
    playCommand = new Command("Play", Command.SCREEN, 1);
```

LISTING 9.4     continued

```
    helpCommand = new Command("Help", Command.HELP, 2);
    aboutCommand = new Command("About",
        Command.SCREEN, 3);
    exitCommand = new Command("Exit", Command.EXIT, 4);
        addCommand(playCommand);
    addCommand(helpCommand);
    addCommand(aboutCommand);
    addCommand(exitCommand);
    setCommandListener(this);
}

public void commandAction(Command c, Displayable s)
{
    if (c.equals(playCommand))
    {
        // The Play Command has been selected.
    }
    else if (c.equals(helpCommand))
    {
        // The Help Command has been selected.
    }
    else if (c.equals(aboutCommand))
    {
        // The About Command has been selected.
    }
    else if (c.equals(exitCommand))
    {
        // The Exit Command has been selected.
        game.exit();
    }
}
}
```

To create commands, add them as a global variable, construct them using new, then plop them on a screen using the addCommand() method.

To actually catch the commands, implement a CommandListener and register it using the setCommandListener() method.

## Creating Help and About Alert Screens

An alert is a screen that shows data to the user and waits for a certain period before proceeding to the next screen. An alert generally contains some descriptive text, an optional image icon, and several special commands—usually OK and, optionally, CANCEL. Figure 9.6 illustrates an example.

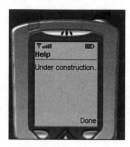

*FIGURE 9.6*   The Help alert.

### The Alert Class

The `javax.microedition.lcdui.Alert` class makes it easy to create alerts. The intended use of an alert is to inform the user about information, errors, and other exceptional conditions. Every alert can have an `javax.microedition.lcdui.AlertType` class associated with it to provide an indication of its nature.

An `Alert`'s constructor accepts four parameters:

- Title (for example, "Help" or "About")

- Alert text

- Alert image (may be set to null if not needed)

- Alert type

After constructing an alert, an application should set the alert timeout. The timeout may be set to infinity by using the `setTimeout(Alert.FOREVER)` method. In this case, the alert is considered to be modal—forcing the user to hit the OK or CANCEL command to dismiss it.

> **WARNING**
>
> If you put too much content in a timed alert, the alert dialog will scroll, and might automatically become a modal alert.

The following alert types are defined:

- ALARM—Alerts the user to an event for which the user has previously requested to be notified. For instance, "You are out of time!"

- CONFIRMATION—Confirms an action. For example, "Are you sure you want to quit this game?"

- ERROR—Alerts the user to an erroneous operation. For example, "No Network Connection Detected."

- INFO—Provides non-threatening information to the user. For example, "Congrats! You just passed level one."

- WARNING—Warns the user of a potentially dangerous operation. For example: "Hitting the OK button will erase your saved game. Are you sure you want to do this?"

Alerts do not accept application-defined commands. As such, some of the command-relevant methods inherited from Screen will throw exceptions. Methods useful in the Alert class are the following:

- getDefaultTimeout()—Returns the default time for showing an alert. This is either a positive value, which indicates a time in milliseconds, or the special value FOREVER, which indicates that alerts are modal by default.

- getTimeout()—Gets the timeout for the current alert box. This is either a positive value, which indicates a time in milliseconds, or the special value FOREVER, which indicates that this alert is modal.

- setTimeout(int time)—Sets the timeout for the alert box. This must either be a positive time value in milliseconds, or the special value FOREVER.

- getType()—Returns the type of the alert.

- setType(AlertType type)—This method sets the type of the alert.

- getString()—Returns the text string used in the alert.

- setString(String str)—Sets the text string used in the alert.

- getImage()—Gets the image used in the alert.

- setImage(Image img)—Sets the image used in the alert.

Alerts are a great and easy way to add Help or About screens to your game.

Listing 9.5 shows how to implement a Help alert screen and an About alert screen.

*LISTING 9.5*    Implementing Help and About Screens

```java
import javax.microedition.lcdui.*;

public class StartForm extends Form
    implements CommandListener
{
  private Game game;
  private Command playCommand;
  private Command helpCommand;
  private Command aboutCommand;
  private Command exitCommand;

  public StartForm(Game game)
  {
    super("Micro Racer");
    this.game = game;
    StringItem item = new StringItem(
        "Welcome to Micro Racer!", null);
    append(item);
    playCommand = new Command("Play", Command.SCREEN, 1);
    helpCommand = new Command("Help", Command.SCREEN, 2);
    aboutCommand = new Command("About",
        Command.SCREEN, 3);
    exitCommand = new Command("Exit", Command.SCREEN, 4);
        addCommand(playCommand);
    addCommand(helpCommand);
    addCommand(aboutCommand);
    addCommand(exitCommand);
    setCommandListener(this);
  }

  public void commandAction(Command c, Displayable s)
  {
    if (c.equals(playCommand)) {}
    else if (c.equals(helpCommand))
    {
      String str = "Under construction.";
      Alert alert = new Alert("Help", str, null,
          AlertType.INFO);
      alert.setTimeout(Alert.FOREVER);
      game.getDisplay().setCurrent(alert, this);
    }
```

**LISTING 9.5**   continued

```
  else if (c.equals(aboutCommand))
  {
    StringBuffer buf = new StringBuffer("");
    buf.append("Developed by David Fox");
    buf.append("and Roman Verhovsek.\n");
    Alert alert = new Alert("About", buf.toString(),
        null, AlertType.INFO);
    alert.setTimeout(Alert.FOREVER);
    game.getDisplay().setCurrent(alert, this);
  }
  else if (c.equals(exitCommand))
  {
    game.exit();
  }
 }
}
```

When putting an alert on the screen, the display's `setCurrent()` method is called with two parameters. The second parameter is the screen that should be shown after the alert is dismissed.

## Splash Screens

A *splash screen* is an informational screen that introduces the game with specific logo and text. It is shown during a game's startup, and usually turns off after a period of time. You can use the `Alert` class to create such a screen, but oftentimes you will want more control and may want to show several images along with several text elements.

In these cases, the `Canvas` or `Form` classes can be used instead. A `Canvas` is the most flexible type of screen, but you must implement your own scrolling and component positioning. The `Canvas` class is discussed in much more detail in Chapter 14, "Low-Level Approach."

An easier solution is the `Form` object, which is discussed in Chapter 13. For now, check out Listing 9.6 to see how a simple intro screen, shown in Figure 9.7, is created.

*LISTING 9.6*   A Form Object Splash Screen

```java
import java.util.*;
import javax.microedition.lcdui.*;

public class IntroForm extends Form
{
  private Game game;
  private Form form;

  public IntroForm(Game game, Form form)
  {
    super("");
    this.game = game;
    this.form = form;
    Image image = null;
    try
    {
      image = Image.createImage("/logo.png");
    } catch (Exception ex) {}
    ImageItem item = new ImageItem(null, image,
        ImageItem.LAYOUT_CENTER, null);
    append(item);
    Task task = new Task();
    Thread thread = new Thread(task);
    thread.start();
  }

  public class Task implements Runnable
  {
    private final int DELAY = 5000;

    public void run()
    {
      try
      {
        Thread.sleep(DELAY);
      } catch (Exception ex) {}
      game.getDisplay().setCurrent(form);
    }
  }
}
```

**FIGURE 9.7**    The splash screen.

The `IntroForm` constructor takes two parameters: a reference to a MIDlet (so that we can access the current display object) and a reference to the form that must replace the current one. An invoked thread waits for five seconds, then makes the change to the new form.

An image is loaded using the static method `Image.createImage()` where the file-name should start with a slash (/) to indicate that the image is in the same directory or JAR file as the MIDlet class.

To call up the intro dialog, your main MIDlet Game class would use code similar to the following:

```
public void startApp()
{
  display = Display.getDisplay(this);
  StartForm form = new StartForm(this);
  IntroForm introForm = new IntroForm(this, form);
  display.setCurrent(introForm);
}
```

# Global Properties

Part of the challenge of writing a professional game is being sure it runs as smoothly as possible, no matter what the operating system, device, screen resolution or colors, or language.

You can accomplish a great deal by sniffing out a MIDlet's various application and system properties.

## Getting Application Properties

The `getAppProperty(String key)` method within the `MIDlet` class provides the program with a mechanism to retrieve named properties from the application management software. These properties are retrieved from the combination of the application descriptor file (JAD) and the manifest (built within every JAR). For example, one could call the following methods on the Hello World program:

```
System.out.println("Vendor: " +
  getAppProperty("MIDlet-Vendor"));
 System.out.println("MIDlet: " +
  getAppProperty("MIDlet-Version"));
```

Doing so would produce the following output in the debug console:

```
Vendor: Sun Microsystems
MIDlet Version: 1.0
```

## Getting System Properties

MIDP includes four valid system properties:

- `microedition.profiles`—Returns the available profile (for example, `MIDP-1.0`)

- `microedition.locale`—Returns the current locale of the device (for example, `en-US` for United States English).

- `microedition.platform`—Returns the current phone being used. For example, `Motorola i85s`.

- `microedition.encoding`—Returns the type of `String` encoding this phone uses. Every CLDC implementation supports the ISO8859_1 (Latin 1) encoding. But Japanese phones, for example, will support the SJIS (Shift-JIS) encoding.

The values of these properties can be retrieved using the static method `getProperty(String key)` in the `System` class. This method gets the system property indicated by the specified key.

The `microedition.locale` property is very important for games and other apps that want to achieve international support. The locale is represented by two values. The first one is a two-letter code defined in the ISO-639 standard, and the second one is a two-letter code defined by ISO-3166, separated by a hyphen.

## Creating a Global Cache Class

Let's begin writing our first game class. Most games, not to mention other MIDP applications, will want a nice place to store global variables and other values that might need to be accessed throughout. To accomplish this, we will build a `Cache` class.

One important global value is the language that the player speaks. Listing 9.7 shows a simple Cache class that can handle English and Slovakian.

*LISTING 9.7*   The Cache Class

```
public class Cache
{
  public static final int ENGLISH = 0;
  public static final int SLOVENE = 1;

  private int language;

  private Cache() {}

  static
  {
    String locale =
        System.getProperty("microedition.locale");
    if (locale == null)
      language = ENGLISH; // Default value
    else
      if (locale.startsWith("si")
        language = SLOVENE;
      else
        language = ENGLISH; // Default
  }

  public static int getLanguage()
  {
    return language;
  }
}
```

Note that the Cache class' constructor is private. Because of this, the class can't be instantiated; all methods are going to be static.

## Summary

Hopefully, this chapter gives you an idea of how simple it is to get up and running using MIDP.

And this is just the beginning. We've already accomplished quite a bit: Our game has an intro screen, a main user interface menu, a help screen, and the ability to be readable in both Eastern Europe and the United States.

Throughout the next few chapters, we will be adding more to our racing game, creating a more complex game interface, graphics, animations, sprites, sounds, and more—much, much more!

# 10

# Making the Most of Limited Resources

**IN THIS CHAPTER**

- The Limitations
- Memory Limitations
- Displays
- Breaking Through the Limitations

Games are one of the most powerful factors forcing computer users to upgrade to better hardware. The latest games run on up-to-date machines with powerful processors, lots of working memory, and fast video acceleration and 3D-rendering cards. Fortunately, PCs are expandable, with lots of empty slots for additional cards. When a slick new game comes out, fans can easily swap in a new video card or add more memory chips.

On the other hand, most small J2ME devices offer what's inside and nothing more. They don't usually provide any extension slots, although PDAs such as the Palm, iPaq, or Handspring do offer basic expansion ports.

Here's another crazy fact: The micro devices that users buy today will most likely have been in use for a year or two already, and users are generally tied to their mobile phone or other micro device for a few years.

If you want to develop games for micro devices, then, you have to be acutely aware of a target device's limitations. And you have to face the fact that these limits won't be improved upon anytime soon.

## The Limitations

Most J2ME MIDP devices can fit in your hand. Several years ago, mobile devices were very expensive and geared toward business people. Today, almost 90% of all mobile phone users own a device for personal use, especially in Europe and Asia.

By looking at the mobile scene in Japan, and based on predictions by European mobile operators such as Vodafone, Deutsche Telecom, and Telefonica, as well as American operators Sprint PCS, Nextel, and Voicestream, entertainment is going to become the number one mobile application. As better games hit the market, mobile users will demand faster processors and more memory. Hopefully this will create a mutually beneficial relationship between consumers, phone manufacturers, and game developers, with better games driving better hardware and vice versa.

However, no matter how advanced hardware gets, there will always be three problematic areas for games on micro devices:

- Processor speed

- Memory

- Video

## Processor Paucity

A lot goes on under the hood in a typical game. Games must move the sprites, calculate new positions, check for collisions, and paint everything. Artificial intelligence adds additional processing.

All this functionality is supported by multithreading, where separate actions are executed at the same time. Threading is discussed in much more detail in Chapter 12, "Multithreaded Game Programming."

In reality, however, only one thread is executed at any given time. The processor execution time is sliced into small time chunks, and each slice is used to execute a given thread's code. For slow human eyes, the fast execution of different threads makes it seem like many things are happening at the same time.

When all is said and done, the execution time of all the threads must be under a certain maximum. This maximum is usually dictated by the frame rate of the game. For example, to achieve 16 frames per second, the complete execution cycle must be invoked in under 62.5 milliseconds. That's possible only if the processor is powerful enough to execute the code needed for each animation frame in that time.

As you will soon see, most micro device processors are not powerful enough to deliver animations of 16 frames per second.

## Memory Madness

Even if a processor was powerful enough, memory can dictate whether a device will support a given game. Although the CPU affects the overall speed of a game, memory problems can crop up at any time, because new objects are constantly being created.

### Video Vex

Different micro devices also offer different screen resolutions. Although more and more color displays are coming out, especially in Japan, most mobile phones are still black and white. Drawing operations can be executed with different speeds on different devices. The more pixels a screen has, the more time is needed to draw a complete screen.

Most PDAs, for example, have large screens, generally 160×160 pixels or more. This makes for slower drawing times compared to smaller devices with the same processors.

### Processors of the Future

The microprocessor is the brain and heart of every device. The J2ME CLDC specification doesn't force the hardware manufacturers to conform to any special processor, or even keep to a specific processor speed. Rather, any 16- or 32-bit processor can be supported.

Although Nokia, Siemens, and Motorola currently offer high-end mobile devices (such as the Nokia Communicator 9110, Motorola Accompli A008, and Siemens SL45i), these devices are expensive and geared toward a business audience. The most addicted game players are young and don't have a lot of their own money to spend on devices. As such, most of the gaming will likely be done on phones with very slow, cheap processors.

## Memory Limitations

Memory is the place where the brain of the device stores its data, and where the list of things that need to be done (the execution code) is located. The J2ME memory model can be split into three sections:

- Working memory—Where the device stores data needed only during the lifetime of the game. When the game is terminated, everything in this memory is forgotten. When the game is started up, the complete execution code is also copied here as the classes are loaded. This memory also holds all bitmap images created from PNG files.

- Storage memory—Where the device stores RMS data in its own local database. When the game is terminated or the device is turned off, the information stored here remains.

- Application memory—Where the device stores installed games and other applications. This memory can take the same place as storage memory.

All these memories have their limitations, depending on free memory. Although working and storage memory have an impact on the game execution, the application memory dictates how large the game can be and how many games can be installed onto a given device.

## Working Memory

When the game is started up, it is first copied from the application memory into the working memory and then executed. In fact, only the classes that the classloader needs (the starting classes) are copied. Other classes are loaded upon their first instantiation. If games are too large to fit into working memory, the device notifies the user with an out-of-memory warning.

That restriction is one of the reasons why J2ME devices ask developers to restrict the size of their applications. Another reason is the fear that larger applications would crash the mobile network. If all 2G mobile networks are capable of 9600 bytes per second, an application with a size of 50KB needs almost a minute to be transferred from the Internet into the application memory. If thousands of users try to download a large popular game at once, then the network might become clogged.

During execution, a game constantly allocates memory for primitive data and objects. The created information takes up more memory space and can be divided into three groups:

- Static data—Created when the class is loaded into the working memory. It occupies part of the memory and stays there as long as the game lives.

- Global data—Created when the instance of the class is created. This stays in memory as long as the object is alive. When the object is destroyed by the garbage collector, the data disappears too.

- Local data—Created each time the method that creates the variables is executed. At the end of the method, local variables become candidates for garbage collection. Local data is created and destroyed so often that is one of the biggest reasons for memory fragmentations.

### Memory Fragmentation

*Memory fragmentation* happens when working memory is completely allocated with smaller objects. After a time, some of those objects are destroyed and some parts of the memory space are cleaned up. If developer checks for available memory, the device will return the correct value. But when the game tries to allocate a large object in memory, the object can't be placed anywhere because there is not enough consecutive room for it. The memory looks like Swiss cheese—a lot of empty space, but none of it in one clean block.

A good implementation of garbage collection should take care of this problem. Most J2ME virtual machines, however, don't have enough room for a good implementation. Chapter 11, "Making the Most of it: Optimizations," contains tips and tricks for getting around this problem.

In general, the key to avoiding fragmentation and other memory issues is to avoid constantly allocating and de-allocating objects. Instead, try to create every object you need ahead of time. For example, you can create a pool of sprites. When you need a new object, grab an unused sprite from the pool instead of creating a new one. When you're done with the object, drop it back into the pool.

### Memory Matters

All in all, it is important to build a compatibility list for any game you release. You should carefully check the specification for any device you are targeting, because every gadget has a different amount of working memory. For example, the Siemens SL45i has 128KB of available working memory, the Motorola i85 has 256KB, and the Motorola Accompli A008 has 640KB. Some larger games will only run on certain devices.

## Storage Memory

Games also need memory for persistent storage of data, such as the current status, high scores, and so on. When the device is turned off, the storage stays intact and nothing is forgotten. This memory is usually larger than the working memory, and uses a different type of hardware, such as flash memory, a multimedia memory card, or even a small disk drive.

For example, the Siemens SL45i has a 32MB multimedia memory card (MMC) that can be replaced with a larger one, and is completely available for J2ME application and database storage. With J2ME applications averaging 30KB for each JAR file, each MMC can hold more than a thousand games! On the other hand, the Motorola Accompli A008 uses internal memory limited to 1.6MB.

Internal memories are smaller than memory cards, but are also faster. Speed can be important. The Siemens' MMC is very slow, and Siemens also suggests that developers use their non-standard File I/O API instead of local storage (RMS). The Accompli's RMS, because of its large memory, is also quite slow. On the other hand, the Motorola i85 and similar phones can manipulate the RMS relatively quickly.

RMS speed also has a lot to do with the Java implementation. The Java virtual machine for iDEN devices was developed in Florida, and the KVM for the Accompli A008 was built in Sweden. Apparently, developers in warm weather do a better job implementing database storage than those up north!

## Displays

Screen resolution is one of the largest problems for game developers. If displays were standard on every J2ME device the way they are on personal computers, we could fix all images to one size everything would look fine.

Unfortunately, the graphics resolution of J2ME devices starts at 96×54 pixels, but is usually much higher (101×80 on the Siemens SL45i, or 240×234 on the Motorola Accompli A008). PDAs have even larger screens.

Additionally, some devices offer double buffering on the screen, while others do not.

## Breaking Through the Limitations

Ultimately, game producers will have to make some tough decisions. On the one hand, it's a fine idea to support every J2ME device and make more income from a game. But, if you want your game to look really good, some lower-end devices will have to be excluded. Unfortunately, most mobile gamers will own cheaper devices with smaller screens, smaller amounts of memory, and slower processors.

### Detecting the Minimum Speed

If your game is running too fast, users will be unable to play it. Enemies will move at the player too quickly, not giving the player enough time to dodge. If your game is running too slowly, it will become boring.

Finding the right execution speed is key. To accomplish this, your game should set a frame rate and try to achieve this rate no matter how slow or fast the device being used is.

### Frame Rate

A *frame rate* is exactly what it sounds like—the rate at which one still frame flashes by, creating the appearance of motion. For example, think of a Bugs Bunny cartoon. Normally, a cartoon flickers by at 16 frames per second (FPS). This is quick enough for the human eye to believe that the image is "moving." If the frame rate slows down, the eye begins to see choppiness and flickering.

In order for a game to achieve 16 FPS, the device would need to paint each frame in under 62.5 milliseconds. This is not feasible on most micro devices, given most processor and screen paint speeds. However, games are not as detailed as cartoons. Game characters are made up of larger pixels, and usually things don't change that much per frame. As such, a frame rate of 10 frames per second is acceptable, and gives the game 100 milliseconds to process and paint each frame. Chapter 17, "Sprite Movement," delves into the finer points of sprite movement and painting.

## Multiple Display Support

As new J2ME devices come out, your game will need to support new screen resolutions and color depths. One solution is to have different JAR files for each J2ME device. The difference between all those JAR files would be in the images within, as well as minor changes to the code that displays the image. For example, sprites on a device with a screen resolution of 200×200 pixels should be twice as large as those that are meant for a device with a 100×100 pixel screen.

It is a good idea to design your game into two separate classes:

- Logical classes—This part represents the game itself, together with the game's artificial intelligence. This should be where 90% of all game functionality takes place.

- Visual classes—This part is responsible for painting on the screen and information that depends heavily on the device specifications, such as screen size, image size, movement values, and so on. This code can either read in parameters and adjust drawing sizes on-the-fly, or can be totally rewritten for each new device.

Another approach is to use the lowest common denominator for all devices. For example, let's say that you want to support the following screen resolutions: 96×80, 120×64, and 102×72. Simply paint the game at 96×64 pixels and center the game in the screen. The empty space on the devices with larger screen resolutions can be filled out with a border image.

## Black and White World

It would be a mistake to attempt to use color images in your game. Although most phones in Japan have color screens, most small devices around the world only have black and white screens.

When a device paints an image, the image's colors are translated into colors that are actually supported. If a phone can only paint in black or white, a colorful image will be reduced to an odd-looking smear.

As such, be sure to create all game images as black and white bitmaps. You can then scale up for better devices.

# Summary

Limitations exist. That's life. Throughout this book, however, we will strive to break through the limitations. We will focus on how to create games that look as good as they can possibly look, no matter what the device is. The key lies in finding the right game execution speed and reducing the game's memory usage.

It is important to benchmark the processor speed, working memory size, storage memory size, and display for any device you want to target. You can then adjust your game's frame rate, graphics size and color depth, or artificial intelligence as appropriate.

The next chapter contains a slew of tips for optimizing the speed, size, and flexibility of your game code.

•

# 11

# Making the Most of It: Optimizations

**IN THIS CHAPTER**

- A Limited World
- Making Code Optimal
- Code Size Reductions
- Speeding Up the Code
- Using Less Memory
- Power Consumption

So you've finished your game. It's time to break out the champagne. But then you load your game onto your favorite Java device and get an out-of-memory message. What now?

Well, you basically have two choices: Only release the game on devices that have enough speed and memory, or rewrite, optimize, and strip your game down to make it fit.

## A Limited World

Most devices that run MIDP are very limited in memory size, processor power, display resolution, and connectivity. Manufacturers have made sacrifices in the hopes of creating devices that are portable, battery-powered, and cheap. Initially, most handheld devices were intended for business users who wanted to check e-mail or do an Internet search out of the office. More and more, however, manufacturers are gearing these devices to a broader audience. An audience thirsting for good games. And even though we're beginning to see more color screens, better sound capabilities, and faster processors, handheld devices are always going to be pretty restricted compared to their big brother, the PC.

Because of these steep limitations, developers—especially game developers—must focus like mad on making applications smaller, faster, economical, and optimal.

## Making Code Optimal

Making game code optimal is not an easy task. As a matter of fact, half the work in game development for small devices is in the optimization stage. But with experience, you will learn where typical problems are and how to solve them.

Code optimization can be divided into five categories:

- Optimizations to reduce code size
- Optimizations to speed up the code execution
- Optimizations to decrease memory usage
- Optimizations to increase device availability
- Optimizations to increase network performance

## Code Size Optimizations

When a game is installed onto a device via a synch cable or over the network, the JAR file is unpacked into the device's storage memory. Every time the game is executed, the execution byte code (Java classes) are copied into the working memory (*heap memory*) and processed. The larger the classes are, the less heap memory is left for the game. The less heap memory, the slower things run and the greater the chances that the game will run out of memory completely. So, given all that, making game classes as small as possible is of the utmost importance.

## Making Code Faster

According to specification, devices that run J2ME CLDC have 16- or 32-bit processors with low frequencies, in the range between a few megahertz (smart phones), to a few hundred (Windows CE-based devices). The higher the clock speed is, the more power-hungry devices are. Unfortunately, all small devices are limited by their batteries or accumulators—and most devices aim to have at least 24 hours of continuous battery usage. As such, device manufacturers have purposely installed low-powered chipsets. Making code run fast, then, is another key goal of micro game development.

## Decreasing Memory

Devices have different ranges of available working memory. Smart phones only have between 128KB and 256KB of heap memory. Developers who write games in native assembly code, or a low-level languages such as C++, can easily compact their code to be as efficient as possible. Java developers, however, must deal with a lot of overhead, such as memory allocation  (*object construction*) and deallocation (*garbage collection*). A chunk of memory is also eaten up by the Java Virtual Machine (KVM), which runs the byte code. As you begin to create Java games and test them on real devices, you'll probably run across out-of-memory error messages.

## Device Availability

Different actions, such as the background display light or vibrations, might consume extra power and force the device into off-line mode. With correct development, and by avoiding the overuse of various calls, your game can have a better impact on a device's lifetime.

## Network Performance

If your game is multiplayer-capable, then you'll need to send and receive messages over the network. In most cases, this network is awfully slow, with high latency and limited bandwidth. As such, it is important to make sure that every packet your game deals with is as compressed as possible.

More information about network optimization can be found in Chapter 20, "Connecting Out: Wireless Networking."

# Code Size Reductions

Making the execution code or JAR file smaller has several positive impacts on devices and game players:

- The smaller a JAR file is, the less time it takes to download it over the Internet. With fewer bytes to transfer, gamers will be charged less by their mobile operators, and be online and playing much faster.

- The smaller execution code is, the less time it takes to install, verify, and execute a game. Users will not have to wait for delays between stages.

- The less space classes take, the more heap memory is left for the game. Games usually allocate large tables (for example, for level design, a list of enemies, and so on) might run out of memory if there's not enough elbow room.

- Some devices have explicit limits on the size of a JAR file. For example, i-mode applications may not be larger than 10 kilobytes.

Please note that code size optimizations are not always sufficient. Often times, game functionality must be stripped down or simplified.

There are three techniques used to perform code reduction:

- Shorten the names of variables and methods in the code.

- Avoid a pure object-oriented way of programming.

- Make the image sizes smaller.

## Obfuscators and Name-Shortening

When developing in an assembly language, every variable or method is represented by an address (16- or 32-bit in small device processors) that points to a memory cell. Whatever mnemonic a developer uses for a variable or method name, the size of the variable in memory stays the same (2 or 4 bytes). Needless to say, Java is not like assembly language. Instead, Java's focus is on making code easy to write and maintain. Typical variable and method names might be `GoldMonster` or `LowLevelInterfaceControl`. In the world of desktop computing, where machines have a few hundred extra megabytes to play around with, there's usually no need to give these names a second thought. But in the limited world of handhelds, every little byte counts:

- Each letter in the name of the class adds an additional byte to the execution code.

- Each letter in the name of the public method adds an additional byte to the execution code. Protected and private methods don't have any impact on the class size.

- Each letter in the name of the public variable adds an additional byte to the execution code. Protected and private variables don't have any influence on the size of the class. Also, the name length of local variables and parameters don't change the size of the class.

- Every letter in the name of the constructor adds an additional byte to the class file.

Does this mean that you should try to write a game using tiny method and variable names? Imagine changing all method names like `moveEnemy()`, `drawScene()`, and `makeNextMove()` into `a()`, `b()`, and `c()`. Not fun! The length of the class file would immediately be shortened, but the source code would be muddled and impossible to maintain.

There is a better solution. Instead of making the source code dirty and unreadable, developers can use a special application called an *obfuscator*.

An obfuscator's main job is to protect applications against illegal decompilation by making the code hard to read and difficult to unravel. The obfuscator is run only when the code is ready to be released. It takes normal Java files and outputs tight, special class files. Luckily for J2ME developers, most obfuscators will also drastically shorten class, variable, and method names. An obfuscator's output code is typically 5 to 20 percent smaller than original class files. The size of the reduction is based on the number of classes, methods, and variables.

There are many different obfuscators on the market, some available commercially and some free. Check them out:

- IBM's JAX (`http://www.alphaworks.ibm.com/tech/JAX`)

- RetroGuard (`http://www.retrologic.com/`)

- Jshrink (`http://www.e-t.com/jshrink.html`)

- Condensity (`http://www.condensity.com/`)

For example, to run Jax on a class, you would use the following code fragment:

```
java jax TestClass.class
```

Jax will output the compressed class into a Zip file called `TestClass_jax.zip`.

> **NOTE**
>
> Note that you may not want to change the name of your main MIDlet class. Most obfuscators let you specify classes whose names should not be changed.

## The Object-Oriented Dilemma

Java is an object-oriented language. Developers typically separate their code into many different objects, each represented by a separate class. Each class has number of public methods and variables available to other classes, and then has private methods for the class' internal usage.

With good object-oriented design, programmers can easily reuse pre-developed components and speed up the development cycle. Code is also more tightly written and separated by functionality. For example, a game may typically have a separate class for game logic and one for actually drawing visual graphics.

The following illustrates a typical object-oriented approach, in which two different classes will use the same method name to achieve different functionality. Class `Ext1` sets the global variable to the same value as the parameter, and class `Ext2` sets it to the square value of the parameter:

```
public abstract class Base
{
  protected int value;

  public abstract void setValue(int value);
}
```

```
public class Ext1 extends Base
{
  public void setValue(int value)
  {
    this.value = value;
  }
}

public class Ext2 extends Base
{
  public void setValue(int value)
  {
    this.value = value * value;
  }
}
```

This type of programming is very useful if you want to create an abstract concept that acts differently at different times. For example, you might have a RaceTrack interface that returns different values depending on whether the track is in the country or the city.

The result of the three classes listed above, however, is that they take up 654KB worth of storage space. Another option is to use a non-object-oriented approach, and put all three classes into one:

```
public class Base
{
  public static final int EXT1 = 0;
  public static final int EXT2 = 1;

  private int type;
  private int value;

  public Base(int type)
  {
    this.type = type;
  }

  public void setValue(int value)
  {
    switch (type)
    {
      case EXT1:
```

```
        this.value = value;
        break;
    case EXT2:
        this.value = value * value;
        break;
    default:
    }
  }
}
```

In this case, the execution code only takes up 431 bytes. The code size is reduced by one third!

Although it is not recommended that you abandon all object-oriented techniques altogether, you should be aware of not over-designing your game into too many classes. A good rule of thumb is to design and build your game in a way that is easiest for you, and when you are ready to release the game, combine classes that don't offer much extra functionality.

---

**WARNING**

Some devices, such as the Siemens Java phone, have a 16KB class size limit. In this case, it may make sense to split big classes into several objects.

---

## Image Size Reduction

Graphics are the centerpiece of most modern games. Graphics are everywhere—in the introductory animation, in sprites, and in cutscenes. These image files can really add up.

Everything that a J2ME game needs is stuffed into one JAR file. Too many individual images can quickly inflate the JAR file beyond its suggested maximum size.

The PNG image format used with MIDP has a large amount of overhead. PNG files are 24-bit and include a complete palette in the PNG header. If you put twenty image files in your JAR file, you will also be putting in 20 copies of the same palette.

One idea is to squeeze images together by putting them into one image file, like a filmstrip. That way, one file can have multiple images, but only one palette. To grab the image from this filmstrip, your program must clip the screen appropriately. More information about clipping can be found in Chapter 14, "Low-Level Approach."

Another means of reducing the JAR file size is to move images off the local JAR file and onto the network. This way, images are downloaded over HTTP from a Web server as they are needed. The images can even be stored in the device's local database. More information about downloading and storing images can be found in Chapter 16, "Managing Your Sprites."

## Speeding Up the Code

In the world of game development, animation and gameplay are often expressed as *frames per second,* or *FPS*. A typical 3D console game may animate millions of polygons at 24 FPS. The time it takes for a human eye to judge a series of still images as "moving" ranges from 20 to 30 frames per second. Any less than that and the animation or film begins to look choppy, like an old Charlie Chaplin movie.

On handheld devices, users are much more forgiving. As long as a game animates at 10 frames per second or better, things will appear relatively smooth.

However, running 10 FPS is far from easy. For example, if the animation consists of a UFO sprite flying across the screen, then every frame of the game must move the sprite, recalculate the position using complex physics, look for collisions, and so on. To achieve 10 FPS, all of this must be done in fewer than 100 milliseconds.

Here are some cold hard facts about mobile devices and processor power:

- The processors are 16- or 32-bit.

- The frequency of the processors is extremely low compared to PCs. For example, the Siemens SL45i runs at 13MHz, and the Motorola Accompli A008 runs at 33MHz.

- To provide low power consumption, the processors have the smallest possible number of transistors. That means there's no floating-point support, no extra memory management units, and so on.

Given these parameters, a thoughtlessly developed J2ME game will run at only 1 or 2 frames per second. No game player in the world will stand for that.

The following optimizations can help speed up your game's execution:

- Optimize the call for garbage collection.

- Void constructing new objects.

- Use static methods instead of object methods.

- Speed up the screen repainting.

## Dealing with the Garbage Collector

For many developers, Java's memory management is one of its most attractive features. A Java developer never has to deal directly with memory allocation and deallocation. When an object is created, Java automatically grabs the memory it needs. When the object is no longer needed, you simply set it to null. Java's garbage collector destroys the object and cleans up the memory after the destruction.

Garbage collection only reclaims memory when it determines that the object is unreachable from any part of the application. Since the Java language specifications don't provide any rules for how the garbage collection should be invoked, each JVM uses its own implementation. The garbage collector generally runs in its own thread and at its own pace.

J2ME MIDP devices are limited not only to the heap memory, but also to the memory needed for implementation of the device's Kilobyte virtual machine. In order to make the KVM small, some functionality has been stripped down or implemented in a more primitive way. As such, garbage collection is usually not very sophisticated on handheld devices. Sometimes creating too many objects can confuse the garbage collector and cause an out-of-memory situation.

To avoid application crash situations, you should call garbage collection manually whenever possible. The process can be invoked by calling

```
System.gc();
```

or

```
Runtime.getRuntime().gc();
```

In other words, the second you are done using any object and reach a good spot in your game to pause, set it to null and notify the garbage collector. A good time to call the garbage collector is after your screen paints. That way, the garbage collector will not kick up in the middle of animations, making sprites seem choppy or inconsistent.

## The Constructorless Way

A constructor is called every time a class is created. When the constructor is called, two steps are involved during class instantiation:

- Memory space needed for the object is allocated.

- Any additional code in the constructor method is called. The constructor may also call a constructor of the parent class.

Both steps usually take quite a bit of time. Creating too many classes within your game loop will cause needless delays. Instead, you should create any objects you need before the main game loop actually begins. Of course, you must be careful here: Too many created objects might cause an out-of-memory situation.

One good design pattern is to use a pool of created objects that are available to the application as necessary. When the object is needed, it can be borrowed from the pool. After using it, the application returns the object back to the pool for later reuse.

### Math Classes

Custom-created mathematical classes in particular can cause lots of constructor problems. For example, many MIDP programs will have a class simulating floating-point numbers. Often, it is tempting to create each number as a separate object:

```
Float number1 = new Float(100);
```

Making each number its own object is convenient. You can easily call various methods on the number to add it, subtract it, and so forth. The big problem with this approach, however, is that each new mathematical operation takes extra time and memory for object construction and garbage collection. If a lot of small objects are created during the game execution, the memory might become fragmented. If memory becomes too fragmented, a new large object can't be created even if there is plenty of memory left, because there is not enough clean, consecutive memory space.

A better way of implementing a mathematical library is to create one singleton class that is always accessible. This class can have static methods that allow mathematical functions to be called at any time.

## Static Methods

Static methods belong to entire classes, not to individual objects. A program can call a static method without constructing a new object. As such, using lots of static methods can speed up your game's execution time and increase the size of available heap memory.

Of course, there is also a downside: Static methods can only call other static methods, and only access static variables. This limits their usability.

A good example of static methods usage can be found in a the `Cache` class detailed in Chapter 9, "Creating A MIDlet." This class holds all game-wide information, such as the language, screen resolution, list of sprites, and so on. You should strive to put any commonly used variables or other info as static variables within static classes.

## The Fast-Draw

A game is a series of actions that constantly repeat. A typical game animation loop will usually perform the following actions:

- Read in user input

- Calculate new position of sprites

- Animate the background

- Check for collisions

- Draw the complete scene

Calculating sprite position can take a nice chunk of available cycle time. The more complex a game is, the more intricate the game's artificial intelligence (AI) is. One helpful technique is to place the game's AI in a separate thread, so that animation isn't waiting on game logic.

Another blocking point is collision detection. The more sprites you have, the more collision detection routines you will need to run. Chapter 16 contains several techniques for speeding up collision detection.

Obviously, you want to strive to get through the game loop as quickly as possible. The faster you can get all the calculations done with, the faster your frame rate will be. However, some frames may finish much more quickly than others. This means that your animations may appear a bit herky-jerky, with sprites sometimes racing across the screen and sometimes moping.

Some devices support double buffering. These devices accept all paint calls and execute them on an offscreen image located in device memory. When the paint() method is complete, the device will automatically flush the offscreen image onto the device's display. If double buffering is not supported, you will need to implement it yourself to avoid screen-flickering. Creating this additional offscreen image can take some more free memory, and the extra drawing routine can take additional more time.

When double buffering, try not to clear and redraw every sprite on your entire game screen each and every frame. Instead, you can merely delete pieces of the scene where the sprite was located before the new movement occurred. You can then draw the sprite at its new location.

Another good idea is to keep track of your frame rate by checking the system clock. You may even want to slow down extra-fast frames using the Thread.sleep() method.

More information about these and other animation techniques can be found in Chapter 17, "Sprite Movement."

In the end, though, the main graphical bottleneck is the device's graphics driver. The driver's main job is to connect an application paint call with the device's actual display. Unfortunately, the driver is not optimized like the ones found in personal computers, and doesn't have any additional accelerators for fast painting. In fact, many micro devices take more than 100 milliseconds to paint a typical screen.

Micro Java game developers will have to separate all Java-enabled devices into two groups: Those that are fast enough and those that are hopeless. For example, smart phones such as Motorola's i85 and Siemens' SL45i are faster than PDA-like phones with big screens such as the Motorola Accompli A008.

## Using Less Memory

When a game executes, it usually needs to allocate lots and lots of memory. Every sprite, image, game state, and other piece of the virtual world will require a bit of memory. Since devices have a limited amount of memory, games should strive to create each level or scene only as needed.

Memory usage can also be controlled by using some smart coding techniques. Two of the most frequent memory problems occur while creating text and using lists.

### String **Versus** StringBuffer

After a `String` object is created, the contents of the object can't actually be changed. Whenever you modify a `String`, you are actually creating one or more new `String` objects. That means the concatenation of two `Strings` actually creates three separate objects. The same problem occurs with other `String` operations such as inserting characters, converting to uppercase, or parsing out a substring.

A much more efficient way to manipulate character arrays is the `StringBuffer` class. `StringBuffer` objects automatically expand as needed. For example, if you concatenate two `StringBuffers`, then a new array is created and the old arrays are copied within. `StringBuffer` operations are much faster than using `Strings`.

Here's an example of using a `StringBuffer` instead of a `String`:

```
public class StringLib
{
  private StringLib() {}

  public static String getTime(int time)
  {
```

```
    StringBuffer buf = new StringBuffer();
    buf.append("""Time: """);
    int seconds = time / 1000;
    int minutes = seconds / 60;
    int hours = minutes / 60;
    seconds = seconds - minutes * 60;
    minutes = minutes - hours * 60;
    buf.append(hours);
    buf.append(":");
    buf.append(format(minutes));
    buf.append(":");
    buf.append(format(seconds));
    return buf.toString();
  }

  private static String format(int value)
  {
    String str = String.valueOf(value);
    str = (str.length() == 1 ? "0" + str : str);
    return str;
  }
}
```

The getTime() method cuts the time (provided in milliseconds) into separate chunks representing hours, minutes, and seconds. Because the default length of a StringBuffer object is 16 characters, there is no need for the object to expand itself.

If you were to use String objects in the preceding code in place of a StringBuffer, the application would need to create six string constants and five Strings for concatenations.

Note, however, the format() method in the preceding code. There is only one concatenation at most. In this case, it makes more sense to use two small Strings rather than one large StringBuffer.

## Arrays Versus Vector and Hashtable

Arrays in Java are a special kind of object. They are created by using either the new operator, or in a combined declaration, creation, and initialization statement. An array represents a 32-bit address that points to a list of indexed values. Values may be of primitive types or classes. The biggest problem in using arrays is that you need to set the size of your array in advance. If you need to enlarge the array, you must create a larger one and copy the values from the old array into the new one (by calling the System.arraycopy() method).

A much easier approach is to use the Vector class. The Vector object is used to store an array of objects, and it can grow automatically as needed. The class also offers a wide range of methods for adding, inserting, finding, and deleting objects. All methods are synchronized to guard against one thread changing the data currently being used by another thread.

The Hashtable class is similar to the Vector class, allowing you to store an unlimited number of objects keyed to a particular value.

Unfortunately, the convenience and safety of a Vector or Hashtable comes at a price. A lot of overhead memory is used to create a Vector or Hashtable, and locking and releasing the Vector and Hashtables reduces your program's execution speed.

When it comes to your own games, try to use arrays whenever possible.

## Power Consumption

The last important optimization technique has to do with the lifetime of a device's battery. Some phones are not very good with using power for graphics and program execution. Some phones might run out of battery power if the user plays a game for an hour or two.

Some of the biggest power-eating problems in games are

- Whenever a game key is pressed, the display light turns on for a moment. Some devices have the ability to turn the light off manually, but most users don't bother to use this feature.

- During the game execution, your game may produce sounds. Sounds may be turned off, but then your gameplay suffers.

- Some devices support vibrations, and games may use them for special effects.

Pure MIDP devices don't support backlight, advanced sounds, or vibrations. However, some devices, such as the Siemens SL45i and the i-mode series 503 have an additional game API that enables those effects. As tempting as it may be to use some of these neat features, you should do so sparingly to avoid totally sapping battery power.

## Summary

As you can see, Micro Java game development is a tricky business. However, by focusing carefully on your game's file size, execution speed, memory bounds, battery life, and networking protocol, you can achieve some remarkable things.

One thing J2ME programming teaches you is to be resourceful. In subsequent chapters, we will go into more detail about creating optimized routines that balance functionality with speed and size.

# 12

# Multithreaded Game Programming

**IN THIS CHAPTER**

- Threads
- Extending the `Thread` Object
- Implementing the `Runnable` Interface
- Thread Priorities
- Thread States
- Synchronizations and Deadlocks
- `wait()` and `notify()`
- Timers
- Making Threads Better

When games are running on a mobile device, many different pieces of code must be executed simultaneously. This includes actions such as checking the keyboard, moving the sprites, detecting sprite collision, planning the game's artificial intelligence, and of course, repainting. If a developer has to put all those tasks into a list and execute the list step by step, just waiting for a new key pressed event could pause the game. A much better approach would be to put tasks into different lists, and permit each list to execute at the same time. For example, one task can check the keyboard as the other task executes other parts of the code. Fortunately, when calling the `repaint()` method, only a request for a new painting is sent, without waiting for the repaint itself. This is done in a completely different task. A question arises: Can you do such a thing in J2ME? The answer is yes. This multitasking capability can be achieved simply by using Java's multithreading capabilities.

## Threads

A *thread* is a path taken by a program during execution. By executing through several paths, an application is quicker, flexible, and non-blockable. If a program can be split into separate tasks, it is often easier to program the algorithm as a separate task or thread. Such programs deal with multiple independent tasks. The popularity of threading increased when graphical interfaces became the standard for all devices, from desktop computers to small intelligent devices. The reason for threading's success is the user's perception of better program performance—and performance is extremely important in games!

When developing threads for games, the following questions arise:

- How many threads does the game need?
- What should be the animation frame-rate?
- How do you manipulate data using a thread?
- Do you use the `Thread` class, `Runnable` interface, or `Timer` class?

The answer to the first question is that at least three threads are required. One thread is used for drawing the graphic scene, one for reading input events (for example, keyboard, pen, and so on), and one for manipulating the sprites. Fortunately for the game developers, the first two threads are already automatically implemented, and developers don't need to implement additional threads. The easiest way to implement the third thread is by using the `Canvas` class that represents the game graphics area where the game is happening. Additional threads can be used for artificial intelligence to make the game more attractive.

If a developer wants to attract a gaming audience, a lot of work must be done in the area of the graphics. Usually today's games make a lot of effort to convince players by making magnificent introductory animations. But Java-enabled mobile devices are too limited in resources to offer the same effects. Mobile developers need to focus more on the games themselves. Providing animated action is possible with implementation of the *animation thread*. Such a thread is used to offer animated scenes with a fixed frame-rate.

Animation adds a great deal to the user interface, but unfortunately the devices currently available on the market are not fast enough, so higher animation frame-rates are not possible. There are many ways to implement animation, which can differ in speed from device to device. This book will show you the simplest solution: taking the lowest common denominator. The lowest acceptable frame-rate is ten frames per second. This means that a thread must execute the loop every 100 milliseconds.

The thread can have multiple methods to manipulate its data, but it should have these two required methods:

- `start()`—To start the thread (game)
- `stop()`—To stop the thread (game)

## Extending the Thread **Object**

Within the Java virtual machine, a `java.lang.Thread` object encapsulates the details of how a particular system approaches the multithreading.

The following methods are important for the Thread class:

- `currentThread()`—This method returns a reference to the currently executing thread object.

- `yield()`—This method causes the currently executing thread object to temporarily pause and permit other threads to execute.

- `sleep(long millis)`—This method causes the currently executing thread to sleep (temporarily cease execution) for the specified number of milliseconds. The thread does not lose ownership of any monitors. This method is very useful for managing the game speed that must produce a fixed frame-rate. The developer's responsibility is to measure the time of execution and to sleep the rest of the time to achieve the correct time (for example, 100 milliseconds for 10 frames per second).

- `start()`—This method causes the thread to begin execution. The Java Virtual Machine calls the run method of this thread. The result is that two threads are running concurrently: the current thread (which returns from the call to the start method) and the other thread (which executes its run method). The start method is very important for starting the game.

- `run()`—Subclasses of Thread should override the run() method to provide functionality such as sprite movement, calling the repaint() method and executing artificial intelligence tasks.

- `isAlive()`—This method tests whether the thread is *alive*. A thread is alive if it has been started and has not yet died.

- `setPriority(int newPriority)`—This method changes the priority of the thread.

- `getPriority()`—This method returns the thread's priority.

- `activeCount()`—This method returns the current number of active threads in the Java Virtual Machine.

- `join()`—This method waits for the thread to die.

Listing 12.1 illustrates how to implement a thread using the Thread class.

*LISTING 12.1*   The GameCanvas Thread Example

```java
public class GameCanvas
{
  private final int DELAY = 100;

  private GameThread thread;
  private boolean running;

  public GameCanvas()
  {
  }

  public void start()
  {
    running = true;
    thread = new GameThread();
    thread.start();
  }

  public void stop()
  {
    running = false;
  }

  public class GameThread extends Thread
  {
    public void run()
    {
      while (running)
      {
        // Move sprites
        // Check collisions
        // Repaint
        try
        {
          Thread.sleep(DELAY);
        } catch (Exception ex) {}
      }
    }
  }
}
```

A special flag called running is used to notify the thread whether it can continue. When the flag is set to false by a stop() method, the thread finishes. The constant DELAY defines the sleep time for each loop. The developer should be aware that sleep time alone doesn't provide the animation frame-rate because execution time also contains times needed for moving sprites, collision detection, and calling the paint() method, which is executed in a separate thread. In reality, the speed is much lower, depending on the CPU speed of the mobile device.

## Implementing the Runnable Interface

Another way to create a thread is to implement the java.lang.Runnable interface. This interface is designed to provide a common protocol for objects that want to execute code while they are active. For example, Runnable is implemented by the Thread class. Being active simply means that a thread has been started and has not yet been stopped. In addition, Runnable provides the means for a class to be active while not subclassing Thread. The class is free to extend some other class, in this case Canvas. A class that implements Runnable can run without subclassing Thread by instantiating a Thread instance and passing itself in as the target. In most cases, the Runnable interface should be used if you are only planning to override the run() method and no other Thread methods.

Runnable has only one method:

- run()—When an object implementing the Runnable interface is used to create a thread, starting the thread causes the object's run method to be called in that separately executing thread. The general contract of the run method is that it may take any action whatsoever. Usually, a game provides its own functionality within this method (such as sprite movement and calculations).

Listing 12.2 shows how to implement a thread using the Runnable interface.

**LISTING 12.2**  The GameCanvas Runnable Example

```
public class GameCanvas implements Runnable
{
  private final int DELAY = 100;

  private Thread thread;
  private boolean running;

  public GameCanvas()
  {
  }
```

*LISTING 12.2*    continued

```
public void start()
{
  running = true;
  thread = new Thread(this);
  thread.start();
}

public void stop()
{
  running = false;
}

public void run()
{
  while (running)
  {
    // Move sprites
    // Check collisions
    // Repaint
    try
    {
      Thread.sleep(DELAY);
    } catch (Exception ex) {}
  }
}
}
```

As with the extended Thread object, a special flag called running is also used to notify the thread whether it can continue. When the flag is set to false by a stop() method, the thread finishes. The developer should be aware that, as in the Thread class, sleep time alone doesn't provide the animation frame-rate. If developer wants to have a fixed frame-rate, thus freezing the execution of every frame at one tenth of a second, the easiest approach is to use the Timer class, which will be discussed later in this chapter. Timers may not be connected to the hardware clock itself, which can fire the timer events on time.

## Thread Priorities

Each thread can have its own thread priority. By looking closer at the multithreading mechanism implemented in the Java virtual machine, you see that only one thread is ever executed at a given time (on single-processor machines). It is the system's responsibility to slice the time and execute the specific thread within one time slice. How often the thread appears in a specific time is indicated by the priority. A higher priority means more frequent execution, and such threads also run faster. The following constants define priorities:

- MIN_PRIORITY—The minimum priority that a thread can have (value 1)

- NORM_PRIORITY—The default priority assigned to a thread (value 5)

- MAX_PRIORITY—The maximum priority that a thread can have (value 10)

The priority can be any integer number between MIN_PRIORITY and MAX_PRIORITY. If it is out of this range, java.lang.IllegalArgumentException is thrown.

## Thread States

Depending on what the thread is doing, it can have different thread states. Each thread can have one of four states:

- New state—This is the state of a newly created thread. The start() method is used to activate the thread, assign some resources to it, and move it to a runnable state. A newly started thread always executes a run() method.

- Runnable state—In this state, the thread is on the virtual machine's list of runnable threads. When it gets to run depends on its priority, the characteristics of the JVM, and the activity of other threads.

- Blocked state—A thread can be moved to the list of blocked threads as a result of entering a wait() method, calling the sleep() method, or calling one of the blocking I/O methods that the JVM manages.

- Dead state—A thread becomes dead when it exits the run() method that it started. A dead thread can't be reanimated.

By using the isAlive() method, the developer can find out if the thread is still alive. A thread is alive if it is starting, running, or blocked. Dead threads are not alive, and the call to the method returns false in this case.

## Synchronizations and Deadlocks

In theory, any Thread can access any object within a Java program. To prevent the programming chaos that would result from multiple threads modifying the same object at the same time, Java uses the monitor mechanism wherein the synchronized keyword is used. The monitor mechanism is built into the Object class, thus insuring that all Java objects can use it.

The Java virtual machine has control over a lock variable attached to each object. This lock variable is used to implement a monitor mechanism that can control threads' access to the object. The monitor mechanism is used only when the synchronized keyword has been used to label a block of code. When a thread attempts to enter a synchronized block of code, the virtual machine checks whether the lock is available. If no other thread has the lock, the current thread locks the object. If the lock already exists, the current thread becomes blocked and can't proceed until the lock is released. When the thread leaves the synchronized block, the lock is automatically released, and the next blocked thread in a blocked list may proceed.

A *deadlock* occurs when two threads are trying to gain control of object and each one has a lock on a resource that the other needs to proceed. Unfortunately, Java has no mechanism to detect or control deadlock situations. It is a programmer's responsibility to plan objects and threads so that after the thread acquires the lock on the object, it will be able to complete the synchronized code, or at least call its wait() method.

## wait() **and** notify()

If two threads require more cooperation in the use of an object that can't be obtained with a simple synchronized access, the wait() and notify() methods can be used.

The wait() method has three forms:

- wait()—This method causes the current thread to wait until another thread invokes either the notify() method or the notifyAll() method for this object. The current thread must own this object's monitor. The thread releases ownership of this monitor and waits until another thread notifies threads waiting on this object's monitor to wake up, through a call to either the notify() method or the notifyAll() method. The thread then waits until it can re-obtain ownership of the monitor and resumes execution. Only a thread that is the owner of this object's monitor should call this method.

- wait(long timeout)—This method causes the current thread to wait until either another thread invokes the notify() method or the notifyAll() method for this object, or a specified amount of time has elapsed.

- wait(long timeout, int nanos)—This method causes the current thread to wait until another thread invokes the notify() method or the notifyAll() method for this object, some other thread interrupts the current thread, or a certain amount of real time has elapsed.

The `notify()` method wakes up a single thread that is waiting on the object's monitor. If any threads are waiting on the object, one of them is chosen to be awakened. The choice is arbitrary and occurs at the discretion of the implementation. The thread waits on an object's monitor by calling one of the `wait` methods. The awakened thread will not be able to proceed until the current thread relinquishes the lock on the object. The awakened thread will compete in the usual manner with any other threads that might be actively competing to synchronize on the object. The `notifyAll()` method wakes up all threads that are waiting on the object's monitor.

## Timers

If you want to execute tasks that take different amounts of time during sprite movement and collision detection, the simplest way is to use the `java.util.Timer` class. The `Timer` class makes it easy for threads to schedule tasks for future execution in a background thread. Tasks may be scheduled for one-time execution, or for repeated execution at regular intervals. Timer tasks should complete quickly. If a timer task takes excessive time to complete, it "hogs" the timer's task execution thread. This can, in turn, delay the execution of subsequent tasks, which might bunch up and execute in rapid succession when the offending task finally completes. By default, the task execution thread does not run as a daemon thread, so it is capable of keeping an application from terminating. If a caller wants to terminate a timer's task execution thread rapidly, the caller should invoke the timer's `cancel()` method.

The following methods are part of the `Timer` class:

- `schedule(TimerTask task, long delay)`—This method schedules the specified task for execution after the specified delay. Games should call this method when execution of the task doesn't depend on fixed execution rate. Each task is executed within a specified amount of time (for example, every 100 milliseconds), but the execution of the task can exceed that time.

- `schedule(TimerTask task, Date time)`—This method schedules the specified task for execution at the specified time.

- `schedule(TimerTask task, long delay, long period)`—This method schedules the specified task for repeated fixed-delay execution, beginning after the specified delay. Subsequent executions take place at approximately regular intervals separated by the specified period.

  If the execution is delayed for any reason (such as garbage collection or other background activity), subsequent executions will be delayed as well. In the long run, the frequency of execution will generally be slightly lower than the reciprocal of the specified period.

- schedule(TimerTask task, Date firstTime, long period)—This method schedules the specified task for repeated fixed-delay execution, beginning at the specified time. This is similar to preceding method.

- scheduleAtFixedRate(TimerTask task, long delay, long period)—This method schedules the specified task for repeated fixed-rate execution, beginning after the specified delay. Subsequent executions take place at approximately regular intervals, separated by the specified period.

  If the execution is delayed for any reason, two or more executions will occur in rapid succession to catch up. In the long run, the frequency of execution will be the exact reciprocal of the specified period.

  A game should use this method if the timeframe must be fixed. However, if the execution time of the task is larger than is allowed, the number of threads will constantly increase. J2ME devices are unfortunately resource-limited, and might eventually crash.

- scheduleAtFixedRate(TimerTask task, Date firstTime, long period)— This method schedules the specified task for repeated fixed-rate execution, beginning at the specified time. This is similar to the preceding method.

- cancel()—This method terminates this timer, discarding any currently scheduled tasks. It does not interfere with a currently executing task if it exists. After a timer has been terminated, its execution thread terminates gracefully, and no more tasks can be scheduled on it.

You need to implement your own TimerTask class and create a TimerTask object if you want to use the Timer class. The run() method needs to be implemented containing the thread functionality. Listing 12.3 contains an implementation of threading using the Timer class.

*LISTING 12.3*   The GameCanvas Timer Example

```
import java.util.*;

public class GameCanvas
{
  private final int DELAY = 100;

  private Timer timer;

  public GameCanvas()
  {
  }
```

*LISTING 12.3*   continued

```
public void start()
{
  GameTask task = new GameTask();
  timer = new Timer();
  timer.scheduleAtFixedRate(task, 0, DELAY);
}

public void stop()
{
  running = false;
}

public class GameTask extends TimerTask
{
  public void run()
  {
    // Move sprites
    // Check collisions
    // Repaint
  }
}
}
```

This code is similar to the implementation of the Thread class, where the developer writes Thread's own inner class. Timer executes the task every 100 milliseconds. If the task takes more then 100 milliseconds, a new task will still be invoked on time. This means that at a specific time, there might be a bunch of threads running, which can slow down the device. Another approach would be to use the schedule() method, but the application would lose the fixed scheduling necessary during game execution.

## Making Threads Better

The problem with timers is that they don't provide additional control methods for tasks like threads do. You can still use the Thread class instead by implementing a similar functionality as found in the Timer class, as seen in Listing 12.4.

*LISTING 12.4*   A Similar Functionality to the Timer Example

```java
public class GameCanvas
{
  private final int DELAY = 100;

  private GameThread thread;
  private boolean running;

  public GameCanvas()
  {
  }

  public void start()
  {
    running = true;
    thread = new GameThread();
    thread.start();
  }

  public void stop()
  {
    running = false;
  }

  public class GameThread extends Thread
  {
    public void run()
    {
      while (running)
      {
        long time = System.currentTimeMillis();
        // Move sprites
        // Check collisions
        // Repaint
        time = System.currentTimeMillis() - timer;
        try
        {
          if (time < DELAY)
              Thread.sleep(DELAY - (int)time);
        }
```

**LISTING 12.4**   continued

```
        catch (Exception ex) {}
    }
  }
 }
}
```

In the run() method, you measure the time of functionality execution by calling the
System.currentTimeMillis() method. If the execution time is less then 100 milliseconds, the run method sleeps until it receives a reminder. Otherwise, it executes the
next loop.

## Summary

Through the use of multithreading, games become faster and manage different tasks
at the same time—which was not easy to achieve in older systems. While the game
waits on the player's keyboard, joystick, or touch-screen commands, it can paint on
the screen, calculate new positions of the sprites, and manage its artifical intelligence. Multithreading can be done using threads or timers. Timers are much easier
to use, because a game can execute the task in a fixed timeframe. However, because
Java did not initially have the Timer class, a lot of ported games opt to use the
Thread class instead. The next chapter will introduce high-level GUI components,
and how to use them for game development.

# PART IV

# Let the Games Begin!

## IN THIS PART

**13** High-Level Graphical User Interfaces

**14** Working with Graphics: Low-Level Graphical User Interfaces

**15** Entering The Land Of Sprites

**16** Managing Your Sprites

**17** Sprite Movement

**18** J2ME Audio Basics

**19** Be Persistent: MIDP Data Storage

**20** Connecting Out: Wireless Networking

# 13

# High-Level Graphical User Interfaces

**IN THIS CHAPTER**

- The Screen Class
- Forms and Alerts
- Lists
- Text Boxes
- Items
- Additional Libraries

Most games, especially those that involve a lot of action, don't concern themselves with a high-level graphical interface. High-level elements are those you'd typically find in a data entry form, including text boxes, pull-down selection menus, and check boxes.

Instead, games are focused on more detailed graphics—stuff like backgrounds, animations, and sprites. This type of low-level graphics manipulation is discussed in the next chapter.

However, a game isn't all about action. Even the most graphically advanced game needs a start menu, or a form for the user to enter their name when she achieves a high score. When new levels are loaded, you might want to show players a gauge component to indicate how much has been downloaded so far. Players might also need choice components to select the difficulty of levels.

And so, high-level GUI components are important after all. Luckily, MIDP makes high-level GUIs extremely easy to implement.

This chapter will discuss the basics of Java GUI development as it pertains to game programming. The emphasis will be on graphics fundamentals, as well as the development of custom components for our applications to use. The key lies in the Screen class.

## The Screen Class

The javax.microedition.lcdui.Screen class is a superclass of all GUI components that can be put on a screen. Such components can also contain other components. The Screen class itself has methods to set and get the values of the title bar and ticker text. It usually has automatic component positioning and scolling mechanisms, so developers don't need to bother with such things.

---

**NOTE**

The layout policy in most devices is vertical. In forms, a new line is usually started for focusable items such as a TextField, DateField, Gauge, or ChoiceGroup. If the size of a form is greater than the size of the display, then the user will usually be able to scroll downward. There is usually no horizontal scrolling.

String items and images, which do not involve user interaction, behave differently than other widgets. Several strings, for example, are drawn horizontally unless the newline character (\n) is embedded in the string. Content is wrapped (for text) or clipped (for images) to fit the width of the display.

---

## Forms and Alerts

The javax.microedition.lcdui.Form class is one of the most commonly used child classes of the Screen class. It is the only one that is a container in which developers can place different GUI objects.

Items that are placed in forms are descended from the javax.microedition.lcdui.Item class. The Form class is similar to the java.awt.Panel class in J2SE.

The Alert class is a special type of form used for notification purposes. Like the Form class, when an Alert is shown it occupies the complete screen.

## Lists

The javax.microedition.lcdui.List class is a successor of the Screen class and is used to present a list of choices to the user. A list can be exclusive (acting like a set of radio buttons), multiple (acting like a set of check boxes), or implicit (acting like a selecting menu).

The user generally accesses an item in the list by using the up and down arrow keys to choose the item. The item can then be selected using the phone's main Select button.

Most of the behavior in a list is common with the class javax.microedition.lcdui.ChoiceGroup, and the common API is defined in the interface javax.microedition.lcdui.Choice.

When a list is present on the display, it also takes up the entire screen. Traversing a list or scrolling through its items does not trigger any application-visible events. The system only notifies the application when a list item is actually selected. The notification of the application is done within the commandAction() method. An example of the List class in action can be seen in Figure 13.1.

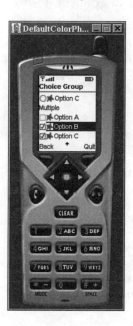

*FIGURE 13.1*    A Java List object.

## List Types

There are three types of lists:

- IMPLICIT—This list acts like a selection menu. When an item is selected, the application is immediately notified.

- EXCLUSIVE—Acts like a set of radio buttons. The select operation changes the selected element in the list. The application, however, is not notified until the user explicitly triggers a command such as Done. You must be sure to add and handle this command.

- MULTIPLE—Acts like a set of check boxes. The select operation toggles the selected state of the current element. The application is not notified.

IMPLICIT lists can be used to construct menus by treating each element like a logical command. In this case, no application-defined commands have to be created. The application just has to register a CommandListener that is called when a user selects an item.

For example, you might create an explicit list with three operations: Start Game, Quit Game, and Instructions. Start Game is considered the default operation.

Because the list is of type IMPLICIT, when a player selects a given command, the commandAction() method is called, and the SELECT_COMMAND parameter is passed in.

## Choices, Choices

The javax.microedition.lcdui.Choice interface defines an API for a user interface component implementing a selection from a predefined number of choices. The UI components that implement Choice are List and ChoiceGroup.

Each element of a Choice is composed of a text string and an optional image. If the application provides an image, the implementation can choose to ignore the image if it exceeds the capacity of the device to display it. If the implementation displays the image, it will be displayed adjacent to the text string as a sort of icon, and the pair will be treated as a unit.

After a Choice object has been created, elements may be inserted, appended, and deleted, and each element's string part and image part can be obtained and set. Elements within a Choice object are referred to by their indexes, which are consecutive integers starting from zero.

There are three types of choices: IMPLICIT-CHOICE (valid only for lists), EXCLUSIVE-CHOICE, and MULTIPLE-CHOICE.

When a Choice is present on the display, the user can interact with it indefinitely. These traversing and scrolling operations do not cause application-visible events. The system notifies the application only when some application-defined command is fired, or when the selection state of a ChoiceGroup is changed. When a command is fired, a high-level event is delivered to the listener of the Screen.

The following important methods  can be found in the javax.microedition.lcdui.Choice interface:

- size()—Gets the number of elements present.
- getString(int elementNum)—Gets the text part of the element referenced by elementNum value.
- getImage(int elementNum)—Gets the image part of the element referenced by elementNum.

- `append(String stringPart, Image imagePart)`—Appends an element to the choice group. The added element will be the last element listed. The size of the group grows by one.

- `insert(int elementNum, String stringPart, Image imagePart)`—Inserts an element into the choice just prior to the element specified. The group size grows by one.

- `delete(int elementNum)`—Deletes the element referenced by `elementNum`. The group size shrinks by one.

- `set(int elementNum, String stringPart, Image imagePart)`—Sets the element referenced by `elementNum` to the specified element, replacing the previous contents of the element.

- `isSelected(int elementNum)`—Gets a Boolean value indicating whether this element is selected.

- `getSelectedIndex()`—Returns the index number of an element in the choice that is selected.

- `getSelectedFlags(boolean[] selectedArray)`—Queries the state of a choice and returns the state of all elements in the Boolean array called `selectedArray`.

- `setSelectedIndex(int elementNum, boolean selected)`

  For `MULTIPLE`, this method simply sets an individual element's selected state.

  For `EXCLUSIVE`, this can be used only to select any element. In other words, the selected parameter must be true. When an element is selected, the previously selected element is deselected.

  For `IMPLICIT`, this can be used only to select any element. The selected parameter must be true. When an element is selected, the previously selected element is deselected.

- `setSelectedFlags (boolean[] selectedArray)`—Attempts to set the selected state of every element in the `Choice` using the Boolean array.

Lists can be used as menus and track/level selectors. Listing 13.1 shows an example menu. A car racing game can use this menu to select a type of track.

*LISTING 13.1* Choosing a Track

```
import javax.microedition.lcdui.*;
import javax.microedition.midlet.*;

public class Tracks extends List
    implements CommandListener
```

*LISTING 13.1*    Continued

```java
{
  private MIDlet midlet;
  private GameCanvas nextForm;
  private Form previousForm;

  private Command backCommand = new
      Command("Back", Command.SCREEN, 1);

  private static String trackNames[] =
      {"City", "Forest", "Mountain"};

  private static int lengths[] =
      {1000, 1400, 800};

  public Tracks(MIDlet midlet, GameCanvas nextForm,
      Form previousForm)
  {
    super("Tracks:", List.IMPLICIT, trackNames, null);
    this.midlet = midlet;
    this.nextForm = nextForm;
    this.previousForm = previousForm;
    addCommand(backCommand);
    setCommandListener(this);
  }

  public void commandAction(Command c, Displayable s)
  {
    if (c.equals(List.SELECT_COMMAND))
    {
      int trackID = getSelectedIndex();
      nextForm.setLength(lengths[trackID]);
      nextForm.setSpeed(Float.createFloat(2, 400));
      nextForm.initEnemies();
      Display.getDisplay(midlet).setCurrent(nextForm);
      nextForm.start();
    }
    else if (c == backCommand)
    {
      Display.getDisplay(midlet).setCurrent(previousForm);
    }
  }
}
```

The application memorizes the previous and next form so that forward and backward navigation is available. All list options are passed as an array of strings. When the Select key is pressed, it invokes a special SELECT_COMMAND event. In the command listener, when the event is caught, the track's id is read from the list and the game is started (usually by starting a thread). The track is shown in Figure 13.2.

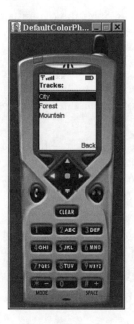

**FIGURE 13.2**    The race track selection list.

## Text Boxes

A javax.microedition.lcdui.TextBox class is another Screen class successor that allows the user to enter and edit text. It has a maximum size, which is the maximum number of characters that can be stored in the object at any time (its capacity). This limit is enforced when the TextBox's instance is constructed, when the user is editing text within, as well as when the application program calls methods that modify its contents. The maximum size is the maximum stored capacity, and is unrelated to the number of characters that can be displayed at any given time.

The text contained within a TextBox may be more than can be displayed at one time. If this is the case, the implementation will usually let the user scroll down through the box to view and edit any part of the text. This scrolling occurs transparently to the application.

Important methods are the following:

- getString()—Gets the contents of the TextBox as a string value.

- setString(String text)—Sets the contents of the TextBox as a string value, replacing the previous contents.

- getChars(char[] data)—Copies the contents of the TextBox into a character array starting at index zero. Array elements beyond the characters copied are left unchanged.

- setChars(char[] data, int offset, int length)—Sets the contents of the TextBox from a character array, replacing the previous contents. Characters are copied from the region of the data array starting at array index *offset* and running for *length* characters.

- insert(String src, int position)—Inserts a string into the contents of the TextBox. The string is inserted just prior to the character indicated by the position parameter. The current size of the contents is increased by the number of inserted characters. The resulting string must fit within the current maximum capacity.

- insert(char[] data, int offset, int length, int position)—Inserts a subrange of an array of characters into the contents of the TextBox.

- delete(int offset, int length)—Deletes characters from the TextBox.

- getMaxSize()—Returns the maximum size of characters that can be stored in this TextBox.

- setMaxSize(int maxSize)—Sets the maximum size (number of characters) that can be contained in this TextBox. If the current contents of the TextBox are larger than maxSize, the contents are truncated to fit.

- size()—Gets the number of characters that are currently stored in this TextBox.

- getCaretPosition()—Gets the current input position.

- setConstraints(int constraints)—Sets the input constraints of the TextBox.

- getConstraints()—Gets the current input constraints of the TextBox.

## Items

The javax.microedition.lcdui.Item class is the big daddy of them all. Any user interface component that can be added onto a Form must derive from Item. All Item objects have a label field, which is a string that is attached to the item. The label is typically displayed near the component when it is displayed within a screen and has the following methods:

- setLabel(String label)—Sets the label of this object.

- getLabel()—Gets the label of this object.

In some cases, when the user attempts to interact with the item, the system will switch to a system-generated screen where the actual interaction takes place. If this occurs, the label will generally be carried along and displayed within this new screen in order to provide the user with some context for the operation.

## Item State Listening

Sometimes it is useful to know if a user is selecting one of your items. You can have a form listen to a item by using the following static method:

Form.setItemStateListener(ItemStateListener)

When a user does something interesting with a user interface component, the listener's itemStateChanged(Item item) method will be triggered. Such changes include

- Changing the set of selected values in a ChoiceGroup

- Adjusting the value of an interactive Gauge

- Entering a new value into a TextField

- Entering a new Date into a DateField

The listener is not called if the application (as opposed to the user) changes the value of an interactive item.

## Choices

A javax.microedition.lcdui.ChoiceGroup is a group of selectable elements intended to be placed within a Form. The group may be created with a mode that requires a single choice to be made, or one that allows multiple choices.

Each device implementation is responsible for providing the graphical representation of these modes, and must provide visually different graphics for different modes. For example, some devices might use radio buttons for the single choice mode and check boxes for the multiple-choice mode. Choices implement the javax.microedition.lcdui.Choice interface and therefore have the same methods as lists.

## Dates

A `javax.microedition.lcdui.DateField` is an editable component for presenting date and time information that can be placed into a `Form`.

You can create an instance to accept a given date, a given time, or both. This input mode configuration is accomplished by calling the `DATE`, `TIME`, or `DATE_TIME` static fields of this class. Figure 13.3, for example, shows a typical date and time selection screen.

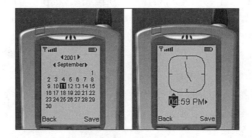

*FIGURE 13.3*    Displaying date and time.

Methods for manipulating the date and time include the following:

- `getDate()`—Returns the date value of this field. The returned value is null if the field value is not initialized. The `Date` object is constructed according to the rules of a locale-specific calendaring system and defined time zone. In the `TIME` mode field, the date components are set to the *zero epoch* value of January 1st, 1970. If a `Date` object presents time beyond one day from this zero epoch, then this field is in the *not initialized* state, and this method returns null. In the `DATE` mode field, the time component of the calendar is set to zero when constructing the date object.

- `setDate(Date date)`—Sets a new value for this field. Null can be passed to set the field state to the not initialized state. The input mode of this field defines what components of the passed `Date` object is used. In `TIME` input mode, the date components must be set to the zero epoch value of January 1st, 1970. If a `Date` object presents time beyond one day from the zero epoch, then this field is in the not initialized state.

  In `TIME` input mode, the date component of the `Date` object is ignored, and the time component is used to the precision of minutes.

  In `DATE` input mode, the time component of the `Date` object is ignored.

  In `DATE_TIME` input mode, the date and time components of `Date` are used, but only to the precision of minutes.

- `getInputMode()`—Gets the input mode for this date field. Valid input modes are DATE, TIME, or DATE_TIME.

- `setInputMode(int mode)`—Sets the input mode for this date field. Valid input modes are DATE, TIME, or DATE_TIME.

- `setLabel(String label)`—Sets the label of the Item. If the label is null, it specifies that this item has no label.

## Progress Meters

Often times, it's a good idea to show a load bar to a user as a bunch of graphics or classes are loaded from the network or from storage memory. The `javax.microedition.lcdui.Gauge` class implements a bar graph display of a value intended for use in the form of a progress meter. Figure 13.4 shows a typical gauge.

**FIGURE 13.4**    An interactive and non-interactive gauge.

The values accepted by the Gauge object are small integers in the range zero through a maximum value established by the application. The application is expected to normalize its values into this range. The device is also expected to normalize this range into a smaller set of values for display purposes. Doing so will not change the actual value contained within the object. The range of values specified by the application may be larger than the number of distinct visual states possible on the device, so more than one value may have the same visual representation.

Applications can set or retrieve the Gauge's value at any time, regardless of the interaction mode. The user is prohibited from moving the value outside the established range. The expected behavior is that the application sets the initial value, then allows the user to modify the value thereafter. However, the application is not prohibited from modifying the value even while the user is interacting with it.

The Gauge class has the following important methods:

- setValue(int value)—Sets the current value of this Gauge object. If the value is less than zero, zero is used. If the current value is greater than the maximum value, the current value is set to be equal to the maximum value.

- getValue()—Gets the current value of this Gauge object.

- setMaxValue(int maxValue)—This sets the maximum value of this Gauge object. The new maximum value must be greater than zero, otherwise an exception is thrown. If the current value is greater than the new maximum value, the current value is set to be equal to the new maximum value.

- getMaxValue()—Gets the maximum value of this Gauge object.

- isInteractive()—Tells whether the user is allowed to change the value of the Gauge.

- setLabel(String label)—Sets the label of the Item. If the label is null, it specifies that this item has no label.

An example of a progress meter in use can be seen in Listing 13.2.

*LISTING 13.2*   The ProgressForm Example

```
import javax.microedition.lcdui.*;
import javax.microedition.midlet.*;

public class ProgressForm extends Form
implements CommandListener, Runnable
{
  private final int MAX = 10;

  private MIDlet midlet;
  private Form nextForm;
  private Gauge gauge;
```

**LISTING 13.2**    Continued

```
private StringItem label;
private Command nextCommand = new
    Command("Next", Command.SCREEN, 1);

public ProgressForm(MIDlet midlet, Form nextForm)
{
  super("Loader");
  this.midlet = midlet;
  this.nextForm = nextForm;
  addCommand(nextCommand);
  setCommandListener(this);

  gauge = new Gauge("", false, MAX, 0);
  append(gauge);
}

public void commandAction(Command c, Displayable s)
{
  if (c.equals(nextCommand))
  {
    Thread thread = new Thread(this);
    thread.start();
  }
}

public void run()
{
  for (int i = 0; i < MAX; i++)
  {
    // Do something
    gauge.setValue(i + 1);
  }
  Display.getDisplay(midlet).setCurrent(nextForm);
}
}
```

Progress meters are often used during the execution of segmented actions that are quite slow (for example, loading images and levels over the network). Users want some kind of feedback that showing that the device is not frozen. The value MAX should have the number of items to be done (such as number of images). When pressing the Next soft key, a new thread is invoked.

### StringItem**s**

The javax.microedition.lcdui.StringItem class is a simple item that can contain a string. This is used to create a display-only text label. Both the label and the textual content of a StringItem can be modified by the application. The visual representation of the label may differ from that of the textual contents.

To manipulate a StringItem, use the following methods:

- getText()—Gets the text contents of the StringItem, or null if the StringItem is empty.

- setText(String text)—Sets the text contents of the StringItem. If text is null, the StringItem is set to be empty.

- setLabel(String label)—Sets the label of the Item. If the label is null, it specifies that this item has no label.

### ImageItem**s**

Similar to StringItem, the javax.microedition.lcdui.ImageItem class provides layout control when Image objects are added to a Form. Each ImageItem object contains a reference to an Image object. This image must be immutable. The value null may be specified for the image contents of an ImageItem. If this occurs (and if the label is also null), the ImageItem will occupy no space on the screen.

Each ImageItem object contains a layout field that is combined from the following values:

- LAYOUT_DEFAULT—Use the default formatting of the container of the image.

- LAYOUT_LEFT—Image should be close to left edge of the drawing area.

- LAYOUT_RIGHT—Image should be close to right edge of the drawing area.

- LAYOUT_CENTER—Image should be horizontally centered.

- LAYOUT_NEWLINE_BEFORE—A new line should be started before the image is drawn.

- LAYOUT_NEWLINE_AFTER—A new line should be started after the image is drawn.

Because of device constraints such as limited screen size, the implementation might choose to ignore layout directions.

There are some implicit rules on how the layout directives can be combined:

- LAYOUT_DEFAULT cannot not be combined with any other directive. In fact, any other value will override LAYOUT_DEFAULT because its value is 0.

- LAYOUT_LEFT, LAYOUT_RIGHT, and LAYOUT_CENTER are meant to be mutually exclusive.

- It usually makes sense to combine LAYOUT_LEFT, LAYOUT_RIGHT, and LAYOUT_CENTER with LAYOUT_NEWLINE_BEFORE and LAYOUT_NEWLINE_AFTER.

Important methods within ImageItem are the following:

- getImage()—Gets the image contained within the ImageItem, or returns null if there is no contained image.

- setImage(Image img)—Sets the image object contained within the ImageItem. The image must be immutable. If img is null, the ImageItem is set to be empty.

- getAltText()—Gets the text string to be used if the image exceeds the device's capacity to display it.

- setAltText(String text)—Sets the alternate text of the ImageItem, or null if no alternate text is provided.

- getLayout()—Gets the layout directives used for placing the image.

- setLayout(int layout)—Sets the layout directives.

- setLabel(String label)—Sets the label of the Item. If the label is null, it specifies that this item has no label.

## Text Inputs

The javax.microedition.lcdui.TextField class is an editable text component that may be placed into a Form, as seen in Figure 13.5).

You can give a text field an initial value. It also has a maximum size, which is the maximum number of characters that can be stored in the object at any time. This limit is enforced when the TextField instance is constructed, when the user is editing text within the TextField, as well as when the application program calls methods on the TextField that modify its contents. The maximum size is the maximum stored capacity and is unrelated to the number of characters that may be displayed at any given time. The number of characters displayed and their arrangement into rows and columns are determined by the device.

The TextField shares the concept of input constraints with the TextBox object. The different constraints allow the application to request that the user's input be restricted in a variety of ways. The implementation is required to restrict the user's input as requested by the application. The following constants can be used to restrict the character set:

*FIGURE 13.5*    A typical text password field.

- ANY—The user is allowed to enter any type of text at all. This is the default.

- EMAILADDR—The user is allowed to enter an e-mail address.

- NUMERIC—The user is allowed to enter only an integer value. The implementation must restrict the contents to consist of an optional minus sign followed by an optional string of numerals.

- PHONENUMBER—The user is allowed to enter a phone number. The phone number is a special case, since a phone-based implementation may be linked to the native phone dialing application. The implementation might automatically start a phone dialer application that is initialized so that pressing a single key would be enough to make a call. The call must not be made automatically without requiring the user's confirmation. The exact set of characters allowed is specific to the device and to the device's network, and can include non-numeric characters.

- URL—The user is allowed to enter a URL, such as http://www.yahoo.com.

- PASSWORD—The text entered must be masked so that the characters typed are not visible. The actual contents of the text field are not affected, but each character is displayed using a mask character such as *. The character chosen as the mask character is implementation-dependent. This is useful for entering confidential information such as passwords or PINs. A password box is shown in Figure 13.5.

- CONSTRAINT_MASK—The mask value for determining the constraint mode. The application should use the logical AND operation with a value returned by getConstraints() and CONSTRAINT_MASK to retrieve the current constraint mode, as well as to remove any modifier flags such as the PASSWORD flag.

The implementation may provide special formatting for the value entered. For example, a PHONENUMBER field may be separated and punctuated as appropriate for the phone number conventions in use, grouping the digits into country code, area code, prefix, and so on. Note that in some networks a + prefix is part of the number, and is returned as a part of the string.

## Tickers

A special type of item that can be added to any screen is a *ticker*. The javax.microedition.lcdui.Ticker class implements a scrolling ticker-tape, which is a piece of text that runs continuously across the display. The direction and speed of scrolling are determined by the implementation. While animating, the ticker string scrolls continuously. That is, when the string finishes scrolling off the display, the ticker starts over at the beginning of the string.

There is no API provided for starting and stopping the ticker. The ticker always scrolls continuously. Some devices might automatically pause the scrolling for power consumption purposes; for example, if the user doesn't interact with the device for a certain period of time. The implementation should resume scrolling the ticker when the user interacts with the device again.

The same ticker can be shared by several Screen objects. This can be accomplished by calling the setTicker() method on all such screens. Typical usage is for an application to place the same ticker on all its screens. When the application switches between two screens that have the same ticker, a desirable effect is for the ticker to be displayed at the same location on the display and to continue scrolling its contents at the same position. This gives the illusion of the ticker being attached to the global display, instead of to each screen.

You can construct and add a ticker object as follows. Just drop the following code into any form class:

```
Ticker ticker = new Ticker("Please wait! Loading...");
setTicker(ticker);
```

## Additional Libraries

If you want to extend the user interface further, you might want to check out some other toolkits.

A site called Trantor in Germany offers a package known as kAWT. Grab it from http://www.trantor.de/kawt/index.html.

kAWT is a lightweight version of Java's AWT, specially tailored for J2ME. There are versions for the Palm as well as for MIDP. It enables your MIDlets to use standard

Java widgets such as panels and containers, and makes the MIDlet code truly upwardly compatible with applets. For example, a typical panel is shown in Figure 13.6.

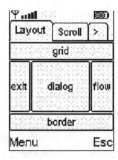

**FIGURE 13.6**    Using kAWT in J2ME.

The only caveat is that kAWT will suck away an additional 27K or so of memory.

## Summary

As you can see, a high-level user interface is pretty simple to throw together. Creating your game menus, load bars, alert boxes, input boxes, and other such interface items is really easy. Just create a quick Form, drop in the items you want, and off you go!

But obviously the real meat of a game is in the graphics. For that, you need to draw images directly onto the screen. The Canvas class is a special type of screen that makes this possible, and the next chapter has all the details you'll need....

# 14

Working with Graphics:
Low-Level Graphical
User Interfaces

**IN THIS CHAPTER**

• The Canvas Class

• Painting on the Screen

• Drawing Images

Let's face facts—graphics are the heart of gaming, and good graphics consist of writing and animating all sorts of images on a device's screen.

The MIDP UI component that supports this low-level approach is the javax.microedition.lcdui.Canvas class. This is the class where all the action happens.

## The Canvas Class

Canvas handles low-level events and allows you to draw directly onto the device's display. The Canvas class, just like the Screen class, implements the javax.microedition.lcdui.Displayable interface. Just like a Form, an Alert, or any other type of screen, you can easily create and display multiple Canvases using the setDisplay() method.

For example, in the car racing game we have been creating, a list screen is used to select the track you want to race on, and a Canvas subclass would implement the actual game.

Canvases require applications to subclass them because the paint() method is declared abstract. The paint() method is where you actually put the pedal to the metal and draw things onto the screen.

Other methods found in the Canvas class are the following:

- getWidth()—Gets the width of the display in pixels.

- getHeight()—Gets the height of the display in pixels.

- isDoubleBuffered()—Checks whether the device uses double buffering when painting on the canvas.

- hasPointerEvents()—Checks whether the device supports pointer press and release events. Most phones do not have touch screens and pointers. Most PDAs (such as the Palm) however, do support pointers.

- hasPointerMotionEvents()—Checks whether the device supports pointer motion events (pointer is dragged).

- hasRepeatEvents()—Checks whether the device can generate repeat events when the key is kept down. Some mobile phones can deal with this, but many do not.

- getKeyCode(int gameAction)—Gets a key code that corresponds to the specified game action on the device.

- getKeyName(int keyCode)—Gets an informative key string for a key.

- getGameAction(int keyCode)—Gets the game action associated with the given key code of the device.

- keyPressed(int keyCode)—Called when a key is first pressed.

- keyRepeated(int keyCode)—Called when a key is repeated (held down).

- keyReleased(int keyCode)—Called when a key is released.

- pointerPressed(int x, int y)—Called when the pointer is pressed on a coordinate (x,y).

- pointerReleased(int x, int y)—Called when the pointer is released on the coordinate (x,y).

- pointerDragged(int x, int y)—Called when the pointer is dragged to the new coordinate (x,y).

- repaint(int x, int y, int width, int height)—Requests a repaint for the specified region of the screen.

- repaint()—Requests a repaint for the entire canvas.

- showNotify()—Called immediately prior to this canvas being made visible on the display. If you need to do something to the canvas right before it is shown, do it here.

- `hideNotify()`—Called shortly after the canvas has been removed from the display. This is a good place to clean up any objects and free up some extra memory.

- `paint(Graphics g)`—Renders the canvas. The application must implement this method in order to paint any graphics.

## Canvas **Events**

Canvas makes it easy to handle game actions, key presses, and pointer manipulations. Special methods are also provided to let you know what the current device can handle.

Using the `keyPressed()` method, for example, you can detect any time a user hits a soft key, a menu key, a cursor (arrow) key, or a number key on the phone's keypad. The MIDP API also includes a special set of game keys, which are usually mapped to the arrow keys and the main "send" or "fire" key. Games should use game actions instead of key codes whenever possible.

Event-handling methods are not declared abstract, and their default implementations are empty. That means they do nothing. This allows you to override only the methods you actually need.

Most mobile phones do not have a touch screen, where the user uses a stylus or mouse-like cursor to point to a location on the screen. Instead, most user input on micro devices is via the keypad.

Every key is assigned a special key code. The key code values are unique for each hardware key. The following key codes are defined:

- `KEY_NUM0` to `KEY_NUM9` for numeric 0 through 9 keys

- `KEY_STAR` for the * key

- `KEY_POUND` for # key

These key codes correspond to keys on an ITU-T standard telephone keypad. Other keys may be present on the keyboard, and they will have key codes different from those listed previously. In order to guarantee portability, applications should use only the standard key codes.

Most games use arrow keys and fire keys. The MID Profile defines the following game actions:

- `UP`, `DOWN`, `LEFT`, and `RIGHT` for navigation keys. Almost every phone now features these cursor keys.

- GAME_A, GAME_B, GAME_C, and GAME_D for special keys. This usually corresponds to the soft keys immediately beneath the screen.

- FIRE for a select key. This is usually in the center of the cursor keys, or is the phone's main Send or Talk key. For example, the Siemens SL45i maps the fire key to the left soft key.

Each key code may be mapped to at most one game action, but it may be associated with more than one key code. The application can translate a key code into a game action using the getGameAction() method, and it can translate a key code into a game action using the getKeyCode() method.

## Custom Commands

You can also add your own custom commands, as discussed in Chapter 9, "Creating a MIDlet." Simply register a command listener and implement the public void commandAction(Command c, Displayable s) method.

Commands will be mapped to keys and menus in a device-specific way.

## Creating a Game Key and Pointer Handler

Unlike a relatively static business application, a game needs to be extremely responsive to user input. When a player hits or holds down the right cursor key to move his car to the right, the game sure as heck better be able to keep up.

Most J2ME devices use a separate thread for receiving keyboard commands. When a player presses a phone key, the key fires an event which is immediately transferred to the game. For example, when a user hits the right key, the keyPressed(int keycode) method is called. The keycode will equal RIGHT. As long as the player is pressing this key, we need to make sure to animate the race car to the right.

Now, as soon as the player releases the key, the keyReleased(int keycode) method is called. The game should be smart enough to immediately stop the race car's rightward movement.

As such, a typical action game doesn't really need to trigger a series of events when a key is pressed. Rather, a game needs to keep track of an *input state*.

This is easily done. Just create a global variable called *key* and change the variable as keys are pressed or released:

```
private int key;

public void keyPressed(int keyCode)
{
```

```
    key = getGameAction(keyCode);
}

public void keyReleased(int keyCode)
{
    // We set this to zero to indicate nothing is pressed.
    key = 0;
}
```

If you want the gameplay to be slightly different, you could ignore the keyReleased() method. This would make it so that your car responded to more realistic steering wheel physics: To straighten the race car's direction, the player would have to press the opposite direction key.

Instead of using the system above, you may optionally use the keyRepeated() method to determine if a key is continuously held down. However, some phones do not support this method and other phones wait quite a while before calling the method. To achieve smooth, 10 frames per second action, you should implement your own "repeat detection."

Note that some older phones may not have game keys at all. As such, when creating an action game, it is a good idea to handle not only game (cursor) keys, but keypad keys. Use the following numeric key for compatibility with older phones:

- Key 2 for up
- Key 8 for down
- Key 4 for left
- Key 6 for right
- Key 5 for fire

In Chapter 17, "Sprite Movement," we will tie this key variable in with the sprite movement thread.

## Handling Touch Screens

More expensive devices such as PDAs will have large touch screens with a minimal set of keys. In this case, you can use the pointerPressed() and pointerReleased() methods. To find out if a device supports the touch screen events, call the hasPointerEvents() method.

Similar to key events, pointer events are fired by touching the screen. The x and y coordinate of where the stylus is touching will be returned. Your game should define the screen area that is sensitive to screen touches.

For example, in our racing game, you can define the width of the screen in the game's Cache class. You can then treat any pointer presses on the right side of the screen as steering to the right. Touching the left side of the screen will steer left. Lifting the pointer will stop the car's side-to-side movement.

The code to handle this is listed here:

```
public void pointerPressed(int x, int y)
{
  if (x < getWidth() / 2)
      key = LEFT;
  else
      key = RIGHT
}

public void pointerReleased(int x, int y)
{
  key = 0;
}
```

You can also draw your own virtual command keys onto the game screen. In such a case, you'd create special screen areas reserved for navigation.

## Painting on the Screen

The javax.microedition.lcdui.Graphics class is an abstract class that represents the actual device's display.

The Graphics class provides simple 2D geometric rendering capabilities. You can easily use graphics to draw primitive lines, rectangles, and arcs. You can also fill in your rectangles and arcs with a solid color. Rectangles with rounded corners can also be specified.

Using Graphics, you can also easily draw text Strings or, most importantly, images. The only explicit drawing operation provided in the Graphics class is pixel replacement. The destination pixel value is simply replaced by the current pixel value specified in the graphics object being used for rendering. No facility for combining pixel values, such as raster-ops or alpha blending, is provided.

The Graphics class can be rendered directly to the display or to an offscreen image buffer, depending on the device. A graphics object for rendering to the display is passed to the Canvas paint() method. This is the only means by which a graphics object destined for the display can be obtained.

The default coordinate system's origin (0,0) is at the upper left-hand corner of the screen. The X-axis direction is positive towards the right, and the Y-axis direction is positive downwards. All coordinates are specified as integers.

Important methods within `Graphics` include the following:

- `translate(int x, int y)`—Translates the origin of the graphics context to the point (x, y) in the current coordinate system.

- `getTranslateX()`—Gets the X coordinate of the translated origin of this graphics context.

- `getTranslateY()`—Gets the Y coordinate of the translated origin of this graphics context.

- `setStrokeStyle(int style)`—Sets the stroke style used for drawing lines, arcs, rectangles and rounded rectangles.

- `getStrokeStyle()`—Gets the stroke style used for drawing operations.

- `getColor()`—Gets the current color.

- `getRedComponent()`—Gets the red component of the current color.

- `getGreenComponent()`—Gets the green component of the current color.

- `getBlueComponent()`—Gets the blue component of the current color.

- `getGrayScale()`—Gets the current grayscale value of the color being used for rendering operations.

- `setColor(int red, int green, int blue)`—Sets the current color to the specified RGB values.

- `setColor(int RGB)`—Sets the current color to the specified RGB value.

- `setGrayScale(int value)`—Sets the current grayscale to be used for all subsequent rendering operations.

- `getFont()`—Gets the current font.

- `setFont(Font font)`—Sets the font for all subsequent text rendering operations.

- `getClipX()`—Gets the X offset of the current clipping area relative to the coordinate system origin of this graphics context.

- `getClipY()`—Gets the Y offset of the current clipping area relative to the coordinate system origin of this graphics context.

- `getClipWidth()`—Gets the width of the current clipping area.

- `getClipHeight()`—Gets the height of the current clipping area.

- `clipRect(int x, int y, int width, int height)`—Intersects the current clip with the specified rectangle. The resulting clipping area is the intersection of the current clipping area and the specified rectangle.

- `setClip(int x, int y, int width, int height)`—Sets the current clip to the rectangle specified by the given coordinates.

- `drawLine(int x1, int y1, int x2, int y2)`—Draws a line between the coordinates (x1,y1) and (x2,y2).

- `drawRect(int x, int y, int width, int height)`—Draws the outline of the specified rectangle.

- `fillRect(int x, int y, int width, int height)`—Fills the specified rectangle with the current color.

- `drawRoundRect(int x, int y, int width, int height, int arcWidth, int arcHeight)`—Draws the outline of the specified rounded corner rectangle.

- `fillRoundRect(int x, int y, int width, int height, int arcWidth, int arcHeight)`—Fills the specified rounded corner rectangle with the current color.

- `drawArc(int x, int y, int width, int height, int startAngle, int arcAngle)`—Draws the outline of a circular or elliptical arc covering the specified rectangle.

- `fillArc(int x, int y, int width, int height, int startAngle, int arcAngle)`—Fills a circular or elliptical arc covering the specified rectangle.

- `drawString(String str, int x, int y, int anchor)`—Draws the specified string using the current font and color.

- `drawSubstring(String str, int offset, int len, int x, int y, int anchor)`—Draws the specified substring using the current font and color.

- `drawChar(char character, int x, int y, int anchor)`—Draws the specified character using the current font and color.

- `drawChars(char[] data, int offset, int length, int  x, int y, int anchor)`—Draws the specified characters using the current font and color.

- `drawImage(Image img, int x, int y, int anchor)`—Draws the specified image by using the anchor point.

## Working with Colors

In J2ME, images are expressed using 24 bits per pixel. This means that J2ME, in theory, can handle full-color images. To define each pixel's color, three bytes are used—8 bits for the red component, 8 for the green, and 8 for the blue. Because most micro devices don't support all 24 bits, they map colors requested by the application into colors available on the device. For example, even though J2ME may support millions of colors, a device may only be able to handle black, white, and gray.

The current color of the `Graphics` object can be set by calling the `Graphics.setColor()` method. The color's red-green-blue components can be set separately or as an integer value. For example, the color red can be set using

```
setColor(255, 0, 0);
```

or

```
setColor(0xff0000);
```

The methods `getRedComponent()`, `getGreenComponent()`, and `getBlueComponent()` return the values of the current color. Currently, most mobile phones in the USA and Europe are black and white, offering only a few shades of gray. To see how the color is mapped into a gray scale, use the `getGrayScale()` method.

## Stroke Types

Lines, arcs, rectangles, and rounded rectangles may be drawn with either a `SOLID` or a `DOTTED` stroke style set by the `Graphics.setStrokeStyle()` method. For the `SOLID` stroke style, drawing operations are performed with a one-pixel wide pen that fills the pixel immediately below and to the right of the specified coordinate. Drawn lines touch pixels at both endpoints. Drawing operations under the `DOTTED` stroke style will touch a subset of pixels that would have been touched under the `SOLID` stroke style. The frequency and length of dots is implementation-dependent.

## Drawing Lines

To draw a line, use the `Graphics.drawLine()` method. It accepts four parameters: x1, y1, x2, and y2. The parameters set two points on the screen (x1,y1) and (x2,y2), and a line is drawn between them. The current color and stroke style are used to draw the line.

To create a dotted line in the middle of the road for our car racing game, you could use code similar to

```
public void paint(Graphics g)
  {
    g.setStrokeStyle(Graphics.DOTTED);
    g.drawLine(getWidth() / 2, 0, getWidth() / 2,
        getHeight() - 1);
  }
```

This code snippet uses the `Canvas` `getWidth()` method to get the display's width so the line is put in the middle. Figure 14.1 shows the result of the `paint()` method.

*FIGURE 14.1*    A dotted line.

## Drawing Rectangles

To draw a rectangle, the `drawRect()` method is used. Much like `drawLine()`, it also accepts four parameters: x, y, width, and height. The point (x,y) sets the upper-left coordinate of the rectangle and then draws the box with the given width and height. The rectangle can be solid or dotted, and is drawn in the currently specified color.

You can also draw filled rectangles with the `fillRect()` method. The current color is used as the fill. The resulting rectangle will cover an area that is (width+1) pixels wide and (height+1) pixels tall.

To draw the edges of the road, we could add on to our dotted line and use this code:

```
public void paint(Graphics g)
  {
    g.setStrokeStyle(Graphics.DOTTED);
    g.drawLine(getWidth() / 2, 0, getWidth() / 2,
        getHeight() - 1);
    g.setStrokeStyle(Graphics.SOLID);
    g.fillRect(0, 0, (getWidth() - ROAD_WIDTH) / 2,
        getHeight());
    g.fillRect((getWidth() + ROAD_WIDTH) / 2, 0,
        (getWidth() - ROAD_WIDTH) / 2, getHeight());
  }
```

The fillRect() method is called twice: once to create the left edge of the road, and once to create the right. Setting a solid style doesn't affect the filled rectangles, but will be used later for further drawings. To give the road a fixed width, the ROAD_WIDTH constant is used.

Figure 14.2 illustrates our new road.

*FIGURE 14.2*    The side of the road.

## Drawing Rounded Rectangles

To draw a rectangle with rounded corners, use the drawRoundRect() method. Similarly, you can fill a round rectangle using the fillRoundRect() method.

Both of these methods accept six parameters—four of them are equal to parameters in drawRect() and fillRect(), and two additional parameters provide the horizontal and vertical diameters of the arc at all four corners.

## Drawing Arcs

With the drawArc() method, you can draw the outline of a circular or elliptical arc covering a specified area on your device's screen. The resulting arc begins at a specific angle and extends a set number of degrees to the next angle. Angles start at 0 degrees, which is similar to the 3 o'clock position.

A positive value indicates a counter-clockwise rotation of the angle, whereas a negative value indicates a clockwise rotation. The center of the arc is the center of the rectangle whose origin is (x,y) and whose size is specified by the width and height arguments. Similarly, the fillArc() method fills a circular or elliptical arc covering the specified rectangle.

## Fonts

The javax.microedition.lcdui.Font class represents fonts and their font metrics. Fonts cannot be created by applications, but are defined in the system. Your game should query for a given font based on its attributes, and the system will provide the font that matches your requested attributes as closely as possible.

The Font class has the following attributes:

- Style
- Size
- Face

The following styles are available for the font:

- STYLE_BOLD
- STYLE_ITALIC
- STYLE_PLAIN
- STYLE_UNDERLINED

The supported font sizes are

- SIZE_LARGE—The largest font the device can display. Usually corresponds to a point size of 16.
- SIZE_MEDIUM—Corresponds to a medium-sized font.
- SIZE_SMALL—The smallest font the device can handle. Usually refers to a point size of 8.

Finally, the various faces you can ask for are

- FACE_MONOSPACE—A monospace font, where each character is equally wide.
- FACE_PROPORTIONAL—A font where letters are proportional to each other.
- FACE_SYSTEM—The standard font used on this system.

So, to get a bold, medium-sized, and monospaced font, you would use

```
Font newfont = Font.getFont(Font.FACE_MONOSPACE,Font.STYLE_BOLD,
➥Font.SIZE_MEDIUM) ;
```

You can then set the font in the paint method using

```
g.setFont(newfont);
```

## Drawing Strings

To draw a string, you can use the following methods:

- drawString()
- drawSubstring()
- drawChar()
- drawChars()

The drawString() method draws the specified string using the current font and color. The (x,y) position is the position of the anchor point defined by the parameters. In a similar way, the drawSubstring() method can be used to draw only part of a given string.

If you want to draw individual characters, or if you are dealing with an array of characters in lieu of a string, you can use the drawChar() and drawChars() methods.

To draw the racing game's "heads up display" interface information, which contains the lives left, time left, and score, you could use the code as follows:

```
public void paint(Graphics g)
{
  g.setStrokeStyle(Graphics.DOTTED);
  g.drawLine(getWidth() / 2, 0, getWidth() / 2,
      getHeight() - 1);
  g.setStrokeStyle(Graphics.SOLID);
  g.fillRect(0, 0, (getWidth() - ROAD_WIDTH) / 2,
      getHeight());
  g.fillRect((getWidth() + ROAD_WIDTH) / 2, 0,
      (getWidth() - ROAD_WIDTH) / 2, getHeight());
  g.drawString("Score:", (getWidth() - ROAD_WIDTH) /
      2 + 1, 0, Graphics.TOP | Graphics.LEFT);
}
```

This creates a status line, shown in Figure 14.3.

# Drawing Images

Drawing primates and strings is all well and good, but what we're really here for is to draw some graphics!

To drop an image on a canvas, use the Graphics.drawImage() method. Simply specify at which point the graphic should be drawn.

*FIGURE 14.3*   Drawing the score.

In most cases, the upper left corner of your graphic should be drawn at the given point. As such, you should usually pass Graphics.TOP and Graphics.LEFT into the drawImage() method.

Note that, if you desire, your image can be drawn in different positions relative to the anchor point by passing in different anchor constants.

Valid constants include the following:

- BASELINE—Images should be aligned with the baseline of any text to be drawn at the given anchor point.

- BOTTOM—Images should be aligned with the bottom of the given anchor point.

- HCENTER—Images should be centered horizontally around the given anchor point.

- LEFT—Images should be aligned with the right of the given anchor point.

- RIGHT—Images should be aligned with the right of the given anchor point.

- TOP—Images should be aligned with the top of the given anchor point.

- VCENTER—Images should be centered vertically around the given anchor point.

## The Image Class

The javax.microedition.lcdui.Image class holds graphical image data. Images exist only in offscreen memory, and will not be painted on the display unless an explicit command is issued by the application (such as within the paint() method of a Canvas) or when an Image object is placed within a form screen or an alert screen.

Images are either *mutable* or *immutable*, depending upon how they are created. Immutable images are generally created by loading image data (usually as a Portable Network Graphics, or PNG file) from resource bundles, from files, or from the network. They may not be modified once they are created.

Mutable images are created in offscreen memory. The application might paint into them after having created a `Graphics` object expressly for this purpose.

The `Image` class supports images stored in the PNG format, version 1.0.

The following methods are part of the `Image` class:

- `createImage(int width, int height)`—Creates a new, mutable image for off-screen drawing.

- `createImage(Image source)`—Creates an immutable image from a source image.

- `createImage(String name)`—Creates an immutable image from decoded image data obtained from the named resource.

- `createImage(byte[] imageData, int offset, int length)`—Creates an immutable image, which is decoded from the data stored in the specified byte array at the specified offset and length. The data must be in a self-identifying image file format supported by the implementation, such as PNG.

- `getGraphics()`—Creates a new `Graphics` object that renders to this image.

- `getWidth()`—Gets the width of the image in pixels.

- `getHeight()`—Gets the height of the image in pixels.

- `isMutable()`—Checks whether this image is mutable. Mutable images can be modified by rendering to them through a `Graphics` object obtained from the `getGraphics()` method of this object.

## Clipping

As we delve into more advanced animation techniques, you'll notice that it often makes sense to deal with a specific portion of the canvas at a given time. You will often want to create a little rectangle within the drawing area. Any draw commands issued inside the rectangle are registered. Anything outside the clipping region is ignored.

To set the current clip rectangle on the current `Graphics` screen, use the `Graphics.setClip()` method. Just pass in two sets of coordinates to create a rectangle.

After `setClip()` has been called, any rendering operations will have no effect outside the clipping area. This method is useful for implementing image transparency. We will discuss how to draw transparent images in Chapter 15, "Entering the Land of Sprites."

## Translating

Another advanced rendering technique involves moving the base origin of all drawing functions to a different point. For example, any time you pick an (x,y) coordinate position in which to paint a line, draw text, or drop an image, the canvas assumes that you are doing so based on the upper left corner at point (0,0).

If you like, you can translate the origin of the graphics context to any point you wish. To do so, just call the `translate()` method. All coordinates used in subsequent rendering operations on this graphics context will be relative to this new origin.

Note that the effect of calls to `translate()` are cumulative. If you set the new origin to (10,10) and then set it to (10,10) again, you will actually be drawing based on point (20,20).

## Double Buffering

Double buffering is a key technique used when drawing graphics. Because a screen's repaint is unpredictable, if you were to paint graphics directly to the device screen, you would notice a yucky flickering. This is because the screen might begin painting a new frame before it has fully finished drawing the last one.

Double buffering enables you to assemble a sort of offscreen "preview" of the exact way you want your screen to appear *before* it is painted. The way it works is that you draw all your sprites and other graphics onto an offscreen image that is the same size as the actual device screen. This offscreen image acts a buffer. When you are done drawing, you simply draw the entire offscreen image onto the "live" screen.

Many J2ME devices support double buffering themselves, but some devices, such as the Accompli A008, do not. To check whether your device supports this feature, call

```
isDoubleBuffered();
```

If the method returns false, you will need to implement your own double buffering. This can be done as follows:

```
private Image scene = Image.createImage(getWidth(),
    getHeight());
private Graphics g = scene.getGraphics();

public void paint(Graphics gr)
{
  g.setStrokeStyle(Graphics.DOTTED);
  g.drawLine(getWidth() / 2, 0, getWidth() / 2,
      getHeight() - 1);
  g.setStrokeStyle(Graphics.SOLID);
```

```
    g.fillRect(0, 0, (getWidth() - ROAD_WIDTH) / 2,
        getHeight());
    g.fillRect((getWidth() + ROAD_WIDTH) / 2, 0,
        (getWidth() - ROAD_WIDTH) / 2, getHeight());
    g.drawString("Score:", (getWidth() - ROAD_WIDTH) /
        2 + 1, 0, Graphics.TOP | Graphics.LEFT);
    gr.drawImage(scene, 0, 0, Graphics.TOP |
        Graphics.LEFT);
}
```

In the example above, an additional Image object is added to the code. This represents the offscreen image. We will set the Graphics variable g to point to this image instead of the actual device screen, which is actually passed in as gr.

Notice that the size of the offscreen image must be the same as the size of the display, which we grab from the getWidth() and getHeight() method of Canvas.

When painting on the screen, all painting is in reality done to the offscreen image. In the last line of our paint routine, the full frame is rendered onto the real screen.

## Summary

The Canvas class, along with Image, Font, and other such classes, gives you a lot of direct control. Using these classes, you can achieve endless graphical effects.

In later chapters we will delve more deeply into these classes, creating fully animated sprites that can easily be moved around the game screen, making your game come alive.

# 15

# Entering the Land of Sprites

**IN THIS CHAPTER**

• Sprites

• Image Files

• Collision Detection

• Image Transparency

Sprites are one of the most important components in any graphical game. A *sprite* is, simply put, any graphic that appears on your screen. A sprite is every monster, every fireball, every tree, and every ladder. Some sprites move around the screen, some sprites have animations, and some will affect the game when something else collides with them.

Throughout this book, we will be building a game called Micro Racer. The goal of the game is simple: You are a car racing down a track. Enemy cars speed at you from the opposite direction. You must avoid these cars. You can pick up various weapons and objects along the way to help you repair your car, move faster, or blast enemies off the track.

This chapter will show you how to create the basic building block of all action games—a simple but robust `Sprite` class.

## Sprites

Suppose we want to model an ordinary scene straight from the real world. What do we see? People walk the sidewalks. Cars drive through the streets. Birds fly beneath the clouds. People, cars, and birds are objects that represent our physical world.

At any given time, these objects have positions that can be termed as absolute. From a given vantage point, every object is a certain horizontal distance, vertical distance, and depth away—this can be expressed as x, y, and z coordinates.

Many of these objects are also moving at a certain velocity and certain direction—again, things that can be expressed in terms of x, y, and z. Clouds move slowly, cars move quickly.

Finally, these objects may interact with each other. What happens when a bird hits a person? What happens when a car does? All the objects that make up the gameworld are known in game terminology as sprites.

## Sprite Properties

In order to create and work with standard sprites in a two-dimensional gameworld, you will need to be able to access and set various properties. These include the following:

- x position—The position x represents the horizontal coordinate of the sprite, measured in pixels. If the sprite's x and y position are inside the visible display area, then the sprite is drawn on the screen. The leftmost column of the screen is known as x position 0, the rightmost column of a 100-pixel-wide screen would be x position 99.

- y position—This represents the vertical coordinate of the sprite. The top row of the screen is y position 0, and the bottom row of a 100-pixel-long screen would be y position 99.

- Velocity Vx—This represents the horizontal speed of the sprite. In other words, in every frame the sprite will move Vx pixels. If Vx is a negative value, the sprite moves to the left, otherwise it moves to the right.

- Velocity Vy—This is the vertical speed of the sprite If Vy is negative, the sprite will move up, otherwise the sprite will move downward. If both Vx and Vy are set to 0, then the sprite is stationary and does not move.

- Width—Represents the width of the sprite graphic. Together with the x position, it defines the right edge of the sprite on the x coordinate.

- Height—Represents the height of the sprite graphic. Together with the y position, it defines the bottom edge of the sprite on the y coordinate.

- Image—Points to the graphical representation of the sprite that is encoded in PNG format. The image file might contain a series of animated images that are defined by a frame number.

- Frame—If a sprite is to be animated, it will contain more than one frame. This property enables you to set the current frame.

- Visibility—During the game, some sprites might be disabled because they were hit, or they might be eliminated because they have moved off the screen. The visibility flag shows or hides the sprite.

Besides these properties, sprites can also have their own energy value, hit points, dollar value, number of lives, and many more properties that are different from game to game.

## Animating Frames

Some sprites might just contain one frame. For example, an arrow flying through the air might just consist of one simple image. However, sprites are at their most beautiful and interesting when they are animated. For example, a man walking might consist of three frames:

1. A man with both legs down.

2. A man with the right leg extended.

3. A man with the left leg extended.

You could then animate the man by calling the frames in sequence: 1,2,1,3,1,2, and so on.

If your game features a character being shown from the top down, you might want to create different frames for each direction the character can face.

The Sprite class that we will create must be able to handle multiple frames. The easiest way to do this is to put all of a Sprite's frames in one file, known as a *filmstrip* file. For example, Figure 15.1 shows a blown-up version of the car we are going to use in our racing game.

Notice that the two images in Figure 15.1 are nearly identical. The rightmost image, however, has white stripes in its tires. When these two frames are cycled quickly, it creates the illusion of speedy tire movement.

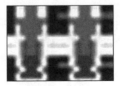

*FIGURE 15.1*    Creating a car filmstrip file.

Notice that the width of the image in Figure 15.1 is twice as wide as the actual frame we want to show. This leads to the following simple formula:

```
filmstrip_width = frame_width * num_frames
```

## The Sprite Class

You can easily extend the Sprite class, detailed in Listing 15.1, to add additional properties.

*LISTING 15.1*    Adding to the Sprite Class

```java
import javax.microedition.lcdui.*;

public class Sprite
{
  private Image image;
  private int x;
  private int y;
  private int vx;
  private int vy;
  private int width;
  private int height;
  private int numFrames;
  private int frame;
  private boolean visible;

  public Sprite(Image image, int width, int height,
      int numFrames)
      throws Exception
  {
    this.image = image;
    this.width = width;
    this.height = height;
    this.numFrames = numFrames;
    if (image.getHeight() != height)
        throw new Exception("Height not correct.");
    if (image.getWidth() / numFrames != width)
        thro new Exception("Width not correct.");
  }

  public Image getImage()
  {
    return image;
  }

  public int getX()
  {
```

**LISTING 15.1**    continued

```java
    return x;
  }

  public void setX(int x)
  {
    this.x = x;
  }

  public int getY()
  {
    return y;
  }

  public void setY(int y)
  {
    this.y = y;
  }

  public int getVx()
  {
    return vx;
  }

  public void setVx(int vx)
  {
    this.vx = vx;
  }

  public int getVy()
  {
    return vy;
  }

  public void setVy(int vy)
  {
    this.vy = vy;
  }

  public int getWidth()
  {
    return width;
  }
```

*LISTING 15.1*    continued

```
public int getHeight()
{
  return height;
}

public int getFrame()
{
  return frame;
}

public void setFrame(int frame)
    throws Exception
{
  if (frame < 0 || frame > numFrames - 1)
      throw new Exception ("Not correct frame number.");
  this.frame = frame;
}

public boolean isVisible()
{
  return this.visible;
}

public void setVisible(boolean visible)
{
  this.visible = visible;
}
}
```

By default, sprites are inactive when they are first created. You pass in the number of frames. The Sprite class ensures that the image used for the sprite is wide enough to handle the given number of frames. An exception is thrown if the image width is not correct:

```
if (image.getWidth() / numFrames != width)
      thro new Exception("Width not correct.");
```

**NOTE**

A sprite's position and speed should ideally use floating-point numbers. Since J2ME does not include floating-point libraries, the next chapter will show you how to simulate floating-point numbers.

By default, the first frame of a sprite (with the numerical value of 0) is shown.

## Image Files

Images are the heart of sprites. Our Sprite classes must be able to load and properly display sprites.

### Loading Included Images

Before an image can be used, it must be loaded from the resource file using the Image.createImage() method. In J2ME, the only resource file is in the JAR file, where all classes are located. Listing 15.2 shows what the loading procedure looks like. We will add this procedure to our global Cache class that contains all game-wide objects and variables.

Notice that images are loaded within a static block. This block is executed when the class is first loaded, generally before the first application's method starts.

> **NOTE**
>
> To use images with the Wireless Toolkit, drop your PNG files into the res directory of your current project. When you build and package the MIDlet, images will be taken from here automatically.

*LISTING 15.2*   Loading an Image Resource

```
static
{
  String locale =
      System.getProperty("microedition.locale");
  language = ENGLISH; // Default value
  if (locale != null && locale.startsWith("si"))
      language = SLOVENE;     try
  {
    carImage = Image.createImage("/car.png");
  }
  catch (Exception ex) {}
}
```

### Loading Images Over the Network

Some devices have limitations on the size of JAR files. NTT DoCoMo iApplis, for example, may not be more than larger than 10 kilobytes. Other phones have limitations of 30–50 kilobytes.

The reason for this limitation has to do with slow 2G mobile networks with 9600bps bandwidths. If hundreds of users were to download a large Java game at the same time, it could overload the network.

---
**WARNING**

Over a 9600bps network, 10 kilobytes of data can take 10 seconds to download. Because mobile users will probably only wait one minute at the most, applications should always be smaller than 50 kilobytes (with an average size of 30 kilobytes).

---

JAR files not only contain game classes, but also include images. If your game has 20 or so sprites, this can easily take up a good 10K of additional room.

Given the size limitations of JAR files, it often makes sense to download images from the network as needed. The raw image data can then be stored in the phone's internal data records. The next chapter shows you to how grab images on-the-fly. Chapter 19, "Be Persistent: MIDP Data Storage," shows you how to store these images on the phone for later use.

## Image Size Reduction

A good game will generally include many attractive graphics. The more characters, enemies, obstacles, and backgrounds you can draw, the richer your gameworld will be.

In MIDP, all the images you use must be in PNG format. PNG is a compressed format that uses all 24 bits as its color palette. If you take an in-depth look at a PNG file, you will notice the following:

- Header—This part contains basic information about the image, such as the image's size. Most importantly, a large chunk of the header contains information about the color palette the image uses.

- Data part—Contains the value for each pixel in the image.

Because a PNG file's header is so large, the more files you use, the more memory you are taking up. Because most images will use the same color palette, this amounts to wasted space.

Putting all the frames of a sprite in one filmstrip file, as in Figure 15.1, solves this problem. A lot of different images will have only one header.

The question then becomes, how does your MIDlet extract each frame from the filmstrip? Luckily, MIDP enables us to clip images as we draw them. The game needs to create a clip rectangle that equals the width of the frame. The image must then be positioned in such a way that the current frame of the image is located in the clipping rectangle.

Clipping an image takes some extra drawing time, however. As such, creating separate filmstrips for each sprite (as opposed to putting every frame of every sprite in one huge file) makes a lot of sense.

## Drawing the Sprites

A sprite is meaningless unless it can be dealt with and drawn. A robust sprite engine must include not only the sprite data, but a `SpriteManager` class capable of storing collections of sprites. The engine also needs to include a rendering component to actually draw the sprites onto the screen.

Listing 15.3 shows how to integrate a `paint()` method into the `Sprite` class. By making each `Sprite` responsible for painting itself, you give it absolute control over its own visual fate. The main `paint()` method in your game, `Canvas`, simply needs to go through the list of sprites and individually call `paint()` on each one.

*LISTING 15.3*    Adding the `paint()` Method

```
public void paint(Graphics g)
{
  g.setClip(x, y, width, height);
  g.drawImage(image, x - frame * width, y,
      Graphics.TOP | Graphics.LEFT);
  g.setClip(0, 0, Cache.width, Cache.height);
}
```

The `paint()` method is pretty simple:

1. The clipping rectangle is set to the current x and y position, at the current width and height. This ensures that only one frame is drawn at a time.

2. The image itself is then drawn so that the frame we want corresponds with the upper left corner of the clipping rectangle. For example, if we want to draw the second frame of an animation, where each frame is 20 pixels wide, we offset the image's x position by 20.

3. The clipping rectangle is then re-sent to equal the full screen width and height.

## Collision Detection

Sprite collision detection is an essential attribute of any game engine. *Collision detection* lets you know when two sprites are touching. Pretty much every game is based on this principal: Bullet hits soldier, monster touches elf, pinball bumps into flipper, Bill Gates grabs money bags, shoes touch lava, and so on.

In our Micro Racer game, when the player's car collides with an enemy car, we will deduct one unit of energy. If the player loses all 100 energy units, the game is over. We'll also throw obstacles into the game. If the player's car hits an oil slick, for example, it will veer off to the side. Finally, we'll include power-ups. When the player's car touches a wrench, its damage will be fixed automatically.

The question is, how can we implement fast but accurate collision detection on small, slow, resource-limited devices?

### Basic Collision Detection

The simplest form of collision detection is generally the fastest form. Each sprite and its image are treated as a rectangle. If one sprite's rectangle overlaps another sprite's rectangle, as in Figure 15.2, then we consider the sprites as having collided. Notice that in the figure there is a 4×2 section of overlapping rectangles.

To implement this type of detection, you need to take the x position, y position, width, and height of two sprites and then do some simple math, as shown in Listing 15.4.

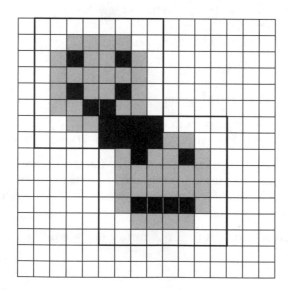

*FIGURE 15.2*   Simple collision between two sprites.

*LISTING 15.4*   Adding Collision Detection to the Sprite

```
public boolean collide(Sprite sprite)
{
  if ((x + width) > sprite.getX() &&
      x < sprite.getX() &&
      (y + height) > sprite.getY() &&
      y < sprite.getY())
          return true;
  return false;
}
```

Unfortunately, this is a very primitive form of detection. Most sprites are not actually rectangular. A racing car, for example, is shaped more like an I. Using this form of collision detection, the game might deduct energy from your car, even if the car doesn't actually touch an enemy.

Additionally, you might want to only detect collision within a certain part of a sprite. For example, when a knife hits a monster, you might want to deduct two hit points if the knife stabs the monster's face, and only one hit point if the knife hits the body.

The next chapter discusses how to implement a more advanced form of collision detection.

## Creating Child Sprites

The Sprite class contains everything we need to draw and move sprites, but it doesn't have a lot of personality. To really make a game swing, child classes need to be created for various sprites, each containing their own properties and methods.

In our Micro Racer game, for example, we will have two types of sprites—the player and the enemy.

### Building the Player Sprite

Many games feature a hero or protagonist. This is known as a *player sprite*. In our racing game, the red car is the player sprite. A player sprite is treated differently than other sprites. It represents the one unique object that defines how the game will progress.

In our racing game, the player sprite contains one additional property—energy. This property lets us know how often collisions have occurred. When energy reaches zero, the game is over. If the car can reach the end of a track without losing all its energy, the energy value is reset and the player is given a score.

A player child class is shown in Listing 15.5.

*LISTING 15.5*    The Player Sprite Child Class

```
import javax.microedition.lcdui.*;

public class Player extends Sprite
{
  protected int energy;

  public Player(Image image, int width, int height,
      int numFrames, int energy)
    throws Exception
  {
    super(image, width, height, numFrames);
    this.energy = energy;
  }

  public int getEnergy()
  {
    return energy;
  }

  public void setEnergy(int energy)
  {
    this.energy = energy;
  }
}
```

The Player class constructor calls its parent constructor, passing up most of the values. The only additional value helps set the car's initial energy.

A more advanced Player class might contain even more information, such as the amount of money the car's owner has made, the damage to various parts of the car, the number of bonus points the player has gained, and so on. We will flesh out this class in the final chapter of the book, "Micro Racer: Putting it All Together."

### Opponents

To keep things simple, enemy cars are represented using the basic Sprite class. However, a more advanced version of Micro Racer might include various types of enemies, each with its own attributes, personality, and artificial intelligence driving routines.

## Image Transparency

Every PNG image is rectangular. However, a typical sprite itself usually has a much more interesting shape. For example, a bouncing ball would be circular. To make sprites seem realistic, not like strange blocks, it is important to set one color within every PNG file as the background, or *transparent color*.

When you create a PNG file using Photoshop or another design application, you can specify one of the colors to be transparent. When each pixel of a PNG image is rendered, this transparent color will be masked out and not drawn.

Unfortunately, the MIDP specification does not demand that image transparency be supported. Because J2ME is so limited, most manufacturers have only implemented the minimum MIDP requirements. As such, many phones, such as the Motorola i85s, do not support PNG transparency. This means that an image will appear with a blockish border around it, such as the bottommost sprite in Figure 15.3. This effect will look especially odd when two sprites overlap. The nontransparent corner of one sprite will paint over another sprite, slicing bits of it off.

Luckily, there are several means of achieving transparency so that an image appears more realistic, as with the topmost smiley face in Figure 15.3:

- Sprites can be drawn with primitive drawing methods.

- Sprites can be drawn with smaller image chunks.

- Sprites can be drawn into precise, clipped areas.

### Drawing by Pixels

If your sprite is simplistic, there's no need to use a PNG file at all. Instead, you can create the image using MIDP primitive methods such as drawLine(), drawRect(), fillRect(), and so on.

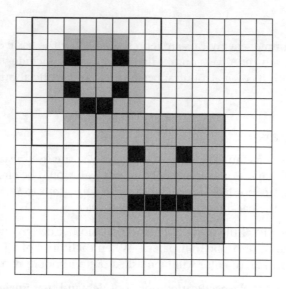

*FIGURE 15.3*    Without image transparency.

Drawing primitives is also much faster than rendering a PNG using drawImage().
However, there are also weaknesses to this approach:

- If your image gets complicated, you might need to use tons of drawing
  methods. This produces larger source code and execution code, resulting in a
  larger JAR file size.

- Because PNG images are not used in this approach, all image design must be
  done by a Java programmer, who must be artistic enough to plot every pixel
  within the source code. A game artist will not be able to design and easily
  tweak images.

  In theory, you could get around this problem by creating a tool to convert a
  PNG image or any other array of bits into a set of drawLine() calls. However,
  this would involve lots of extra work.

- Although primitive graphical methods, in general, are faster then drawImage(),
  calling dozens of primitive methods can be very slow.

In Listing 15.6, the Player class draws its car one line at a time using the drawLine()
method. By calling other methods, the number of code lines can be significantly
reduced. All coordinates are based on the (x, y) position of the sprite. The car
appears in Figure 15.4.

FIGURE 15.4    Drawing a car using primitives.

LISTING 15.6    Creating a Car Using Primitives

```
public void paint(Graphics g)
{
  g.drawLine(x + 2, y + 1, x + 2, y + 3);
  g.drawLine(x + 7, y + 1, x + 7, y + 3);
  g.drawLine(x + 3, y + 2, x + 6, y + 2);
  g.drawLine(x + 4, y + 3, x + 4, y + 5);
  g.drawLine(x + 5, y + 3, x + 5, y + 5);
  g.drawLine(x + 3, y + 6, x + 3, y + 10);
  g.drawLine(x + 6, y + 6, x + 6, y + 10);
  g.drawLine(x + 4, y + 7, x + 4, y + 8);
  g.drawLine(x + 5, y + 7, x + 5, y + 8);
  g.drawLine(x + 2, y + 11, x + 2, y + 11);
  g.drawLine(x + 7, y + 11, x + 7, y + 11);
  g.drawLine(x + 3, y + 12, x + 6, y + 12);
  g.drawLine(x, y + 9, x, y + 13);
  g.drawLine(x + 1, y + 9, x + 1, y + 13);
  g.drawLine(x + 8, y + 9, x + 8, y + 13);
  g.drawLine(x + 9, y + 9, x + 9, y + 13);
}
```

## Drawing a Sprite's Chunks

Another means of achieving transparency is to separate the image into a few image chunks. Each chunk would be rectangular, but they could be combined together to form a nonrectangular graphical object.

To create this, your game artist will need to draw images for sprites and later split the images into many small rectangulars. You will then need to position these rectangles relative to each other to "put them together" in the way the artist intended.

This approach works if you have a small amount of chunks and a relatively rectangular-shaped object, such as with the simplistic car in our racing game. However, this approach makes it very hard to draw circular objects.

## Implementation of Image Transparency

The last approach involves clipping each rectangular part of the image, then drawing the image on the screen. This is similar to the previous approach, except the work of dividing up the image into rectangular components is done programmatically, rather than by an artist.

Listing 15.7 shows a way to define an unlimited number of rectangular clipped areas using a two-dimensional array of integers that holds each rectangle's (x, y) position as well as its width and height.

*LISTING 15.7*    Using Many Clipping Rectangles

```
protected int areas[][] = {{2, 1, 6, 3}, {3, 4, 4, 5},
    {0, 9, 10, 14}};


public void paint(Graphics g)
{
  for (int i = 0; i < areas.length; i++)
  {
    g.setClip(areas[i][0], areas[i][1], areas[i][2],
        areas[i][3]);
    g.drawImage(image, x - frame * width, y,
        Graphics.TOP | Graphics.LEFT);
  }
  g.setClip(0, 0, Cache.width, Cache.height);
}
```

In this case, the image is drawn three separate times, and three separate clipping rectangles are created. This method takes more than three times as long as drawing a plain, nontransparent image.

## Summary

We now have a `Sprite` class, a good basis for creating the rest of our game. But we're still dealing with some severe limitations—we need a way to download images over the network, a way for the game to handle and keep track of all our sprites, and a way to achieve better collision detection. All these techniques, and more, will be discussed in the next chapter.

# 16

# Managing Your Sprites

**IN THIS CHAPTER**

- Networked Game Components

- Advanced Collision Detection

- The Sprite Manager

This chapter shows you how to create a sprite manager. The SpriteManager class is an important part of any game, acting as a container in which to add sprites. This makes it easy to retrieve, manipulate, move, and draw groups of sprites.

This chapter will also cover advanced sprite techniques, such as retrieving images from the network, and creating more advanced collision detection to make games more accurate and realistic.

## Networked Game Components

A game does not only consist of the code. Rather, the game code is usually just an engine that loads up all sorts of other data and manipulates it.

Because most mobile devices place severe limitations on the size of JAR files, it makes a whole lot of sense to retrieve game components separately, over the network. In fact, this might be part of your game's business model: You might give away the first level, but then charge players to download further levels. Each level could come with its own sounds and audio.

A typical game includes the following:

- Images—Different mobile devices can handle differ-ent types of images. Some devices have large color screens. Others only have tiny black and white displays. By retrieving your files over the network, you can grab optimized images that are appropriate for the device being used.

- Sounds—Audio files are currently not supported by MIDP. Some extension profiles, however, such as the Siemens Game API and the DoCoMo iAppli API support audio files. Eventually, it might even be possible to stream MP3 files over the network. For more information, check out Chapter 22, "iAppli: Micro Java with a Twist," and Chapter 23, "Siemens Game API."

- Levels, missions, or tracks—Some mobile devices such as the Siemens SL45i store applications on multimedia memory cards. This is a great plus for users, because they can store a few thousand applications on each card. However, this portability has a downside for the game developer. A user can easily upload a commercial game from a memory card onto a personal computer, then illegally distribute the game to other users. To solve this problem, you can distribute your game without any levels. Each level must then be downloaded over the network separately. Each download can be monitored and charged.

The process of downloading any of these data types is similar:

1. Connect to a server.

2. Download the image, audio, or game level as a byte array.

3. Convert it into the format your game requires.

## Downloading Images

Listing 16.1 shows how to load images over a network. Because every MIDP phone supports the HTTP protocol, simply place your images on any public Web server. When your application starts, it connects to the server and grabs the needed images.

*LISTING 16.1*    Loading Images from Afar

```
public static Image carImage;
static
{
  try
  {
    carImage = loadImage(
        "http://www.foo.com/images/car.png");
  } catch (Exception ex) {}
}

public static Image loadImage(String url)
{
  byte buffer[] = null;
  try
  {
    HttpConnection conn = (HttpConnection)
```

***LISTING 16.1***   continued

```
      Connector.open(url);
  try
  {
    int length = (int)conn.getLength();
    buffer = new byte[length];
    DataInputStream in = conn.openDataInputStream();
    in.read(buffer);
    in.close();
    return Image.createImage(buffer, 0,
        buffer.length);
  }
  finally
  {
    conn.close();
  }
  }
  catch (Exception ex) {}
  return null;
}
```

The `loadImage()` method is relatively simple: An HTTP connection to a Web server is created. The server returns the length of the image. A byte array of that length is then created, and the image is downloaded into the array. This array is then passed into the `Image.createImage()` method, and a new Java image is returned.

More information about the `Connector` class can be found in Chapter 20, "Connecting Out: Wireless Networking."

## Downloading Other Media Types

Grabbing other media types can work in a similar fashion. Pretty much every API allows you to construct sounds, images, or other objects using a simple byte array.

When you create your game components, be sure to write a game engine or level editor that can input and output byte arrays as necessary. Ideally, your entire game state should be able to be compressed into a byte array.

Additionally, your images and other multimedia can be saved onto the device's storage memory for future games. Chapter 19, "Be Persistent: MIDP Data Storage," shows you how to achieve this.

## Advanced Collision Detection

In the previous chapter we talked about a way of detecting sprite collision using overlapping rectangles. This type of collision detection is very inaccurate. For instance, if the transparent corners of a ball sprite touch the corners of another ball sprite, your game will think they have collided. The player, however, will see two balls move past each other without touching. Luckily, there are several advanced detection techniques that can be used to eliminate this problem:

- Collision detection with multiple levels—A sprite is divided into different areas, called *levels*. The largest area is called the *root level*, and has no parent. Every other level can contain other levels, and also lies within a parent level. This enables you to create various zones within your sprite. For example, you will be able to tell when a missile hits the side, edge, or center of an enemy barracks. Or, if you just need to know whether the sprite was hit at all, you merely look at the parent level.

- Collision detection with multiple areas—A nonrectangular sprite is divided into different rectangular parts. Detection within each of these small rectangles occurs separately.

- Bitmasked collision detection—This involves two images: The original sprite image and a sprite mask. The mask image is a two-colored (black and white) bitmap, wherein the white color represents the presence of the sprite, and the black color its absence. This approach is the most accurate, but also the slowest.

Each of the above solutions will be discussed in the following sections.

### Solution 1: Multiple Levels

Figure 16.1 shows how the image of a ball can be separated into two levels. The larger rectangle surrounds the entire ball. The smaller rectangle, which is a child of the larger rectangle, denotes the center of the ball. When a collision occurs, the game is told which level was hit.

Each level is represented by a quadruplet that holds the upper-left coordinate (x, y) of the area, as well as the width and height. In Listing 16.2 the quadruplets are hard-coded, but they could just as easily have been provided as parameters in the Sprite's constructor.

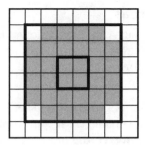

*FIGURE 16.1*   Multiple levels of collision.

*LISTING 16.2*   Creating Collision Levels

```
protected int areas[][] = {{0, 0, 10, 14},
    {3, 2, 4, 11}};

public int collide(Sprite sprite)
{
  for (int i = 0; i < areas.length; i++)
  {
    if ((areas[i][0] + areas[i][2]) > sprite.getX() &&
        areas[i][0] < sprite.getX() &&
        (areas[i][1] + areas[i][3]) > sprite.getY() &&
        areas[i][1] < sprite.getY())
            return i;
  }
  return -1;
}
```

The code presumes that levels in the array are presented in order from the outer area
to the inner one. The collide() method tests whether a given sprite has collided
with a specific area. The method returns an integer value that represents the level
number. The root level has a value 0. If there is no collision, the value -1 is returned.
This can let you know whether a sprite has hit the outer edge of another sprite, or
the direct center. You can then react accordingly.

The example shows how basic area detection can occur. In reality, you would need to
check each area of one sprite against each area of another sprite. If one sprite has *m*
areas, and the other one has *n* areas, the game would need to make *m×n* comparisons
for one collision. That can slow down your game considerably.

## Solution 2: Multiple Areas

Any digital nonrectangular image can be partitioned into a finite number of rectangular parts. For example, the circle in Figure 16.2 has been divided into three rectangles. If your image has any extra pixels along its edges, they can be divided into a rectangle that is only 1 pixel square.

When your program tries to detect whether two sprites have collided, it can check every rectangle of one sprite against every rectangle of another. This type of collision detection is 100% accurate. However, the more rectangles your sprite is made up of, the more checking iterations there are that must be performed.

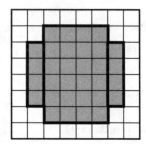

*FIGURE 16.2*   Multiple areas of collision.

Area collision detection can be implemented similarly to level detection. Simply create an array of quadruplets (x, y, width and height), as in Listing 16.3.

*LISTING 16.3*   Creating Collision Areas

```
protected int areas[][] = {{2, 1, 6, 3}, {3, 4, 4, 5},
    {0, 9, 10, 14}};

public boolean collide(Sprite sprite)
{
  for (int i = 0; i < areas.length; i++)
  {
    if ((areas[i][0] + areas[i][2]) > sprite.getX() &&
        areas[i][0] < sprite.getX() &&
        (areas[i][1] + areas[i][3]) > sprite.getY() &&
        areas[i][1] < sprite.getY())
            return true;
  }
  return false;
}
```

The collide() method returns true if at least one of the parts collide with another sprite.

When you actually build your game, you should experiment with various types of collision detection and various numbers of areas. Because current Java devices are quite slow, you might want to limit your sprites to one or two areas at most.

## The Sprite Manager

A sprite manager's main jobs are to manage a list of different sprites and to provide the capability to manipulate those sprites.

When defining the manager, the following methods should be implemented:

- addSprite(Sprite sprite)—Adds a new sprite into the manager at the end of the list.

- insertSprite(Sprite sprite, int position)—Adds a new sprite into the manager at the given position.

- getSpritePosition(Sprite sprite)—Returns the sprite's position number associated to the given sprite. The first sprite is at the position 0. The value -1 is returned if the sprite was not found.

- getSprite(int index)—Returns the sprite associated with the given index.

- deleteSprite(Sprite sprite)—Deletes the given sprite from the manager.

- deleteSprite(int position)—Deletes a sprite from the given position from the manager.

- paint(Graphics g)—Draws all the sprites onto the given Graphics object. The sprites are drawn in order from 0 to getLength()-1.

- size()—Returns the number of sprites in the manager.

Listing 16.4 shows the implementation of the SpriteManager class, using all the preceding methods.

*LISTING 16.4*   The SpriteManager Class

```
import java.util.*;
import javax.microedition.lcdui.*;

public class SpriteManager
{
  private Vector list;
```

**LISTING 16.4**   continued

```java
public SpriteManager()
{
  list = new Vector();
}

public void addSprite(Sprite sprite)
{
  list.addElement(sprite);
}

public void insertSprite(Sprite sprite, int position)
{
  list.insertElementAt(sprite, position);
}

public int getSpritePosition(Sprite sprite)
{
  for (int i = 0; i < list.size(); i++)
  {
    Sprite comparableSprite = (Sprite)list.elementAt(i);
    if (sprite.equals(comparableSprite))
        return i;
  }
  return -1;
}

public Sprite getSprite(int index)
{
  return (Sprite)list.elementAt(index);
}

public void deleteSprite(Sprite sprite)
{
  deleteSprite(getSpritePosition(sprite));
}

public void deleteSprite(int position)
{
  list.removeElementAt(position);
}
```

*LISTING 16.4*   continued

```java
public int size()
{
  return list.size();
}

public void paint(Graphics g)
{
  for (int i = 0; i < list.size(); i++)
  {
    Sprite sprite = (Sprite)list.elementAt(i);
    sprite.paint(g);
  }
}
}
```

The manager uses a Vector object for storing sprites. If sprites need to have unique IDs, Vector could be replaced with Hashtable. Your game can use several managers to hold each group of sprites. For example, you might want to organize things so that you have one manager for opponent vehicles, one for obstacles, one for background elements, and so on.

Sprites are always added at the end of the list. All searches are linear, and are fast enough for small amount of sprites. For larger games, you can implement more advanced search mechanisms such as sorting via binary trees. The paint() method simply draws all the sprites in the list in order as they're put in the list.

## Drawing Optimizations

Look closely at the paint() method in Listing 16.4. The SpriteManager class is drawing sprite images, even if they are located beyond the bounds of the current screen. This will slow down the game, because a huge number of unnecessary actions are invoked. Your game might have hundreds of sprites in memory, but only one or two drawn on the screen at any given time. Instead, painting should be done as in Listing 16.5.

*LISTING 16.5*   Improved Painting

```java
import java.util.*;
import javax.microedition.lcdui.*;
```

*LISTING 16.5*   continued

```java
public class SpriteManager
{
  private Vector list;
  private int width;
  private int height;

  public SpriteManager(int width, int height)
  {
    this.width = width;
    this.height = height;
    list = new Vector();
  }

  public void paint(Graphics g)
  {
    for (int i = 0; i < list.size(); i++)
    {
      Sprite sprite = (Sprite)list.elementAt(i);
      if ((sprite.getX() + sprite.getWidth() > 0) &&
          (sprite.getX() < width) &&
          (sprite.getY() + sprite.getHeight() > 0) &&
          (sprite.getY() < height))
          sprite.paint(g);
    }
  }
  ...
}
```

The sprite manager stores the values of the screen's width and height. Both values are very important, because they represent boundaries. The paint() method walks through the manager's sprite list and checks whether each sprite lies inside the screen.

## Enhancing Sprite Collision

To apply the sprite manager to our Micro Racer game, you can create one SpriteManager group for all the enemy cars. You can then figure out whether your player sprite has collided with an enemy by creating collision detection within the SpriteManager class, as illustrated in Listing 16.6.

**LISTING 16.6**   Adding Collision Detection

```
public boolean collide(Sprite sprite)
{
  for (int i = 0; i < list.size(); i++)
  {
    Sprite comparableSprite = (Sprite)list.elementAt(i);
    if (sprite.collide(comparableSprite))
        return true;
  }
  return false;
}
```

The `collide()` method checks whether the player sprite (which should be passed in as a parameter) has collided with any of the enemy sprites. If there is a collision, the method returns `true`.

Moving through the list with a larger number of sprites can significantly slow down the game. One possible optimization would be to put the sprites in a correct order within the list, and only check the sprites that are on the screen. The ones that are offscreen could never collide with the player sprite.

## Summary

Now we're getting someplace! We have a fully functional game with a hero, a group of enemies, and a means of figuring out whether any fender-benders have occurred. However, the game is still pretty simplistic. After all, none of our sprites are actually moving yet! The next chapter finally makes sprites spritely, showing you how to actually animate and move them around within a game loop.

# 17

# Sprite Movement

**IN THIS CHAPTER**

- Floating-Point in J2ME
- Game Initialization
- Movement
- Piecing It All Together

So far, we've managed to create a bunch of sprites and draw them on the screen. But we're not painting a still life here; we're programming a game!

To make a game a game, it must read input events from the keyboard or the screen and move sprites accordingly. The game must also set up initial conditions, check controls for game operability, and provide artificial intelligence for computer-controlled characters or game moves.

## Floating-Point in J2ME

Before we get too excited, though, there's one thing we're going to have to get out of the way: MIDP does not support floating-point math.

Why is floating-point math important for games? Imagine a game hero that can move in different directions, such as the enemy cars in our Micro Racer game. You'll want the cars to move at a constant speed, regardless of which direction the sprite is moving. To create this type of smooth movement, you would use a pair of simple trigonometric formulas:

```
Vx = V * cos(tau)
```

and

```
Vy = V * sin(tau)
```

where `tau` is an angle starting at the 3 o'clock position and increasing counterclockwise, as illustrated in Figure 17.1.

Unfortunately, the results of these formulas are going to involve decimal places. If you round things off, movement becomes nonlinear.

Additionally, 3D games are becoming very popular. It's conceivable that 3D engines, or *isometric* engines (games that simulate depth of scene, such as the view of a maze by peeking over its outer wall), will soon be feasible on smaller devices. In order to transform 3D polygons and draw 3D worlds, accurate linear algebra and trigonometric functions are imperative. This involves precise floating-point support.

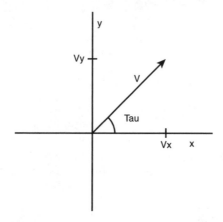

*FIGURE 17.1.*   Velocity components.

## Cheating the System

Even if your target device doesn't support floating-point numbers, you can easily develop your own floating-point library, or even buy it from software companies specializing in such libraries.

When developing a floating-point math library, there are a few questions to be answered:

- Should the floating-point library be based on IEEE or fixed-point arithmetic?

- What is the level of precision that the game needs?

- How fast is the target device?

The IEEE standard enables you to implement 32-, 64-, or higher-bit floating-point numbers, and to perform arithmetic on them. However, this standard is very difficult to implement and requires a lot of memory.

A more simplistic solution is to use fixed-point arithmetic, directly mapping floating-point numbers to integers. We will just imagine a decimal point between the third and fourth digits.

The weakness of using fixed-point arithmetic is that you are limited in how many decimal spots you can use after the floating point. However, the precision is generally good enough to suit the needs of sprite movement.

To achieve the best precision, you should use a long integer, because it is the largest numerical format in the Java language. Long integers offer 64 bits for floating-point number representation.

Because most devices have small screens and relatively coarse sprite movement, most sprite math usually involves real numbers in the range between 0.001 and 1000.000. Because you'll need four digits to represent 1.000, its integer value would be 1000. Further, the integer value of 1000.000 would be 1000000.

Our custom floating-point library must also implement common mathematical functions. For example, the trigonometric sine function can be calculated using an interactive formula. This approach is very precise if a high enough number of iterations are performed. Unfortunately, it is difficult to predict how many loops are needed to calculate sine with precision, and each loop eats up precious time.

A much faster approach is to use pre-calculated value tables (a list of values) for each function. The table for sine can have the results for angle values of 0, 10, 20, and so on, all the way to 90°. If a game needs to find the sine of 6°, the library uses linear interpolation to calculate it based on neighboring results. The more values that are in the table, the more precise results can be. More precision can also be achieved by interpolating through more points. Listing 17.1 implements a basic floating-point library for J2ME.

**LISTING 17.1**    The Float Class

```
public class Float
{
  // The value of the number 1.
  public static final long VALUE_ONE = 1000;

  // The value of PI, to three decimal places.
  public static final long PI = 3142;

  // A sine table with 10 values.
  private static final long SIN_TABLE[] =
  {
    0, 173, 342, 500, 643, 766, 866, 940, 985, 1000
  };

  // A cosine table with 10 values.
  private static final long COS_TABLE[] =
```

**LISTING 17.1**   continued

```java
{
  1000, 985, 940, 866, 766, 643, 500, 342, 173, 0
};

private Float() {}

// Create a float from a round integer.
public static long createFloat(long integer)
{
  if (integer > Long.MAX_VALUE / Float.VALUE_ONE)
      throw new RuntimeException(
          "Integer too large.");
  return integer * Float.VALUE_ONE;
}

// Create a float from a round integer and a decimal fraction.
public static long createFloat(long integer,
    long fraction)
{
  if (integer > Long.MAX_VALUE / Float.VALUE_ONE)
      throw new RuntimeException(
          "Integer too large.");
  if (fraction > Float.VALUE_ONE - 1)
      throw new RuntimeException("Fraction too large.");
  return integer * Float.VALUE_ONE + fraction;
}

// Get the integer value.
public static long getInteger(long value)
{
  return value / Float.VALUE_ONE;
}

// Get the decimal fraction value.
public static long getFraction(long value)
{
  return value % Float.VALUE_ONE;
}

// Add two floats.
public static long add(long value1, long value2)
{
```

**LISTING 17.1**   continued

```
    return value1 + value2;
  }

  // Subtract two floats.
  public static long sub(long value1, long value2)
  {
    return value1 - value2;
  }

  // Multiply two floats.
  public static long mul(long value1, long value2)
  {
    return value1 * value2 / Float.VALUE_ONE;
  }

  // Divide two floats.
  public static long div(long value1, long value2)
  {
    return value1 * Float.VALUE_ONE / value2;
  }

  // Get the inverse of a float.
  public static long inv(long value)
  {
    return Float.div(Float.VALUE_ONE, value);
  }

  // Get the absolute value of a float.
  public static long abs(long value)
  {
    if (value < 0)
      value = - value;
    return value;
  }

  // Get the sign of a float.
  public static long sign(long value)
  {
    return (value < 0 ? -1 : 1);
  }
```

*LISTING 17.1*    continued

```
// Perform the sine function on a float.
public static long sin(long value)
{
  value = value % Float.createFloat(360);
  long sign = 1;
  if (value > Float.createFloat(180))
  {
    value = value - Float.createFloat(360);
    sign = -1;
  }
  long abs = Float.abs(value);
  if (abs > Float.createFloat(90))
      abs = Float.createFloat(180) - abs;
  if (abs == Float.createFloat(90))
      return Float.createFloat(1);
  if (abs == Float.createFloat(0))
      return Float.createFloat(0);
  int x1 = (int)Float.getInteger(Float.div(abs,
      Float.createFloat(10)));
  int x2 = x1 + 1;
  long y1 = SIN_TABLE[x1];
  long y2 = SIN_TABLE[x2];
  long k = Float.div(Float.sub(y2, y1),
      Float.sub(x2, x1));
  return sign * Float.add(y1,
      Float.mul(k, Float.sub(abs, x1)));
}

// Perform the cosine function on a float.
public static long cos(long value)
{
  value = value % Float.createFloat(360);
  long sign = -1;
  if (value > Float.createFloat(180))
  {
    value = value - Float.createFloat(360);
  }
  if (value >= Float.createFloat(-90) &&
      value <= Float.createFloat(90))
  sign = 1;
  long abs = Float.abs(value);
```

**LISTING 17.1**   continued

```
    if (abs > Float.createFloat(90))
        abs = Float.createFloat(180) - abs;
    if (abs == Float.createFloat(90))
        return Float.createFloat(0);
    if (abs == Float.createFloat(0))
        return Float.createFloat(1);
    int x1 = (int)Float.getInteger(
        Float.div(abs, Float.createFloat(10)));
    int x2 = x1 + 1;
    long y1 = COS_TABLE[x1];
    long y2 = COS_TABLE[x2];
    long k = Float.div(Float.sub(y2, y1),
        Float.sub(x2, x1));
    return sign * Float.add(y1,
        Float.mul(k, Float.sub(abs, x1)));
}


// Perform the tangent function on a float.
public static long tan(long value)
{
    return Float.div(Float.sin(value), Float.cos(value));
}


// Convert a value from radians to degrees.
public static long toDeg(long value)
{
    return Float.div(Float.mul(
        value, Float.createFloat(180)), Float.PI);
}


// Convert a value from degrees to radians.
public static long toRad(long value)
{
    return Float.div(Float.mul(value, Float.PI),
        Float.createFloat(180));
}
}
```

Listing 17.1 creates a library that isn't complete, but offers enough functionality to move sprites in a game. All functions are static, enabling any other class to easily access the methods.

The float value is represented as a long integer. You must carefully keep track of numbers you use in the game—some long integers will actually be floating-point numbers.

The constant VALUE_ONE represents the number 1.0, and the number of zeros shows how many decimal places are reserved after the decimal point. You can change this value to offer different levels of precision. By increasing the constant, the maximum float value decreases.

Some values in mathematical libraries are represented as constants. The most commonly used constants are *pi* ($\pi$) and *E*. Because the game needs only trigonometric functions, the constant *E* is not needed. *Pi* has the value 3.142 to provide the highest precision possible with three decimal places after the decimal point.

A floating-point number can be created with two createFloat() methods. One method accepts just an integer value, and the other accepts an additional fraction part. If method parameters exceed the maximum value, an exception is thrown. To retrieve the integer part of a floating number, your game can call the getInteger() method. To retrieve the fraction part, call the getFraction() method.

Addition and subtraction are done in the traditional way. When multiplying, however, the result must be divided with the VALUE_ONE constant at the end to keep the result at the same decimal point precision. During division, the result is multiplied by VALUE_ONE to keep the same decimal point precision. To avoid additional precision losses, the numbers must be multiplied before dividing them.

There are also two tables in the code with results for major angles of sine and cosine. Both tables can be easily merged because they are mirrored. However, it is sometimes quicker to have more tables and less execution code.

## Game Initialization

Now we're almost ready to move some sprites.

First off, however, each sprite's initial condition must be set. Sprites must be placed at their starting positions and given initial values (for example, level of energy, x velocity, y velocity, and so on). If your game contains a timer, it should be reset. When your game is over, the initial conditions should be set once again.

Listing 17.2 expands Micro Racer's GameCanvas class to initialize the player sprite as well as the enemy sprites.

**LISTING 17.2**    Initializing It All

```
private SpriteManager enemyList;
private int length;

public GameCanvas()
{
  Cache.width = getWidth();
  Cache.height = getHeight();
  try
  {
    player = new Player(Cache.carImage,
        Cache.carImage.getWidth(),
        Cache.carImage.getHeight(), 1, INIT_ENERGY);
    // Place the player in the center of the screen
    player.setX(Float.createFloat((Cache.width -
        player.getWidth()) / 2));
    // Place the player at the very bottom
    player.setY(Float.createFloat(Cache.height -
        player.getHeight()));
    player.setVisible(true);
  } catch (Exception ex) {}
}

public void initEnemies()
{
  enemyList = new SpriteManager(Cache.width,
      Cache.height);
  int size = length / Cache.height - 1;
  Random rnd = new Random();
  // Create "size" enemies.
  for (int i = 1; i <= size; i++)
  {
    try
    {
      Sprite sprite = new Sprite(Cache.enemyImage,
          Cache.enemyImage.getWidth(),
          Cache.enemyImage.getHeight(), 1);
      // Set the X position of the sprite randomly
      int x = rnd.nextInt() % (ROAD_WIDTH -
          Cache.enemyImage.getWidth());
      x = (x < 0 ? -x : x);
      sprite.setX(Float.createFloat((Cache.width -
```

*LISTING 17.2*    continued

```
        ROAD_WIDTH) / 2 + x));
    // Scatter the sprites around the at various Y positions
    sprite.setY(Float.createFloat(- i *
        Cache.height));
    // Set the downward velocity to "speed"
    sprite.setVy(speed);
    enemyList.addSprite(sprite);
  } catch (Exception ex) {}
  }
}

public void setSpeed(long speed)
{
  this.speed = speed;
}

public void setLength(int length)
{
  this.length = length;
}
```

In Listing 17.2, the player's race car is constructed and set at a default location at the bottom center. Afterwards, a sprite manager is created, and different enemy sprites are put in the list by calling the addSprite() method. The number of sprites is carefully calculated to put no more than four opponent cars on one screen at a time. The x position of each enemy is random, using the nextInt() method from Java's Random class. The x, y and velocity values are created as floating-point numbers.

## Movement

In Micro Racer, the movement of the hero sprite depends on which keys the player presses. On the other hand, the movement of enemy sprites is determined by game intelligence. Enemy movement can be accomplished in different ways:

- Predefined movement—The opponent sprites have their initial positions and velocities. These values never really change throughout the game.

- Smart movement—The opponent sprites have their initial positions. Each car's velocity (direction and speed) is determined during the course of the game. For example, an opponent basketball player could always be running toward the ball.

- Artificial intelligence (AI) movement—Opponent sprites use a custom artificial intelligence engine. This engine evaluates the history of the sprite's movement, learns from its mistakes, predicts what the player is going to do next, and defines the movement of sprites accordingly. A simple example of AI movement is in chess, where the computer can search through a tree of legal moves, calculating which combination of future moves will have the best effect—that is, avoiding traps, leading to the capture of an opponent's piece, and checkmate.

For starters, we'll keep things simple with our game. We will use predefined movement to position opponent cars randomly, keeping a reasonable number of cars on the screen at one time.

When the user selects a track to play using the Tracks form, the track's length will be set by calling the setLength() method, and the speed of enemy vehicles will be set using the setSpeed() method. In this way, each new track is more challenging than the last.

### The Movement Routine

Movement occurs by creating a special game thread. This thread will continue running as long as the game is in progress. Any game actions can be handled in this loop. We can create a game thread in Listing 17.3.

*LISTING 17.3*   Creating a Game Thread

```
public class GameThread extends Thread
{
  public void run()
  {
    while (running)
    {
      long time = System.currentTimeMillis();
      moveSprites();
      // Check collisions
      repaint();
      serviceRepaints();
      time = System.currentTimeMillis() - time;
      try
      {
        if (time < DELAY)
            Thread.sleep(DELAY - (int)time);
```

*LISTING 17.3*    continued

```
        }
        catch (Exception ex) {}
    }
  }
}
```

The moveSprite() routine, which actually handles the movement of each sprite, is detailed in Listing 17.4.

*LISTING 17.4*    Moving the Sprites

```
private void moveSprites()
{
  switch (key)
  {
    case Canvas.LEFT:
        if (Float.getInteger(player.getX()) >
            (Cache.width - ROAD_WIDTH) / 2)
            player.setX(Float.sub(player.getX(),
            Float.createFloat(2)));
        break;
    case Canvas.RIGHT:
        if (Float.getInteger(player.getX()) +
            player.getWidth() <
            (Cache.width + ROAD_WIDTH) / 2)
            player.setX(Float.add(player.getX(),
            Float.createFloat(2)));
        break;
  }
  for (int i = 0; i < enemyList.size(); i++)
  {
    Sprite sprite = enemyList.getSprite(i);
    sprite.setY(Float.add(sprite.getY(),
        sprite.getVy()));
  }
}
```

Finally, we make sure to paint all our sprites in the paint() method of GameCanvas. This can be found in Listing 17.5.

*LISTING 17.5*    Painting Sprites

```
public void paint(Graphics gr)
{
""    // All the other paint functions happen here…
  // ...
  // Then we paint the enemy list
  enemyList.paint(g);
  // And then the player...
  player.paint(g);
  // And then drop it all onto the real screen
  gr.drawImage(scene, 0, 0, Graphics.TOP |
      Graphics.LEFT);
}
```

The movement magic happens in the moveSprites() method. This method does the following:

- Move the hero sprite. The race car moves either to the left if the player is holding down the left arrow key, or to the right if the player is holding down the right arrow key. Movement occurs by adding or subtracting 2 pixels (as a floating-point number) from the vehicle's current x position. If the race car hits either side of the track, movement stops.

- Move opponent sprites. Opponent movement, for now, is pretty simple. Each enemy car is moved a set number of pixels down the screen. The enemy's current y position is increased by the enemy's current y velocity. An enemy can be slowed down or sped up by changing the y velocity value.

## Piecing It All Together

We now have all sorts of sprites moving around the game screen. All that remains now is to handle sprites when they interact, and to determine how the game ends.

### Handling Collision Detection

Whenever your car touches an enemy car, it loses some energy. That means collision detection is essential. Because our Sprite class already has collision detection routines, it's just a matter of detecting and handling collisions. A method could be created as follows:

```
private void checkCollision()
{
  if (enemyList.collide(player))
```

```
        player.setEnergy(player.getEnergy() -
            COLLIDE_ENERGY);
    if (player.getEnergy() <= 0)
        running = false;
}
```

This method checks for a collision. If one occurs, the COLLIDE_ENERGY value is deducted from the player's energy. If the energy reaches zero, then we stop running the game loop.

It's important for players to know where they stand in a game at any given time. As such, the energy value is drawn at the top of the screen at all times. We'll also let the player know how much time has passed:

```
public void paint(Graphics gr)
{
  ...
  g.drawString("E:" + player.getEnergy(), (getWidth() -
      ROAD_WIDTH) / 2 + 1, 0, Graphics.TOP |
      Graphics.LEFT);
  g.drawString("T:" + (timer / 10) + "." + (timer % 10)
      + "s", getWidth() / 2 + 1, 0, Graphics.TOP |
      Graphics.LEFT);
  ...
}
```

## Endgame: Losing or Winning

A game isn't much of a game unless you either lose or win it. In our Micro Racer game, you win if your car successfully reaches a track's finish line before losing all its energy. If your energy reaches zero, however, the game is over.

To set the finish line's location, we add this bit of code to the initEnemies() method:

```
private long line;

public void initEnemies()
{
    line = - Float.createFloat(length);
    ...
}
```

Recall that length is a global variable, which is set from the Tracks class. Each track has a different length.

The finish line can then be painted in the paint method:

```
public void paint(Graphics gr)
  {
    ...
    g.drawLine((getWidth() - ROAD_WIDTH) / 2,
        (int)Float.getInteger(line),
        (getWidth() + ROAD_WIDTH) / 2,
        (int)Float.getInteger(line));
    ...




  }
```

Finally, we'll create a method to detect whether the finish line has been crossed. If it is successfully crossed, we'll set the finished global flag to true, and stop running the game loop:


```
  private void checkFinishLine()
  {
    if (Float.getInteger(line) > Cache.height)
    {
      running = false;
      finished = true;
    }
  }
```

## The Final Game Thread

Okay, now let's piece this all together. The key is to add the appropriate methods to the GameThread loop. Listing 17.6 implements a game thread that checks for car collisions, checks whether the finish line has been crossed, increments the timer, and handles the endgame gracefully.

**LISTING 17.6**    The Final Game Loop

```
public class GameThread extends Thread
{
  public void run()
  {
    while (running)
    {
      long time = System.currentTimeMillis();
      moveSprites();
      checkCollision();
      checkFinishLine();
      timer++;
      repaint();
      serviceRepaints();
      time = System.currentTimeMillis() - time;
      try
      {
        if (time < DELAY)
            Thread.sleep(DELAY - (int)time);
      }
      catch (Exception ex) {}
    }
    if (finished)
    {
      // Tell the user the score.
      // Send the score to a high-score server..
    }
    else
    {
        // Tell the player that the game is over...
    }
    // Finally, return the the original menu form
    Display.getDisplay(midlet).setCurrent(form);
  }
}
```

Figure 17.2 shows the game in action.

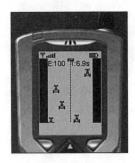

*FIGURE 17.2*   The game in action.

## Summary

And so there you have it—a fully functional game. Although it might not be on par
with *Quake* or *Tomb Raider*, Micro Racer is definitely a cute enough little action game
to play during boring business meetings. The final version of the game is far from
complete. In the remaining chapters, we'll add sounds, supercharge the game for
Siemens or NTT DoCoMo phones, store data locally, and even add a multiplayer-
networking component.

# 18

# J2ME Audio Basics

**IN THIS CHAPTER**

• Sounds Are (Barely) Possible!

Blockbuster games combine a rich story, beautiful graphics, smooth playability, mood-inducing background music, and startling sound effects. Mobile game designers must get used to working around severe limitations on all of these elements. But of all the sacrifices a MIDP developer must make, no other component is quite as inadequate as music and audio effects. MIDP sound support is virtually nil.

That being said, many phone operators are beginning to introduce extension APIs with excellent sound capabilities. Check out Chapter 23 for a full overview of the Siemens API.

## Sounds Are (Barely) Possible!

Most early MIDP devices were not originally intended as gameplaying or digital entertainment machines. While it may seem ironic that a telephone doesn't come with built-in audio hardware, that is sadly often the case.

The latest batch of phones and other devices, however, are much more impressive. Many phones now have the capability to play fancy ring-tones, chirpy sound effects, and even MP3 music files.

Even the simplest phone, however, usually has the capability to emit a few simple beeps and blips. These sounds are triggered as part of the phone's user interface—whenever you select a menu option, whenever an alert dialog pops up, or if an alarm is triggered.

MIDP allows you to use its Alert class to invoke simple system sounds. The Alert class, discussed in Chapter 13, "High-Level Graphical Interfaces," is used when a game needs to display an important dialog box notification. Alerts are typically used to present information about the game, such as instructions, credits, and so on. Sometimes an alert box will pop up as a gameplay warning, or even as a user-friendly way of catching a programming error.

MIDP lets you define various types of alerts using the AlertType class. Some phones attach unique sound effects to each of these alert types.

These types are

- Information—Communicates some sort of non-crucial data to the player. The associated sound is usually very short and subtle. This sound can be played several times throughout the cycle of a game to express some sort of common game event.

- Confirmation—Confirms a user's actions. The associated sound is usually succinct but noticeable.

- Warning—Warns the user about a potentially dangerous operation. The sound is often sharp and of a long duration. In general, it makes sense to play a warning sound during major game events, such as when the character is about to die or when the game is over.

- Alarm—A very noticeable sound intended to alert the user about a predefined event. Alarm sounds can last for a very long time. Games should use such a sound rarely.

- Error—Alerts the user that something erroneous or problematic has just occurred. The associated sound is generally short but grating and negative.

The AlertType—class doesn't have any public constructor. To use it, you can grab one of five static objects: AlertType.INFO, AlertType.CONFIRMATION, AlertType.WARNING, AlertType.ALARM and AlertType.ERROR. Each of these objects only has one method: playSound(), which plays the defined alert sound. The method takes an instance of the Display class as a parameter.

For example, if we wanted to spice up the car game we have been developing, we can add a short sound effect (Info) whenever the user collides with another car; a blaring horn (Error) when the car's energy drops to zero, and a long wail (Alarm) when the game is over.

Listing 18.1 shows a modified version of the checkCollision() and checkFinishLine() methods.

**LISTING 18.1**   Modified Versions of `checkCollision()` and `checkFinishLine()` Methods

```
private void checkCollision()
{
  if (enemyList.collide(player))
  {
    player.setEnergy(player.getEnergy() -
        COLLIDE_ENERGY);
    AlertType.INFO.playSound(Display.getDisplay(
        midlet));
  }
  if (player.getEnergy() <= 0)
  {
    running = false;
    AlertType.ERROR.playSound(Display.getDisplay(
        midlet));
  }
}

private void checkFinishLine()
{
  if (Float.getInteger(line) > Cache.height)
  {
    running = false;
    finished = true;
    AlertType.ALARM.playSound(Display.getDisplay(
        midlet));
  }
}
```

## Summary

Unfortunately, the sound capabilities of today's Micro Java devices leave a lot to be desired. Future versions of MIDP will definitely focus much more on rich and varied effects, background music, and other audio features.

In the meantime, there are many vendor-specific extensions by companies like Siemens enabling more impressive grooves.

# 19

**IN THIS CHAPTER**

- RecordStore Overview

- RecordStore in Practice

- More RecordStore Joy

# Be Persistent: MIDP Data Storage

So, now we've got some data we'd like to store persistently on our J2ME device—the images for the car's weapons. By storing these directly on the device, we don't have to download them every time the MIDlet fires up. Fine, but how do you do it across so many diverse devices, most of which are without hard drives or even file systems?

As with most things in the J2ME scheme of things, data storage is in the mix, but it's rather different than you might be used to, and requires a little limited-device common-sense to use effectively and efficiently.

To take advantage of J2ME's data access capabilities, we'll need to make use of the classes and interfaces in a core MIDP package we haven't yet touched, the javax.microedition.rms package. (The "rms" acronym stands for Record Management System.) This package's RecordStore class is our key to data storage and handling.

## RecordStore **Overview**

Before we dive into coding, let's take a look at RecordStore's quirks and limitations. Here's what the class javadocs say:

> "…A record store consists of a collection of records which will remain persistent across multiple invocations of the MIDlet. The platform is responsible for making its best effort to maintain the integrity of the MIDlet's record stores throughout the normal use of the platform, including reboots, battery changes, etc."

It's worth paying attention to that last bit—the platform will make "its best effort" to keep persistent data safe and sound. For the most part, we can assume that any given device will follow through, but we'll really need to account for the possibility that the storage might get wiped, and that we'll need to rebuild it if it's not found.

Working with a `RecordStore` is rather like working with a database, or with a `RandomAccessFile` from J2SE's `java.io` package. You create and access a `RecordStore` using a unique `String` ID (up to 32 Unicode characters long), and you can then add, read, set, or delete individual records of data within it. There are a bevy of new exceptions to handle with a `RecordStore`, which we'll touch on later.

A `RecordStore` is associated only with the MIDlet suite that created it. Any `RecordStore` created by any MIDlet within a suite is available to all other MIDlets in the same suite. However, you can't access a `RecordStore` in another suite.

When you add a new piece of data to a `RecordStore`, it's added via the `addRecord()` method, which returns a unique `recordId` `int` primitive that can be used to access the same record later on. The `recordId` is guaranteed to start at 1 for the first record of a new `RecordStore`, and will increment by one for each record subsequently added to it.

This `recordId` number increments *absolutely*, regardless of any record deletions. In other words, if you add three records to a new `RecordStore` upon creating it, their `recordId`s will be 1, 2, and 3 in the order in which they were added. If you then delete the second record and add an entirely new one, the `recordId`s will be 1, 3, and 4. Bearing this in mind, we'll use this behavior to our advantage to keep track of our images consistently—if perhaps inflexibly—although we'll hint at how to handle records in a more arbitrary fashion toward the end of the chapter (using a `RecordEnumeration`).

Data is stored and retrieved to and from individual records only as byte arrays, and so must be packed into byte arrays for storage, then unpacked to rebuild and use as needed by the MIDlet. We'll build some methods for doing this simply with our data.

The amount of `RecordStore` storage space depends wholly upon the device, and is generally shared with the MIDlet storage. In other words, don't believe you've got megabytes of memory to dump data into. You might only have some tens of kilobytes, if even that. Keep only what you need, and clear out what you don't. So, when the car's images need to change, we'll completely replace the older data with the new stuff.

Likewise, there's no guarantee that data access *speed* will be anything remarkable. Don't worry too much: accessing an individual record will likely only take a few milliseconds, but it may very well be *much* slower than using normal Java variable objects on the VM's memory heap. Furthermore, for many devices (for example,

Palm Pilots), writing to memory storage is often considerably slower than reading from it, usually because of well-considered memory-locking and security.

The key here for us is that the data is persistent across "multiple invocations of the MIDlet." This is RecordStore's best use, instead of storing and retrieving data on the fly during a MIDlet's normal operation. The rule of thumb is that for any data which *should* be persistent, it should be moved from normal runtime variables into the RecordStore before the MIDlet shuts down. The MIDlet should then unpack the record data into those variables when it starts up again.

Finally, a RecordStore is thread-safe. It is synchronized so that only a single running thread can access a record at a time. Remember, it's still up to the developer to make sure that, if there are multiple threads in a given MIDlet that may potentially access the same record, that they do so with some intelligence. In other words, if one thread adds records to a store and a second thread only retrieves records, the second one should be smart enough not to retrieve a particular record until the first thread has actually added it.

Those are the basic ups and downs of RecordStores, so now let's see what they can do!

## RecordStore **in Practice**

A RecordStore isn't built via a constructor like most other objects; rather, it's effectively requested from the client device via a static method call:

```
RecordStore openRecordStore(String recordName, boolean createIfNecessary)
```

If a RecordStore specified by the recordName argument exists on the device, it's found and returned. If it doesn't exist and the createIfNecessary Boolean argument is true, a new RecordStore is built and returned. If an exception is thrown, it might not exist, or the device might not be able to create any new RecordStores (possibly not enough spare memory). Other useful RecordStore methods available are described in the following sections.

### addRecord()

```
int addRecord(byte[] data, int offset, int numBytes)
```

This is the single method used to add new data to a RecordStore. The data *must* be handled as a byte array, and will be stored in the new record as such. You can specify the offset index in the data array and the number of bytes to actually store. If successfully added (without generating an exception), the method will return the recordId int for the new record. Because this is a write operation, the RecordStore is blocked to all other accesses until the record is fully written and added successfully.

### getRecord()

getRecord(int recordId)

This returns a copy of the byte array stored at the location specified by recordId. Note that it indeed returns a copy; changing the copy won't alter the record in any way. If the recordId doesn't exist in the record, this will throw an InvalidRecordIDException.

getRecord(int recordId, byte[] buffer, int offset)

Instead of returning the byte array, this method inserts a copy of the record's array into the supplied buffer array, beginning at the offset index in the buffer. It then returns an int representing the number of bytes copied into the buffer. Note that this could result in an ArrayIndexOutOfBounds exception if the buffer is too small to accommodate the record's array from the offset index.

### setRecord()

setRecord(int recordId, byte[] newData, int offset, int numBytes)

This is used similarly to the addRecord() method, but it wholly replaces the record at the recordId specified. The recordId remains in the RecordStore, but now points to the new data. The offset can be used to point at a starting index in the newData array, along with numBytes, to indicate the range of newData's indices that will actually be stored as its own array in the record.

### deleteRecord()

deleteRecord(int recordId)

This deletes the record in the store associated with the recordId. The recordId value is effectively gone from the RecordStore and will not be reused.

### getLastModified()

long getLastModified()

This returns the last time the record store was modified.

## getNextRecordID()

`int getNextRecordID()`

Returns the `recordId` that would be assigned to the next record added. This is useful when we need to check up on the `recordId` status without actually adding a record.

## getNumRecords()

`int getNumRecords()`

Returns the number of records currently in the `RecordStore`. This has no relation to the `recordId` status.

## getSize()

`getSize()`

Returns the total size, in bytes, used by the `RecordStore`.

## getSizeAvailable()

`getSizeAvailable()`

This returns the total bytes still available in the device's storage for the `RecordStore` to use. For some games and applications, this will be a key method to confirm how much to rely upon the local device storage, and to scale that reliance appropriately.

## deleteRecordStore()

`deleteRecordStore(String recordName)`

This is a static class method, and it completely removes a `RecordStore` from the device's persistent memory storage. This is unrecoverable, and any data remaining in the `RecordStore` is lost. If you need to reset a `RecordStore` and start from scratch (at `recordId == 1`), you'll need to delete it and create a new one.

## EnumerateRecords()

`RecordEnumeration enumerateRecords(RecordFilter filter, RecordComparator` ➥`comparator, boolean keepUpdated)`

We'll look a little at enumerating `RecordStores` later in the chapter. Enumeration allows for some greater flexibility in record handling, at the cost of some efficiency.

`RecordStore` **Exceptions**

These are the new exceptions we can catch when dealing with `RecordStores`. Just about every method shown so far will need to be contained in a try-catch block, and can potentially throw at least one of the following:

- `RecordStoreExeption`—This is the most generic of the `RecordStore`'s exceptions, and is the super class of most of the others.

- `RecordStoreNotFoundException`—This is thrown whenever the `RecordStore` requested isn't found in the device's storage.

- `RecordStoreNotOpenException`—This is thrown whenever an attempt at access (read/write/whatever) is executed on a `RecordStore` that hasn't been properly opened for use by the MIDlet.

- `RecordStoreFullException`—This can be a big one, the `RecordStore` has no memory space left available to store new records.

- `InvalidRecordIDException`—One of these is thrown whenever a `recordId` is used that doesn't exist in the `RecordStore`. This can actually be useful to catch and discard while iterating through a `RecordStore` up to its `getNextRecordID()` value.

## The Game's New Methods

Whoops! Let's just hang on a second; there are a couple more J2ME caveats to consider before we start implementing anything, this time regarding the `Image` class. This isn't your dad's old reliable J2SE `Image` class; it's rather more restrictive and we'll have to hurdle the following issues:

- Once an `Image`, always an `Image`. There are no `PixelGrabbers` or other useful classes to pull the raw image data from an `Image` object.

- You can't just point the `Image` class at a likely URL and hope to pop out anything better than a null. To get our remote image files on the server downloaded and looking good on the device, we'll need to access them as binaries. In other words, as byte arrays.

What this means for us is that we're going to be keeping two versions of the `Images` in memory. One version will be the binary source byte array, and the other will be the resulting displayable `Image`.

We're going to define the methods in a generic form, so that they're not hard-coded only to handling the weapon `Images` and data.

Here they are, in brief:

- `public byte[][] getImageDataFromStore()`—If the `RecordStore` is present, this will rebuild each weapon `Image`'s source byte array from the records found and return a two-dimensional byte array for all `Images` found. If the method returns null, it couldn't find its `RecordStore` (or experienced some other device issue), and the MIDlet will have to download the images over the Internet.

- `public void storeImageData(byte[][] imageData)`—Before the MIDlet shuts down, this method will delete the current `RecordStore` (if present), build a new `RecordStore`, and pack the supplied byte arrays into records. If the method can't create the `RecordStore`, or there isn't enough room for the data, the method will simply return without issue. This means that the MIDlet will load the images over the Internet the next time it runs.

  As stated previously, a `RecordStore` returns a predictable ordering of `recordId` ints when adding records to it, starting at `recordId == 1` for the very first record added, and incrementing by one for each subsequent record added. We'll use this behavior to keep our `Images` in the same order in the `RecordStore` as they will be in the `Images` array.

  The static ints already a part of the `Weapon` class will come in handy to properly index and ID the records `Weapon.FLAME` (`== 0`) and `Weapon.OIL` (`== 1`).

- `protected boolean removeImageStore()`—The last method we'll need will simply delete the `RecordStore` completely. Since it's possible we might only partially build the `RecordStore` before running into problems, it's only proper to make sure it's removed from the device's storage space, and not just leave it littering up the MIDlet neighborhood.

The MIDlet will also need some new member variables:

```
private static final String IMAGE_STORE = "CarDB";
private Image[] weaponImages;
private byte[][] weaponImageSource;
private RecordStore imageDB;
```

The `Image` array, `weaponImages`, will be used to handle the weapon `Image` objects on the client and the `IMAGE_STORE` string will be used to uniquely identify the `RecordStore` for consistent access from session to session.

## Writing the Code

As shown previously, `RecordStore` usage is heavy on exception handling. For our purposes, it's good enough to use a catchall approach (pardon the Java pun) and just catch most exceptions in general.

Let's start off with the method to clear the `RecordStore`. It returns a Boolean that's true if the `RecordStore` was successfully removed (or simply didn't exist), and false if a different exception is encountered.

```
protected boolean removeImageStore()
{
    try
    {
    if (imageDB != null
    {
        imageDB.closeRecordStore();
    }
    RecordStore.deleteRecordStore(IMAGE_STORE);
    }
    catch (RecordStoreException rse)
    {
        // The RecordStore didn't exist to delete
        // in the first place. Shouldn't be a
        // problem.
        return true
    }
    catch (Exception e)
    {
        // Something happened we can't handle
        return false;
    }
    // Removed successfully
    return true;
}
```

Now let's build the first method, which grabs image data from the `RecordStore`.

First, we'll check whether the `RecordStore` of images even exists, and if not, just return null so that the MIDlet will know to get the images over the Internet. Then, we'll verify that the `RecordStore` is properly built (that is, simply has some records).

```
public byte[][] getImageDataFromStore()
{
    imageDB = null;
    try {
        imageDB = RecordStore.openRecordStore(IMAGE_STORE, false);

        // Get the number of records present
        int numRecords = imageDB.getNumRecords();
```

```
        // Make sure the RecordStore actually *has* some records
        if (numRecords == 0)
        {
            // The RecordStore seems to be whacked, so delete it
            // and abort
            removeImageStore();
            return null;
        }
```

Now let's set up the temporary variables needed to unpack the Images. If there's an issue, just return null and move on.

```
        byte[][] allRecordData = new byte[numRecords][];
        byte[] data = null;

        // Note that we're counting the records from 1,
        // not from 0.
        for (int i = 1; i <= numRecords; i++)
        {
            data = null;
            data = imageDB.getRecord(i);
            // Note that the array index is one less than the
            // recordId.
            allRecordData[i-1] = data;
        }

        // All done, close the RecordStore
        imageDB.closeRecordStore();

        // Success!
        return allRecordData;
    }
    catch (Exception e)
    {
        // There was a problem somewhere above.
        // Make sure the RecordStore is removed.
        removeImageStore();

        // And abort
        return null;
    }
}
```

As you can see, it's all pretty straightforward. Here's the sister method:

```
public void storeImageData(byte[][] imageData)
{
```

First, let's remove the old `RecordStore` and start a new one by calling `removeImageRecord()`. Remember the Boolean it returns? If it returns false, we abort because it might mean an issue with the `RecordStore` facility in general, which we can't handle.

Removing the `RecordStore` before writing to it isn't strictly necessary, but it will let us handle the same number of images from one session to another cleanly, without the need to monitor the record numbers and ids too closely.

```
If (!removeImageRecord())
{
    return;
}
```

Next, we build the `RecordStore` anew.

```
imageDB = null;

try {
    // This creates a new RecordStore
    imageDB = RecordStore.openRecordStore(IMAGE_STORE, true);
```

Now, let's make absolutely sure there's enough storage space for our byte arrays. This isn't really needed, as adding the actual data will result in an exception if there's not enough room, but it will let us stop the process before actually writing anything to the store.

```
int totalSize = 0;
for (int i = 0; i < imageData.length; i++)
{
    totalSize += imageData[i].length;
}

if (totalSize > imageDB.getSizeAvailable())
{
    // bad news, just abort and return
    removeRecordStore();
    return;
}
```

```
            // If we made it to here, it looks good and we'll likely succeed.
            for (int i = 0; i < imageData.length; i++)
            {
                imageDB.addRecord(imageData[i], 0, imageData[i].length);
            }

            imageDB.closeRecordStore();
        }
        catch (Exception e)
        {
            // Clean up and abort
            removeImageStore();
        }
    }
}
```

As you should expect, writing the records is a little more involved than simply reading them, because there's more chance that things could go wrong.

### The MIDlet Changes
In the game MIDlet's code, we'll need to handle things as follows:

```
weaponImageSource = getImageDataFromStore();
if (weaponImageSource == null)
{
    // We couldn't build the data from
    // the RecordStore so we need to
    // get them via the Internet.

    weaponImageSource = getImageDataFromServer();

    if (weaponImageSource == null)
    {
        // Now we're in trouble, we couldn't
        // build the images any which way
        // so we'll need to inform the user
        // and possibly abort the game…
    }
}

// We got the data, now build the images

weaponImages = new Image[weaponImageSource.length];
for (int i = 0; i < weaponImageSource.length; i++)
```

```
{
    weaponImages[i] = Image.createImage(weaponImageSource[i], 0,
    ➥ weaponImageSource[i].length);
}
```

Okay, the `Images` are built! Now, when the user is done playing and closes out the MIDlet, the `weaponImageSource` array should still be alive and kept up-to-date with any weapon image changes, so we simply call

```
storeImageData(weaponImageSource);
```

That's it! The game can now store and retrieve its weapon images from the `RecordStore`.

## More `RecordStore` Joy

Storing a byte array used to create an `Image` is about as simple as it gets for images, but with the right combination of classes, we can actually use records and their byte array data more simply and with greater flexibility for other types of objects. We'll also get into `RecordEnumerator` handling here. Consider the following class in Listing 19.1.

**LISTING 19.1**    The `CarStore` Class

```
public class CarStore
{
    // These two static final ints will
    // be used to filter the records via
    // a RecordFilter implementation.
    public static final int CASH_RECORD = 1;
    public static final int WEAPON_RECORD = 2;

    // The player's current weapons
    private Weapon[] weapons;

    // The player's current cash
    private int cash;

    // Build a new CarStore and set the
    // members
    CarStore(int cash, Weapon[] weapons) {
        this.cash = cash;
```

LISTING 19.1   continued

```
        this.weapons = weapons;
    }

    // get the current cash
    public int getCash()
    {
        return cash;
    }

    // get the current weapons array
    public Weapon[] getWeapons()
    {
        return weapons;
    }

    // Writes the cash and weapon data to a new
    // RecordStore.
    public void writeToStore()
    {
        try
        {
            // Let's make sure we're dealing with a fresh new RecordStore
            // (because we're still relying a little on recordId ordering)
            // and remove it if it's still in device storage.
            RecordStore.deleteRecordStore("MyCoolCar");

        }
        catch (Exception e)
        {
            // Shouldn't be a showstopper, so continue
        }

        // Now we can build the RecordStore from scratch
        try
        {
            // Let's make sure we're dealing with a fresh new RecordStore
            // (since we're still relying a little on recordId ordering)
            // and remove it if it's still in device storage.
            RecordStore.deleteRecordStore("MyCoolCar");
```

**LISTING 19.1**    continued

```java
// Now we'll create a new one.
RecordStore carDB = RecordStore.openRecordStore("MyCoolCar", true);

// Build some reusable data handling objects.
ByteArrayOutputStream bout = new ByteArrayOutputStream();
DataOutputStream dout = new DataOutputStream(bout);
byte[] data = null;

// Build some simple weapon description Strings
// just to show the breadth of functionality we
// have here.  This array is keyed to Weapon.FLAME
// and Weapon.OIL, which are 0 and 1, respectively.

String[] weaponName = { "Flamer", "Oil" };

// First, we're going to write the player's
// current cash to the car's RecordStore
// We'll id the record as a cash record...
dout.writeByte(CASH_RECORD);

// and then write the cash amount
dout.writeInt(cash);

// and now bundle the Stream into a byte
// array and write a new record.  It's
// the very first record in the RecordStore,
// so we know it'll have the recordId of 1.
data = bout.toByteArray();

// Add the array to the RecordStore
carDB.addRecord(data, 0, data.length );

// and reset the Streams to
// properly handle the Weapons.
bout.reset();

// Iterate through the car's Weapons array
for (int i = 0; i < weapons.length; i++)
{
    // Write the weapon record tag..
    dout.writeByte(WEAPON_RECORD);
```

*LISTING 19.1*    continued

```
                    // Write the weapon name to the stream
                    dout.writeUTF(weaponName[weapons[i].getWeaponType()]);

                    // Write the weapon type...
                    dout.writeInt(weapons[i].getWeaponType());

                    // Write the weapon's ammo
                    dout.writeInt(weapons[i].getWeaponAmmo());

                    // and finally, the Weapon's time value
                    dout.writeInt(weapons[i].getWeaponTime());

                    dout.flush();

                    // Pack the Byte Stream (aka the Data Stream)
                    // into the data byte array...
                    data = bout.toByteArray();

                    // Add the array to the RecordStore
                    carDB.addRecord(data, 0, data.length );

                    // and reset the Streams to
                    // properly handle the next Weapon.
                    bout.reset();
                }
                carDB.closeRecordStore();
                dout.close();
                bout.close();

            }
            catch (Exception e)
            {
                // handle exceptions here...
            }
}
```

Okay, that puts the cash and the weapons data into a RecordStore. To get it out,
we're going to do things differently and use a RecordEnumerator with a custom
implementation of the RecordFilter interface. If you noticed, the CASH_RECORD and
WEAPON_RECORD values were written as bytes to their respective records before any of
the other data. We'll use that byte to filter the records. Setting aside the CarStore
class for a moment, here's our CarItemFilter class, shown in Listing 19.2.

*LISTING 19.2*    The CarItemFilter Class

```
class CarItemFilter implements RecordFilter
{
    // This will contain the car item id
    // we'll be looking for in the records.
    private byte filterValue;

    // Builds a new CarItemFilter for the
    // specific car record id we want to
    // find
    public CarItemFilter(int filterInt)
    {
        filterValue = (byte)filterInt;
    }


    // This is the RecordFilter method used
    // by the RecordEnumeration to determine
    // if the record is a "match" and needs
    // to be included in its enumeration.
    public boolean matches(byte[] candidate)
    {
        if (candidate == null || candidate.length == 0)
        {
            return false;
        }

        // Since, in the CarStore.writeToStore() method,
        // we wrote the item type byte to the records
        // before anything else, the byte at index 0
        // should be our id to filter.
        return (candidate[0] == filterValue);
    }
}
```

Alright! Now we're ready to get our data back out of the RecordStore. Here's the CarStore method that will do it for us:

```
public void readStore()
{
    try
    {
        // Open the RecordStore built above...
```

```
        RecordStore carDB = RecordStore.openRecordStore
➥("MyCoolCar", false);

        // Build some reusable data handling objects.
        ByteArrayInputStream bin = null;
        DataInputStream din = null;
        byte[] data = null;

        // First, we'll get the cash record out and set
        // the cash value.  Remember that this record
        // was added before any other so we know it's
        // at recordId == 1.
        data = carDB.getRecord(1);

        // Set up the streams to read back the
        // stored variables
        bin = new ByteArrayInputStream(data);
        din = new DataInputStream(bin);

        // discard the CASH_RECORD byte
        din.readByte();

        // and now grab the actual cash value stored.
        cash = din.readInt();

        // clean up for the weapons handling
        din.close();
        bin.close();

        // Prepare the Weapons array for the new data
        // (We build it to (getNumRecords()-1) to account
        // for the cash record.)
        weapons = new Weapon[carDB.getNumRecords()-1];

        // The following sets up a RecordEnumeration
        // object with our CarItemFilter RecordFilter
        // and a null RecordComparator which means
        // it will simply iterate the weapon records
        // in no particular order.  We're assuming, here,
        // that the Weapon records found won't need to be
        // in a certain sequence but can be rebuilt
        // willy-nilly.  You can always build your
```

```
// own RecordComparator to put the enumeration into
// some specific order.
CarItemFilter filter = new CarItemFilter(WEAPON_RECORD);
RecordEnumeration re = carDB.enumerateRecords(filter, null, false);

// Prepare the necessary temp variables and
int count = 0;
String weaponName = "";
int type = 0;
int time = 0;
int ammo = 0;
while (re.hasNextElement())
{
    // This next call returns the record's byte array and
    // advances the RecordEnumerator's pointer to the record
    // beyond the one returned.
    data = re.nextRecord ();

    // Set up the streams...
    bin = new ByteArrayInputStream(data);
    din = new DataInputStream(bin);

    // Read and discard the weapon record id
    din.readByte();

    // Read back the weapon name String
    weaponName = din.readUTF();
    System.out.println("Got the Weapon name: "+weaponName);

    // Read the weapon type...
    type = din.readInt();

    // Read the weapon's ammo
    ammo = din.readInt();

    // and finally, the Weapon's time value
    time = din.readInt();

    // Now rebuild the weapon into the
    // weapons array.
    weapons[count++] = new Weapon(type, time, ammo);
```

```
            // Clean up
            din.close();
            bin.close();
        }
    }
    catch (Exception e)
    {
        // handle exceptions here...
    }
  }
}
```

The `RecordEnumeration`'s behavior can be further refined by building an implementation of `RecordComparator`. For example, we could easily implement one and make a `RecordEnumerator` to return weapon records ordered according to the ammo value.

> **NOTE**
>
> Using filters and comparators slows down the process. Using null for both ensures the fastest record retrieval possible with a `RecordEnumerator`, but will return all the records in the `RecordStore` in no specific guaranteed order.

There's one last interesting bit we haven't touched on yet with `RecordStores`. You can add a `RecordListener` to a `RecordStore` via its `addRecordListener()` method. The class implementing `RecordListener` will then be notified any time any record is added, changed, or deleted from the `RecordStore`.

## Summary

In this chapter we looked at when (and when not) to use J2ME's `RecordStore` class, along with its limitations and practical work-arounds. Now you know how to directly store and retrieve data from a `RecordStore`, get a helping hand from the `java.io` package, and use `RecordFilters` and `RecordEnumerations` to store and retrieve data flexibly and consistently.

# 20

# Connecting Out: Wireless Networking

**IN THIS CHAPTER**

- J2ME Networking Overview
- MIDP Networking
- Setting Up Your Game Server
- Data Format
- Making a Multiplayer Car Racing Game

Above all else, a mobile phone's true purpose is to connect people together over vast distances. Single player games on phones are well and good, but the tiny graphics window and puny processors will never compete with the likes of Microsoft's Xbox, Sony's PlayStation 2, or Nintendo's GameCube.

Rather, the mobile games that are most likely to be successful and awe-inspiring will involve lots of players cooperating, competing, and sharing an experience. A well-done wireless game can bring people together in ways previously unimaginable.

## J2ME Networking Overview

In the world of Java Standard Edition, large and intricate `java.io.*` and `java.net.*` packages are used to great effect. These packages contain pretty much any type of networking class you want: `Socket`, `DatagramSocket`, `ServerSocket`, and so on. Each class has different methods and different ways of being used.

In the world of J2ME, however, we don't have the luxury of being quite so complete. For starters, we have no idea what type of network transport protocol a phone is using. Devices that work over circuit-switched networks can use streaming always-on connections such as the Transport Control Protocol (TCP). However, packet-switched networks may only be able to handle their network data in discrete, non-guaranteed packets, using a protocol such as the User Datagram Protocol (UDP). What's a poor phone to do?

The CLDC's Connection interface was created to be as general as possible. The Connection class is a catch-all that can, in theory, handle pretty much any network connection. A special class known as the Connector can tap into any CLDC class that extends from the Connection interface.

The Connection interface is an ultra simple, ultra-generalized networking class with only two methods: open() and close().

There are several more specialized interfaces that extend from Connection. These are illustrated in Figure 20.1.

- InputConnection—This points to a device from which data can be read. Use the openInputStream() method to return an input stream.

- OutputConnection—This points to a device from which data can be written. Use its openOutputStream() method to talk to the outside world.

- StreamConnection—Combines input and output connections. The StreamConnectionNotified interface waits for a connection to be established and then returns a StreamConnection.

- ContentConnection—Extends StreamConnection and deals with metadata about the given connection.

- DatagramConnection—A point that can send or receive datagrams.

Every Connector's open method takes in a String with the familiar syntax: "protocol:address;parameters". For example, to open up a typical HTTP connection

```
Connector.open("http://java.sun.com/developer");
```

to open a socket

```
Connector.open("socket://108.233.291.001:1234");
```

and to open a datagram connection

```
Connector.open("datagram://www.myserver.com:9000");
```

For example, to connect to a server, simply have the MIDlet use the Connector class:

```
Datagram dgram = dc.newDatagram(message, msglength,"datagram://
➥www.myserver.com:9000");
dc.send(dgram);
dc.close();
```

You can even theoretically connect to a serial or infrared port if your phone or J2ME device supports the interface:

```
Connector.open("comm:0;baudrate=9600');
```

Or even open a local file, if the device has a file system:

```
Connector.open("file:/myFile.txt");
```

Get the idea?

When you call the `Connector` class, it sniffs out the protocol you are using and looks for an applicable `Connection` class to use. This makes it exceptionally easy to swap out one protocol for another—merely change the `String` passed to the `open()` method.

**NOTE**

The CLDC itself does not actually implement any protocols. The MIDP is required to support the HTTP protocol, but not necessarily sockets or datagrams. These protocols may or may not be supported by specific phones. As such, it is recommended that you use HTTP for all your game communications, so that the same game will work on pretty much any MIDP-compliant phone.

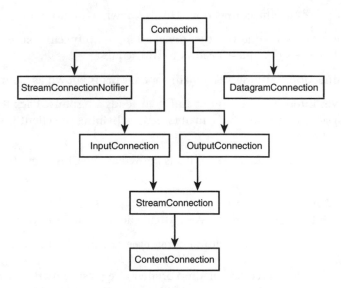

*FIGURE 20.1*   The `Connection` interfaces.

# MIDP Networking

The MIDP specification makes it extremely easy to pass data back and forth using HTTP. To do this, MIDP adds the `HttpConnection` interface to the `Connector` suite, allowing for HTTP protocol access. The `HttpConnection` interface, extending from `javax.microedition.io.ContentConnection`, handles everything you could want to request or respond to an HTTP connection.

Every Motorola i85s phone, for example, has its own static IP address. Having one phone communicate with another is only a matter of simple peer-to-peer networking. Have one phone connect to the other's IP address using HTTP and communicate away!

More often, though, your phone will connect to an outside server machine. This server can be used as a gateway for almost any type of game traffic or other network communication. For instance, a gateway can be set up to access an entire database of sports scores, then stream only the latest requested scores to a MIDlet as part of a real-time sports fantasy game.

## A Little Info About HTTP

The *Hyper Text Transport Protocol (HTTP)* is the protocol that you use each time you surf the Web. It is a request-response protocol that works like this:

1. The client sets up the connection. This is known as Setup mode.

2. The client sends a request to the server, asking for a specific piece of data. It can add all sorts of request headers to this request.

3. The connection to the server remains open. This is known as Connected mode.

4. The server interprets the request and then sends a response back to the client. The response might also have many headers, helping the client interpret the response body.

5. The connection is then closed. This is known as the Closed mode.

### HTTP Setup Mode

So, to set up a HTTP connection on your MIDP client, create the connection

```
HttpConnection c = (HttpConnection)Connector.open("http://www.myserver.com/");
```

You can then change the request method or alter a request property. By default, the request method is GET, which means that all parameters are passed in along with the URL.

You can also use the POST method, which passes all data and parameters as a separate chunk, thus enabling you to send much bigger packets of data:

```
c.setRequestMethod(HttpConnection.POST);
```

Use the following to set some of the HTTP headers:

```
c.setRequestProperty("User-Agent","Profile/MIDP-1.0 Configuration/CLDC-1.0");
c.setRequestProperty("Content-Length","100");
```

At any time, you can call various methods to get the status or other information about the HTTP connection. For example

- getURL—Gets the full URL.

- getProtocol—Gets the protocol from the URL.

- getHost—Gets the URL's host.

- getPort—Gets the port from the URL.

- getFile—Gets the file portion of the URL.

- getRequestMethod—Gets the current request method. The default is GET.

- getRequestProperty—Gets the value of a request property.

### Making the HTTP Connection

There are several methods you can call to actually try to connect:

- openInputStream—Read text from the HTTP connection.

- openOutputStream—Write text to the HTTP connection.

- openDataInputStream—Read binary data from the HTTP connection.

- openDataOutputStream—Read binary data from the HTTP connection.

- getLength—Get the length of the current packet of data.

- getType—Get the type of the current packet of data.

- getDate—Get the date when the current packet of data was created.

- getExpiration—Get the expiration date of the current packet of data. This can be found in the "expires" line of the HTTP header.

### Closing Out

To close your HTTP connection, use this method:

- close—Inherited from the Connection interface. Closes out the connection.

## HTTP Example

A typical example of sending some data to a servlet via POST might look like this:

```
HttpConnection c = null;
InputStream is = null;
OutputStream os = null;

c = (HttpConnection)Connector.open(url);

// Set the request method and headers
c.setRequestMethod(HttpConnection.POST);
c.setRequestProperty("User-Agent","Profile/MIDP-1.0 Configuration/CLDC-1.0");
c.setRequestProperty("Content-Language", "en-US");
```

You can then send your data along using an output stream:

```
// Write your data to the output stream
os = c.openOutputStream();
os.write("data");
os.flush();
```

### Response Code

The MIDlet usually asks for the response code to ensure that the data was returned correctly:

```
int rc = c.getResponseCode();
if( rc == HttpConnection.HTTP_OK ) {
// we're good... continue
} else {
// tell the user about the error
}
```

In some cases, the response code might be valid, but not HTTP_OK. For example, you might get HTTP_MOVED_TEMP, which means that the servlet or Web page you requested might have redirected you to another page. You should grab the new URL from the header and open a new connection:

```
int rc = conn.getResponseCode();

switch( rc )
{
 case HttpConnection.HTTP_MOVED_PERM:
 case HttpConnection.HTTP_MOVED_TEMP:
```

```
case HttpConnection.HTTP_SEE_OTHER:
case HttpConnection.HTTP_TEMP_REDIRECT:
 url = conn.getHeaderField( "Location");
 if( url != null && url.startsWith("/*" ))
 {
   StringBuffer b = new StringBuffer();
   b.append( "http://" );
   b.append( conn.getHost() );
   b.append( ':' );
   b.append( conn.getPort() );
   b.append( url );
   url = b.toString();
 }
 // Close the old connection
 c.close();
 // You should open a new connection here
 break;
}
```

### Reading In Data

In any event, eventually you can read in the returned data. You can read in the data as raw bytes using an input stream.

Whenever possible, you should use the content length header information when reading in data. If you try to read more bytes than were sent, the application might just wait forever waiting for new data to come down the pike.

However, you should also prepare for the situation in which you're not sure how much data to expect. In that case, just read in one byte at a time until you get -1, indicating that there are no more bytes to be read.

```
// Open an InputStream to read in the HTTP headers.
is = c.openInputStream();
// Get the length and process the data
int len = (int)c.getLength();
if (len > 0)
{
  byte[] data = new byte[len];
  int actual = is.read(data);
  // do something with the data here
}
else
{
```

```
// If we don't know the length, read in the data
// one character at a time and add it to a byte array.
ByteArrayOutputStream tmp = new ByteArrayOutputStream();
int ch;
while ((ch = is.read()) != -1)
  tmp.write( ch );
data = tmp.toByteArray();
// do something with the data here
}
```

On the other hand, you can read in your data as a data input stream. This lets you read in primitive Java types (such as strings, integers, and so on) in a machine-independent way. The servlet must use a data output stream to write data accordingly:

```
DataInputStream is = new DataInputStream(c.openInputStream());
String msg = is.readUTF();
// Do something with the data
```

### Closing Down Cleanly

You can continue to write and read data if you so desire. Just be sure that the connection is of the "Keep-Alive" variety. More information about keeping connections alive can be found later in this chapter.

In the end, be sure to close all open streams and connections:

```
if (is != null)
  is.close();
if (os != null)
  os.close();
if (c != null)
  c.close();
```

## Working Around HTTP's Limitations

HTTP is known as a *half-duplex* protocol. That means you cannot transmit information in two directions at the same time. If your game is advanced, with unpredictable data packets constantly coming in and going out, you'll want to use a *full-duplex* protocol. But what if your phone only supports HTTP?

### Multiple Connections

One way to achieve full-duplex communication is by having your MIDlet client create multiple connections—one that sends data to the server and one that stays alive, retrieving server data.

The first connection should use chunked transfer encoding. The server creates an open connection and assigns it some sort of unique ID. This ID is sent down to the client.

The client can now create a client-to-server connection with an incredibly large *content-length* heading, passing in the proper ID. The server can then handle request data as it flows in from the client and channel an appropriate response to the open server-to-client connection.

Some servers and proxies may not be able to handle a request with a long content length heading, buffering the request and waiting for the request to be completed. In this case, the client can break each message into a chunk and send it as a new, individual request. The client should send the ID along with each request, either as a custom header element or as part of the payload. The server can then parse this ID number and send the appropriate response back to the client.

### The Power of the Proxy

Of course, you can write your game server using any networking protocol you want. You can tap into the game server via an HTTP *proxy*. A proxy is a servlet or other server-side component that reads in HTTP messages sent from your MIDlet and translates them into another protocol which it then transmits to the game server. Likewise, a proxy will take server messages and translate them into HTTP messages, queuing them up and sending them out to your MIDlet as necessary.

Using a proxy will add extra latency to your game's communications. But it will also allow you to write games that support different network protocols. For example, devices that support datagrams can use them. If a ConnectionNotFoundException is thrown, the game can revert to using HTTP via a proxy instead.

## Setting Up Your Game Server

Your remote game server can, of course, be another mobile device. This lets you achieve true peer-to-peer gameplay.

To accomplish this, create an endless loop that listens to a port and waits for some data. If you are sure your target device supports datagrams, for example, you could write something like this:

```
int receiveport = 91;
DatagramConnection dc = ( DatagramConnection)Connector.open("datagram://:
➥"+receiveport);
while (true)
{
    dgram = dc.newDatagram(dc.getMaximumLength());
    dc.receive(dgram);
```

```
    reply = new String(dgram.getData(), 0,dgram.getLength());
}
```

Alternatively, you could write a dastardly simple server in Java Standard Edition (or any other language), running as an application on any network-enabled PC.

For instance, the meat of your server could handle datagrams as follows:

```
DatagramSocket receiveSocket = null;
DatagramPacket receivePacket = new DatagramPacket(bytesReceived,
➥bytesReceived.length);
receiveSocket.receive(receivePacket);
```

For the sake of this chapter, however, we will focus on HTTP and use a Java servlet to handle the HTTP communications.

Servlets are perfect for dealing with HTTP, because they have been designed from the ground up for request-response connections.

To use a servlet, you must be using a J2EE Web server, such as Resin, Tomcat for Apache, Weblogic, SilverStream, and so on. You can also configure most other Web servers to support servlets. Tomcat is a free, open-source servlet engine. You can grab it from `http://jakarta.apache.org/site/binindex.html`.

## Data Format

Your game packets can be sent in any format you want. Obviously, you want to try to keep your data as small as possible.

### Doing Your Own Packing

You can pack a lot of information into a byte. For example, you can fit 8 Boolean flag values into each of the 8 bits. The following code line represents false, true, true, false, false, false, true, true:

```
01100011
```

To set this, you could use a function like the following code fragment, passing in an array of 8 Booleans:

```
byte setFlag(boolean[] flag)
{
  // temp starts off as 00000000
  byte temp = 0;
  for (int i=0; i<8; i++)
```

```
  {
    // Set the last bit to 1 if true
    if (flag[i])
        temp += 1;
    // Shift the bits over to the left
    temp = temp << 1;
  }
  return temp;
}
```

Then you can read the values by masking out bits using the bitwise and command (&). For example, to see if the seventh bit is true or false, you can mask your byte with `01000000` (64), and see if the result is `0` (false) or 64 (true):

```
01100011 & 01000000 = 01000000
(99 & 64 = 64)
```

You can also shift the bits over a set amount and compare the first bit. For example, this method returns whether a given flag is true or false:

```
boolean getFlag(byte b,int location)
{
    return (((b >> location) & 1) == 1);
}
```

For the most part you shouldn't need to roll your own bit-packing routines. The `DataInputStream` and `DataOutputStream`, discussed a bit later in this chapter, do a decent job.

## XML

Many people adore eXtensible Markup Language (XML), which formats documents in a highly organized and readable way. XML has some great advantages. For example, it's really easy to figure out what's in this game message:

```
<move><sprite>car</sprite><x>10</x><y>15</y></move>
```

However, XML is very verbose and will create ultra-heavy data packets. There are, however, ways to compress and otherwise optimize XML data.

If you want your MIDlet to parse XML data, you can choose various types of parsers:

- Validating—The document is checked against a DTD. This requires a lot of extra code and time to validate. It is *not* recommended that you ever use a validating XML parser.

- Non-Validating—The document is just read in.

- Single-Step Document Parser—This will parse an entire document and create a document-type-definition (DTD) object that contains a sense of all nodes, children, and branches. The root of the tree is called `kXMLElement`, and each node is an instance. You can grab nodes using methods such as `getChildren()`, `getTagName()`, and `getContents()`. This type of parsing takes tons of time and uses up scads of memory because the entire document must be kept around.

- Incremental—This will take in a line and parse it, putting the data into temporary variables. A sense of the entire document is not retained. This is the smallest and fastest way to parse XML.

There are several good non-validating parsers available for MIDP.

- kXML—A small incremental parser. You can download it from `http://www.kxml.org/` and include the kXML classes with your application.

- NanoXML—A single step parser. Grab a port of NanoXML for J2ME from `http://nanoxml.sourceforge.net/`. You will also need a special version of the XMLElement.java file ported for J2ME: `http://www.ericgiguere.com/micro-java/cldc_xml.html`.

To parse a document incrementally using kXML, just use code similar to the following:

```
InputStreamReader xmldata = new InputStreamReader( c.openInputStream());
XmlParser parser = new XmlParser(new InputStreamReader(xmldata));
try {
    boolean keepParsing = true;

    while( keepParsing )
    {
        ParseEvent event = parser.read();

        switch( event.getType() )
        {
        case Xml.START_TAG:
            // handle the start of a XML tag
            break;
        case Xml.END_TAG:
            // handle the end of a XML tag
            break;
        case Xml.TEXT:
```

```
                    // handle the text inside a tag
                    break;
                case Xml.END_DOCUMENT:
                    // document done
                    keepParsing = false;
                    break;
            }
        }
    }
catch( java.io.IOException e ){ }
```

## Encoding with `DataOutputStream` and `DataInputStream`

Perhaps the easiest way of sending and receiving data is to use Java's predefined data types. For example, nothing could be easier than sending an integer, a `String`, and a boolean, and then reading them directly back in.

The `DataOutputStream` and `DataInputStream` classes make this immensely easy. For example, to write out your variables

```
DataOutputStream os = new DataOutputStream(c.openOutputStream());
os.writeBoolean(true);
os.writeUTF( "Hello World!");
os.writeInt(5);
os.close();
```

and then to read them in

```
DataInputStream is = new DataInputStream(c.openInputStream());
boolean b = is.readBoolean();
String hello = is.readUTF();
int t = = is.readInt();
is.close();
```

# Making a Multiplayer Car Racing Game

So, let's create a game here!

Obviously, it would be nice to modify our car racing action game to have two cars racing on the same track, each trying to reach the finish line first. The latency of most mobile networks, however, makes such a game quite impossible.

Games that require immediate knowledge of where opponents are and what they're doing just don't make sense over low-latency connections. A shooting game just isn't much fun when it takes a second or more for the news of your gunshot to reach your opponent!

The types of multiplayer games presently possible with today's wireless networks are as follows:

- Turn-based games—Almost any board or card game is possible on MIDP.

- Games that read from the same data source—Many games, such as fantasy sports games, involve people competing against each other in a way that doesn't involve direct interaction. You make your decisions, your opponent makes her decisions, and the game is kicked into action.

- Centralized high-score lists, ratings, and rankings.

- Games where the interaction with other players isn't graphical—for example, in our Micro Racing game, you drive the track and win money. You can then spend your money online and buy or sell parts for your car.

- Simple chatting and instant messaging applications.

All this being said, there *is* a clever way to create a two-player racing game:

1. Two players start the game and log into a server.

2. Both clients show two cars on the track.

3. The server sends a "start game" message to both clients.

4. When the game starts, the client uses artificial intelligence to move the opponent's car slowly along the track.

5. Meanwhile, the client sends information to the server about where it is and how much time has elapsed.

6. The server then sends information about the opponent's car as often as possible. Your opponent's car "leaps" forward or backward on the track depending on where it actually is.

Although this system is workable, it is definitely clunky and unsightly. Instead of trying to cheat slow latencies, we're going to use this chapter to create a car part trading system that would be cool and useful to use with the present limitations.

## Design the System

The first step in building the multiplayer aspect of your game is to look at the game design and figure out the minimum amount of data that needs to be sent back and forth, which in our case is the following:

1. You log into the server and enter the Garage. You send in your username.

2. You are sent back a list of all the items available for sale.

3. You are also sent a list of others who are currently hanging out in the Garage.

You have two choices: Buy It! or Sell It!

1. If you decide to buy, you can pick the item you want. A more detailed description is shown to you. You can then click the Buy It! button to make the purchase.

2. If you have enough money, the purchase is made. Money is deducted from your account and you now own the new item. It is automatically installed onto your car (saved into the game's data record). The next time you race, you will reap the advantages of this new engine, tire, or weapon.

**NOTE**

If this game was commercial, the Garage might charge a nominal maintenance fee in real dollars for installing your item.

3. If you decide to sell, you are a shown a detailed list of all your items. You check the items you want to sell. You can then indicate how much money you want to charge for it. You then hit the Sell It! button. As long as you stay logged into the Garage, others users can buy this item.

4. When you log off, any of your goods that didn't sell are taken off the market.

## Special Considerations

Because we're going to be using HTTP as the transport medium, several considerations must be kept in mind:

- Unlike a socket, an HTTP connection is generally not kept alive. Rather, the client must "pull" info from the server as often as it needs it. To figure out whether any of your items have sold, you will need to poll the server constantly to check on the status of your goods. If anything has been sold, you are notified. That item is removed from your inventory and the purchase price is added to your account.

- The connection is stateless. This means that every time you talk to the server, you need to tell it who you are. This is called *session tracking*.

## Polling

Polling can be accomplished by creating a thread, having the thread send a request to the server, and then sleeping for a given number of milliseconds.

In the land of MIDP, however, it is much more efficient and convenient to use a `Timer` and a `TimerTask`.

Create the timer as follows, giving it a pause of 10 seconds:

```
timer = new Timer();
CheckInTimer ci = new CheckInTimer();
timer.schedule(ci,(long)10000,10000);
```

The `CheckInTimer` class can look like this:

```
class CheckIn
{
  CheckIn()
  {
    ConnectServer("checkin",null,this);
  }
}
```

How long the timer should wait to trigger each server call depends on your game design and on the target network. In general, the faster your timer, the more responsive the game—but realistically, wireless networks cannot handle multiple connections spaced less than one second apart.

## Keeping HTTP Connections Alive

By default, HTTP connections are *kept alive*. This means that the same connection will be used for multiple requests. This is useful for any situation where the client will repeatedly send requests to the server.

If you explicitly do not want your connection to stay alive, set the `Connection` header to `"close"`:

```
conn.setRequestProperty( "Connection","close" );
```

To keep the connection alive, you must set a valid `Content-Length` header every time you send some data. This must be set to the size, in bytes, of the data you are about to send:

```
byte data[] = new byte[55];
// Fill in the byte array with data here
c.setRequestProperty("Content-Length",data.length);
```

As long as the game client and game server deals with valid lengths of data, and as long as both parties don't issue the close() command, the client and server can communicate freely on this By default, HTTP connections are *kept alive* This means that the same connection will be used for multiple requests. connection.

### Session Tracking

Although keeping an By default, HTTP connections are *kept alive* This means that the same connection will be used for multiple requests. HTTP connection alive is well and good, it is usually cleaner and easier for a server to close out a connection after every request.

When you surf between several Web pages on a big site, a browser cookie keeps track of who you are and enables the Web server to track a given session. However, MIDP doesn't support cookies.

Rather, the typical method of keeping track of sessions is by sending some sort of identification along with every request. This ID can be part of the message itself, sent in a special request header, or attached to the URL, as seen here:

http://www.testgame.com/servlet/GarageServlet?uname=fox

In our sample game, the MIDlet will tack on a username parameter to *every* message. This lets the server keep track of sessions.

## The Messages

Given our game design parameters, Table 20.1 shows the commands and applicable parameters that will need to be handled.

*TABLE 20.1*   Necessary Game Parameters

| | |
|---|---|
| Uname | Takes the username as a parameter. Must be sent along with every message. |
| Action | login—Logs in to the server. Sends down a list of items and list of other users. |
| | logout—Logs out and notifies you if anything has been sold. |
| | buy—Buy a particular item. |
| | sell—Sell a particular item. |
| | checkin—Just check in to the server to see how things are progressing. |
| Item | When sent along with buy, just include the name of the item you want. |
| Sell | When sent along with sell, you must include the item's name, description, and price, in the format ItemName!A Neat Item!59. |

## Weaknesses

Although the preceding design is functional, it has a lot of weaknesses. Here are just a few:

1. There's no check to be sure two users aren't using the same username. Eventually, the system should include usernames and passwords, and only allow one person to use a particular account name.

2. The amount of money you have and your car's items should be stored on the server in a database. Otherwise, it's easy for a hacker to pretend to have limitless amounts of money.

3. If items were in a database, then the store could be persistent. You wouldn't have to remain logged in to sell your items. Rather, the system could sell items for you and notify you via e-mail when a purchase succeeds.

4. All buy and sell operations should be discrete transactions—that is, a database should "lock" each object whenever a deal is made, to ensure that only one person is buying or selling it at a time.

5. There's no real interaction. It would be nice to have some chat or other social functionality so people can express themselves, and allow the player to get an idea of the other players' personalities.

## The Client Side

It then sends this number to a server. Note that for the sake of testing, it's a good idea to set the server to localhost—that way you can run the server and the client from the comfort of your desktop machine. Eventually, however, you will want to run the servlet on a live Web site and your MIDlet should connect to that URL. Different application servers allow you to set up servlets in different ways. A typical servlet setup will look like this: http://localhost:8080/servlet/GarageServlet.

Note that we created a ServerCallback interface with one method:

```
public void serverResponse( String response);
```

Every major game message is given its own class, each implementing ServerCallback. Each message connects to the server and passes in itself as the callback. That way, when the servlet issues a response, it can be handled by the appropriate class.

The full code listing is as follows:

```
import java.util.*;
import java.io.*;
import javax.microedition.io.*;
import javax.microedition.lcdui.*;
import javax.microedition.midlet.*;
```

```java
public class GarageClient extends MIDlet implements CommandListener
{
  private Display display;
  private Form loginform;
  private Form mainform;
  private Form detailform;
  private Form sellform;
  private Form sellform2;
  private Form itemsoldform;

  // Hard-coded for now. I have 200 dollars.
  public int mybalance = 200;
  // For now, just hard code the item data
  // TODO: Grab this from the database
  public String[] myitemname = {"Turbo Boost","Oil Slick","Wide Tires"};
  public String[] myitemdescript = {"Add 2 To Speed","Releases Oil On
➥Track","Add 1 To Control"};

  // commands
  static final Command LOGIN = new Command("Log In",Command.SCREEN, 1);
  static final Command EXIT = new Command("Exit",Command.EXIT, 2);

  static final Command BUY = new Command("Buy",Command.SCREEN, 1);
  static final Command SELL = new Command("Sell",Command.SCREEN, 1);
  static final Command LOGOUT = new Command("Log Out",Command.SCREEN, 2);
  static final Command REFRESH = new Command("Refresh",Command.SCREEN, 2);

  static final Command BUYIT = new Command("Buy It",Command.SCREEN, 1);
  static final Command SELLIT = new Command("Sell It",Command.SCREEN, 1);
  static final Command BACK = new Command("Back",Command.BACK, 2);

  private TextField usernamefield;
  private TextField pricefield;
  private ChoiceGroup itemgroup;
  String username;
  private Vector itemvector;
  private Vector solditemvector;
  private int price;
  private String usershere;

  Timer timer;
```

```java
// Point to the servlet here...
String url = "http://localhost:8080/servlet/GarageServlet";

public GarageClient()
{
  display = Display.getDisplay(this);
}

public void startApp()
{
  loginform = new Form("The Garage");
  loginform.append("Log In Now");
  usernamefield = new TextField("Username:", "", 10, TextField.ANY);
  loginform.append(usernamefield);
  loginform.addCommand(LOGIN);
  loginform.addCommand(EXIT);
  loginform.setCommandListener(this);

  display.setCurrent(loginform);
}

public void pauseApp()  {   }

public void destroyApp(boolean unconditional) { }

public void commandAction(Command c, Displayable s)
{
  if (s instanceof Form)
  {
      Form obj = (Form) s;
      if (obj == loginform)
      {
          if (c == EXIT)
          {
              notifyDestroyed();
          }
          else if (c == LOGIN)
          {
              username = usernamefield.getString();
              Login l = new Login();
          }
      }
```

```
    else if (obj == mainform)
    {
        if (c == BUY)
        buydetail(itemgroup.getSelectedIndex());
        else if (c == SELL)
            sell();
        else if (c == LOGOUT)
        {
            Logout lo = new Logout();
        }
        else if (c == REFRESH)
        {
Login l = new Login();
        }
    }
    else if (obj == sellform || obj == detailform || obj == itemsoldform)
    {
        if (c == BACK)
            display.setCurrent(mainform);
        else if (c == BUYIT)
        {
            BuyIt bi = new BuyIt(itemgroup.getSelectedIndex());
        }
        else if (c == SELLIT)
pickprice();
    }
    else if (obj == sellform2)
    {
        if (c == BACK)
            display.setCurrent(sellform);
        else if (c == SELLIT)
        {
            String price = pricefield.getString();
            int i = itemgroup.getSelectedIndex();

// Be sure item wasn't already put up for sale
            if (myitemname[i].equals(""))
        return;

            // Marshal data for item in a String
            String theitem = myitemname[i]+"!"+myitemdescript[i]+"!"+price;
```

```
                    // Remove the item from the local list of my items
                    myitemname[i] = "";
                    myitemdescript[i] = "";

                    SellIt si = new SellIt(theitem);
                }
            }
        }
    }

    void CreateMainform()
    {
      mainform = new Form("Items For Sale");
      mainform.addCommand(BUY);
      mainform.addCommand(SELL);
      mainform.addCommand(LOGOUT);
      mainform.addCommand(REFRESH);
      mainform.setCommandListener(this);

      mainform.append("Also Here: "+usershere+"\n");
      mainform.append("My Balance: $"+mybalance+"\n");

      if (itemvector.size() == 0)
      {
        mainform.append("No Items For Sale");
        mainform.append("Come Back Later");

            // Remove the buy button
            mainform.removeCommand(BUY);
      }
      else
      {
          String items[] = new String[itemvector.size()];
          // Now parse out the item name
          for (int i=0; i < itemvector.size(); i++)
              items[i] = ItemName((String)itemvector.elementAt(i));

          itemgroup = new ChoiceGroup("Exclusive",ChoiceGroup.
➡EXCLUSIVE,items,null);

          mainform.append(itemgroup);
      }
```

```
    }

void CreateItemsoldform()
{
  itemsoldform = new Form("Item Sold!");
  itemsoldform.addCommand(BACK);
  itemsoldform.setCommandListener(this);
}


class Login implements ServerCallback
{

Login()
{
    ConnectServer("login",null,this);
}

public void serverResponse(String response)
{
  if (CheckForError(response)) return;

  // Parse out the user list and items for sale

  int uindex = response.indexOf("users");
  int findex = response.indexOf("forsale");
  if (uindex == -1 || findex == -1)
  {
      ShowError("Bad User List or For Sale List Returned");
      return;
  }
  usershere = response.substring(6,findex-1);
  String forsale = response.substring(findex+8);

  // Now parse through the for sale list
  itemvector = new Vector();
  CreateItemVector(forsale,itemvector);
  boolean canbuy = true;

  CreateMainform();

  display.setCurrent(mainform);
```

```
  }
  }

  private void buydetail(int at)
  {
    detailform = new Form("Ready To Buy");
    detailform.addCommand(BUYIT);
    detailform.addCommand(BACK);
    detailform.setCommandListener(this);

    detailform.append(ItemName((String)itemvector.elementAt(at))+"\n");

    // Show the description
    detailform.append(ItemDescription((String)itemvector.elementAt(at))+"\n");

    // Show the price
    String iprice = ItemPrice((String)itemvector.elementAt(at));
    detailform.append("For $"+iprice+"\n");
    try {
    price = Integer.parseInt(iprice);
    }
    catch (NumberFormatException nfe)
    {
        price = 0;
    }

    // Do we have enough money?
    if (price > mybalance)
    {
     detailform.append("You Can't Afford This!");
    detailform.removeCommand(BUYIT);
    }
    display.setCurrent(detailform);
  }

  class BuyIt implements ServerCallback
  {
  int index;

  BuyIt(int itemindex)
  {
    index = itemindex;
```

```
      ConnectServer("buy",itemgroup.getString(itemindex),this);
    }

    public void serverResponse(String response)
    {
      if (CheckForError(response)) return;
      if (response.equals(""))
      {
      // Charge your account
          mybalance -= price;

          // TODO: Add item to your personal database

          // Remove item from local list
      itemvector.removeElementAt(index);

      CreateMainform();
          display.setCurrent(mainform);
      }
      else
          ShowError(response);
    }
    }

    private void sell()
    {
      sellform = new Form("Your Items");
      sellform.addCommand(SELLIT);
      sellform.addCommand(BACK);
      sellform.setCommandListener(this);

      itemgroup = new ChoiceGroup("Exclusive",ChoiceGroup.
➥EXCLUSIVE,myitemname,null);
      sellform.append(itemgroup);
      display.setCurrent(sellform);
    }

    private void pickprice()
    {
      sellform2 = new Form("Choose Sale Price");
      sellform2.addCommand(SELLIT);
      sellform2.addCommand(BACK);
```

```
    sellform2.setCommandListener(this);

    sellform2.append(itemgroup.getString(itemgroup.getSelectedIndex())+"\n");

    pricefield = new TextField("Price:", "", 3, TextField.NUMERIC);
    sellform2.append(pricefield);

    display.setCurrent(sellform2);
}

class SellIt implements ServerCallback
{

SellIt(String item)
{
  ConnectServer("sell", item, this);
}

public void serverResponse(String response)
{
  if (CheckForError(response)) return;

  // Begin polling the server for any updates
  if (timer == null)
  {
      timer = new Timer();
  CheckInTimer ci = new CheckInTimer();
  timer.schedule(ci,(long)10000,10000);
  }
  display.setCurrent(mainform);
}
}

class Logout implements ServerCallback
{

Logout()
{
  if (timer != null)
  timer.cancel();
  ConnectServer("logout",null,this);
}
```

```java
public void serverResponse(String response)
{
  if (CheckForError(response)) return;
  display.setCurrent(loginform);
}
}

class CheckIn implements ServerCallback  {

CheckIn()
{
  ConnectServer("checkin",null,this);
}

public void serverResponse(String response)
{
  if (CheckForError(response)) return;
  int rindex = response.indexOf("sold");
  if (rindex != -1)
  {
      String items = response.substring(rindex+5);
      if (!items.equals(""))
      {
    CreateItemsoldform();
     solditemvector = new Vector();
        CreateItemVector(items,solditemvector);

        // Now parse out the item name
        for (int i=0; i < solditemvector.size(); i++)
        {
         String itemname = ItemName((String)solditemvector.elementAt(i));
         String itemprice = ItemPrice((String)solditemvector.elementAt(i));
           int price = 0;
           try {
             price = Integer.parseInt(itemprice);
           }
           catch (NumberFormatException nfe) { }

           // TODO: Remove the item from the database
       itemsoldform.append(itemname+" sold for $"+itemprice);

           // Add money to your balance
```

```
                    mybalance += price;
            CreateMainform();
            display.setCurrent(itemsoldform);
             }
          }
      }
  }
}


void CreateItemVector(String items,Vector iv)
{
    // Parse through the list of items
    int start = 0;
    int end = 0;
    String item = "";
    end = items.indexOf(',');

    while (end != -1)
    {
     item = items.substring(start,end);
     iv.addElement(item);
     start = end+1;
     end = items.indexOf(',',start);
    }
    item = items.substring(start);
    if (!item.equals(""))
  iv.addElement(item);
}


private boolean CheckForError(String response)
{
   System.out.println("RESP:"+response);
   int ecode = response.indexOf("error");
   if (ecode != -1)
   {
   String therror = response.substring(ecode+6);
   ShowError(therror);
   return true;
   }
   return false;
}
```

```
private void ShowError(String err)
{
  Alert errorAlert = new Alert("Alert",err,null, AlertType.ERROR);
  errorAlert.setTimeout(Alert.FOREVER);
  display.setCurrent(errorAlert);
}

private String ItemName(String item)
{
  int end = item.indexOf('!');
  if (end == -1)
  {
      ShowError("Bad Item Format");
      return "";
  }
  return item.substring(0,end);
  // Horse!mean!669
}

private String ItemDescription(String item)
{
  int start = item.indexOf('!');
  int end = item.indexOf('!',start+1);
  if (end == -1 || start == -1)
  {
      ShowError("Bad Item Format");
      return "";
  }
  return item.substring(start+1,end);
}

private String ItemPrice(String item)
{
  int start = item.indexOf('!');
  int end = item.indexOf('!',start+1);
  if (end == -1 || start == -1)
  {
      ShowError("Bad Item Format");
      return "";
  }
  return item.substring(end+1);
}
```

```
    void ConnectServer(String action,String item,ServerCallback callback)
    {
        ConnectNow cn = new ConnectNow(action,item,callback);
        cn.start();
    }

    public interface ServerCallback
    {
        public void serverResponse( String response);
    }

    class ConnectNow implements Runnable
    {
      String action;
      String item;
      ServerCallback callback;

      ConnectNow( String a,String i,ServerCallback c)
      {
        action = a;
        item = i;
        callback = c;
      }

      public void run()
      {
        HttpConnection c = null;
        InputStream is = null;
        DataOutputStream os = null;
        StringBuffer b = new StringBuffer();

        if (item == null)
            item = "";

        try
        {
          c = (HttpConnection)Connector.open(url);
          c.setRequestMethod(HttpConnection.POST);
          c.setRequestProperty("User-Agent","Profile/MIDP-1.0
➥Configuration/CLDC-1.0");
          c.setRequestProperty("Content-Language", "en-US");
```

```
    os = new DataOutputStream(c.openOutputStream());
    os.writeUTF(username);
    os.writeUTF(action);
    os.writeUTF(item);
System.out.println(username+","+action+","+item);

    int rc = c.getResponseCode();
    if( rc == HttpConnection.HTTP_OK )
    {
      is = c.openDataInputStream();
      int ch;
      while ((ch = is.read()) != -1)
          b.append((char) ch);
    }
    else
    {
     System.out.println("Response Code: "+rc);
       ShowError("Bad Server Response!");
    }
  }
  catch (Exception e)
  {
      ShowError("Problem Connecting to Network");
  }
  finally
  {
    try {
    if (is != null)
      is.close();
    if (c != null)
      c.close();
    if (os != null)
      os.close();
    }
    catch (Exception e)
    {
      ShowError("Problem Closing Network Connection");
    }
  }
  if (b != null)
      callback.serverResponse(b.toString());
  else
```

```
          callback.serverResponse(null);
    }

    void start()
    {
      Thread t = new Thread( this );
      try
      {
        t.start();
      }
      catch( Exception e )
      {
          ShowError(e.toString());
      }
    }
  }

  class CheckInTimer extends TimerTask
  {
    CheckInTimer() { }

    public void run()
    {
      try {
          CheckIn ci = new CheckIn();
      }
      catch (Exception ex) { }
    }
  }
}
```

## The Server Side

The Garage servlet itself is pretty simple—once kicked off, it remains running. It listens for new connections, handles commands, and returns data.

### The Game Data

Encapsulating the game data itself in Java classes is an exceptionally easy way to keep track of things. Eventually, these classes could be turned into Enterprise JavaBeans, enabling all the data to be stored permanently in a database.

Basically, we have two objects we care about: CarItem and CarUser.

For the sake of this simplified demo, `CarUser` merely contains one item—the user's name.

We'll also create an `equals` method to help the servlet figure out whether two users are the same:

```
public class CarUser {
    public String name;

    CarUser (String n) {
        name = n;
    }

    public boolean equals(CarUser cu) {
        return (cu.name.equals(name));
    }
}
```

Meanwhile, the `CarItem` class isn't that much more complicated. It just holds the items that are for sale, their description, and the sale price:

```
public class CarItem {
    public String name;
    public String description;
    public int cost;
    public String ownername;

    CarItem (String n,String d,int c,String o) {
        name = n;
        description = d;
        cost = c;
        ownername = o;
    }
}
```

Note that eventually you could use `CarItem` to keep track of things on both the client side as well as the server side. You could also create special classes that extend `CarItem`—for example, the `Armor` class, `Wheel` class, `Weapon` class, `Booster` class, or `Engine` class.

Let's just concentrate on one of these, the `Weapon` class. The class is relatively simple. It basically just acts as a container to hold several useful variables.

It could, in theory, look like the following code fragment, containing the amount of damage the weapon extracts, the amount of ammunition left, and whether the weapon is situated on the front, side, or back of the car.

```java
public class Weapon extends CarItem
{
  static public final int FRONT = 0;
  static public final int REAR = 1;
  static public final int LEFT = 2;
  static public final int RIGHT = 3;

  public int weapon;
  public int damagepoints;
  public int ammunition;
  public int location;

  Weapon(String name,String descrip,int cost,String ownname,int points,int
➥ammo,int loc)
  {
    super(name,descrip,cost,ownname);
    damagepoints = points;
    ammunition = ammo;
    location = loc;
  }
}
```

To create a flamethrower, you would just use

```java
Weapon ft = new Weapon("flamethrower","Burns Vehicles In Front",
➥100,myname,25,16,Weapon.FRONT);
```

### The Servlet

Running on the `localhost` machine is the `GarageServlet` servlet, which simply waits for HTTP messages.

The full code is as follows:

```java
import java.io.*;
import java.util.*;
import javax.servlet.*;
import javax.servlet.http.*;

public class GarageServlet extends HttpServlet {
```

```java
// Store the users, items for sale, and items sold
private static Vector users = new Vector();
private static Vector forSale = new Vector();
private static Vector sold = new Vector();

    public GarageServlet() { }

    public void doPost(HttpServletRequest request,HttpServletResponse response)
      throws ServletException,IOException
    {
      // Get the input stream
      ServletInputStream in = request.getInputStream();
      DataInputStream din = new DataInputStream(in);

    try {
      String name = din.readUTF();
      String action = din.readUTF();
      String item = din.readUTF();
      din.close();
    SendOutput(name,action,item,response);
    }
    catch (Exception e)
    {
      }
    }

    public void doGet(HttpServletRequest request,HttpServletResponse response)
      throws ServletException,IOException
    {
      // get the input through the URL
      String name = request.getParameter("uname");
        String action = request.getParameter("action");
        String item = request.getParameter("item");
    SendOutput(name,action,item,response);
    }

    private synchronized void SendOutput(String name,String action,String
item,HttpServletResponse response) throws IOException
    {
    PrintWriter out = new PrintWriter (response.getOutputStream(), true);
            response.setStatus( response.SC_OK );
```

```java
        if (name == null)
            return;

        if (action.equals("login"))
        {
            // Be sure we aren't already logged in
            CarUser cu = FindUser(name);
            if (cu == null)
            {
                cu = new CarUser(name);
                  // add to user list
                  users.addElement(cu);
              }

            // send down list of users
            SendUsers(out);
            out.print("&");

            // send down list of items for sale
            SendItemsForSale(out);

            out.close();
        }
        // Otherwise, be sure this user is on the system
        CarUser thisuser = FindUser(name);
        if (thisuser == null)
        {
            SendError(out,"Not Logged In");
            return;
        }
        if (action.equals("logout"))
        {
            // remove this user's items from the for sale list
            CarItem ci = FindItemOwnedBy(name);
            while (ci != null)
            {
                forSale.removeElement(ci);
                ci = FindItemOwnedBy(name);
            }

              // remove user from list
              users.removeElement(thisuser);
```

```java
        NotifyOfItemsSold(out,name);
}
else if (action.equals("buy"))
{
     if (item == null)
     {
         SendError(out,"No Item Specified");
         return;
     }

     // Be sure requested item name is on the list
     CarItem ci = FindItem(item);
     if (ci != null)
     {
         // Remove item from the for sale list
         forSale.removeElement(ci);

         // Add item to sold list
         sold.addElement(ci);
     }
     else
     {
         SendError(out,"Item Not Found");
         return;
     }
}
else if (action.equals("sell"))
{
     if (item == null)
     {
         SendError(out,"No Item Specified");
         return;
     }

      // Parse out the name, descrip, and cost
     String iname = "";
     String descrip = "";
     int cost = 0;
     StringTokenizer st = new StringTokenizer(item,"!");
     try {
     iname = st.nextToken();
     descrip = st.nextToken();
```

```
        try {
         cost = Integer.parseInt(st.nextToken());
        }
        catch (NumberFormatException nfe) {
            SendError(out,"Bad Price");
            return;
        }
        }
        catch (NoSuchElementException  nse) {
            SendError(out,"Bad Item Format");
            return;
        }
        // Create the CarItem object
        CarItem ci = new CarItem(iname,descrip,cost,name);

        // Add item to for sale list
        forSale.addElement(ci);
    }
    else if (action.equals("checkin"))
    {
            NotifyOfItemsSold(out,name);
    }
    else
      SendError(out,"Illegal Action");
    out.close();
}

private static void SendError(PrintWriter out,String error)
{
    out.print("error="+error);
    out.close();
}

private static void SendUsers(PrintWriter out)
{
  out.print("users=");
  for (int i=0; i < users.size(); i++)
  {
      CarUser cu = (CarUser)users.elementAt(i);
      out.print(cu.name);
      if (i != users.size()-1)
          out.print(",");
```

```java
    }
  }

private static void SendItemsForSale(PrintWriter out)
{
  out.print("forsale=");
  for (int i=0; i < forSale.size(); i++)
  {
      CarItem ci = (CarItem)forSale.elementAt(i);
      out.print(ci.name+"!"+ci.description+"!"+ci.cost);
      if (i != forSale.size()-1)
          out.print(",");
  }
  }

private static void NotifyOfItemsSold(PrintWriter out,String owner)
{
  out.print("sold=");
  for (int i=0; i < sold.size(); i++)
  {
      CarItem ci = (CarItem)sold.elementAt(i);
      if (ci.ownername.equals(owner))
      {
          // Remove the item from the sold list
          sold.removeElement(ci);
          out.print(ci.name+"!!"+ci.cost);
      if (i != sold.size()-1)
          out.print(",");
  }
}
}

private CarItem FindItem(String name)
{
for (int i=0; i < forSale.size(); i++)
{
    CarItem ci = (CarItem)forSale.elementAt(i);
    if (ci.name.equals(name))
        return ci;
  }
  // Item not in list
  return null;
```

```
   }

   private CarItem FindItemOwnedBy(String name)
   {
   for (int i=0; i < forSale.size(); i++)
   {
      CarItem ci = (CarItem)forSale.elementAt(i);
      if (ci.ownername.equals(name))
         return ci;
    }
    // Item not in list
    return null;
   }

   private CarUser FindUser(String name)
   {
   for (int i=0; i < users.size(); i++)
   {
      CarUser cu = (CarUser)users.elementAt(i);
      if (cu.name.equals(name))
         return cu;
    }
    // Item not in list
    return null;
    }
}
```

## Playing the Game

First you log into the Garage, as shown in Figure 20.2. You then see a list of who's there (Figure 20.3) and what's for sale (Figure 20.4). You can then choose an item that you're interested in. Detailed information about its abilities and enhancements will be shown to you, as in Figure 20.5. You now have the choice of buying it or bailing out. If you buy it, the price is deducted from your account and you now own it.

**FIGURE 20.2**   Logging in.

**FIGURE 20.3**   Who's here...

***FIGURE 20.4***    ...and what's for sale.

***FIGURE 20.5***    An item's detail.

You might also, of course, decide to sell your own goodies to make some extra money. To do so, just hit the Sell button. A list of all your items appears, as can be seen in Figure 20.6.

FIGURE 20.6   A list of your items.

You simply need to set your sale price, as shown in Figure 20.7. You can set this as high as you want, but if you make your item too costly, you will most likely not get any buyers.

FIGURE 20.7   Choosing a sale price.

As you wait, your MIDlet will automatically poll the server every few seconds for any updated info. If somebody decides to buy your item, you are informed as shown in Figure 20.8.

*FIGURE 20.8*    Your item has been sold!

## Summary

And so there you have it—a full-featured (more or less) multiplayer game component!

In Chapter 19, we created a local data store with game information, such as how much money you have, which objects you own, and so on. Obviously, it makes lots of sense to tie the Garage client to this same data store, so that everything you buy and sell is persistent from one game to the next.

In Chapter 24, "Micro Racer: Putting It All Together" we will tie together the data store, the multiplayer buy-and-sell networking component, as well as all the action components. In the end, we'll have a complete, competitive action game with a built-in online community.

# PART V

# J2ME Extensions

## IN THIS PART

21 PersonalJava, Connected Device Configuration, and Other Micro Java Blends

22 iAppli: Micro Java with a Twist

23 Siemens Game API

# 21

# PersonalJava, Connected Device Configuration, and Other Micro Java Blends

## IN THIS CHAPTER

- Connected Device Configuration (CDC)
- PersonalJava
- PDA Profile
- Java Game Profile
- The J2ME Multimedia Profile

Throughout this book, we've been leaning heavily on designing games for the MIDP—the Micro Java profile designed for today's average mobile phone. But there are other types of Micro Java, too. This chapter gives those types a fair shake.

Some examples of devices that sport other Micro Java blends:

- Personal Digital Assistants (PDA)s such as Palm devices will soon have their own Micro Java profile.

- Many advanced hybrid organizer-phones, such as the Nokia Communicator, use Symbian's EPOC operating system, which supports the Java profile. This is often accompanied by the JavaPhone API.

- More powerful palmtop computers, such as those sporting Microsoft's Windows CE operating system, can run PersonalJava. The Sharp Zaurus SL-5000 runs embedded Linux along with PersonalJava.

- Many set-top digital television boxes, game consoles, and other multimedia devices will come with PersonalJava pre-installed, usually working in conjunction with the JavaTV API.

With the large number of devices supporting PersonalJava and other Java technologies, expect to start playing games in places games haven't traditionally been played before. For example:

- A navigation device in an automobile can help pop out trivia, geography, wordplay, or other fun games during long family road trips.

- A refrigerator can make a game out of guessing its contents. Or a special game can help you diet by forcing you to help Sergeant Heart battle the giant Cholesterol Monster before you can mindlessly reach for a snack.

- Small screens in digital telephones might enable you to engage in simple multiplayer games, puzzles, or adventures with friends while you speak to them.

This chapter will discuss PersonalJava, as well as other forthcoming Micro Java profiles that might be useful for game developers.

## Connected Device Configuration (CDC)

The Connected Device Configuration (CDC) is a J2ME configuration meant for higher-end devices that are more sophisticated than standard mobile phones. For example, the CDC covers smart communicators, pagers, micro laptops, PDAs, and set-top boxes. Specifically, the CDC targets devices with the following attributes:

- Minimum 512K ROM

- Minimum 256K RAM

- Connectivity to a network

- Capability to support the full Java virtual machine

- Some sort of user interface

- Typically running on a 32-bit microprocessor

- A basic user interface

Just as the CLDC uses the Kilobyte virtual machine (KVM) to process bytecode, the CDC has a special C virtual machine (CVM). The CVM supports nearly all the Java 2 virtual machine features, but has a much smaller footprint. More info can be found at http://java.sun.com/products/cdc/cvm/.

The CDC uses the Foundation Profile to flesh out all user interface and network

functionality. More info about the Foundation Profile can be found at
`http://java.sun.com/products/foundation/`.

## J2ME Foundation Profile

The J2ME Foundation Profile is targeted at network-enabled devices that do not
necessarily have a display or otherwise require a GUI. As such, there are no user
interface classes or methods.

A target device will have a minimum 1024KB of ROM and a minimum 512KB of
RAM.

## The Personal Profile

The next release of PersonalJava, which is still in the specification phase, is known as
the Personal Profile for J2ME. This profile will be based on the Java 2 Standard
Edition code and will be compatible with PersonalJava specification versions 1.1
and 1.2.

The Personal Profile will use the CDC and the Foundation Profile as a basis, but will
go on to define GUI and other special features.

The Personal Profile will target micro devices with the following characteristics:

- Minimum 2.5MB ROM available

- Minimum 1MB RAM available

- Robust connectivity to a network

- A graphical user interface display

In effect, the Foundation Profile for J2ME, along with the CDC and the Personal
Profile, is equivalent to the current PersonalJava environment. This means that existing PersonalJava applications will be able to run on more modern J2ME systems.

# PersonalJava

The PersonalJava platform was around before J2ME technologies were finalized. It
was the first Micro Java technology. The current release of PersonalJava is basically a
subset of the JDK 1.1.8 code, along with some Java 2 security and support for native
interfaces. PersonalJava also has a few of its own APIs, such as the Timer API.

Just like standard Java, PersonalJava can run as either applets or applications. Various
devices will include browsers than support PersonalJava applets. Other gadgets, such
as the Nokia 9210 Communicator, have a separate AppletViewer program capable of
running applets. Most PersonalJava devices sport the full PersonalJava Application
Environment (PJAE).

Many small devices currently handle PersonalJava. There are also various runtime libraries, such as Insignia Jeode, SavaJe, and Kada VM, which you can install on top of other operating systems, allowing you to then run PersonalJava apps. More information about these packages can be found in Chapter 2, "The Mobile World."

PersonalJava combines the pros of the Java language with a small, efficient footprint and memory model. Thousands of PersonalJava applications have already been written and deployed for set-top boxes, PDAs, and other systems.

More information about PersonalJava can be found at `http://java.sun.com/products/personaljava/`.

## PersonalJava APIs

PersonalJava supports some form of the following standard Java APIs:

- `java.applet`
- `java.awt`
- `java.awt.datatransfer`
- `java.awt.event`
- `java.awt.image`
- `java.awt.peer`
- `java.beans`
- `java.io`
- `java.lang`
- `java.lang.reflect`
- `java.net`
- `java.util`
- `java.util.zip`

In addition, there are several specific omissions and additions.

## Double Buffering

Many PersonalJava devices have built-in support for double buffering. This allows for flicker-free drawing to the screen without any additional work or overhead.

To check whether your device supports double buffering, call the `public boolean isDoubleBuffered()` method from the `java.awt.Component` or `java.awt.peer.ComponentPeer` packages.

If the device supports double buffering, then all `paint()` and `update()` functions will automatically be drawn to an offscreen buffer. If the method returns `false`, however, you will need to implement double buffering yourself.

### Input Without a Mouse

Your PersonalJava application can deal with special input methods. There are four interfaces in the `com.sun.awt` package that enable you to develop components that use specific means of navigation.

The interfaces include the following:

- `NoInputPreferred`—This component is just meant to display something. It has no navigation at all.

- `KeyboardInputPreferred`—Keyboard support is preferred, if possible. Because many devices won't have an actual keyboard attached, a virtual keyboard might appear on the screen and a user may use that to "type" her message.

- `ActionInputPreferred`—A user can activate this component using the standard input device. Basically, the component should be able to figure out when a user has focused on it (`MOUSE_ENTER`), moved away from it (`MOUSE_EXIT`), or selected/clicked on it (`MOUSE_DOWN` followed by `MOUSE_UP`). This usually involves some sort of pointer, such as a stylus, a finger on a touch screen, or rolling around an arrow cursor with a trackball.

- `PositionalInputPreferred`—Use this interface when it is important to determine the specific x and y coordinates that a user has selected within the actual component.

### Dealing with Unsupported Features

If there's one thing can be generalized about the wide variety of devices that use PersonalJava, it's that there are always exceptions to every rule. Some devices just won't be able to support every PersonalJava feature.

As such, if an implementation does not support an optional package or class, then the `NoClassDefFoundError` will be thrown when the program attempts to access that class.

If only certain methods within a class are not valid on a particular device, the implementation will throw an exception class called `com.sun.lang.UnsupportedOperationException` when the method is accessed. Be sure to catch and handle these exceptions throughout your game.

### The Timer API

PersonalJava has a built-in series of timer events. The main timer call is `com.sun.util.PTimer`. A `PTimer` object can hold specific timer events, each specified by a timer specification. When a timer goes off, it calls the timer specification's `notifyListeners()` method.

To schedule a timer, use the `schedule(PTimerSpec pts)` method and pass in a `PTimerSpec` object.

The `com.sun.util.PTimerSpec` class determines how and when a timer should be triggered. A specification can register `PTimerWentOffListeners` and determine how often `com.sun.util.PTimerWentOffEvent` should be thrown.

You can create two types of timer specifications: `absolute` or `delayed`, using the `setAbsolute(boolean absolute)` method. A delayed timer will go off after a set amount of time has passed. An absolute timer will go off at a specific time.

You can set the time value itself using the `setTime(long time)` method. For delayed timers, this is the delay in milliseconds. For absolute timers, this is the time in milliseconds since midnight, January 1, 1970 (a standard Java clock unit).

Delayed specifications can be set to repeat immediately after being activated using the `setRepeat(boolean repeat)` method. A repeating specification can be set to be regular or non-regular using the `setRegular(boolean regular)` method. A regular specification will go off at a fixed interval, no matter what the system load is or whether it takes a long time to notify listeners. A non-regular timer will only begin to count down after all listeners have been called.

The interface used to deal with a timer is `com.sun.util.PtimerWentOffListener`. Simply implement this interface, create your timer, and then handle the `timerWentOff(PtimerWentOffEvent pte)` method. This method will be called whenever the timer finally goes off.

## Developer Tools

Creating PersonalJava applications is similar to cranking out any other Java application. You write the Java source code files, compile them into bytecode classes using `javac`, and test.

Because PersonalJava has several special classes that aren't in the standard JDK, you can download the compatibility classes from `http://java.sun.com/products/personaljava/pj-cc.html`. You will need these classes to compile PersonalJava applets and applications via the standard JDK environment.

### PersonalJava Emulation Environment

After you've built your class files, it's time to see what they actually look like on a typical PersonalJava device.

You can download the PersonalJava emulation environment from Sun's site (http://java.sun.com/products/personaljava/pj-emulation.html). There are versions available for Solaris and Windows. There are also various packages available, to simulate various devices. You can simulate using the full set of support libraries by using standard Win32 or Motif components. Or you can simulate the minimum platform using the special Touchable component set.

---

**TIP**

To ensure that your PersonalJava application runs on any supported device, use the minimal Touchable set.

---

You can run your applications using the pjava program. You can view applets using the pappletviewer. These two programs work just like their Java Standard Edition counterparts, java and appletviewer.

For example, enter the following line:

```
pjava MyTest.class
```

If all goes well, you'll see your application run. You are now able to thoroughly test it.

### JavaCheck

Another tool enabling you to be sure your code is valid is JavaCheck. This program, available for download at http://java.sun.com/products/personaljava/javacheck.html, analyses applications and applets and ensures that they are compatible with PersonalJava or other Java platforms. JavaCheck reads Platform Specification Files, which have a file extension of .spc. These files define the limits of a given platform. Sun has created .spc files for various Java platforms.

So, to test a PersonalJava application, you would run JavaCheck, load up the PersonalJava spc file as the basis, and then input the classes you want to test. JavaCheck will tell you whether there are any errors or warnings.

Both a command line and GUI version of JavaCheck are available.

### Nokia's PersonalJava Development Environment

The Nokia 9201 Communicator is one of the most popular PersonalJava devices available. The Communicator is both a mobile phone and PDA, running on the

EPOC Operating System. It has a full (mini) keyboard and 12-bit color screen that is 640x200 pixels in size. Check out `http://forum.nokia.com/` for more information.

Nokia and Borland have created a visual Integrated Development Environment (IDE) and Software Development Kit (SDK) to help ease application development. The SDK for the Nokia 9210 can plug into Borland's popular JBuilder product, giving the developer an integrated environment in which to write, test, emulate, and debug applications.

To create a PersonalJava file for the Symbian Platform, you must import two packages that include classes for the Crystal application environment and Symbian's standard EPOC classes:

```
import com.symbian.devnet.crystal.awt.*;
import com.symbian.epoc.awt.*;
```

For example, to install your PersonalJava applet on the Communicator or other Symbian platform systems, you need to follow this process:

1. You must obtain a unique identifier (UID) number. You can obtain this from Symbian's Web site at `http://www.symbiandevnet.com/`.

2. Compile your Java code as usual.

3. Package all classes into a JAR file.

4. Create all graphics as bitmaps.

5. Use the AIF Builder tool that comes with the Nokia SDK to create support files. You will need to type in your UID, the application name, and the application's main class and working directory.

6. The AIF Builder tool also lets you import or edit your application's icons. You need to create two icons: One 25x20 and one 64×50.

7. You can also use this tool to set the application's Caption in 23 different languages!

8. In the end, the AIF Builder will output files to your working directory:

    a. An application information file (`.aif`)

    b. A Symbian application file (`.app`)

    c. A text file with command-line parameters (`.txt`)

    d. A resource file (`.rss`)

    e. A multi-bitmap file (`.mbm`)

9. You can now use the emulator to test your program. Just point it to this working directory and select the main class file.

10. To actually deploy to a Nokia phone, you need to create a package (.PKG) file that lists all components. This is a simple text file that lists all the files necessary to build the installer, including the JAR and any image files. This file also indicates what supported languages are, and what the UID number is. The format looks like this:

```
&EN
#{"Test"}, (0x01010101), 1, 0, 0
"Test.aif" - "!:\system\apps\test\Test.aif"
"Test.app" - "!:\system\apps\test\Test.app"
"Test.txt" - "!:\system\apps\test\Test.txt"
"Test.mbm" - "!:\system\apps\test\Test.mbm"
"Test.jar" - "!:\system\apps\test\Test.jar"
"Test.jpg" - "!:\system\apps\test\Test.jpg"
```

11. Use the makesis command-line tool (available from Nokia or Symbian's site) to package everything together. Just input the .PKG file as a parameter.

12. A .SIS installation file will be created. The .SIS file can then be copied to the device using a serial cable or infrared port, or it can be downloaded from the Internet.

## MIDP Plug-In for PersonalJava

It's possible to run MIDP programs on many PersonalJava devices. For example, Nokia offers a special plug-in program for the Nokia 9210 that emulates the MIDP environment. You can find it at the following URL:
http://forum.nokia.com/files/disclaimer/1,14553,1423,00.html.

## PersonalJava Design Considerations

Because PersonalJava is almost as feature-rich as the full Java 2 Standard Edition, developers might be tempted to write big, meaty applets. However, there are many design constraints to keep in mind:

- Many devices don't have typical input or output devices. Some devices might use touch-screen monitors, speech recognition, styluses, joysticks, virtual keyboards, a simple set of cursor keys on a remote control, levers, buttons, dials, and so on. As such, mouse-only events such as right-clicking, double-clicking, dragging and dropping, and so on are not appropriate. Most buttons or other commands should be available via a single "click" or selection.

- There might not be enough room in memory for images. Any images displayed should be very small. Downloading images from the network as necessary and then disposing of them often makes more sense than packaging them in the application.

- Use `flush` and `dispose` on objects as often as you can, and be sure to set all objects to `null` when you're done with them.

- Watch out for hashtables—they eat memory for breakfast. Try to limit them to a few dozen elements.

- For animation, use PersonalJava's built in automated double-buffering rather than copying graphics onto your screen one frame at a time.

- Instead of spawning your own memory-intensive threads, use PersonalJava's Timer API.

## PDA Profile

The Java community is currently fleshing out a J2ME profile especially for PDA devices and other handheld organizers. This profile will extend and enhance the CLDC, and can be found at `http://jcp.org/jsr/detail/75.jsp`.

It is shaping up to be similar to the MIDP, but with better graphics and user interface features, and less support for wireless network functionality.

The PDA Profile will likely have a user interface toolkit that is a subset of Java Standard Edition's Abstract Window Toolkit (AWT). It might also support infrared beaming and persistent storage of data.

The target platform will have these characteristics:

- A minimum of 512KB total memory (ROM + RAM), and a maximum of 16MB.

- Limited power, usually battery operated.

- A basic user interface; Displays should have a resolution of 20,000 pixels or more.

- A basic pointing device and the capability to accept character input.

## Java Game Profile

Information on the Java Game Profile proposal can be found at `http://jcp.org/jsr/detail/134.jsp`. This proposal is for a J2ME profile that will cover nine areas of game development:

1. 3D modeling and rendering, including effects such as reflection mapping, stencil buffer-based shadow volumes, and so on.

2. 3D physics modeling.

3. 3D character animation.

4. 2D rendering and video buffer management, page flipping, hardware-accelerated BLT, line draw, and rectangular fill.

5. Game message marshalling and network communication.

6. Streaming media and high-quality video playback.

7. Sound effects and background music, including support for such formats as MP3, MIDI, streaming audio, and popular voice codecs.

8. Access and discovery of game controllers such as joysticks, gamepads, and steering wheels.

9. Hardware access. The Java Virtual Machine, under the game profile, will likely be able to access memory outside the Java heap. This will enable the program to load game data and memory more efficiently and to access video graphics memory directly for quicker rendering and special effects.

This will allow for a relatively high-end gaming platform. Development of this profile is very exciting for both Java and gaming enthusiasts. If this profile is successful and receives support from major game console manufactures, a game design studio will be able to create one amazing kick-butt game and deploy it on dozens of different systems. Currently, developers must spend millions of dollars porting their games from one console to another.

The idea is to pare down the Java 2 Standard Edition API, which is focused on database and e-business applications, and create a brand new profile geared exclusively towards games. This profile will likely be based on the CDC and Foundation Profile.

There are many existing APIs that support graphics, sound, and other gaming needs. For example, the Java Media Framework (JMF) API supports streaming of audio and video, the Java3D API handles 3D rendering, and Java2D with its `VolatileImage` and `Graphics2D` classes allow for quick-drawing rendering effects.

The gaming profile will likely leverage as many existing APIs as possible, and spawn a whole new set of Java APIs for things such as physics modeling.

The target platform is high-end consumer game devices, ranging from handsets such as the GameBoy to consoles such as the PlayStation 2 and Xbox.

## The J2ME Multimedia Profile

The J2ME Multimedia Profile can be found at `http://jcp.org/jsr/detail/135.jsp`. This proposed multimedia API specification gives developers high-level access to the sound and multimedia capabilities of J2ME devices.

Although many mobile devices can only produce single monophonic sounds, others feature both sampled, synthetic audio and other rich media types. The J2ME Multimedia Profile will be able to handle, generate, and playback sound in all these formats.

Simple controls will handle the lower common denominator, and additional functions will be available for devices that support more advanced audio.

The Multimedia Profile will also allow for time-based synching of images with audio, using formats similar to SMIL.

## Summary

As there are tons of different types of devices, there are different types of Java. PersonalJava cleverly brings the power of the Java Standard Edition into smaller spaces.

In the next chapter, we'll look at yet another breed of Micro Java—NTT DoCoMo's iAppli profile. This profile will allow you to develop kick-butt Java applications in Japan and beyond.

# 22

# iAppli: Micro Java with a Twist

**IN THIS CHAPTER**

- The Architecture of It All
- iAppli: Like MIDP, But Not Quite
- Developing iApplis

In Chapter 6 we looked at i-mode, NTT DoCoMo's popular wireless network. Just as WAP is too limited for true interactive applications, i-mode is too simplistic for apps such as games that require quick reactions, decent graphics and animations, always-connected networking, and sounds.

Like many other mobile phone manufacturers, NTT DoCoMo decided that Java was the answer. However, at the time of this decision, the MIDP specification was just beginning to be fleshed out and taken seriously. NTT DoCoMo, unfortunately, didn't have time to wait. They also wanted to create a library specially geared toward their particular service, brand, and mobile phone constraints.

So NTT DoCoMo built atop the CLDC basics and came out with their own Micro Java profile. It has lots in common with MIDP, but branches off in some interesting and weird directions.

Instead of MIDLets, NTT DoCoMo's Java apps are known as *iApplis*. The first Java handsets went on sale in Japan in January 2001. A full list of current phones capable of running iApplis can be found in Chapter 2, "The Mobile World."

> **NOTE**
>
> While reading about iApplis on the Web, you might come across the word *keitai*. This is a Japanese word meaning "portable," and is often used in the vernacular to refer to mobile phones (*keitai denwa*).

## The Architecture of It All

iAppli applications can run on any 50*x* series of i-mode phone. The extensions library basically sits atop the CLDC class library. Like MIDP, iApplis are based on a subset of the `java.lang`, `java.io`, `java.util`, and `javax.microedition.io` classes.

iApplis are defined using five special packages: `com.nttdocmo.io`, `com.nttdocmo.util`, `com.nttdocmo.ui`, `com.nttdocmo.net`, and `javax.microedition.io`.

In addition, like MIDP, the i-mode library runs using the KVM. Additionally, various phone manufacturers might add additional functionality and handset-specific libraries.

The architecture looks something like Figure 22.1.

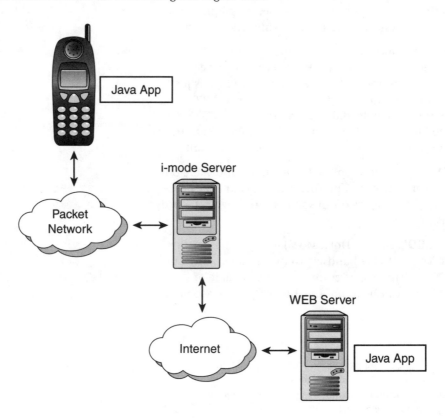

**FIGURE 22.1**    The iAppli architecture.

Basically, the i-mode extension library handles the following:

- User Interface—Graphics and clear interface widgets are a major focus for NTT DoCoMo. For example, iAppli supports i-melody sounds and i-anime animated images.

- Networking—All communication occurs using HTTP. Fully functional client-server application can be run, allowing for true multiplayer gaming or games that change over time based on input from a central server.

- Scratchpad—Applications or data downloaded from the networks can be stored on the mobile phone. This allows for permanent storage of a user's most useful applications. Scratchpad is the storage memory where "files" can be saved and loaded.

- Text Conversion—iAppli handles all Japanese language processing. Just like i-mode's browser, iAppli deals with the Shift JIS (SJIS) Japanese character encoding. Java applications can also display the emoji picture symbols used throughout i-mode.

In addition to providing room for the iAppli classes, media, and ScratchPad, each handset has a Java Application Manager (JAM) that controls the activation of applications in i-mode phone terminals.

## Provisioning

The iAppli architecture makes deploying Java applications really easy. You just drop the application on a Web server. The program is downloaded using HTTP, the same way i-mode formatted cHTML documents are downloaded.

All Java classes, multimedia files, and other data files are packaged in a JAR file and can be downloaded all at once. Alternatively, individual images, sounds, or other pieces of data can be downloaded on-the-fly by the Java application during runtime.

---

**NOTE**

An iAppli program, packaged in a JAR file, can only take up a maximum of 10KB. The phone terminal allocates at least 5KB of room for a ScratchPad. Most Java-enabled i-mode phones will hold at least three JAR files and ScratchPads.

---

Additionally, each iAppli package must include an Application Descriptor File (ADF) with the extension JAM. This is a simple text file, much like a MIDPJAD file, that includes information about how to install, activate, and control applications. It also defines the application's size, its home URL, the size of the ScratchPad needed, and any specific start-up parameters. This can help a handset determine whether the iAppli program will run properly or fit in the available memory.

### The ADF File

Some of the major parameters within the ADF file are detailed in Table 22.1.

Table 22.1    JAM File Properties and Parameters

| | |
|---|---|
| AppName (required) | Application name. This can be a maximum of 16 bytes long. This is the name that appears on the phone's application menu. |
| AppVer | The current version number of the application. |
| PackageURL (required) | The URL from which the JAR file can be downloaded. |
| AppSize (required) | The size of the JAR file. Must be 10240 bytes (10KB) or less. |
| AppClass (required) | The main class name, used to start the application. |
| AppParam | Starting parameters for the main class. An application can call the getArgs() method to access this. |
| KvmVer | Version of KVM, in case you are using a special version. |
| SPsize | Size of ScratchPad needed for this application. |
| LastModified (required) | Last date and time the application was modified. Enables the phone to update the application when necessary. The format is: Dow, DD Mon YYYY HH:MM:SS (Day of the week, Day, Month, Year, Hours, Minutes, Seconds) |
| UseNetwork | You must set this to http when network communication is used. |
| TargetDevice | The brand or version of mobile phone that this application will work on. |
| LaunchAt | iAppli programs can be set to start up every time the phone is turned on, or at specific times, enabling users to set up personal agents that can download news, stocks, weather, gameworld status, or other info according to a regular schedule. |

For example, a sample JAM file named `MySample.jam` might look like this:

```
AppName = MYSampleApp
AppClass = MySample
AppVer = 1.0
PackageURL = http://www.sample.com/MySample.jar
AppSize = 1014
AppParam = arg1 arg2 arg3
LastModified = Fri, 3 Mar 2002 11:11:11
```

### The Provisioning Process

The provisioning process works as follows:

1. A player reaches a content provider's Web page using the standard i-mode browser. A list of various Java games can be presented here. This page is created using cHTML.

2. The player selects the game she wants to play. A message pops up warning the user that the game needs to be downloaded.

3. The JAM file is downloaded. The phone then scans the file and determines whether the application will work on the particular model of handset. For example, if the application uses an extension library that only works on Sony phones and the player is using a Panasonic phone, then a message will be shown telling the player that the application cannot be installed.

4. Likewise, she will be told if there's not enough room on the user's handset. She will usually be given the option to erase other Java applications and free up more memory.

5. If the classes for the game already exist, then the JAR file will only be downloaded if the existing files are out of date.

6. Downloading of the JAR begins. When the download is finished, the player gets a message stating that the application is now stored on the handset. The JAM now has a new applet in its menagerie.

7. The player can now browse her local library of Java applications and select the game. She's off and playing!

All iAppli applications can also operate as standalone apps. For example, a user can enjoy a single-player action game without connecting to the network and incurring network fees of any kind.

### Updating Applications

After an iAppli program has been downloaded, users can activate it directly from the original cHTML i-mode page.

Each JAM file has a `LastModified` entry. If the key is out of date, then the new JAR file will be downloaded and installed. After everything is installed properly, the old JAR file will be deleted. All data in the ScratchPad, however, will remain intact.

### i-mode Extension Tags

To drop an iAppli program within an i-mode cHTML page, you can use the `<OBJECT>` tag as follows:

```
<OBJECT declare id="application.declaration" data="MySampleApp.jam" type="applica-
tion/x-jam">
Here's a Sample IAppli Java Application
</OBJECT>
```

Point to the JAM file using the `data` attribute. You can then have the user download the iAppli as follows:

```
<A ijam="#application.declaration" href="fail.html">Download The Sample App!</A>
```

Note that the `href` attribute points to a URL that will only come up if the application's download fails. This is a good place to put an error or help page.

### Priorities, Priorities

i-mode handsets will give priority to voice phone calls. When a call is received, the iAppli will be paused while the call takes place. When the player hangs up, the iAppli will be resumed.

If e-mail is received, the user will be alerted, but the iAppli will not be interrupted.

---

**WARNING**

If the iAppli is currently sending or receiving data over the network, then some phones will interrupt the data transfer, only to resume it later. Other phone models will simply restart the application. The user will usually have the option to turn this automatic switching on or off.

---

As such, every iAppli should implement the `resume()` method. This method can check to be sure no important data transfers were lost.

## iAppli: Like MIDP, But Not Quite

All iAppli programs run from one main class, which must be derived from the `com.nttdocomo.ui.IApplication` class. When the application starts up, the `start()` method of this main class is run.

The most basic iAppli program would look like this:

```
import com.nttdocomo.ui.IApplication

public class Sample extend IApplication
{
    public IApplication(){
    }

    public void start(){
    }
}
```

When the application is finished, you need to call the `terminate()` method within `com.nettdocomo.ui.IApplication`. The `System.exit()` routine used with standard Java will not adequately shut the program down and clean up all the resources, and will likely throw a security exception.

Other methods within the `IApplication` superclass are the following:

- `String[] GetArgs()`
- `IApplication GetCurrentApp()`
- `String GetSourceUrl()`
- `void resume()`
- `abstract void start()`
- `void terminate()`

## User Interface

Much as with MIDP, iAppli programs enable you to use either a low-level user interface API—drawing pixels directly on the screen—or writing to a high-level API, creating forms using buttons, list boxes, text fields, and other widgets.

All user interface output happens via the `com.nttdocomo.ui.Display` class. Major methods include the following:

- `int getHeight()`—Get the height of the current screen.
- `int getWidth()`—Obtain the width of the current screen.
- `void setCurrent(Frame frame)`—Set the current frame to be shown on screen. This can this a low-level `Canvas` or a high-level `Form`.

### Low-Level UI

Low-level API is based on the `com.nttdocomo.ui.Canvas` class. Methods in this class include the following:

- `Graphics GetGraphics()`
- `int GetKeypadState()`
- `abstract void paint(Graphics g)`
- `void processEvent(int type, int param)`
- `void repaint()`
- `void repaint(int x, int y, int width, int height)`

A low-level implementation of iAppli `Canvas` is almost identical to the way you would do it with the MIDP standard. Basically, all the action happens in the `paint()` method.

You could create a simple `Canvas` class as follows:

```
import com.nttdocomo.ui.*;

public class MyCanvas extends Canvas(){

    MyCanvas(){
    }

    public void paint(Graphics g){
        g.lock();
        g.clearRect(0, 0, 200, 200);
        g.drawString("Hello", 10, 10);
        g.drawRect(5,5, 195, 195);
        g.unlock(true);
    }
}
```

Note the `g.lock()` and `g.unlock()` methods. You should always surround all drawing routines with these functions to draw to an offscreen buffer and create flicker-free graphics.

You could bring the canvas to life by creating an iAppli as follows:

```
import com.nttdocomo.ui.IApplication;

public class HelloIAppli extends IApplication{
    public void start() {
        MyCanvas myCanvas = new MyCanvas();
            Display.setCurrent(myCanvas);
    }
}
```

## Graphics
The `com.nttdocomo.ui.Graphics` class is very similar to the MIDP's `Graphics` class. There are some interesting additions and omissions, however:

- `drawPolyline(int[] xPoints, int[] yPoints, int numPoints)`—Draws a continuous line segment between various sets of points.

- `fillPolygon(int[] xPoints, int[] yPoints, int numPoints)`—Paints a filled polygon with vertices indicated by xPoints and yPoints arrays. There is no corresponding function in the MIDP spec. However, MIDLets do enable you to draw arcs.

- lock()—Begins double buffering.

- setOrigin(int x, int y)—Sets the origin upon which all coordinates will be based.

- setColor(int color)—Sets a color to be used for drawing. Note that you must grab the appropriate color for the given handset using either the getColorOfName(int color) method or getColorOfRGB(int r,int g,int b). For example

  ```
  g.setColor((g.getColorOfName(g.YELLOW)))
  ```

  or

  ```
  g.setColor((g.getColorOfRGB(128,128,128)))
  ```

- unlock(boolean forced)—Ends double buffering. When you lock the graphics context, all drawing occurs in an offscreen buffer. When you unlock the buffer, the entire offscreen image is drawn to the actual screen. If you set unlock()'s forced parameter to true, then the drawing occurs immediately. Otherwise, the graphics are put in a queue and drawn as soon as possible.

### High-Level UI

All high-level UI is achieved by creating a Panel. First off, you can set the title of the panel as follows:

```
setTitle("My Panel");
```

You can then add various user interface elements. Elements will appear in the panel according to the order you add them. You can adjust elements using standard component methods such as setEnabled(), setVisible(), and so on.

Some of the user interface elements are discussed in the following sections.

Label   You can create a text label, choosing the text you want to display and the justification. For example
```
Label lab = new Label("Username:", Label.LEFT);
add(lab);
```

TextBox   You can create a text input box using the TextBox(String text,int columns,int rows,int mode) method.
For example, to create two fields—one for a username (with a default name of "Henry") and one for a password, you would use:

```
TextBox name = new TextBox("Henry", 50, 1, TextBox.DISPLAY_ANY);
TextBox pass = new TextBox(null, 50, 1, TextBox.DISPLAY_PASSWORD);
name.setInputMode(TextBox.KANA);
pass.setInputMode(TextBox.NUMBER);
```

ListBox    The ListBox element is a powerful widget that enables you to create various types of selection menus. Types include the following:

- SINGLE_SELECT—A simple list of choices. The user may select one and only one option.

- RADIO_BUTTON—A list of choices, where each choice is preceded by a small button. The user may select one and only one option. This is shown in Figure 22.2.

- NUMBERED_LIST—A list of choices, each choice preceded by a number, starting from 1.

- CHOICE—A standard options menu choice list.

- MULTIPLE_SELECT—The user may select numerous items. Clicking on a item once selects it, clicking again deselects it.

- CHECK_BOX—A list of choices, each preceded by a check box graphic. The user may select numerous items. When an item is selected, its check box will be filled in (see Figure 22.2).

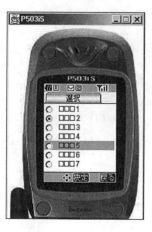

**FIGURE 22.2**    A check box version of ListBox.

For example

```
ListBox lb = new ListBox(ListBox.RADIO_BUTTON);
String items[] = new String[3];
```

```
items[0] = "Choice 1";
items[1] = "Choice 2";
items[2] = "Choice 3";
lb.setItems(items);
add(lb);
```

`Ticker`   This enables you to create a scrolling text ticker, similar to the news ticker-tape in Times Square. The ticker will usually appear at the very top (or bottom) of the screen.

To create the ticker you could use code similar to the following:

```
Ticker tick = new Ticker();
tick.setBackground(Graphics.getColorOfName(Graphics.LIME));
tick.setText("This text will scroll and scroll forever!");
add(tick);
```

`VisualPresenter`   The `VisualPresenter` component enables you to create a scrollable area in which you can plop an image. You can then set various attributes such as `IMAGE_XPOS` and `IMAGE_YPOS`, which indicate where in the `VisualPresenter` the top right corner of the image will be drawn.

For example

```
VisualPresenter vp = new VisualPresenter();
add(vp);
vp.setAttribute(VisualPresenter.IMAGE_XPOS, 0);
vp.setAttribute(VisualPresenter.IMAGE_YPOS, 0);
MediaImage mediaImage = MediaManager.getImage("resource:///myimage.gif");
try {
 mediaImage.use();
} catch (Exception e) { }
Image img = mediaImage.getImage();
int imgWidth = img.getWidth();
int imgHeight = img.getHeight();
vp.setImage(mediaImage);
vp.setSize(Display.getWidth()/2, Display.getHeight()/2);
vp.play();
```

`Button`   Buttons can be created and added very simply:
```
Button but = new Button("Hit Me!");
add(but);
```

You can detect whether the button is hit using a component event listener, which we will discuss in a later section.

**Dialog Boxes**    To create a dialog box, simply designate the type of dialog you want and the dialog box's title. Valid types include the following:

- `DIALOG_INFORMATION`

- `DIALOG_WARNING`

- `DIALOG_ERROR`

- `DIALOG_YESNO`

- `DIALOG_YESNOCANCEL`

You can then add text to the dialog box and detect button presses. The buttons that appear will depend on the type of dialog you use. Various button types that are in the `Dialog` class include `BUTTON_OK`, `BUTTON_CANCEL`, `BUTTON_YES`, and `BUTTON_NO`.

For example:

```
Dialog dialog = new Dialog(DIALOG_INFORMATION,"Hello");
dialog.setText("Hello sir.");
dialog.show();
```

### Handling Events

The event model for iAppli programs is similar to the listener-delegation model used in JDK 1.1.

If you are drawing a bunch of widgets using high-level user interface classes, listeners might not be registered within a component—but only in the container or panel that holds the component.

If you are drawing directly to the screen using the low-level APIs, all events are automatically passed to the `processEvent()` method of the `Canvas` drawing area. This method can be overridden and all events can thus be handled. You do not need to add a special listener.

**Process Event on** `Canvas`    The `Canvas` has its own event listener built in. Just use the `processEvent(int type, int param)` method.
There are two types of events:

- `KEY_PRESSED_EVENT`—A key was pushed.

- `KEY_RELEASED_EVENT`—The key was released.

Various keys can also be sniffed:

- `KEY_0`, `KEY_1`, `KEY_2`, `KEY_3`, `KEY_4`, `KEY_5`, `KEY_6`, `KEY_7`, `KEY_8`, `KEY_9`—One of the numerical keys.

- `KEY_ASTERISK`, `KEY_POUND`—The asterisk (star) or pound (hash) key.

- KEY_LEFT, KEY_UP, KEY_RIGHT, KEY_DOWN—One of the cursor arrow keys.

- KEY_SELECT—The center select key.

- KEY_SOFT1, KEY_SOFT2—One of the soft keys, usually at the top of the keypad.

You could create a Canvas that deals with keypad presses and other events as follows:

```
class HelloCanvas extends Canvas {

    // Put all drawing here, in the paint() method…

    public void processEvent(int type, int param)
        {
        if(type == Display.KEY_PRESSED_EVENT)
            {
                    int key = getKeypadState();
                    if (param == Display.KEY_RIGHT)
                        // The right cursor key was pressed.
            else if(param == Display.KEY_SOFT1)
                // Softkey 1 was pressed.
            else if(param == Display.KEY_SOFT2)
                // Softkey 2 was pressed.
            else if
        }
    }
}
```

**KeyListener on a Panel**    Panels, meanwhile, can implement various listeners. For instance, to detect key presses simply have your panel implement KeyListener. You can then set the panel as the listener within the constructor:
setKeyListener(this);

The panel must then handle two methods:

- keyPressed(Panel panel,int key)

- keyReleased(Panel panel,int key)

This enables the panel to detect any keypress, similar to the processEvent() method of Canvas.

**Component Listener**    Additionally, a panel can implement ComponentListener. This lets the panel deal with any changes to any of its components. For example, to deal with a button

```
public class ButtonTest extends Panel implements ComponentListener
{
 Button btn;

 ButtonTest() {
 btn = new Button("Button");
 this.add(btn);
 setComponentListener(this);

 public void componentAction(Component source, int type, int param)
 {
    if (source instanceof Button && type == BUTTON_PRESSED)
        // Do something!
 }
 }
}
```

**SoftKeyListener**    Your panel or `Canvas` can also implement the `SoftKeyListener` class to deal directly with the two soft keys. Simply add a listener to your panel or `Canvas`'s constructor method:

```
setSoftKeyListener(this);
```

Then set the label you want to appear on the phone's menu. This label is usually placed directly above the soft key:

```
setSoftLabel(Frame.SOFT_KEY_1, "Exit");
```

You can now implement `SoftKeyListener` using the `softKeyPressed()` and `softKeyReleased()` methods. For example

```
public void softKeyPressed(int key)
{
    if (key == Frame.SOFT_KEY_1)
        MainApp.terminate();
}

public void softKeyReleased(int key) {}
```

### Graphics and Sound

iAppli can handle the following formats:

- Still images—GIF 87 and 87a. Unlike MIDP, iApplis support transparent images. This is good news for game programmers!

- Animations—GIF89a animated GIF sequences.

- Sounds—i-Melody file (MLD) format. This is a format similar to MIDI, allowing up to 16 different voices. Most MLD files are less than 1KB in size.

  You can create i-Melody files using various tools. One popular tool is MLD Creator by Naka-Net (`http://www.naka-net.com/SOFT/MLDC/`).

Images and sounds can be loaded using the `com.nttdocomo.ui.MediaManager`'s methods:

- `MediaData getData(String location)`

- `MediaImage getImage(String location)`

- `MediaSound getSound(String location)`

There are two main locations you can read media from:

- You can place images or sounds within the JAR that the iAppli Java classes are packaged in. In this case, you use the `resource` protocol:

```
MediaImage mi = MediaManager.getImage ("resource: ///sample.gif");
```

- You can grab a media file directly from a Web server using the `HTTP` or `HTTPS` protocol:

```
MediaImage mi = MediaManager.getImage ("http: //www.sample.com/images/sample.gif");
```

  or

```
MediaImage mi = MediaManager.getImage( getSourceURL() + "sample.gif" );
```

**Displaying an Image**    To display an image you could use code similar to the following:

```
MediaImage mi = MediaManager.getImage("resource:///sample.gif");

try{
 mi.use();
}
catch(ConnectionException ce){
    // Could not connect.
}catch(UIException ui){
        // Other exception.
}
Image img = mi.getImage();
```

You can now paint using a `VisualPresenter` component.

When you are temporarily done with the image, you can call `unuse()` to free up the memory. If you no longer need the image at all, you can call `dispose()` to unload the image entirely.

**Playing Music**    To play an audio file, use an `AudioPresenter`. The code is similar to the following:

```
AudioPresenter ap;
MediaSound ms;
ap = AudioPresenter.getAudioPresenter();
ms = MediaManager.getSound("resouce:///audio/test.mld");
try {
 ms.use();
}
catch (Exception e) { }
ap.setSound(ms);
```

You can then play the sound at any time by calling

```
ap.play();
```

When finished, call the `stop()` method on your audio presenter and call `unuse()` and `dispose()` on your media sound object to dispose of the sound properly.

**Listening to Your Music**    You can also keep track of an audio clip by having your panel implement `MediaListener`. You can then set the listener as follows:

```
ap.setMediaListener(this);
```

Finally, you must implement the `mediaAction` method as follows:

```
public void mediaAction(MediaPresenter source, int type, int param)
{
 switch (type) {
 case AudioPresenter.AUDIO_PLAYING:
  break;
 case AudioPresenter.AUDIO_COMPLETE:
  break;
 case AudioPresenter.AUDIO_STOPPED:
  break;
 }
}
```

## Networking and Input/Output

There are basically two ways you can get and receive data:

1. Through the network using HTTP or HTTPS communication. The iAppli inputs or outputs data using standard HTTP requests and responses. Java for i-mode applications cannot use non-HTTP(S) protocols such as TCP socket, UDP, and FTP.

2. Read or write from a ScratchPad. Every iAppli is allotted 5KB of ScratchPad space.

### HTTP Connections

In order to use HTTP communications, you have to add the "UseNetwork = http" line to your application's ADF (JAM) file.

Basically, HTTP communications work the same with iApplis as they do with MIDlets. For example, to read data from a servlet on the network (http://www.myhost.com/myservlet) and put it into a byte array called data you would use the following code:

```
HttpConnection http = null;
InputStream in = null;
byte[] data = null;
String URL = "http://www.myhost.com/myservlet";

try
{
 http = (HttpConnection)Connector.open(URL,Connector.READ);
 http.setRequestMethod(HttpConnection.GET);
 http.connect();

 int contentLength = (int)http.getLength();
 in = http.openInputStream();

 data = new byte[contentLength];
 in.read(data);
}
catch(ConnectionException ce)
{
 // Handle a connection exception.
}
catch(Exception e)
{
 // Handle other type of exception
```

```
    }
    finally
    {
     try
     {
      if(in!=null)
      {
      in.close();
      in = null;
      }
      if(http!=null)
      {
      http.close();
      http = null;
      }
     }
     catch(Exception e)
     {
      http = null;
      in = null;
     }
    }
```

To write to the server you would use code similar to the following:

```
http = (HttpConnection)Connector.open(URL, Connector.WRITE);
http.setRequestMethod(HttpConnection.POST);
http.setRequestProperty("Content-Type","application/octet-stream");
DataOutputStream stream = http.openDataOutputStream();
stream.write(data,0,data.length);
stream.close();
http.close();
```

### CAUTION

For security reasons, iApplis can only access the Web site (the exact URL scheme, host name, and port number) from which they were downloaded. Also, be sure to use the host name when communicating with a server, not the IP address.

### ScratchPad

Writing and reading to the ScratchPad is really easy. Simply use `"scratchpad:///0"` as the URL protocol. For example, to write four Unicode characters to the ScratchPad, use the following code:

```
try
{
 OutputStream out = Connector.openOutputStream("scratchpad:///0");
 out.write(0xfe);
 out.write(0xff);
 out.write(0x100);
 out.write(0x101);
 out.close();
}
catch (IOException e)
{
System.out.println("IOException in save");
}
```

And to read those bytes back in

```
try
{
 InputStream in= Connector.openInputStream("scratchpad:///0");
 for(int i=0; i<4; i++)
 {
  System.out.println(in.read());
 }
 in.close();
}
catch (IOException e)
{
 System.out.println("IOException in read");}
}
```

You could also read or write several bytes at a time using `OutputStream`'s `write(String data,int offset,int length)` method. Then read in using the `read(String data,int offset, int length)` method.

## Developing iApplis

Actually designing and creating iApplis is very similar to developing MIDlets. You need to have a Java compiler and JAR tool, which can be found in Sun Microsystem's J2SE toolkit.

My hope is that this chapter will get you off the ground and creating working iApplis. There is also lots of documentation on the Web, though much of it is in Japanese. The full iAppli specification and API can be found in Japanese at `http://www.nttdocomo.co.jp/i/java/index.html`. However, there is now an English version available at `http://www.nttdocomo.co.jp/english/p_s/i/java/index.html`.

If you happen to live in Japan and own an i-mode phone or two, then you're lucky—you can test your games out right on their target platforms. For those in the rest of the world, however, emulators will do the job nicely. Several emulators can be downloaded:

- i-JADE—A tool by Zentek that lets you simulate several iAppli–capable handsets.

  **URL:** `http://www.zentek.com/i-JADE/index.html`.

- IJavaEngine i503—An open source project emulating the i503 handset.

  **URL:** `http://i503.sourceforge.net/`

- IEmulator—A very useful emulator, written in Java.

  **URL:** `http://uni.himitsukichi.com/iap/eindex.html`

Most of the emulators are in Japanese, and will include lots of Japanese menus. If you explore, it should all make sense soon enough. In general, the first menu option on the phone is usually your test application. The second menu option usually allows you to quit. The i-JADE emulator, however, has an English version.

After you've got all the tools, follow these steps:

1. Be sure to include Sun's `cldc` and NTT DoCoMo's `com.nttdocomo` libraries in your classpath, and compile your application. Most emulators have included the necessary classes as part of their own libraries.

   For example, to compile using the classes that come with the i-JADE emulator:

   ```
   c:\jdk1.3\bin\javac -classpath c:\i-jade\i-jade-p.jar MyApp.java
   ```

   Note that you might need to change the name of the JAR file from `i-jade-p.jar`, depending on the version of i-JADE you download. Different handset emulators have slightly different filenames.

2. Test the application using an emulator. Run the emulator using:

   ```
   c:\jdk1.3\bin\java -jar c:\i-jade\i-jade-p.jar
   ```

   The emulator control panel appears, as seen in Figure 22.3. Here you can input either the name of a JAM file (which must point a JAR), or just a single Java class.

If all goes well, you will then see your iAppli run in the emulator window, as in Figure 22.4.

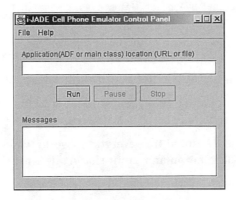

FIGURE 22.3    Inputting a JAM file or Java class.

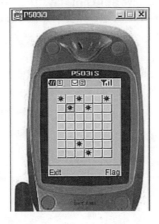

FIGURE 22.4    Emulating a Mine Sweeper game!

3. To actually deploy, you first need to pre-verify your classes. You can use the standard J2ME pre-verify technique discussed in Chapter 9, "First Steps." The pre-verifier also comes with Sun's wireless toolkit:

```
preverify -classpath c:\cldc\classes;c:\i-jade\i-jade-p.jar;c:
➥\myclasses -d c:\myOutput MyApp
```

4. Create the JAM text file, such as myapp.jam.

5. You now need to package your Java classes and all supporting media into a JAR file. Include all GIFs and audio files:

```
c:\jdk1.3\bin\jar cvf MyApp.jar MyApp.class image1.gif image2.gif
```

6. Create a cHTML file with the <OBJECT> tag pointing to your JAR file.

7. Put the cHTML file as well as the JAM text file on a public Web server.

You can now point your i-mode Java-enabled handset to the given Web address and download away!

After you've tested it and ensured that everything works, you can open your game to the public or strike a distribution and profit-sharing deal with NTT DoCoMo.

## Summary

Because iApplis are so similar to MIDlets, it is usually feasible to write games for both systems. It should only take a few hours or days to port a well-written MIDlet so that it will run on NTT DoCoMo's i-mode system. Appendix D lists all the methods and classes that comprise the iAppli profile.

The next few chapters will go into other vendor-specific APIs that can help you write powerful games targeted at specific brands of mobile phones.

# 23

# Siemens Game API

**IN THIS CHAPTER**

- Getting Set Up
- The Game SDK Overview
- Images and Sprites
- Graphic Objects
- Sprites
- TiledBackground
- Flashing
- Good Vibrations
- Music, Sweet Music
- GSM Functions
- Input Output

The Siemens SL45i is more than just one of the first Java phones to be released in Europe—it's actually a lean, mean, fine-tuned gameplaying machine.

To accomplish this, Siemens has put out one of the most advanced Micro Java APIs. The API not only fully supports MIDP, but offers the software developer some additional capabilities:

- Create sprites and sounds using a Game API
- Send SMS messages
- Access the phone book and make calls
- Beam data via the phone's infrared port
- Access the phone's side keys

Motorola, Siemens, and Ericsson have announced that they will band together and create a standard game API. This de facto game API will most likely have many of the same classes and methods discussed in this chapter.

## Getting Set Up

To build a Siemens-specific MIDlet, you must write your code, compile it, pre-verify it, and package it. In other words, the process is exactly the same as creating any other MIDlet.

Siemens has released a full Software Development Kit (SDK) that makes the process easy. You can even integrate the SDK with the Forte development environment if you want. First off, you must have Java 1.3 or later installed. This can be downloaded from
http://java.sun.com/j2se/.

Next, download the Siemens SDK. Go to Siemens' site at `http://www.siemens-mobile.de/` and click on the Developer's Portal. If you don't already have an account, you will need to sign up for one. Signing up is free and painless. Then click on the Wireless Java link to download the latest SDK.

Finally, if you'd actually like to load your MIDlets onto a Siemens phone, you can grab the DataExchange software from `http://www.my-siemens.com/`. Just go to the SL45i page and visit the Downloads and Applications section.

## Compiling

To actually compile, be sure to include the API.jar file in your classpath. Assuming you installed the Siemens SDK to the `C:\Siemens\Java` directory, you could compile the Test.java program as follows:

```
javac -g -bootclasspath C:\Siemens\JavaSDK\lib\API.jar Test.java
```

You can then pre-verify in much the same way:

```
preverify -classpath C:\Siemens\JavaSDK\lib\API.jar;. Test
```

Finally, to package everything together you can use the JAR command:

```
jar cf test.jar Test.class
```

You can now create the JAD *Application Descriptor File (ADF)* as with any other MIDlet. Details on how to do this are discussed in Chapter 9, "Creating a MIDlet."

## Running with the Emulator

The Siemens SDK comes with a neat little SL45i emulator that enables you to launch either JAD files or raw Java classes.

To load up a class file, click on the Start Java Application line in the Commands window. You can select a JAR file, a JAD file, or even a Java class.

After an application has been downloaded on the emulator, you can run it by selecting the Menu command on the phone itself, then choosing Surf/Fun, Java. Select the application you want, then choose the Option command. The application runs, as shown in Figure 23.1.

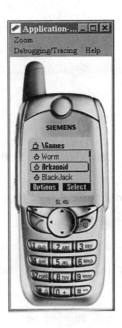

*FIGURE 23.1*   The Siemens emulator.

## Running on the Actual Phone

The easiest way to test your applications out is to copy the class files over using the Siemens DataExchange software.

Connect your phone to your PC using a valid cable—it should come with the phone, or you can obtain one from Siemens. You can now run the DataExchange software:

1. Create a new directory beneath the \java\jam directory.

2. Open the new folder. Copy the class files or the JAR file, as well as any resources (such as images), into the new directory.

3. Open the folder and copy the class files into it.

You can now run the MIDlet!

## Download Your Applet Over the Air

Finally, you can use the phone or emulator to actually download your MIDlet *over the air (OTA)*. To do so, be sure to set up a valid JAD file with a MIDlet-JAR-URL attribute that points to a valid URL:

```
MIDlet-Jar-URL: http://www.myserver.com/MyGame.jar
```

If you want to test the download locally, just point to the phone's local /java/jam directory:

```
MIDlet-Jar-URL: file://a:/java/jam/games/MyGame.jar
```

## The Game SDK Overview

The Siemens game SDK contains everything you might need to create a smooth and quick-moving action game. The SDK classes are in the com.siemens.mp.game package. The classes are

- ExtendedImage—Extended graphical functions for Images.
- GraphicObject—A superclass for game graphics, such as Sprites.
- GraphicObjectManager—Manages and paints GraphicObjects.
- Light—Allows you access the phone's LCD backlight.
- Melody—Plays music.
- MelodyComposer—Creates musical melodies using predefined tones.
- Sound—Allows you to access the phone's sound system.
- Sprite—Allows you to create, move, and animate a game sprite.
- TiledBackground—Allows you to create a background pattern.
- Vibrator—Allows you to access the phone's vibrator.

## Images and Sprites

Images are the main focus of most games. The Siemens API makes it easy to create, manipulate, and render complicated characters and scenes.

### Creating an Extended Image

To create a special Siemens image, just pass a normal Java image into the ExtendedImage class. Because of the way the image might be manipulated, the image width *must* be divisible by eight.

For example

```
ExtendedImage im = new (testimage);
```

You can then modify the image any way you want and use the getImage() method to retrieve a standard Java image.

After you create an `ExtendedImage`, you can perform all sorts of neat modifications. Many methods take a `color` parameter. If you are using 2 bits per pixel, then 0 is the transparent color, 1 is white, and 2 or 3 is black. Otherwise, if you are using only 1 bit per pixel, then 0 is white and 1 is black.

Commands include the following:

- `public void clear(byte color)`—Clears the entire image using the given color.

- `public void setPixel(int x, int y, byte color)`—Allows you to set a given pixel to a specific color.

  Using this command, you can create your own images. For example

  ```
  ExtendedImage im=new ExtendedImage(new Image(24,24));
  im.setPixel(5,0,(byte)1); //black pixel at pos 5,0
  ```

- `public void setPixels(byte[] pixels, int x, int y, int width, int height)`—This lets you create an image using a byte array. Each *bit* of the array indicates the color of the pixel. You can then render this image at a given x,y location. Note that the x location must be divisible by eight.

  For example, to draw a black line that is 8 pixels across and 2 pixels high, create a byte array with two bytes set to –1. The decimal value of –1 is all ones—11111111. You could then draw this line at location 4x1 within an empty image:

  ```
  ExtendedImage im=new ExtendedImage(new Image(24,24));
  byte[] pix=new byte[] { (byte)-1, (byte)-1 };
  im.setPixels(pix, 8, 1, 8, 2);
  ```

Alternatively, you can grab the information from an image using

```
public int getPixel(int x, int y)
```

or

```
public void getPixelBytes(byte[] pixels, int x, int y, int width, int height)
```

## Blitting

To create high-performance graphics, many games will directly modify the video screen, avoiding the overhead of fancy paint and double buffering routes. The process of copying a large array of bits directly into video memory is known as *blitting*.

You can easily blit with any `ExtendedImage`. Simply call the `blitToScreen(int x,int y)` routine, passing in the exact x and y positions you want your image to appear:

```
myimg.blitToScreen(10,15);
```

The most typical usage is to draw all sprites, tiles, and so on to an offscreen image, and then blit that big image onto the screen.

A typical game's paint routine would use a `GraphicObjectManager` to paint all sprites and tiles to an offscreen `ExtendedImage`, as shown in the following code snippet:

```
public void paint(Graphics g)
{
  gameScreen.clear((byte)0);
  try
  {
    gfxManager.paint(gameScreen, 0, 0);
    gameScreen.blitToScreen(0,0);
  }
  catch(Exception e) { }
}
```

## Graphic Objects

Every `Sprite` or `ExtendedImage` you create is a subclass of the `GraphicObject` class. This class basically only has two methods, enabling you to show or hide the graphic:

- `public void setVisible(Boolean visible)`
- `public boolean getVisible()`

You can actually deal with all your objects using the `GraphicObjectManager` class. New objects are added, by default, to the end of the list. When objects are drawn, the first element in the list will be drawn first. Positioning objects in the manager enables you to layer them behind or in front of each other.

The class has the following methods:

- `public void paint(Image image, int x, int y)`—The key routine. Draws all the objects into the given image (usually an offscreen image). The offscreen image must not be transparent. This offscreen image can then be smoothly blitted onto the device's screen.

- `public void addObject(GraphicObject gobject)`—Adds a new object to the object manager at the end of the list.

- `public void insertObject(GraphicObject gobject, int position)`—Adds a new object at a specific location in the list.

- `public int getObjectPosition(GraphicObject gobject)`—Returns the number associated with the given object.

- `public GraphicObject getObjectAt(int index)`—Returns the object at the given index.

- `public void deleteObject(GraphicObject gobject)`—Deletes the given object from the manager.

- `public void deleteObject(int position)`—Deletes the object at the given position from the `ObjectManager`.

- `public void paint(ExtendedImage image, int x, int y)`—Draws all objects to the given `ExtendedImage` offscreen object.

- `public static byte[] createTextureBits(int width, int height, byte[] texture)`—Converts a texture from bytes per pixel into bits per pixel. This enables you to "compress" an image into fewer bytes. For example, the image `{0,0,1,1,1,1,0,0}` would be converted into just one byte: `{60}`.

## Sprites

In Chapter 15, "Entering the Land of Sprites," we discussed what sprites are—basically, any character or graphical object in your game that needs to be animated or moved.

Siemens phones have a special `Sprite` class, a subclass of `GraphicObject`. The `Sprite` class lets you do pretty much anything you can think of:

- `public void setPosition(int x, int y`—This enables you to drop the upper right corner of the sprite at a specific set of coordinates.

- `public void setCollisionRectangle(int x, int y, int width, int height)`—This enables you to create a specific collision rectangle around the sprite. The rectangle can be bigger than the sprite image itself if you want your character to be extra-sensitive, or the rectangle can be small and detect specific collisions. For example, if your sprite is a graphic of a penguin, you can set the collision rectangle around the penguin's head. That way, if a bad guy threw a fish at the penguin's body, a collision would not be detected.

- `public void setFrame(int framenumber)`—This method sets which frame of the animation to draw. The `framenumber` parameter can be set to be anywhere from 0 to the `frameCount-1`.

After your game is running, you can detect where your sprites are and whether or not they've collided with another sprite or a specific point on the screen:

- `public int getXPosition()`—Returns the actual x (horizontal) coordinate.

- `public int getYPosition()`—Returns the actual y (vertical) coordinate.

- `public int getFrame()`—Returns which frame of animation is currently being shown.

- `public boolean isCollidingWith(Sprite other)`—Returns true if the given sprite's collision rectangle is overlapping the other sprite's collision rectangle.

- `public boolean isCollidingWithPos(int x, int y)`—Returns true if the given sprite's collision rectangle overlaps with a specific (x,y) coordinate.

## Creating and Masking a Sprite

A sprite basically consists of two images—a filmstrip of the animated graphic, and a simple black-and-white image representing a *mask*. A mask can be thought of as a specific shape that has been cut out of a black sheet of paper. The shape is then laid atop your graphic, as shown in Figure 23.2. Any pixels not covered by the cut-out will be transparent.

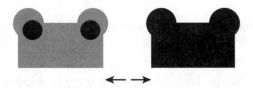

*FIGURE 23.2*    A sprite and its mask.

You can create a mask using most paint programs. Simply throw out the color information from your image, leaving a black silhouette of your sprite.

There are three ways to construct a `Sprite` using the Siemens API:

- `public Sprite(Image source, Image mask, int numFrames)`—This creates a sprite given a source image, a mask image, and a given number of frames. The width of the source and mask image must be divisible by eight.

- `public Sprite(ExtendedImage source, ExtendedImage mask, int numFrames)`—Just like the previous method, except it takes in `ExtendedImages` as the source and mask instead of `Images`.

- `public Sprite(byte[] source, int source_offset, int width, int height, byte[] mask, int mask_offset, int numFrames)`—Yet another way of creating a sprite. Instead of passing in an `Image` object, you can pass in the raw image source and mask data. You must define the width and height of the image so that the byte array can be parsed correctly. The width, of course, must be divisible by eight. You might also begin reading in the bytes at a specific offset.

Each of these constructors will throw an `IllegalArgumentException` if the width of the image is not divisible by eight, if there is the wrong number of frames, or if a transparent color is used as either the source or mask image.

## Sample Code

So, to create a quick game with a few sprites you could use code similar to the following:

```
Image frog=Image.createImage("/frog.png");
Image frogm=Image.createImage("/frog-mask.png");
Sprite frogsprite = new Sprite(frog, frogm, 1);
GraphicObjectManager spriteManager= new GraphicObjectManager();
spriteManager.addObject(frogsprite);
sprite.setPosition(10,10);
spriteManager.paint(offscreen, 0, 0);
```

In your paint method, you could then draw the game screen as follows:

```
g.drawImage(offscreen, 0, 0, Graphics.LEFT | Graphics.TOP)
```

Ultimately, you can layer multiple sprites on top of each other to create a full game, as shown in Figure 23.3.

*FIGURE 23.3*    Multiple sprites.

## TiledBackground

Most games feature not only characters (sprites), but a background world within which the sprites live. The Siemens API includes an easy-to-use `TiledBackground` class that lets you define and draw tiles or patterns across your game screen.

As with `Sprites`, a `TiledBackground` constructor takes three alternative forms:

- `public TiledBackground(Image tilePixels,Image tileMask, byte[] map, int widthInTiles, int heightInTiles)`

- `public TiledBackground(ExtendedImage tilePixels,ExtendedImage tileMask, byte[] map, int widthInTiles, int heightInTiles)`

- `public TiledBackground(byte[] tilePixels, byte[] tileMask, byte[] map, int widthInTiles, int heightInTiles)`

The parameters are as follows:

- `tilePixels`—A Java image, `ExtendedImage`, or byte array that contains the tiles. The total width of the image must be eight. The height can be as long as you want, but the number must be divisible by eight.

- tileMask—This is an 8×8 pixel Java image, ExtendedImage, or byte array with the mask that should be overlaid over the tiles.

- map—This is a byte array that defines how the tiles should be drawn. Each byte represents a separate tile. This concept is explained a bit later in this chapter.

- widthInTiles—The width of the tile map.

- heightInTiles—The height of the tile map.

If the width of the image or mask is not 8, a transparent color is used in the image or mask, or if you define a bigger map than you've actually created, an IllegalArgumentException will be thrown.

Finally, you can determine where within the TileMap the tiles should be drawn using the setPositionInMap(int x, int y) method.

## The Tiles

You can define your tile using any Java image, ExtendedImage, or a byte array.

Although tiles are often geometric, it often makes sense to use a byte array to create the pattern. Each byte in the array should either be 0 (white) or 1 (black). Each pattern within the array should be 8 pixels wide and 8 pixels high.

You can create as many images as you want within a given array. For example, the following code defines an array of two different tiles—the mountains and the forests. If you squint at the zeros and ones, you can almost make out what the pattern will look like. Figure 23.4 corresponds to the tiles created here:

```
final static private byte tiles_pixels[] = {
        0,0,0,0,0,0,0,0, // First tile: The mountain
        0,0,0,0,0,0,0,0,
        0,0,0,0,0,0,0,0,
        0,0,0,1,1,0,0,0,
        0,0,1,1,1,1,0,0,
        0,1,1,1,1,1,1,0,
        1,1,1,1,1,1,1,1,
        1,1,1,1,1,1,1,1,

        0,0,0,1,1,0,0,0, // Second tile: The tree
        0,0,1,1,1,1,0,0,
        0,1,1,1,1,1,1,0,
        0,1,1,1,1,1,1,0,
        0,0,1,1,1,1,0,0,
        0,0,0,1,1,0,0,0,
```

```
        0,0,0,1,1,0,0,0,
        0,0,0,1,1,0,0,0,
};
```

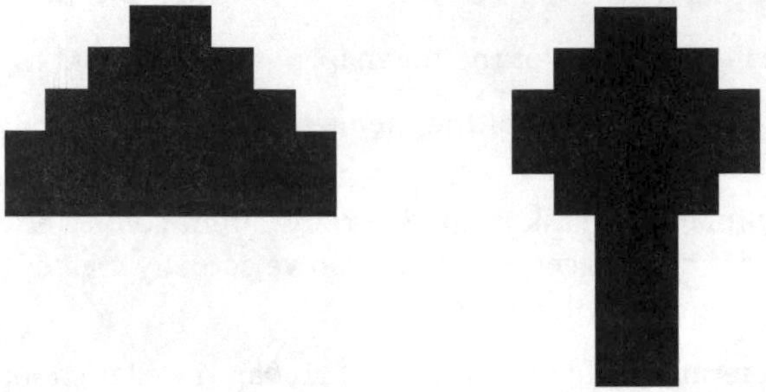

*FIGURE 23.4*    A custom tile.

## The Tile Background

Just as we used a byte array to define each tile, the `TiledBackground` itself can be designed using a byte array. Each byte has a different meaning:

- 0—This tile is transparent.

- 1—This tile is pure white.

- 2—This tile is pure black.

- 3 and up—The is a custom user-defined tile.

For example, you can create a `TiledBackground` as follows:

```
final static private byte map[] = {
0,0,0,0,0,0,0,0, //line with predefined transparent tiles
1,1,1,1,1,1,1,1, //line with predefined white tiles
1,1,1,1,1,1,1,1, //line with predefined white tiles
2,2,2,2,2,2,2,2, //line with predefined black tiles
2,2,2,2,2,2,2,2, //line with predefined black tiles
3,3,3,3,3,4,4,4, //line of hills (3) and trees (4)
3,3,3,3,3,4,4,4, //line with mixed tiles
3,3,3,3,3,4,4,4, //line with mixed tiles
};
```

You could then draw the new `TiledBackground` as follows:

```
TiledBackground tiledBack = new TiledBackground(GraphicObjectManager.
➥createTextureBits(8,16,tiles_pixels), null, map, 8,8);
tiledBack.setPositionInMap(0,0);
GraphicObjectManager spriteManager= new GraphicObjectManager();
spriteManager.addObject(tiledBack);
spriteManager.paint(offscreen, 0, 0); //draw to doublebuffer image
```

You could then draw the double buffer offscreen image in your `paint` method:

```
g.drawImage(offscreen, 0, 0, Graphics.LEFT | Graphics.TOP)
```

A sample tiled screen appears as in Figure 23.5, with a bird sprite in the foreground, a ring pattern set of tiles behind that, an 8-ball graphic in the next layer, and a set of geometric tile shapes in the background. Everything moves at once, smoothly and easily. The code for creating this effect can be found in the `src` directory of the Siemens Toolkit.

*FIGURE 23.5* A tiled background with sprites behind and in front.

Tiling, as you can see, is a great feature that really adds depth and texture to games.

## Flashing

One neat little trick your game can perform is to flash the phone's backlight. This is a great way of getting the player's attention. You can flash things whenever your hero gets hit, whenever you open a new door to your dungeon, or even create an atmospheric game with real-time day and night.

To do this, just use the Light class. It couldn't be simpler:

```
Light.setLightOn();
```

or

```
Light.setLightOff();
```

**WARNING**

Be cautious, though: Every time you flash on the light, you are wasting extra battery power. Be sure to test your game out, so that it doesn't sap away all the phone's energy too quickly.

## Good Vibrations

There is something mobile phones offer that most other gaming appliances cannot—vibrations. Most modern mobile phones have the capability to produce acute vibrations when the user is called as a means of silently letting the user know that somebody is trying to reach him.

Of course, the vibrator can also be used for more entertaining purposes. For example, when player flies a spaceship through a swarm of meteors, the device can vibrate after every collision.

Siemens offers a MIDP extension that enables you to manipulate the device's vibrator. To produce vibration, the com.siemens.mp.game.Vibrator class is used. The class provides the following static methods:

- triggerVibrator(int duration)—Activates the vibrator for a given number of milliseconds. The method should be used to provide shakings and collisions.

- startVibrator()—Activates the vibrator and keeps it on.

- stopVibrator()—Deactivates the vibrator.

So, you could add vibrations to the racing game that we have been developing using code similar to the following:

```
private void checkCollision()
{
  if (enemyList.collide(player))
  {
    player.setEnergy(player.getEnergy() -
        COLLIDE_ENERGY);
    Vibrator.triggerVibrator(100);
  }
}
```

When two sprites collide together, the vibrator's static method `triggerVibrator()` is called. The vibrator is invoked for a duration of 100 milliseconds.

## Music, Sweet Music

One thing that is notably lacking from most MIDP games is decent sound. The Siemens classes comprise one of the best mobile sound APIs on the market.

To play sounds, you need only access the `com.siemens.mp.game.Sound` class. This class has only one static method: `playTone(int freq, int time)`.

This method plays a tone of the specific frequency for a specified amount of time given in milliseconds. For example, to play a tone at 400Hz for 100 milliseconds, you would use the following line:

```
com.siemens.mp.game.Sound.playTone(400, 100);
```

If you are musically inclined, you can combine many of these calls together to perform neat sound effects.

### Melodies

In addition to the generic `Sound` method, the Siemens API also enables you to take predefined musical notes and piece them together, creating rich and beautiful sounding themes, sound effects, and melodies. Siemens extensions offer the `com.siemens.mp.game.Melody` class to play melodies composed with the `com.siemens.mp.game.MelodyComposer` class.

The melodies are based on the custom ring-tones that Siemens users can download to personalize their phones. The melodies have the following features:

- Three full octaves and 8 notes above the third octave
- Multiple note durations, from 1/16 to a whole note, including dotted notes.

For example, you can use various durations of the musical notes C, D, E, F, G, A, H (The H replaces the B in the Siemens API), as well as others, to easily compose complex, rich tunes.

### Composing Like a Virtuoso

The `MelodyComposer` class has the following methods:

- `setBPM(int bpm)`—Sets beats per minute (the default value is 60bpm).

- `appendNote(int note, int length)`—Appends a predefined note of predefined length to the melody composer. All predefined notes are represented as constants. A list of valid notes appears in Table 23.1. Valid lengths can be found in Table 23.2.

- `getMelody()`—Returns the instance of the `Melody` object.

- `resetMelody()`—Resets the composed melody.

- `length()`—Counts the tones in the composed melody.

- `maxLength()`—Returns the maximum allowed size of a melody.

*TABLE 23.1*    Notes You Can Play With

| | |
|---|---|
| NO_TONE | Silence |
| TONE_C0–TONE_C4 | The C note played at various octaves |
| TONE_CIS0–TONE_CIS4 | The C semitone note played at various octaves |
| TONE_D0–TONE_D4 | The D note played at various octaves |
| TONE_DIS0–TONE_DIS4 | The D semitone note played at various octaves |
| TONE_E0–TONE_E4 | The E note played at various octaves |
| TONE_F0–TONE_F4 | The F note played at various octaves |
| TONE_FIS0–TONE_FIS4 | The F semitone note played at various octaves |
| TONE_G0–TONE_G4 | The G note played at various octaves |
| TONE_GIS0–TONE_GIS4 | The G semitone note played at various octaves |
| TONE_A0–TONE_A4 | The A note played at various octaves |
| TONE_AIS0–TONE_AIS3 | The A semitone note played at various octaves |
| TONE_H0–TONE_H3 | The H note played at various octaves |
| TONE_MARK | Sets a marker at a specific point, enabling you to create a variant to be repeated |
| TONE_PAUSE | Pauses the melody |
| TONE_REPEAT | Repeats the melody *n* times from the beginning. Set *n* in the length parameter |
| TONE_REPEAT_MARK | Repeat *n* times from the last TON_MARK call |
| TONE_REPEV | Repeat forever from the very beginning of the melody |
| TONE_REPEV_MARK | Repeat forever from the last TON_MARK call |

**TABLE 23.1**   continued

| | |
|---|---|
| TONE_REPON | Repeat *n* times from the beginning, then continue on |
| TONE_REPON_MARK | Repeat *n* times from the preceding TON_MARK call, then go on |
| TONE_STOP | Stop the current sequence |

**TABLE 23.2**   Tone Length Values

| | |
|---|---|
| TONELENGTH_1_1 | A whole length |
| TONELENGTH_1_16 | 1/16 length |
| TONELENGTH_1_2 | 1/2 length |
| TONELENGTH_1_32 | 1/32 length |
| TONELENGTH_1_4 | 1/4 length |
| TONELENGTH_1_64 | 1/64 length |
| TONELENGTH_1_8 | 1/8 length |
| TONELENGTH_DOTTED_1_1 | A whole length, dotted. A dotted note is equivalent to adding half the beats to the note. For example, if you dot a full-length note, you get a note that is 1 and a half beats long. |
| TONELENGTH_DOTTED_1_16 | 1/16 length, dotted |
| TONELENGTH_DOTTED_1_2 | 1/2 length, dotted |
| TONELENGTH_DOTTED_1_32 | 1/3 length, dotted |
| TONELENGTH_DOTTED_1_4 | 1/4 length, dotted |
| TONELENGTH_DOTTED_1_64 | 1/64 length, dotted |
| TONELENGTH_DOTTED_1_8 | 1/8 length, dotted |

There are many Siemens ring tones published on the Web. If you a do a simple search, you can find numerous tunes to use in your games. For example, the song "Say You'll Be There" by the Spice Girls can be created using the following sequence:

```
Ais2(1/8) Ais3(1/8) F3(1/8) Gis3(1/8) Dis3(1/8) Cis3(1/16) Ais2(1/8) P(1/16)
➥F3(1/8) Dis3(1/8) Cis 3(1/16) A2(1/8) P(1/16) F3(1/8) Dis3(1/8)
➥Cis3(1/8 ) Gis2(1/16) Cis3(1/16) C3(1/16) Gis2(1/16) Ais2(1 /8) Ais3(1/8)
➥F3(1/8) Gis3(1/8) Dis3(1/8) Cis3(1/1 6) Ais2(1/8) P(1/16) F3(1/8)
➥Dis3(1/8) Cis3(1/16) A2(1/8) P(1/16) F3(1/8) Dis3(1/8) Cis3(1/8)
```

**Playing the Melody**

After a melody is composed, you can retrieve the Melody object using getMelody(), then calling the play() method within the melody to start the tune a-crankin'. The melody can be stopped by calling the stop() method.

For example, to play a little ditty when the game is over, use the following code:

```
private void checkCollision()
{
```

```
// Other stuff goes here...
if (player.getEnergy() <= 0)
{
    running = false;
    MelodyComposer  comp = new MelodyComposer();
    comp.setBPM(120);
    try
    {
      comp.appendNote(MelodyComposer.TONE_E1,
          MelodyComposer.TONELENGTH_1_4);
      comp.appendNote(MelodyComposer.TONE_D1,
          MelodyComposer.TONELENGTH_1_2);
      comp.appendNote(MelodyComposer.TONE_C3,
          MelodyComposer.TONELENGTH_1_4);
    } catch (Exception ex) {}
    Melody melody = comp.getMelody();
    melody.play();
  }
}
```

A `MelodyComposer` object is constructed without any parameters. To make the melody quick, the beats per minute value is doubled to 120bpm. When the energy goes below zero, the melody E-D-C is played, with the D duration stretched `getMelody()`, then calling the twice as long as the other notes.

## GSM Functions

The `com.siemens.mp.gsm` package enables you to perform phone-specific functions, such as accessing the phone book, dialing a voice call number, or sending an SMS message.

### Making a Call

Would you like to create a game that actually dials the police department if your character performs an illegal action? Although it is highly *not* recommended to do so, you can using the Siemens API!

Simply call the static `start()` method of the `com.siemens.mp.gsm.Call()` object, passing in the phone number:

```
Call.start("212-555-1212");
```

Note that once you begin a call, the currently running Java application will automatically be terminated. An `IllegalArgumentException` is thrown if the number is in an illegal format, or if the phone does not allow calls to be made from Java.

## Accessing the Phone Book

To get all the Missed Dialing Numbers (MDN) currently within the phone's address book, call the getMDN() method within the com.siemens.mp.gsm.PhoneBook object:

```
String n[] = PhoneBook.getMDN();
```

If all goes well, a String array with all the numbers will be returned.

## SMS Messages

Yes, it's true! You can send an SMS message using the Siemens API. To do so, just activate the static send() method within the com.siemens.mp.gsm.SMS object, passing in the destination's phone number and the message you want to send:

```
SMS.send("212-555-1231","Hi there!");
```

Most phones will display a dialog box asking the user to confirm whether or not she wants to actually send the SMS.

If the number or the text message is missing or in an incorrect format, an IllegalArgumentException will be thrown. If the SMS network is not available, an IOException will be thrown.

# Input Output

The Siemens API not only lets you send SMS messages and initiate calls, but it also enables you to load and save files to the local file system, or send or receive data via the mobile phone's serial or infrared port.

## Sending and Receiving Data

To actually send some data, use the com.siemens.mp.io.Connection class. Construct the Connection class as follows:

```
Connection conn = new Connection(String connectTo);
```

The connectTo parameter can be one of several values:

- SMS:*number*—Connects via SMS to a specific phone number.
- IRDA:—Connects through the infrared port.
- INTERNAL:—Connects through the phone's internal port.

You can then call the send(byte[] data) method to actually send some data. To get a response, use the setListener(ConnectionListener listener) method.

To create a listener, just create a class that implements
`com.siemens.mp.io.ConnectionListener`. You must then add this method to the
class

```
public void receiveData(byte[] data)
```

If any data is received from the given port, this method will be triggered.

## Saving and Loading Files

The Siemens SL45i phone, unlike many other mobile devices, has an explicit file
system with directories that you can read or write to.

The `com.siemens.mp.io.File` package contains a bunch of methods that enable you
to easily create a file, write to a file, read from a file, or even delete a file.

For security reasons, you may only access files beneath the current Java applet's path.
As such, only relative pathnames are valid, and you may not access parent directories using the `..` directive.

The first time you run the `File` class, a special storage directory will be created
beneath your applet's directory.

- `public int open(String filename)`—Opens a file named `filename` and
  prepares the file for reading or writing, in binary (untranslated) mode. If the
  specified file does not already exist, it will be created. Returns a file descriptor
  integer that can be used to access the file.

- `public int close(int fileDescriptor)`—Closes the file associated with the
  given `fileDescriptor`.

- `public int write(int fileDescriptor, byte[] buf, int offset, int
  numBytes)`—Writes `numBytes` from the byte array `buf` at a given offset into the
  file associated with `fileDescriptor`. Writing will begin at the current position
  of the file pointer. After writing a set number of bytes, the file pointer is
  increased by that number. To change the pointer, use the `seek()` method.

- `public int read(int fileDescriptor, byte[] buf, int offset, int
  numBytes)`—Reads `numBytes` (or less) from the file associated with
  `fileDescriptor` into the byte array `buf` at a given offset. The read operation
  begins at the current position of the file pointer. After the read operation, the
  file pointer points to the next unread character. The method returns the total
  number of bytes read. If the value is less than zero, an error has occurred.

- `public static int debugWrite(String filename,  String infoString)`—A
  useful way of creating debug logs for your program; this method adds a given
  string to the indicated filename.

- `public static int exists(String filename)`—Returns true if the given file-name exists.

- `public int seek(int fileDescriptor, int seekpos)`—Moves the file pointer for the specified `fileDescriptor` to the specified `seekpos` location.

- `public int length(int fileDescriptor)`—Returns the length of the file. Length will be less than zero if there is an error.

- `public static int delete(String fileName)`—Removes a specific file from the storage directory. Returns –1 if successful.

- `public static int spaceAvailable()`—Returns how many free bytes are currently available within the phone's file system.

- `public static int rename(String source, String dest)`—Renames the given source file to the new destination name.

- `public static int copy(String source,String dest)`—Copies the given source file as a new file with the destination name.

## Summary

Although the API in this chapter applies only to the Siemens SL45i phone, it also gives you a glimpse of where J2ME profiles are heading.

With better graphic rendering, slicker sprites, tiled backgrounds, delightful audio, and telephonic features, it's possible to design and develop truly kick-butt games.

# PART VI

# Micro Racer

## IN THIS PART

**24** Micro Racer: Putting It All Together

# 24

# Micro Racer: Putting It All Together

**IN THIS CHAPTER**

- The Bad News
- The Good News
- Putting Together the Pieces
- One Game Running Everywhere

In this chapter, we'll take all the pieces of half-baked gameness from other chapters and blend them together to achieve a full-fledged, professional version of Micro Racer. But first, let's recap.

## The Bad News

The bad news, plainly put, is that programming advanced games for handheld devices is a total pain. Compared to a desktop system, the screens are miniscule, the user interface is barbaric, the memory is limited, network connectivity is slow and choppy, and the processor is laughable.

Programming in a language like Java only adds a layer onto this hard-to-digest cake. Sun's Kilobyte virtual machine (KVM) gets its name because it takes up a few kilobytes of space. But even those few bytes are wasteful. The KVM also usurps a fair bit of memory. In addition, Java classes have the added overhead of a slow startup. While startup is going on, the KVM is going through the class, allocating heap space and verifying the bytecode.

Additionally, a Java programmer is restricted to the capabilities of the virtual machine. Because Java must work on a wide variety of devices, it is written for the lowest common denominator.

For example, here are some big stumbling blocks:

- No transparent images. Without transparency, overlapping sprites look really prickly. Any image that might overlap another image or background element will need to be rectangular in order to look good!

- You cannot grab, copy, or edit the pixels of RGB images on-the-fly. This means that ultra-cool graphic effects like fading in, explosions, and dynamic shadows are impossible.

- There is no fill-polygon or fill-triangle method, which makes rendering 3D images quite difficult.

- You cannot copy raw pixel data to the screen (known as *blitting*). This makes it unfeasible to do any texture-mapping or particle effects, and so on.

- Other than elementary system beeps, there is no audio at all. I'll say that again: There is no audio at all!

- There is no floating-point math. This makes some 3D and physics, and even sprite movement, difficult.

- There is no native support or *Java Native Interface (JNI)*. That means you can't dial the phone, work with any of the ringtones, work with any native user interface widgets, and so on.

Additionally, Anfy Team in Italy has put together a detailed list of gaming and graphics-related stuff that MIDP is missing. You can see it at `http://www.anfyteam.com/dev/j2me/midpimage.html`.

Because of all the restrictions on a small device, there is no way of fitting in a *just-in-time (JIT) compiler*. This means that code will run quite slowly. In fact, while playing around with some casual tests, a J2ME application runs about three to eight times slower than a native Palm application written in a compiled language, such as C.

So is J2ME like war—good for absolutely nothing?

## The Good News

Throughout this book we have discussed techniques to sidestep or deal with many of the preceding problems. You have learned how to create your own transparency, make the most out of slow networks, and simulate floating-point math.

In addition, more and more manufacturers are coming out with snazzier extensions to MIDP, allowing for image manipulation, transparency, and enhanced audio. i-mode phones come with some great sound and graphics features out of the box. Siemens, with their nifty game API, are the first to deliver on the promise of extensions. Other companies such as Ericsson and Nokia have game APIs in store and are likely to follow suit. Of course, using one of these APIs means that your game will only work on one particular brand of phone.

It's important to remember that Java is perhaps the easiest modern language to develop in. With garbage collection of old objects and the lack of memory allocation and pointers, it's a great way to create quick prototypes and develop them out into full apps. The object-oriented nature of Java makes it easy to maintain, enabling developers to make sweeping code changes with a little modification to a superclass.

Writing a native handheld application requires countless hours of debugging, emulating, testing, deploying, re-debugging, and packaging. Write to the wrong memory location, and you can easily fry the machine.

If you waste a little memory on a desktop or server application, nobody will bat an eye. But when dealing with a tiny space like a mobile phone, every bad byte hurts. Memory leaks in Java are possible, but they are *much* easier to avoid.

Perhaps the most compelling argument for using Java is that—you guessed it—you can write once and run everywhere. A game written for a Motorola cell phone can also run on a Nokia, an Ericsson, a Siemens, or a Palm. The same code could even be compiled and run as an applet in a Web browser, as an application on a million-dollar server machine, in your car's dashboard, or—eventually—in a Java-powered neural link to your own brain!

Finally, don't forget about the promise of wireless devices. Although it might seem silly to try to achieve a rich, meaningful immersion on a tiny 100×100 pixel screen, there's one thing mobile phone games give you that even the best consoles can't provide: Micro games are always with you, and can be played anywhere you go. This not only means that games can now be more convenient, but wholly new types of games can be designed that take advantage of new lifestyles.

## Putting Together the Pieces

So what do we have here?

- In Chapters 15, 16, and 17, we developed a sprite system and figured out how to create, move, and animate our hero (the race car) and the enemy cars. We also figured out how to detect and deal with collisions.

- In Chapter 18, we added sound.

- In Chapter 19, we discussed ways of saving information as the local database record. This is a useful way of keeping track of how much money you have to spend, and what special attributes your car has.

- In Chapter 20, we created the Garage, an online community you can visit to buy and sell car parts.

So what really remains is to tie everything together. Basically, our game needs to become more than a simple action game—we need to create a complex data structure that lets the player know how good her car is. We need to structure the car in terms of its chassis, engine, tires, weapons, and power-ups. This way, when the player goes online to the Garage to buy components, these items will have meaningful values.

Right now, the car doesn't have any weapons at all! Let's look at how to add some simple weapons, such as oil slicks, machine guns, and flamethrowers.

Another important element will be power-ups. We should scatter ammo, tires, new weapon types, and more throughout the track so that players can spiff up their current weapon. This will make it worth more if they try to sell it online.

To deal with this new complexity and power, we should also create smarter computer-controlled opponents. Some of the enemies can have weapons of their own! This will involve more advanced artificial intelligence techniques.

Finally, we should create several types of tracks to make the game more interesting, and inspire players to try various levels.

Whew! Can we do it?

## Adding Weapons

To add weapons, all we need to do is create a Weapon class. In theory, various weapons can extend from this class, modifying variables and overriding methods as necessary.

To avoid having too many classes, however, we can start by packing several similar weapons within the same class. The class in Listing 24.1 handles a flamethrower and oil slick.

**LISTING 24.1**   The Weapon Class

```
public class Weapon
{
  private int weapontime = 5;
  private int weaponammo = 5;
  private String name;
  private String description;
  public static final int FLAME = 0;
  public  static final int OIL = 1;
  private int weapontype = FLAME;
  private boolean upforsale = false;
  private String displayname = "";

  Weapon(int type,int time,int ammo,String n,String d)
  {
```

*LISTING 24.1*    continued

```
    weapontype = type;
    weapontime = time;
    weaponammo = ammo;
    name = n;
    description = d;
    displayname = name.substring(0,5);
}

public int getWeaponTime()
{
  return weapontime;
}

public void setWeaponTime(int t)
{
  weapontime = t;
}

public int getWeaponAmmo()
{
  return weaponammo;
}

public void setWeaponAmmo(int a)
{
  weaponammo = a;
}

public int getWeaponType()
{
    return weapontype;
}

public void setWeaponType(int t)
{
    weapontype = t;
}

public boolean fire()
{
    if (—weaponammo <= 0)
    {
```

**LISTING 24.1**   continued

```
      weaponammo = 0;
   return false;
    }
    return true;
}

public void setName(String n)
{
  displayname = n.substring(0,5);
    name = n;
}

public String getName()
{
    return name;
}

public void setDescription(String n)
{
    description = n;
}

public String getDescription()
{
    return description;
}

public boolean getUpForSale()
{
  return upforsale;
}

public void setUpForSale(boolean u)
{
  upforsale = u;
}

public String getDisplayName()
{
  return (displayname +": "+weaponammo);
}
}
```

Notice how each weapon has five main variables that need to be set when the weapon is constructed:

- Time—How long the weapon lasts when it is triggered. For example, a flamethrower might stay "on" for five frames.

- Ammo—How many units of ammunition the weapon currently has. Every time the weapon is used (by calling the fire() method), this number is decremented.

- Type—The type of weapon used. This will help the graphics engine figure out which image to paint.

- Name—The name of the weapon. This can change as the player upgrades it in the Garage.

- Description—A good description of the weapon. This will be important when the player tries to sell it online.

The actual visual weapon frames themselves can be loaded using the Cache class:

```
public static Image oilImage;
public static Image flameImage;


static
{
  flameImage = Image.createImage("/flame.png");
  oilImage = Image.createImage("/oil.png");
}
```

Our existing GameCanvas class can then handle the weapon as shown in Listing 24.2. This listing just shows the parts of the class relevant to dealing with a weapon.

*LISTING 24.2*    Adding Weapons to GameCanvas

```
public class GameCanvas extends Canvas
{
  private Sprite theweapon;
  private boolean weaponon = false;
  private int weaponcount = 0;
  private Weapon weapon;

  public GameCanvas(Game midlet, Form form)
  {
    try
```

*LISTING 24.2*    continued

```
  {
     // Use weapon 0 for now
     weapon = game.cs.getWeapons()[0];
     theweapon = new Sprite(Cache.flameImage,10,14, 2);
     theweapon.setX(Float.createFloat((Cache.width - player.getWidth()) / 2));
     theweapon.setY(Float.createFloat(Cache.height - (player.getHeight()
➡ *2) - 14));
     theweapon.setVisible(true);
  }
  catch (Exception ex)
  {
     System.out.println("Problem Creating Sprites!");
  }
}

public void keyPressed(int keyCode)
{
  key = getGameAction(keyCode);
  // When the fire key is pressed, trigger the weapon.
  if (key == FIRE)
  {
    if (!weaponon && weapon.fire())
    {
    weaponon = true;
        weaponcount = 0;
    }
  }
}

public void paint(Graphics gr)
{
  // Paint other things
  ...
  // Paint the racecar
  ...
  // Draw the weapon
  theweapon.setX(player.getX());
  if (weaponon)
  {
        // Draw flame in front
        if (weapon.getWeaponType() == Weapon.FLAME)
        {
```

**LISTING 24.2**   continued

```
            theweapon.setVisible(true);
        }
        // See if the weapon should be switched off
        if (++weaponcount > weapon.getWeaponTime())
        {
            weaponon = false;
            theweapon.setVisible(false);
        }
        theweapon.paint(g);
    }
    // Draw other interface items here
    ...
    if (weapon != null)
    {
        g.drawString(weapon.getDisplayName(), (getWidth() - ROAD_WIDTH) /
            2 + 1, 15, Graphics.TOP | Graphics.LEFT);
    }
    gr.drawImage(scene, 0, 0, Graphics.TOP | Graphics.LEFT);
}

private void checkCollision()
{
    // Did enemy hit weapon?
    if (weaponon)
    {
        Sprite collidedwith = enemyList.collideSprite(theweapon);
        // Get rid of enemy.
        if (collidedwith != null)
            enemyList.deleteSprite(collidedwith);
    }
}
}
```

This is how it works:

1. The weapon is initialized as a sprite. For now, we'll just use one type of weapon, the flamethrower. Notice that the weapon is retrieved from the cs object in the game. This is our data store object, which we will discuss later in this chapter.

2. When the user hits the FIRE button, the weapon is triggered. The weaponcount is set to zero.

If the weapon has no more ammo, then it will not fire. See the `fire()` method in the Weapon class.

3. The next time the car is painted, the weapon sprite is drawn in the appropriate place, which is generally right in front of the car. More advanced weapons, like missiles, can even move across the screen.

   The `weaponcount` is incremented. If the `weaponcount` is more than the `weapontime`, then the weapon is switched off. The weapon will no longer be painted.

4. If an enemy car collides with the weapon, the enemy is removed from the board.

   If you want, you can modify the Micro Racer code to treat collisions more realistically. For example, you could deduct a certain number of hit points from the enemy. Various weapons would exert various types and amounts of damage. If the enemy's hit count reached zero, then a fantastic crashing animation would be shown as the enemy exploded in a ball of flame.

The final game, with weapons and all, appears in Figure 24.1.

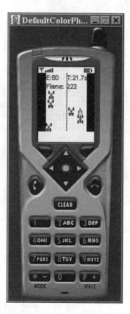

**FIGURE 24.1**    Toasting enemies with our new flamethrower.

## Better Enemies: Artificial Intelligence

It doesn't take a whole lot to make our enemies smarter. Right now, cars are randomly dropped on the track and simply move downward. Let's spice things up a bit by making some enemies move back and forth randomly. Let's also change the velocity, so some cars are faster than others.

This isn't really artificial intelligence (it's more like artificial stupidity). But at least it makes things a little more interesting. To add real artificial intelligence, you'd want to give different drivers personality traits—some would be aggressive, some timid, and so on. Various cars would react to where you go and what weapons you fire in complex and human-like ways. Additionally, enemy cars would need to react to each other. They should not bump against each other or, as is currently the case, overlap with each other.

First, create some random starting positions and velocities using a better initEnemies() method:

```
public void initEnemies()
{
  ...
  enemyList = new SpriteManager(Cache.width, Cache.height);
  int size = length / Cache.height * 4 - 1;
  Random rnd = new Random();
  for (int i = 1; i <= size; i++)
  {
    try
    {
      Sprite sprite = new Sprite(Cache.enemyImage,
          Cache.enemyImage.getWidth(), Cache.enemyImage.getHeight(), 1);
      // Figure out where the enemy starts
      int x = rnd.nextInt() % (ROAD_WIDTH -
          Cache.enemyImage.getWidth());
      x = (x < 0 ? -x : x);
      // Draw at a random X
      sprite.setX(Float.createFloat((Cache.width - ROAD_WIDTH) / 2 + x));
      // Scatter the enemy's Y position
      sprite.setY(Float.createFloat(- i * Cache.height / 4));
      // Modify the speed slightly
      x = rnd.nextInt() % 1000;
      long veer = Float.createFloat(0,x);
      long newspeed = Float.add(veer,enemyspeed);
      sprite.setVy(newspeed);
```

```
        // Move the enemy back and forth
        x = rnd.nextInt() % 2;
        long sidemove = Float.createFloat(x);
        sprite.setVx(sidemove);
        enemyList.addSprite(sprite);
      } catch (Exception ex) {}
    }
  }
```

Then, in the moveSprites() method, be sure that an enemy doesn't drive off the road. If a car swerves too far to the left or right, reverse its horizontal (x) velocity:

```
private void moveSprites()
  {
    ...
    for (int i = 0; i < enemyList.size(); i++)
    {
      Sprite sprite = enemyList.getSprite(i);
      sprite.setY(Float.add(sprite.getY(), sprite.getVy()));
      // Make sure not hitting the side walls
      sprite.setX(Float.add(sprite.getX(), sprite.getVx()));
      if ((Float.getInteger(sprite.getX()) < (Cache.width - ROAD_WIDTH) / 2) ||
          (Float.getInteger(sprite.getX())  +
           sprite.getWidth() > (Cache.width + ROAD_WIDTH) / 2))
      {
            // Move in other direction
            sprite.setVx(-sprite.getVx());
      }
    }
    ...
  }
```

## Better Control

As it stands, the timer in Micro Racer doesn't serve much of a purpose. After all, the player's race car can only move at one speed. Well, it shouldn't be too hard to make things more interesting. For starters, we should use the up and down arrow keys to speed up or slow down our racecar.

This is simple enough, and occurs in the moveSprites() method, which works with a global myspeed variable:

```java
private long myspeed = 0;

private void moveSprites()
{
  switch (key)
  {
    case Canvas.LEFT:
        if (Float.getInteger(player.getX()) >
            (Cache.width - ROAD_WIDTH) / 2)
            player.setX(Float.sub(player.getX(),
            Float.createFloat(2)));
        break;
    case Canvas.RIGHT:
        if (Float.getInteger(player.getX()) + player.getWidth() <
            (Cache.width + ROAD_WIDTH) / 2)
            player.setX(Float.add(player.getX(),
            Float.createFloat(2)));
        break;
    case Canvas.UP:
      if (Float.getInteger(myspeed) > 10)
      break;
  myspeed = Float.add(myspeed,1);
      for (int i = 0; i < enemyList.size(); i++)
      {
        Sprite sprite = enemyList.getSprite(i);
        sprite.setVy(Float.add(sprite.getVy(),myspeed));
      }
      break;
    case Canvas.DOWN:
      if (Float.getInteger(myspeed) < -10)
      break;
  myspeed = Float.sub(myspeed,1);
      for (int i = 0; i < enemyList.size(); i++)
      {
        Sprite sprite = enemyList.getSprite(i);
        sprite.setVy(Float.add(sprite.getVy(),myspeed));
      }
      break;
  }
  ...
}
```

Notice that the longer you hold down the up button, the more each enemy's velocity increases. The finish line's velocity will also increase, as will the power-ups.

The total effect of this is that everything will move downward at a faster rate, making it seem like you are speeding up!

To really get the most of this effect, we'll position the race car slightly above the bottom of the screen by modifying the Y position in the `GameCanvas` constructor:

```
player.setY(Float.createFloat(Cache.height - (player.getHeight() *2)));
```

## Adding Power-Ups

To add a power-up, we just need to create a few random `Sprites` in the `GameCanvas` class. This part is pretty easy, and similar to adding enemies. The only difference is that power-ups don't move from side to side!

For the sake of simplicity, let's just create two types of power-ups—one that gives you an extra point of ammo, and one that gives you anywhere from 5 to 20 dollars. We'll scatter these power-ups throughout the track.

First off, create a new power-up graphic and load it using the global `Cache` class:

```
public static Image powerupImage;
static
  {
    try
    {
      powerupImage = Image.createImage("/power.png");
    } catch (Exception ex) {}
  }
```

Simply create another class-wide `SpriteManager` object to hold the power-ups, and throw in a new `initPowerups()` method as follows:

```
  private SpriteManager powerUpsMoney;

  public void initPowerups()
  {
    powerUpsMoney = new SpriteManager(Cache.width, Cache.height);
    // The number of power ups is half the number of enemies.
    // That seems fair!
    int size = (length / Cache.height * 4 - 1) / 2;
    Random rnd = new Random();
    for (int i = 1; i <= size; i++)
```

```
  {
    try
    {
      Sprite sprite = new Sprite(Cache.powerupImage,Cache.powerupImage.
➥getWidth(), Cache.powerupImage.getHeight(), 1);
      // Figure out how where to put it...
      int x = rnd.nextInt() % (ROAD_WIDTH - Cache.enemyImage.getWidth());
      x = (x < 0 ? -x : x);
      // Draw at a random X
      sprite.setX(Float.createFloat((Cache.width - ROAD_WIDTH) / 2 + x));
      // Scatter the power ups Y position
      sprite.setY(Float.createFloat(- i * Cache.height / 4));
      powerUpsMoney.addSprite(sprite);
    } catch (Exception ex) {}
  }
}
```

You can call initPowerups() in your Tracks class, right after you call initEnemies(). This enables you to give different tracks different types or amounts of goodies.

To create the weapon power-ups, you would simply create yet another SpriteManager instance called powerUpsWeapon. You can then paint your power-ups within the GameCanvas in the exact same way you paint your enemies:

```
public void paint(Graphics gr)
{
  ...
  // paint power ups first since they are on the ground
  powerUpsMoney.paint(g);
  powerUpsWeapon.paint(g);
  // Then paint other things
  ...
}
```

Likewise, you can move the power-ups based on your car's current speed:

```
private void moveSprites()
{
  ...
  for (int i = 0; i < powerUpsMoney.size(); i++)
  {
    Sprite sprite = powerUpsMoney.getSprite(i);
```

```
    long powerUpSpeed = myspeed;
    if (Float.getInteger(powerUpSpeed) <= 3)
        powerUpSpeed = Float.createFloat(3);
    sprite.setY(Float.add(sprite.getY(), powerUpSpeed));
    }
    ...
}
```

Finally, you can check when your race car touches a power-up. Remove the power-up and award more ammo as follows:

```
private void checkCollision()
{
  ...
  // Did we hit a power up?
  Sprite collidedwith = powerUpsWeapon.collideSprite(player);
  if (collidedwith != null)
  {
      // Remove the power up
      powerUpsWeapon.deleteSprite(collidedwith);
      Random rnd = new Random();
      // Add 1 ammo point
      weapon.setWeaponAmmo(weapon.getWeaponAmmo()+1);
  }
  collidedwith = powerUpsMoney.collideSprite(player);
  if (collidedwith != null)
  {
      // Remove the power up
      powerUpsMoney.deleteSprite(collidedwith);
      Random rnd = new Random();
      // Add from 5 to 15 dollars
      int x = rnd.nextInt() % 15;
      x = (x < 0 ? -x : x);
      x += 5;
      game.cs.setCash(game.cs.getCash()+x);
  }     ...
}
```

The game.cs variable seen in the preceding code is discussed in the next section. It points to your CarStore class, which handles all weapons and cash and keeps the values persistent from game to game. Your final game will have little power-up blobs, as shown in Figure 24.2:

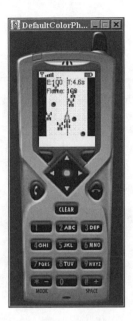

*FIGURE 24.2*  Adding power-ups across the track.

## Tying In the Game with the Data Store

To make Micro Racer interesting, data has to be persistent from game to game—how much money you have, which weapons you've got, how much ammo each weapon has, and so on. The more inventory we make persistent, the more continuous and meaningful objects in the gameworld become.

To create storage for money and weapons, check out the CarStore class from Chapter 19, "Be Persistent: MIDP Data Storage." We will modify it slightly so that it reads and writes each weapon's name and description, along with the ammo, weapon time, and weapon type:

```
// Write the weapon's name
dout.writeUTF(weapons[i].getName());

// Write the weapon's description
dout.writeUTF(weapons[i].getDescription());
```

And for reading

```
// Read the Weapon's name
name = din.readUTF();
```

```
System.out.println("Got the Weapon name: "+name);

// Read the Weapon's description
description = din.readUTF();
```

The trick now is to create a global `CarStore` class. We'll call it `cs` and put it in our Game class, as shown in Listing 24.3.

*LISTING 24.3* Creating a Car Store and Dealing with It

```
import javax.microedition.midlet.*;
import javax.microedition.lcdui.*;

public class Game extends MIDlet
{
  private Display display;

  public static CarStore cs = new CarStore();

  public StartForm form;

  public GarageClient garage;

  public void startApp()
  {
    // To begin, read values from storage
    if (!cs.readStore())
    {
        // If we have problem use default values....
        cs.setCash(100);
        Weapon[] weapons = new Weapon[2];
        weapons[0] = new Weapon(Weapon.FLAME, 6, 7,"Flame Thrower",
➥"Toasts Cars In Front");
        weapons[1] = new Weapon(Weapon.OIL, 15, 2,"Oil Slick","Makes
➥Cars Slide");
        cs.setWeapons(weapons);
    }
    // Be sure we have at least SOME ammo
    for (int i=0; i < cs.getWeapons().length; i++)
    {
        if (cs.getWeapons()[i] != null && cs.getWeapons()[i].getWeaponAmmo()
➥ <= 0)
            cs.getWeapons()[i].setWeaponAmmo(10);
```

**LISTING 24.3** continued

```
    }
  garage = new GarageClient(this);
  display = Display.getDisplay(this);
  form = new StartForm(this);
  display.setCurrent(form);
}

public void pauseApp() {}

public void destroyApp(boolean b)
{
    System.out.println("DestroyApp() called.  Writing data to RecordStore");
    System.out.println("Writing to the store!");
    cs.writeToStore();
}

public Display getDisplay()
{
  return display;
}

public void exit()
{
  destroyApp(false);
  notifyDestroyed();
}
}
```

This is what happens in the preceding code:

1. When the game begins, it attempts to read the current list of weapons and the current amount of cash from storage.

2. If the reading fails, it might be because this is the first time the game has been played. The game gives the player some default values: Seven rounds of a basic flame thrower, two oil slicks, and $100 cash.

3. If the reading succeeds, then the CarStore class will contain an array of weapons as well as the current amount of cash. You can grab these items any time throughout the game by using cs.getWeapons() or cs.getCash().

4. When the game is over, destroyApp() is automatically called. The game takes this final opportunity to store the current list of weapons and current cash balance.

That's it! By putting this code in the constructor of StartForm, the player can display the current balance and weapon list on the start screen the next time the game is started:

```
append("Cash: "+game.cs.getCash());
for (int i=0; i < game.cs.getWeapons().length; i++)
{
  append("Weapon#"+(i+1)+": "+game.cs.getWeapons()[i].getName());
}
```

The starting form will appear as in Figure 24.3.

**FIGURE 24.3**    Showing our current balance and weapons.

## Tying In the Offline Game with the Online Garage

The final task in creating our game is to make it truly multiplayer-capable by merging the storage components and online components. The key to doing this is clever and robust data structures. We already have a Weapon class, which has everything we need to know about a weapon, and we have the persistent CarStore class.

So, all we need to do is tie together the `GarageClient` code from Chapter 20, "Connecting Out: Wireless Networking." Just strip out all the code that makes `GarageClient` a main MIDlet and turn it into an ordinary class.

**Changing** `GarageClient`
You can construct the class as follows, passing in a reference to the game class:

```
private Game game;
GarageClient(Game g)
{
        game = g;
}
```

To trigger everything, we can create a public `Login` method within the `GarageClient` as follows:

```
public void Login()
{
  game.getDisplay().setCurrent(loginform);
}
```

Finally, we need to go through the `GarageClient` class and find all the local variables that contain the amount of cash a player has or which weapons the player wants to buy or sell. We need to replace all these variables with a connection to the `CarStore` class. For example, in the `commandAction()` method, we can deal with a player's `SELLIT` command as follows:

```
else if (c == SELLIT)
{
  String price = pricefield.getString();
  int i = itemgroup.getSelectedIndex();

  // Be sure item wasn't already put up for sale
  if (game.cs.getWeapons()[i].getUpForSale())
    return;

  // Marshal data for item in a String
  String theitem = game.cs.getWeapons()[i].getName()+"!"+game.cs.getWeapons()
➥[i].getDescription()+"!"+price;

  // Remove the item from the local list of my items
  game.cs.getWeapons()[i].setUpForSale(true);
```

```
  SellIt si = new SellIt(theitem);
}
```

## Changing the Game Client

Likewise, our main Game class can have a global pointer to the garage:

```
public GarageClient garage;

public void startApp()
{
  garage = new GarageClient(this);
}
```

## Adding the Garage to the Game Menu

To access the Garage, just add another command to the main menu within the
StartForm class:

```
private Command garageCommand;

public StartForm(Game game)
{
  ...
  garageCommand = new Command("Garage!", Command.SCREEN, 2);
  addCommand(garageCommand);
  ...
}

public void commandAction(Command c, Displayable s)
{
  if (c.equals(garageCommand))
  {
    game.garage.Login();
  }
}
```

## Now You're Online!

That's pretty much it. A player need only select the Garage command from the main
menu to reach the online Garage. The player will then be able to sell her current
weapons, as you can see in Figure 24.4.

*FIGURE 24.4*    Hawking weapons online.

## Future Work

Micro Racer would be even better if it had various types of engines, wheels, chassis, and more. These items could then be added onto any car to achieve better speed, more energy, more accurate control, and so on.

It would also be nice if the various tracks did more than run at different speeds and lengths. It would be nice to actually make a mountain track with plenty of twists and turns, a forest track full of fallen trees, and a city track with intersections, pedestrians, and maybe even police cars.

The biggest addition to the game could be in its graphics. The artwork could be modified based on which track you selected. New tracks with new challenges could even be added weekly to a special game server and then downloaded to the phone.

It would also be nice if the car was more realistic looking, and if the car graphic itself seemed to veer and animate as you moved to the side or hit the brakes. The game could also use some killer death animations, for the times when you destroy an enemy—or an enemy knocks you off the road.

Clearly, Micro Racer "1.0" is only a beginning.

# One Game Running Everywhere

If your game uses pure MIDP and only pure MIDP, then it should be easy to deploy it to almost any phone. Although the means of downloading or installing a JAR file differs from brand to brand, the same code should work without too many problems.

But what if you want to make the most out of each type of phone? It would be nice to create a game that used the best graphic and sound features of each device. For example, using the Siemens API, our driving game might have a neat, energetic soundtrack playing in the background. When the player's car crashes, you might also want the phone to vibrate.

## The Magic of Interfaces

To use the same code base for various extension APIs, simply create interfaces for any external features. For example, let's suppose we want a special sound to play and the phone to vibrate when the player's car crashes. Create an interface called `CrashCarEffect` as shown in Listing 24.4.

*LISTING 24.4*   The `CrashCarEffect` Interface

```
public interface CrashCarEffect
{
    public void ICrashed();
}
```

Now write two classes that implement `CrashCarEffect`. One will be a dummy class for a basic MIDP phone that does absolutely nothing, and is shown in Listing 24.5.

*LISTING 24.5*   The `DummyCrash` Class

```
public class DummyCrash implements CrashCarEffect
{
    public void ICrashed() { }
}
```

The other will be a special class that only works on Siemens phones, seen in Listing 24.6.

*LISTING 24.6*   The `SiemensCrash` Class

```
import javax.microedition.midlet.*;
import javax.microedition.lcdui.*;
import com.siemens.mp.game.*;
```

*LISTING 24.6*   continued

```
public class SiemensCrash implements CrashCarEffect
{
  public void ICrashed()
  {
    // Vibrate a bit
    Vibrator.triggerVibrator(100);
    // Play a defeat sound
    MelodyComposer  comp = new MelodyComposer();
    comp.setBPM(120);
    try
    {
      comp.appendNote(MelodyComposer.TONE_E1,
          MelodyComposer.TONELENGTH_1_4);
      comp.appendNote(MelodyComposer.TONE_D1,
          MelodyComposer.TONELENGTH_1_2);
      comp.appendNote(MelodyComposer.TONE_C3,
          MelodyComposer.TONELENGTH_1_4);
    } catch (Exception ex) {}
    Melody melody = comp.getMelody();
    melody.play();
  }
}
```

Now, in your game code, use the `System.getProperty()` function to figure out what device the player is using. You can then dynamically load the appropriate class using `Class.forName()` and `newInstance()`.

For example, we can modify the `checkCollision()` method in our game's GameCanvas class, as seen in Listing 24.7.

*LISTING 24.7*   Using Different Classes for Different Phones

```
private void checkCollision()
{
  if (enemyList.collide(player))
      player.setEnergy(player.getEnergy() - COLLIDE_ENERGY);
  if (player.getEnergy() <= 0)
  {
      CrashCarEffect tempclass = null;
      String vendor = System.getProperty("microedition.platform");
      try {
      if( vendor != null && vendor.indexOf("Siemens") != -1 )
        tempclass = (CrashCarEffect)Class.forName("SiemensCrash")
```

*LISTING 24.7*   continued

```
➥.newInstance();
      else
       tempclass = (CrashCarEffect)Class.forName("DummyCrash").newInstance();
      }
      catch (Exception e) { }
      if (tempclass != null)
        tempclass.ICrashed();
      running = false;
   }
 }
```

Although the `SiemensCrash` class will not compile using the Wireless Toolkit or standard MIDP development tools, you can toss it into the JAR file anyway. It will just be ignored by phones that do not support it. Alternatively, you could create two different JAR files—one for Siemens users and another for everyone else.

Using the same technique, you can create special interfaces for every major game event, then create device-specific classes for iAppli, Siemens, and so on.

## Summary

What more is there to say?

Throughout this chapter, we've combined all the code we've accumulated so far to create a pretty cool little game (if we do say so ourselves).

However, keep in mind that Micro Racer is a work in progress. We encourage you to take this code and really flesh it out, creating various types of weapons, car parts, tracks, enemies, online community features, and so on.

You should also dust off your artistic skills, or partner up with a good game designer. Better animations and graphics will go a long way toward making Micro Racer seem enticing, sleek, and professional. Better yet, just take some of the concepts you've learned and create something *truly* original! You have a blank game canvas in front of you. Get out there and wow them!

# PART VII

# Appendixes

## IN THIS PART

**A** Low-Level GUI Classes

**B** MIDP 1.1

**C** Siemens Game API

**D** The iAppli API

# A

# Low-Level GUI Classes

## Game Classes

The following listing contains a brief description of commonly used J2ME GUI classes. All the following classes are in the `javax.microedition.lcdui` package.

- `Alert`—Shows data to the user and waits for a certain period of time.

- `AlertType`—Designates the nature of an Alert.

- `Canvas`—Handles low-level events and draws to the display.

- `ChoiceGroup`—A group of selectable elements.

- `Command`—A user action.

- `DateField`—An editable component for presenting date and time information.

- `Display`—Represents the manager of the display and input devices for the device.

- `Displayable`—A superclass of all Screens that can be put on the display.

- `Font`—Text fonts and font metrics.

- `Form`—A Screen that contains common user interface items.

- `Gauge`—A bar graph display.

- `Graphics`—Allows for drawing and 2D geometric rendering.

- `Image`—Holds graphical image data.

- `ImageItem`—Adds an Image to a Form or to an Alert.

- `Item`—A superclass for components that can be added to a `Form` and `Alert`.

- `List`—A `Screen` containing a list of choices.

- `Screen`—An abstract superclass defining the display at any given time.

- `StringItem`—Holds a string.

- `TextBox`—Allows the user to enter and edit text.

- `TextField`—An editable text component.

- `Ticker`—A piece of text that scrolls continuously across the display.

The associated interfaces are

- `Choice`—Components that can be selected from a predefined number of choices.

- `CommandListener`—Receives high-level events.

- `ItemStateListener`—Receives events that indicate changes in the internal state of the interactive items within a `Form` screen.

The hierarchy is as follows:

```
java.lang.Object
        javax.microedition.lcdui.AlertType
        javax.microedition.lcdui.Command
        javax.microedition.lcdui.Display
        javax.microedition.lcdui.Displayable
            javax.microedition.lcdui.Canvas
            javax.microedition.lcdui.Screen
                javax.microedition.lcdui.Alert
                javax.microedition.lcdui.Form
                javax.microedition.lcdui.List (implements
                javax.microedition.lcdui.Choice)
                javax.microedition.lcdui.TextBox
            javax.microedition.lcdui.Font
            javax.microedition.lcdui.Graphics
            javax.microedition.lcdui.Image
            javax.microedition.lcdui.Item
```

javax.microedition.lcdui.ChoiceGroup (implements
javax.microedition.lcdui.Choice)

javax.microedition.lcdui.DateField

javax.microedition.lcdui.Gauge

javax.microedition.lcdui.ImageItem

javax.microedition.lcdui.StringItem

javax.microedition.lcdui.TextField

javax.microedition.lcdui.Ticker

Complete method listings for each of these classes are provided throughout the rest of this appendix.

## javax.microedition.lcdui.AlertType

- AlertType()

- boolean playSound(Display display)

## javax.microedition.lcdui.Command

- Command(String label, int commandType,int priority)

- int getCommandType()

- String getLabel()

- int getPriority()

- String to String()

## javax.microedition.lcdui.Display

- void callSerially(Runnable obj)

- Displayable getCurrent()

- static Display getDisplay(MIDlet c)

- boolean isColor()

- int numColors()

- void setCurrent(Alert alert, Displayable next)

- void setCurrent(Displayable next)

## javax.microedition.lcdui.Displayable

- void addCommand(Command cmd)
- boolean isShown()
- void removeCommand(Command cmd)
- void setCommandListener(CommandListener l)

## javax.microedition.lcdui.Canvas

- Canvas()
- int getGameAction(int keyCode)
- int getHeight()
- int getKeyCode(int gameAction)
- String getKeyName(int keyCode)
- int getWidth()
- boolean hasPointerEvents()
- boolean hasPointerMotionEvents()
- boolean hasRepeatEvents()
- protected void hideNotify()
- boolean isDoubleBuffered()
- protected void keyPressed(int keyCode)
- protected void keyReleased(int keyCode)
- protected void keyRepeated(int keyCode)
- protected abstract void paint(Graphics g)
- protected void pointerDragged(int x, int y)
- protected void pointerPressed(int x, int y)
- protected void pointerReleased(int x, int y)
- void repaint()
- void repaint(int x, int y, int width, int height)
- void serviceRepaints()
- protected void showNotify()

## javax.microedition.lcdui.Screen

- Ticker getTicker()

- String getTitle()

- void setTicker(Ticker newTicker)

- void setTitle(String newTitle)

## javax.microedition.lcdui.Alert

- Alert(String title)

- Alert(String title,String alertText,Image alertImage, AlertType alertType)

- void addCommand(Command cmd)

- int getDefaultTimeout()

- Image getImage()

- String getString()

- int getTimeout()

- AlertType getType()

- void setCommandListener(CommandListener l)

- void setImage(Image img)

- void setString(String str)

- void setTimeout(int time)

- void setType(AlertType type)

## javax.microedition.lcdui.Form

- Form(String title)

- Form(String title, Item[] items)

- int append(Image image)

- int append(Item item)

- int append(String str)

- void delete(int index)

- Item get(int index)

- void insert(int index, Item item)

- void set(int index, Item item)

- void setItemStateListener(ItemStateListener iListener)

- int size()

## javax.microedition.lcdui.List

- List(String title, int listType)

- List(String title, int listType, String[] stringElements, Image[] int append(String stringElement, Image imageElement)

- void delete(int index)

- Image getImage(int index)

- int getSelectedFlags(boolean[] selectedArray_return)

- int getSelectedIndex()

- String getString(int index)

- void insert(int index, String stringElement, Image imageElement)

- boolean isSelected(int index)

- void set(int index, String stringElement, Image imageElement)

- void setSelectedFlags(boolean[] selectedArray)

- void setSelectedIndex(int index, boolean selected)

- int size()

## javax.microedition.lcdui.TextBox

- TextBox(String title, String text, int maxSize, int constraints)

- void delete(int offset, int length)

- int getCaretPosition()

- int getChars(char[] data)

- int getConstraints()

- int getMaxSize()

- String getString()

- void insert(char[] data, int offset, int length, int position)

- void insert(String src, int position)

- void setChars(char[] data, int offset, int length)

- void setConstraints(int constraints)

- int setMaxSize(int maxSize)

- void setString(String text)

- int size()

## javax.microedition.lcdui.Font

- int charsWidth(char[] ch, int offset, int length)

- int charWidth(char ch)

- int getBaselinePosition()

- static Font getDefaultFont()

- int getFace()

- static Font getFont(int face, int style, int size)

- int getHeight()

- int getSize()

- int getStyle()

- boolean isBold()

- boolean isItalic()

- boolean isPlain()

- boolean isUnderlined()

- int stringWidth(String str)

- int substringWidth(String str, int offset, int len)

## javax.microedition.lcdui.Graphics

- void clipRect(int x, int y, int width, int height)
- void drawArc(int x, int y, int width, int height, int startAngle, int arcAngle)
- void drawChar(char character, int x, int y, int anchor)
- void drawChars(char[] data, int offset, int length, int x, int y, int anchor)
- void drawImage(Image img, int x, int y, int anchor)
- void drawLine(int x1, int y1, int x2, int y2)
- void drawRect(int x, int y, int width, int height)
- void drawRoundRect(int x, int y, int width, int height, int arcWidth, int arcHeight)
- void drawString(String str, int x, int y, int anchor)
- void drawSubstring(String str, int offset, int len, int x, int y, int anchor)
- void fillArc(int x, int y, int width, int height, int startAngle, int arcAngle)
- void fillRect(int x, int y, int width, int height)
- void fillRoundRect(int x, int y, int width, int height, int arcWidth, int arcHeight)
- int getBlueComponent()
- int getClipHeight()
- int getClipWidth()
- int getClipX()
- int getClipY()
- int getColor()
- Font getFont()
- int getGrayScale()
- int getGreenComponent()
- int getRedComponent()

- int getStrokeStyle()

- int getTranslateX()

- int getTranslateY()

- void setClip(int x, int y, int width, int height)

- void setColor(int RGB)

- void setColor(int red, int green, int blue)

- void setFont(Font font)

- void setGrayScale(int value)

- void setStrokeStyle(int style)

- void translate(int x, int y)

## javax.microedition.lcdui.Image

- static Image createImage(byte[] imageData, int imageOffset, int imageLength)

- static Image createImage(Image image)

- static Image createImage(int width, int height)

- static Image createImage(String name)

- static Image createImage(byte[] imageData, int offset, int imageLength)

- Graphics getGraphics()

- int getHeight()

- int getWidth()

- boolean isMutable()

## javax.microedition.lcdui.Item

- String getLabel()

- void setLabel(String label)

## javax.microedition.lcdui.ChoiceGroup

- ChoiceGroup(String label, int choiceType)
- ChoiceGroup(String label, int choiceType, String[] stringElements, Image[] imageElements)
- int append(String stringElement, Image imageElement)
- void delete(int index)
- Image getImage(int index)
- int getSelectedFlags(boolean[] selectedArray_return)
- int getSelectedIndex()
- String getString(int index)
- void insert(int index, String stringElement, Image imageElement)
- boolean isSelected(int index)
- void set(int index, String stringElement, Image imageElement)
- void setSelectedFlags(boolean[] selectedArray)
- void setSelectedIndex(int index, boolean selected)
- int size()

## javax.microedition.lcdui.DateField

- DateField(String label, int mode)
- DateField(String label, int mode, TimeZone timeZone)
- Date getDate()
- int getInputMode()
- void setDate(Date date)
- void setInputMode(int mode)

## javax.microedition.lcdui.Gauge

- Gauge(String label, boolean interactive, int maxValue, int initialValue)

- int getMaxValue()

- int getValue()

- boolean isInteractive()

- void setMaxValue(int maxValue)

- void setValue(int value)

## javax.microedition.lcdui.ImageItem

- ImageItem(String label, Image img, int layout, String altText)

- String getAltText()

- Image getImage()

- int getLayout()

- void setAltText(String text)

- void setImage(Image img)

- void setLayout(int layout)

## javax.microedition.lcdui.StringItem

- StringItem(String label, String text)

- String getText()

- void setText(String text)

## javax.microedition.lcdui.TextField

- TextField(String label, String text, int maxSize, int constraints)

- void delete(int offset, int length)

- int getCaretPosition()

- int getChars(char[] data)

- int getConstraints()

- int getMaxSize()

- String getString()

- void insert(char[] data, int offset, int length, int position)
- void insert(String src, int position)
- void setChars(char[] data, int offset, int length)
- void setConstraints(int constraints)
- int setMaxSize(int maxSize)
- void setString(String text)
- int size()

## javax.microedition.lcdui.Ticker

- Ticker(String str)
- String getString()
- void setString(String str)

# B
# MIDP 1.1

## Main Packages

MIDP 1.1 consists of the following packages:

- java.io
- java.lang
- java.util
- javax.microedition.io
- javax.microedition.lcdui
- javax.microedition.midlet
- javax.microedition.rms

## java.io Class Hierarchy

```
java.lang.Object
    java.io.InputStream
        java.io.ByteArrayInputStream
        java.io.DataInputStream (implements
        java.io.DataInput)
    java.io.OutputStream
        java.io.ByteArrayOutputStream
        java.io.DataOutputStream (implements
        java.io.DataOutput)
        java.io.PrintStream
    java.io.Reader
        java.io.InputStreamReader
```

```
java.lang.Throwable
    java.lang.Exception
        java.io.IOException
            java.io.EOFException
            java.io.InterruptedIOException
            java.io.UnsupportedEncodingException
            java.io.UTFDataFormatException
java.io.Writer
    java.io.OutputStreamWriter
```

## java.io **Interface Hierarchy**

```
java.io.DataInput
java.io.DataOutput
```

## java.lang **Class Hierarchy**

```
java.lang.Object
    java.lang.Boolean
    java.lang.Byte
    java.lang.Character
    java.lang.Class
    java.lang.Integer
    java.lang.Long
    java.lang.Math
    java.lang.Runtime
    java.lang.Short
    java.lang.String
    java.lang.StringBuffer
    java.lang.System
    java.lang.Thread (implements java.lang.Runnable)
    java.lang.Throwable
        java.lang.Error
```

```
                     java.lang.VirtualMachineError
                          java.lang.OutOfMemoryError
                 java.lang.Exception
                     java.lang.ClassNotFoundException
                     java.lang.IllegalAccessException
                     java.lang.InstantiationException
                     java.lang.InterruptedException
                     java.lang.RuntimeException
                          java.lang.ArithmeticException
                          java.lang.ArrayStoreException
                          java.lang.ClassCastException
                          java.lang.IllegalArgumentException
                              java.lang.IllegalThreadStateException
                              java.lang.NumberFormatException
                          java.lang.IllegalMonitorStateExecption
                          java.lang.IllegalStateException
                     java.lang.IndexOutOfBoundsException
                     java.lang.ArrayIndexOutOfBoundsException
                 java.lang.StringIndexOutOfBoundsException
                 java.lang.NegativeArraySizeException
                 java.lang.NullPointerException
                 java.lang.SecurityException
```

# java.lang Interface Hierarchy

```
        java.lang.Runnable
```

# java.util Class Hierarchy

```
        java.lang.Object
             java.util.Calendar
             java.util.Date
```

```
java.util.Hashtable

java.util.Random

java.lang.Throwable

    java.lang.Exception

        java.lang.RuntimeException

            java.util.EmptyStackException

            java.util.NoSuchElementException

java.util.Timer

java.util.TimerTask (implements java.lang.Runnable)

java.util.TimeZone

java.util.Vector

    java.util.Stack
```

## java.util **Interface Hierarchy**

```
java.util.Enumeration
```

## javax.microedition.io **Class Hierarchy**

```
java.lang.Object

    javax.microedition.io.Connector

    java.lang.Throwable

        java.lang.Exception

            java.io.IOException

                javax.microedition.io.ConnectionNotFoundException
```

## javax.microedition.io **Interface Hierarchy**

```
javax.microedition.io.Connection

    javax.microedition.io.DatagramConnection

    javax.microedition.io.InputConnection

        javax.microedition.io.StreamConnection

            javax.microedition.io.ContentConnection

                javax.microedition.io.HttpConnection
```

```
javax.microedition.io.OutputConnection
        javax.microedition.io.StreamConnection
                javax.microedition.io.ContentConnection
                        javax.microedition.io.HttpConnection
        javax.microedition.io.StreamConnectionNotifier
java.io.DataInput
        javax.microedition.io.Datagram
java.io.DataOutput
        javax.microedition.io.Datagram
```

## javax.microedition.lcdui Class Hierarchy

See Appendix A.

## javax.microedition.lcdui Interface Hierarchy

See Appendix A.

## javax.microedition.midlet Class Hierarchy

```
java.lang.Object
        javax.microedition.midlet.MIDlet
        java.lang.Throwable
                java.lang.Exception


javax.microedition.midlet.MIDletStateChangeException
```

## javax.microedition.rms Class Hierarchy

```
java.lang.Object
        javax.microedition.rms.RecordStore
        java.lang.Throwable
                java.lang.Exception
                        javax.microedition.rms.RecordStoreException
```

```
javax.microedition.rms.InvalidRecordIDException

javax.microedition.rms.RecordStoreFullException

javax.microedition.rms.RecordStoreNot
FoundException
```

```
javax.microedition.rms.RecordStoreNotOpenException
```

## javax.microedition.rms Interface Hierarchy

```
javax.microedition.rms.RecordComparator

javax.microedition.rms.RecordEnumeration

javax.microedition.rms.RecordFilter

javax.microedition.rms.RecordListener
```

# C

# Siemens Game API

## Game Classes

Programming with the Siemens Game API is discussed in depth in Chapter 23, "Siemens Game API." The Siemens Game API consists of the following classes:

```
java.lang.Object
com.siemens.mp.game.Light
com.siemens.mp.game.MelodyComposer
com.siemens.mp.misc.NativeMem
com.siemens.mp.game.ExtendedImage
com.siemens.mp.game.GraphicObject
com.siemens.mp.game.Sprite
com.siemens.mp.game.TiledBackground
com.siemens.mp.game.GraphicObjectManager
com.siemens.mp.game.Melody
com.siemens.mp.game.Sound
com.siemens.mp.game.Vibrator
```

`com.siemens.mp.game.Light`

- `Light()`
- `static void setLightOff()`
- `static void setLightOn()`

`com.siemens.mp.game.MelodyComposer`

- `MelodyComposer()`
- `void appendNote(int note, int length)`

- Melody getMelody()
- int length()
- static int maxLength()
- void resetMelody()
- void setBPM(int bpm)

## com.siemens.mp.game.ExtendedImage

- ExtendedImage(Image image)
- void blitToScreen(int x, int y)
- void clear(byte color)
- Image getImage()
- int getPixel(int x, int y)
- void getPixelBytes(byte[] pixels, int x, int y, int width, int height)
- void setPixel(int x, int y, byte color)
- void setPixels(byte[] pixels, int x, int y, int width, int height)

## com.siemens.mp.game.GraphicObject

- GraphicObject()
- boolean getVisible()
- void setVisible(boolean visible)

## com.siemens.mp.game.Sprite

- Sprite(byte[] pixels, int pixel_offset, int width, int height, byte[] mask, int mask_offset, int numFrames)
- Sprite(ExtendedImage pixels, ExtendedImage mask, int numFrames)
- Sprite(Image pixels, Image mask, int numFrames)
- int getFrame()
- int getXPosition()

- `int getYPosition()`

- `boolean isCollidingWith(Sprite other)`

- `boolean isCollidingWithPos(int xpos, int ypos)`

- `void setCollisionRectangle(int x, int y, int width, int height)`

- `void setFrame(int framenumber)`

- `void setPosition(int x, int y)`


## com.siemens.mp.game.TiledBackground

- `TiledBackground(byte[] tilePixels, byte[] tileMask, byte[] map, int widthInTiles, int heightInTiles)`

- `TiledBackground(ExtendedImage tilePixels, ExtendedImage tileMask, byte[] map, int widthInTiles, int heightInTiles)`

- `TiledBackground(Image tilePixels, Image tileMask, byte[] map, int widthInTiles, int heightInTiles)`

- `void setPositionInMap(int x, int y)`


## com.siemens.mp.game.GraphicObjectManager

- `GraphicObjectManager()`

- `void addObject(GraphicObject gobject)`

- `static byte[] createTextureBits(int width, int height, byte[] texture)`

- `void deleteObject(GraphicObject gobject)`

- `void deleteObject(int position)`

- `GraphicObject getObjectAt(int index)`

- `int getObjectPosition(GraphicObject gobject)`

- `void insertObject(GraphicObject gobject, int position)`

- `void paint(ExtendedImage eimage, int x, int y)`

- `void paint(Image image, int x, int y)`

```
com.siemens.mp.game.Melody
```
- void play()
- static void stop()

```
com.siemens.mp.game.Sound
```
- Sound()
- static void playTone(int tone_freq, int tone_time)

```
com.siemens.mp.game.Vibrator
```
- Vibrator()
- static void startVibrator()
- static void stopVibrator()
- static void triggerVibrator(int duration)

## Siemens GSM Classes

These classes allow the Java program to access the phone's functions. The classes descend from java.lang.Object:

- com.siemens.mp.gsm.Call
- com.siemens.mp.gsm.PhoneBook
- com.siemens.mp.gsm.SMS

```
com.siemens.mp.gsm.Call
```
- Call()
- static void start(String number)

```
com.siemens.mp.gsm.PhoneBook
```
- PhoneBook()
- static String[] GetMDN()

```
com.siemens.mp.gsm.SMS
```

- SMS()

- static int send(String number, String data)

# Input/Output Classes

The Siemens IO classes, descending from java.lang.Object, include the following:

- com.siemens.mp.io.Connection

- com.siemens.mp.io.File

- interface com.siemens.mp.io.ConnectionListener

```
com.siemens.mp.io.Connection
```

- Connection(String connectTo)

- void send(byte[] data)

- static void setListener(ConnectionListener listener)

```
com.siemens.mp.io.File
```

- File()

- int close(int fileDescriptor)

- static int copy(String source, String dest)

- static int debugWrite(String fileName, String infoString)

- static int delete(String fileName)

- static int exists(String fileName)

- int length(int fileDescriptor)

- int open(String fileName)

- int read(int fileDescriptor, byte[] buf, int offset, int numBytes)

- static int rename(String source, String dest)

- int seek(int fileDescriptor, int seekpos)

- static int spaceAvailable()

- int write(int fileDescriptor, byte[] buf, int offset, int numBytes)

```
public interface ConnectionListener
   • void receiveData(byte[] data)
```

# D

# The iAppli API

## Packages

The iAppli API contains five major packages:

- `com.nttdocomo.io`—Input/output over the network (using HTTP) and to/from the ScratchPad.

- `com.nttdocomo.lang`—The standard language constructs specific to iApplis.

- `com.nttdocomo.net`—Networking support classes.

- `com.nttdocomo.ui`—The user interface, image, sound, and canvas components.

- `com.nttdocomo.util`—Other supporting utility classes.

## `com.nttdocomo.io` Interfaces

There is just one class for input and output:

```
java.lang.Object
java.lang.Throwable
java.lang.Exception
java.io.IOException
com.nttdocomo.io.ConnectionException
```

## `com.nttdocomo.io` Interfaces

Define the communication with HTTP. Extend from both `InputConnection` and `OutputConnection`:

```
javax.microedition.io.Connection
 javax.microedition.io.InputConnection
  javax.microedition.io.StreamConnection
   javax.microedition.io.ContentConnection
    com.nttdocomo.io.HttpConnection
 javax.microedition.io.OutputConnection
  javax.microedition.io.StreamConnection
   javax.microedition.io.ContentConnection
    com.nttdocomo.io.HttpConnection
```

## com.nttdocomo.lang

Called if an unsupported operation or method is called during runtime.

```
java.lang.Object
 java.lang.Throwable
  java.lang.Exception
   java.lang.RuntimeException
    com.nttdocomo.lang.UnsupportedOperationException
```

## com.nttdocomo.net

Converts a character string into a valid URL format. This handles Chinese or Japanese characters.

```
java.lang.Object
 com.nttdocomo.net.URLDecoder
 com.nttdocomo.net.URLEncoder
```

## com.nttdocomo.ui

```
java.lang.Object
 com.nttdocomo.ui.AudioPresenter—An audio control class that implements com.nttdo-
 como.ui.MediaPresenter.
```

com.nttdocomo.ui.Component—All high-level API components derive from com.nttdocomo.ui.Component.

com.nttdocomo.ui.Button—Defines a button, implements com.nttdocomo.ui.Interactable.

com.nttdocomo.ui.ImageLabel—Defines a still image.

com.nttdocomo.ui.Label—Defines a non-editable character string.

com.nttdocomo.ui.ListBox—A list box component that implements com.nttdocomo.ui.Interactable.

com.nttdocomo.ui.TextBox—A text input component that implements com.nttdocomo.ui.Interactable.

com.nttdocomo.ui.Ticker—A ticker component that scrolls text to the left.

com.nttdocomo.ui.VisualPresenter—A component that displays visual media, implements com.nttdocomo.ui.MediaPresenter.

com.nttdocomo.ui.Display—Displays the current screen and processes keystrokes or other input.

com.nttdocomo.ui.Font—Controls the calligraphic text style, size, and family.

com.nttdocomo.ui.Frame—The actual visual frame itself. Superclass of com.nttdocomo.ui.Canvas.

com.nttdocomo.ui.Canvas—An abstract low-level display class that draws pixels to the screen.

com.nttdocomo.ui.Dialog—A dialog box.

com.nttdocomo.ui.Panel—A high-level UI display class, capable of holding UI components.

com.nttdocomo.ui.Graphics—Controls all drawing function in the Canvas class.

com.nttdocomo.ui.IApplication—The main class that starts, stops, and manages the application.

com.nttdocomo.ui.Image—Holds the actual image data.

com.nttdocomo.ui.MediaManager—A media management processing class.

com.nttdocomo.ui.PhoneSystem—Accesses and handles the settings of the mobile phone.

com.nttdocomo.ui.ShortTimer—A basic interval timer function, implements com.nttdocomo.util.TimeKeeper.

java.lang.Throwable

java.lang.Exception

```
java.lang.RuntimeException
```

`com.nttdocomo.ui.UIException`—A common exceptional class for problems related to the user interface.

## com.nttdocomo.ui **Interfaces**

There are several interfaces to support the UI classes:

```
com.nttdocomo.util.EventListener
```

`com.nttdocomo.ui.ComponentListener`—Defines the listener, handling any events that occur to a component.

`com.nttdocomo.ui.KeyListener`—Defines the listener that corresponds to key presses while the high-level UI is being displayed.

`com.nttdocomo.ui.MediaListener`—Defines the listener that corresponds to media events, such as a sound starting or stopping.

`com.nttdocomo.ui.SoftKeyListener`—Defines the event listener of the software key in the high-level UI.

`com.nttdocomo.ui.FocusManager`—Manages which component in a `Panel` currently has focus.

`com.nttdocomo.ui.Interactable`—Defines a component that can be interacted with on-the-fly.

`com.nttdocomo.ui.LayoutManager`—Defines where components are placed in a `Panel`.

`com.nttdocomo.ui.MediaPresenter`—Defines the media type.

`com.nttdocomo.ui.MediaResource`—Resource management superclass of `MediaData`, `MediaImage`, and `MediaSound`.

`com.nttdocomo.ui.MediaData`—Defines something that is media.

`com.nttdocomo.ui.MediaImage`—A graphic image.

`com.nttdocomo.ui.MediaSound`—An audio sound.

## com.nttdocomo.util

The `Timer` class allows events to be triggered on a regular basis:

```
java.lang.Object
com.nttdocomo.util.Timer
```

## com.nttdocomo.util **Interfaces**

Defines all listeners, for events or timers:

com.nttdocomo.util.EventListener

com.nttdocomo.util.TimerListener

com.nttdocomo.util.TimeKeeper

## IApplication

The IApplication class starts the program and manages everything. Your program should derive from this class. The actual classes in IApplication are as follows:

IApplication()—Constructor.

java.lang.String[] GetArgs()—Gets the starting parameters of the application.

static IApplication GetCurrentApp()—Gets the current application instance.

java.lang.String GetSourcecUrl()—The URL from which the application was originally downloaded.

void resume()—Called after the application has been interrupted, due to a voice phone call or other pause event.

abstract void start()—Called when the application first executes.

void terminate()—Ends the application cleanly.

# Index

## Numbers

1G (first generation) wireless networks, 86

2.5G (second and a half generation) wireless networks, 87

2G (second generation) wireless networks, 86-87

3G (third generation) wireless networks, 88

6035 SmartPhone, 32

## A

<A> tag, 142

A-GPS (Assisted GPS), 154

about screens, 194-195

abstract void paint() method, 413

abstract void start() method, 413

Abstract Window Toolkit. *See* AWT

ACCEPT action type, 117

accept command type (<do> tag), 102

accesskey attribute (<A> tag), 142

action games, examples of, 10

<ACTION > tag, 117-118

ActionInputPreferred method, 399

activeCount() method (Thread class), 227

addCommand() method, 191

addCommand(Command cmd) method, 188

addRecord() method (RecordStore class), 331

addSprite(Sprite sprite) method, 301

ADF (Application Descriptor File), 409-410, 430

Advanced Mobile Phone Services. *See* AMPS

adventure games, 11

advertising, 20-21

AI (artificial intelligence), 317

Airtouch (Verizon) Web site, 126

ALARM alert, 193

Alarm alerts, 326

Alert class, 192-197, 242, 325, 481, 485

Alert(String title) method, 485

Alert(String title,String alertText,Image alertImage, AlertType alertType) method, 485

Alerts, 192, 326

AlertType class, 326, 481, 483

AlertType getType() method, 485

AlertType() method, 483

Alien Fish Exchange, 60

align attribute, 143

Alphaworks Web site, 213

alt attribute, 104

Ammo variable, 459

**AMPS (Advanced Mobile Phone Services), 86**

**Anagram, 53**

**anchor tag, 94-95**

**Anfy Team Web site, 454**

**Angle Of Arrival.** *See* AOA

**animation**

EMS (Enhanced Messaging Service) and, 133

sprite frames, 279

threads, 226

**ANY Text Field, 256**

**AOA (Angle Of Arrival), 155**

**APIs (Application Programming Interfaces), 6**

CLDC, 168

extension interfaces, 476-478

PersonalJava supported, 398

Siemens game, 499

**AppClass parameter, 410**

**append (Item item) method, 187**

**append(Image img) method, 187**

**append(String str) method, 187**

**append(String stringPart, Image imagePart) method, 245**

**appendNote(int note, int length) method, 444**

**applets**

Alert class, 192-197

Cache class, 198-199

creating, 175-180

Display class, 183-184

Form class, 185-188

life cycles, 181-183

MIDlet class, 197

properties, 198

Screen class, 184-185

**appliances, 25**

**Application Descriptor File (ADF), 430**

**application layer (WAP protocol stack), 89**

**application memory, MIDP devices, 203**

**Application Programming Interfaces.** *See* APIs

**Application Descriptor File.** *See* ADF

**application.vnd.wap.wmlscriptc, 108**

**application/vnc.wap.wmlc, 108**

**AppName parameter, 410**

**AppParam parameter, 410**

**AppSize parameter, 410**

**AppVer parameter, 410**

**architecture**

iApplis, 408-409

SMSC (Short Message Service Center), 125

WAP (Wireless Application Protocol), 89-91

**arcs (Graphics class), 269**

**areas, 298, 300-301**

**arrays, memory usage, 221-222**

**artificial intelligence, 18, 317**

listing effects of, 16

Micro Racer, 463-464

**Asia, mobile telephone support, 27-28**

**Assisted GPS.** *See* A-GPS

**AT modem command, 127**

**AT&T Wireless Web site, 126**

**attributes**

accesskey, <A> tag, 142

align, 143

behavior, 144

data, 412

direction, 144

emptyok, 98

format, 99

height, 143

href, 94, 412

hspace, 143

id, 93

iname, 100

ivalue, 100

label, 101

loop, 144

maxlength, 98

name

<A> tag, 142

<do> tag, 101

input fields, 98

<INPUT> tag, 140

onpick, 99

select tag, 100

size

input fields, 98

<SELECT> tag, 141

src, 104

title, 93, 98

type

<do> tag, 102

input fields, 99

value, 99

input fields and, 99

<select> tag, 100

vspace, 143

width, 143

**audio**

EMS (Enhanced Messaging Service) and, 133

engines, 18

files, 295

listening to, 422

playing, 422

**automotive navigation systems, 25**

**AWT (Abstract Window Toolkit), 404**

**Axion, 68**


**B**

<b> tag, 96

**BACK command, 189**

**background art, 15**

**background music, 15**

**Banana Battle, 64**

**Bandai networks, 79**

**BASELINE constant, 272**

**batteries, power consumption, 222**

**behavior attribute, 144**

**billing category (Location Based Services), 151**

**Billionaire, 77**

**bitmasked collision detection, 298**

**black and white displays, 207**

**Blackjack, 52**

<BLINK> tag, 139

**blitting, 433-434, 454**

**BlockBuster Web site, 66**

**blocked state, threads, 231**

<BLOCKQUOTE> tag, 139

**Blue Factory games, 63-64**

**Bluetooth**

data rate, 148

development kits, 148

Java and, 149

OBEX protocol, 149

operating radius, 147

RFCOMM protocol, 149

Service Discovery Protocol, 149

uses for, 148

**boolean hasPointerEvents() method, 484**

**boolean hasPointerMotionEvents() method, 484**

**boolean hasRepeatEvents() method, 484**

**boolean isBold() method, 487**

**boolean isColor() method, 483**

**boolean isDoubleBuffered() method, 484**

**boolean isInteractive() method, 491**

**boolean isItalic() method, 487**

**boolean isMutable() method, 489**

**boolean isPlain() method, 487**

**boolean isSelected(int index) method, 486, 490**

**boolean isShown() method, 484**

**boolean isUnderlined() method, 487**

**boolean playSound(Display display) method, 483**

**Borland JBuilder, 177**

**BotFighters Web site, 64**

**BOTTOM constant, 272**

<BR> tag, 96, 139

**business models, 20-22**

**Businessman, 80**

**buttons**

creating, 417

radio buttons, 100

**buy parameter, 365**


**C**

**C virtual machine.** *See* **CVM**

**C.media Compact NetFront Web site, 145**

**Cache class, 198-199, 459, 466**

**CALL action type, 118**

**Call class (Siemens game), 502**

**call detail record (CDR), 155**

**calls, GSM functions, 446**

**CANCEL action type, 118**

**CANCEL command, 189**

**cancel() method (Timer class), 233-234**

**CannonBubble, 80**

**Canvas class, 481**

code example file, 414

creating keypad presses, 419

methods, 260-261, 484

MIDP UI, 259-264

**Canvas() method, 484**

**Capcom, 79**

**car racing game, 361-362**

design, 362-363, 365-366

client side, 366, 380

HTTP considerations, 363-365

parameters, 365

server side, 380-382, 388

playing, 388, 390, 392

**car stores, creating for Micro Racer, 470-472**

**cards**

code example, 93

defined, 92

games, 12

id attribute, 93

switching to new, 95

title attribute, 93

Top Trumps, 54

**CarItem class, 381**

**CarItemFilter class, 344, 347**

**Carrier Force, 61**

**CarStore class, 340-343, 470**

**case sensitivity, tags, 92**

**casino games, 52**

**Casio Cassiopeia, 33**

**Casio CdmaOne C452CA, 38**

**CDC (Connected Device Configuration), 167, 396**

CVM (C virtual machine), 396

Foundation Profile, 396

J2ME Foundation Profile, 397

Personal Profile, 397

targeted devices, 396

**CDMA (Code Division Multiple Access 2000), 86, 88**

**CDR (call detail record), 155**

**CelebriQuiz, 64**

**<CENTER> tag, 139**

**Challenge! The Hard Boiled Way, 76-77**

**chance games, 12**

**character sets (i-mode network), 137**

**check boxes, 100, 140**

**checkCollision() method, 327**

**checkers**

Military, 77

Pincer, 77

**checkFinishLine() method, 327**

**checkin parameter, 365**

**Chess, 77**

**Choice interface, 482**

**ChoiceGroup class, 481, 490**

**ChoiceGroup(String label, int choiceType) method, 490**

**ChoiceGroup(String label, int choiceType, String[ ] stringElements, Image[ ] imageElements) method, 490**

**Choices, Item class, 249**

**Chop Suey Kung Fu, 61**

**cHTML (Compact HTML)**

<A> tag, 142

<BLINK> tag, 139

<BLOCKQUOTE> tag, 139

<BR> tag, 139

<CENTER> tag, 139

creating, 137

<DD> tag, 139

development tools, 144

<DIR> tag, 139

<DL> tag, 139

<DT> tag, 139

features, 137

<FORM> tag, 140

<HR> tag, 139

image formats, 143

<INPUT> tag, 140-141

<MARQUEE> tag, 144

<MENU> tag, 139

<META> tag, 139

<OBJECT> tag, 140

<OL> tag, 140

overview, 136-137

<P> tag, 140

<PLAINTEXT> tag, 140

<PRE> tag, 140

<SELECT> tag, 141

structure, 138-139

<TEXTAREA> tag, 141

<UL> tag, 140

**chunks, drawing, 292**

**Cingular Web site, 126**

**classes**

Alert, 192-197, 325, 481, 485

AlertType, 326, 481, 483

Cache, 198-199, 459, 466

Canvas, 259-261, 481

custom commands, 262

events, 261-262

game key, 262-263

methods, 484

pointer handler, 262-263

touch screens, 263-264

CarItem, 381

CarItemFilter, 344, 347

CarStore, 340-343, 470

ChoiceGroup, 481, 490

com.siemens.mp.game package, 432

com.siemens.mp.game.Melody, 443-445

Command, 481, 483

Connector, 351

Connectory class, 350

DataInputStream, 361

DataOutputStream, 361

DateField, 481, 490

Display, 183-184, 481, 483

Displayable, 481, 484

ExtendedImage, 432

File, 448-449

Float, 309-314

Font, 481, 487

Form, 185-188, 481, 485-486

Game, 474, 481

GameCanvas, 315-316, 459, 461-462

Gauge, 481, 490-491

GraphicObject, 432, 434-435

GraphicObjectManager, 432

Graphics, 264-266, 481

    arcs, 269

    colors, 267

    draw strings, 271

    fonts, 269-270

    Images, 271-275

    lines, 267-268

    methods, 488-489

    rectangles, 268-269

    rounded rectangles, 269

    stroke type, 267

IApplication, 509

Image, 272-273, 334-335, 481, 489

ImageItem, 481

Item, 482, 489

java.io package, 493-494

java.lang package, 494-495

java.util package, 495

java.util.Timer class, 233

javax.microedition.io package, 496

javax.microedition.lcdui package, 497

javax.microedition.midlet package, 497

javax.microedition.rms package, 497

Light, 432, 442

List, 482, 486

logical, 207

mathematical, 218

Melody, 432, 443-445

MelodyComposer, 432, 443-445

MIDlet, 181-183, 197

MIDP, 172

RecordStore, 329-331, 336, 339-340

    addRecord() method, 331

    clearing, 336

    code, 335-339

    deleteRecord() method, 332

    deleteRecordStore() method, 333, 336

    EnumerateRecords() method, 333

    exceptions, 334-335

    getLastModified() method, 332

    getNextRecordID() method, 333

    getNumRecords() method, 333

    getRecord() method, 332

    getSize() method, 333

    getSizeAvailable() method, 333

    MIDlet code, 339-340

    RecordEnumerator handling, 340-344, 347

    setRecord() method, 332

    unpacking images, 337-338

Screen, 184, 241-242, 482

    Alert, 242

    Form, 242

    Item, 248-257

    List, 242-247

    methods, 185, 485

    Text Box, 247-248

    Ticker, 257

Simens game, 499-504

size, optimization, 210

Sound, 432

Sprite, 279-283, 432, 435-436

SpriteManager, 301-305

StartForm, 186-188, 474

static method, 218

StringItem, 482, 491

TextBox, 482, 486-487

TextField, 482, 491

Thread

    activeCount() method, 227

    currentThread() method, 227

    getPriority() method, 227

    implementing threads, 228

    isAlive() method, 227

    join() method, 227

    run() method, 227

    Runnable interface, 229-230

    running flag, 229-230

    setPriority() method, 227

    sleep() method, 227

    start() method, 226

    stop() method, 226

timer example, 236-237

yield() method, 227

Ticker, 482, 492

TiledBackground, 432, 438-441

Timer, 233-235

Vibrator, 432, 442-443

visual, 207

Weapon, 456-461, 471, 477-478

classescom.siemens.mp.game.MelodyComposer, 443

CLDC (Connected, Limited Device Configuration), 167-171

Clear button, creating, 140

clients, ServerCallback interface, 366, 380

clipping, Graphics class, 273

clipRect(int x, int y, int width, int height) method, 266

clock speed, optimization, 210

cloning, 9-10

close method, 353

Cocoasoft games, 67-69

code

audio files, 422

buttons, creating, 417

Canvas class, creating, 414

cards, 93, 95

ComponentListener, 420

decks, 93, 95

dialog boxes, creating, 418

execution

reduced size, 211-216

speed. See FPS

HTTP connections, 423-424

hyperlinks, creating, 118

images, displaying, 421

labels, creating, 415

optimization, 209-211

radio buttons, 100

ScratchPad, 424-425

SMIL (Synchronized Multimedia Integration Language) file, 132

SMS (Short Message Service), 130

SoftKeyListener class, 420

table tags, 98

text boxes, creating, 416

text formatting tags, 96

Thread class

implementing threads using, 228

Runnable interface, 229-230

tickers, creating, 417

Timer class, 236-237

timers, 105

variables, 103

VisualPresenter component, 417

WMLScript

document definition tag example, 92

form example, 101

GuessNUmber.wml example, 106-107

header example, 92

RandomGuess.wml example, 107-108

Code Breaker, 52

Code Division Multiple Access 2000. See CDMA 2000

Code Warrior (Metrowerks), 177

collide() method, 301

collision detection, 298

bitmasked, 298

multiple areas, 298, 300-301

multiple levels, 298-299

SpriteManager class, 304-305

sprites, 286-287, 319-320

colors

Graphics class, 267

image display, 207

com.nttdocomo.io package, 505

com.nttdocomo.lang package, 506

com.nttdocomo.net package, 506

com.nttdocomo.ui package, 506-508

com.nttdocomo.ui.MediaManager methods, 421

com.nttdocomo.util package, 508-509

com.siemens.mp.game package, 432

com.siemens.mp.game.Melody class, 443-445

com.siemens.mp.game.MelodyComposer class, 443

com.siemens.mp.gsm package, Siemens SL45i, 446

calls, 446

loading data, 448-449

Missed Dialing Numbers (MDN), 447

receiving data, 447-448

saving files, 448-449

sending data, 447-448

SMS messages, 447

combat games, 10

Command class, 481, 483

Command(String label, int commandType,int priority) method, 483

command-line development, 175

  compiling, 176

  JAR files, 177

CommandListener interface, 482

commands, MIDP, 188-191

Communicator development tool, 401

Compact HTML. *See* cHTML

Compaq iPaq, 33

competition, 49-51

compiling

  applets, 176

  Siemens SL45i, 430

ComponentListener, 419-420

components, 295

  downloading, 296

    images, 296-297

    media types, 297

  images. *See* images

  levels, 296, 298-299

  missions, 296

  personal digital assistants. *See* PDAs

  sounds. *See* sound

  tracks, 296

Condensity Web site, 213

Configuration layer (J2ME), 166

configurations

  CLDC packages, 170

  J2ME, 166-167

Confirmation alerts, 193, 326

Connected Device Configuration. *See* CDC

Connected, Limited Device Configuration. *See* CLDC

Connection class (Siemens game), 503

Connection interface, 350-351

ConnectionListener class (Siemens game), 504

connections

  HTTP, 353-354, 364-365, 423-424

  ScratchPad, 424-425

Connector class, 350-351

CONSTRAINT_MASK, 256

constructors, 217-218

content deals, 21-22

ContentConnection interface, 350

control, Micro Racer, 464, 466

converting images, 104

Cool Vibes, 64

CrashCarEffect interface, 476

createImage(byte[ ] imageData, int offset, int length) method, 273

createImage(Image source) method, 273

createImage(int width, int height) method, 273

createImage(String name) method, 273

credit cards, 25

Cube game, 70

CubeBuster, 80

currentThread() method (Thread class), 227

custom commands (Canvas class), 262

CVM (C virtual machine), 396

**D**

data

  global, 204

  local, 204

  reading in, 355-356

  static, 204

data attribute, 412

Data Clash, 61-62

data formats, 358

  DataInputStream class, 361

  DataOutputStream class, 361

  packets, 358-359

  XML, 360-361

data part, 284

data storage, 329

  Image class, 334-335

  RecordStore class, 329, 331, 336, 339-340

    addRecord() method, 331

    clearing, 336

    code, 335-339

    deleteRecord() method, 332

    deleteRecordStore() method, 333, 336

    EnumerateRecords() method, 333

    exceptions, 334-335

    getLastModified() method, 332

    getNextRecordID() method, 333

    getNumRecords() method, 333

    getRecord() method, 332

    getSize() method, 333

    getSizeAvailable() method, 333

MIDlet code, 339-340

RecordEnumerator handling, 340-344, 347

setRecord() method, 332

unpacking images, 337-338

**DataExchange software (Siemens SL45i), 431**

**datagram layer (WAP protocol stack), 89**

**DatagramConnection interface, 350**

**DataInputStream class, 361**

**DataOutputStream class, 361**

**Date Item class, 250-251**

**Date getDate() method, 490**

**DateField class, 481, 490**

**DateField(String label, int mode) method, 490**

**DateField(String label, int mode, TimeZone timeZone) method, 490**

**<DD> tag, 139**

**dead state, threads, 231**

**deadlocks, threads, 231-232**

**decks**

code examplee, 93

defined, 93

switching to new, 95

**Defender, 10**

**DELETE action type, 117**

**delete command type, 102**

**delete(int elementNum) method, 245**

**delete(int itemNum) method, 187**

**delete(int offset, int length) method, 248**

**deleteRecord() method (RecordStore class), 332**

**deleteRecordStore() method (RecordStore class), 333, 336**

**deleteSprite(int position) method, 301**

**deleteSprite(Sprite sprite) method, 301**

**Description variable, 459**

**design (game design)**

business models, 20

advertising/sponsorships, 20-21

business outlook, 20

content deals, 21-22

subscriptions, charging players for, 22

car racing game, 362-363, 365-366

client side, 366, 380

HTTP considerations, 363-365

parameters, 365

playing, 388, 390, 392

server side, 380-382, 388

overview, 7-8

playtesting, 19-20

preproduction, 8

artificial intelligence, 16

backgroup art, 15

backgroup music, 15

documentation, 16

game levels, 15

genre, selecting, 9-13

global variables, 16

graphical elements, 15

inputs, listing effects of, 15

interfaces, 16

mission statements, 14-15

outputs, 15

questions, 9

restrictions, 13-14

restrictions, 13

rules, defining, 16-17

sound effects, 15

Web site resources, 17

process of, 8

programming, 18-19

prototyping, 17-18

**developer tools (PersonalJava), 400**

IDE (Integrated Development Environment), 402

JavaCheck, 401

Nokia 9201 Communicator, 401

PersonalJava emulation environment, 401

SDK (Software Development Kit), 402

**development environments, 177**

Forte, 178

J2ME Wireless Toolkit, 178-180

MIDlet life cycles, 181-183

WAP applications, 113

**Devices, 3-5**

color displays, 207

displays, 207

embedded chips, 47-48

frame rates, 206

high-end, 28

JavaPhone, 30

JavaTV, 30

PersonalJava 3.0, 28-30

PingTel, 30

Sharp NC-10 IP, 31

Jump, 165

limitations, 201-202

   memory, 202-205

   processors, 202-203

   video, 203, 206

memory

   fragmentation, 204-205

   working, 204

micro, 25-28

minimum speeds, 206

smart cards, 47-48

Waba, 165

**DGPS (differential GPS), 154**

**Dialtones, 14**

**differential GPS.** *See* **DGPS**

**DIG (Disney Internet Group International), 74**

**Digital Bridges Web site, 51**

**<DIR> tag, 139**

**direction attribute, 144**

**directories, src (Siemens Toolkit), 441**

**Disney Internet Group International.** *See* **DIG**

**Display class, 183-184, 481**

**<DISPLAY> tag, 116**

**Displayable class, 481, 484**

**Displayable getCurrent() method, 483**

**displays**

color, 207

MIDP devices, 203, 206

multiple display support, 207

**dispose() method, 422**

**<DL> tag, 139**

**<do> tag, 101**

command types, 102

label attribute, 101

name attribute, 101

type attribute, 102

**documentation, 16**

**Dope Wars, 71-72**

**double buffering, 274-275, 398-399**

**downloading components, 296**

images, 296-297

media types, 297

**Draw Poker, 67**

**draw strings (Graphics class), 271**

**drawArc(), 269**

**drawArc(int x, int y, int width, int height, int startAngle, int arcAngle) method, 266**

**drawChar(char character, int x, int y, int anchor) method, 266**

**drawChars(char[ ] data, int off-set, int length, int x, int y, int anchor) method, 266**

**drawImage(Image img, int x, int y, int anchor) method, 266**

**drawing**

optimizations, 303-304

sprites, 285

   chunks, 292

   pixels, 289-291

**drawLine(int x1, int y1, int x2, int y2) method, 266**

**drawPolyline method(), 414**

**drawRect(), 268**

**drawRect(int x, int y, int width, int height) method, 266**

**drawRoundRect(), 269**

**drawRoundRect(int x, int y, int width, int height, int arcWidth, int arcHeight) method, 266**

**drawString(String str, int x, int y, int anchor) method, 266**

**drawSubstring(String str, int offset, int len, int x, int y, int anchor) method, 266**

**<DT> tag, 139**

**DummyCrash interface, 476**

**Dwango Web site, 62**

## E

**E-OTD (Enhanced Observed Time Differential), 155**

**Eastridge Technology Web site, 213**

**ECMAScript, 105**

**<em> taq, 96**

**EMAILADDR, 256**

**embedded chips, 47-48**

**EmbeddedJava, 48**

**emergency category (Location Based Services), 151**

**emoji, 137**

associations, 138

creating, 137

**emptyok attribute, 98**

**EMS (Enhanced Messaging Service)**

features supported by, 133

overview, 133

**emulator, Siemens SL45i, 430-431**

**enemy players, sprite movement, 316-317**

**engines**

artificial intelligence, 18

audio, 18

graphics, 18

multiplayer, 19

physics, 19

**Enhanced Messaging Service.
See EMS**

**Enhanced Observed Time
Differential. See E-OTD**

**EnumerateRecords() method
(RecordStore class), 333**

**environments (development),
177**

Forte, 178

J2ME Wireless Toolkit, 178-
180

MIDlet life cycles, 181-183

**Ericsson R380, 39**

**Ericsson WapIDE Web site, 113**

**Error alerts, 193, 326**

**Esmertec Jbed Micro Edition
CDLC, 36**

**ETSI (European
Telecommunications
Standards Institute), 123**

**Europe mobile telephone sup-
port, 28**

**European Telecommunications
Standards Institute. See ETSI**

**Eurotel Web site, 127**

**events**

Canvas class, 261-262

KEY PRESSED EVENT, 418

KEY RELEASED EVENT, 418

processEvent() method, 418

**exceptions (RecordStore class),
334-335**

**EXCLUSIVE lists, 243**

**EXCLUSIVE-CHOICE, 244**

**execution codes, reduced size,
211, 213-215**

**EXIT command, 189**

**ExtendedImage class (Siemens
game), 432, 500**

**eXtensible Markup Language.
See XML**

**extension APIs, interfaces,
476-478**

**extensions (J2ME), 5-6**

**ExtremeQuiz, 64**

**Ezos Web site, 145**


# F

**field sets, 101**

**Fight Arena, 57**

**Fight KO, 52**

**File class (Siemens game), 448-
449, 503**

**files**

audio, 295

filmstrip, 279

JAR

command-line develop-
ment, 177

reduced size, 211-216

PNG

data part, 284

header, 284

**fillArc(int x, int y, int width, int
height, int startAngle, int
arcAngle) method, 266**

**fillPolygon() method, 414**

**fillRect(int x, int y, int width, int
height) method, 266**

**fillRoundRect(int x, int y, int
width, int height, int
arcWidth, int arcHeight)
method, 266**

**filmstrip file, 279**

**first generation (1G) wireless
networks, 86**

**Fisupeli, 63**

**Flash SMS, 124**

**flashes, 442**

**Flirtylizer, 64**

**Float class, 309-314**

**floating-points, 307-314**

**FOMA (Freedom of Mobile
Multimedia Access), 88**

**Font class, 481, 487**

**Font getFont() method, 488**

**fonts (Graphics class), 269-270**

**football games (Picofun
Football), 57**

**FootballQuiz, 64**

**Form class, 185-186, 242, 481**

javax.microedition.lcdui.Ite
m, 242

methods, 187-188, 485-486

**<FORM> tag, 140**

**Form(String title) method, 485**

**Form(String title, Item[ ] items)
method, 485**

**format attribute, 99**

**formatting, text formatting
tags, 96**

**Forte, 178**

**Foundation Profile, 396**

**Fours game, 53**

**FPS (frames per second), 206,
216**

constructors, 217-218

memory management, 217

sprite movement, 219-220

static method, 218

**fragmentation (memory), MIDP
devices, 204-205**

Frame property (sprites), 278

frame per second (FPS)

MIDP devices, 206

sprites, 278-279

Freedom of Mobile Multimedia Access. *See* FOMA

Fruit Machine (slots), 52

Fujitsu F503i, 39

full-duplex protocols, 356

FunCaster.com games, 59

FunCaster.com Web site, 59

functions, GSM (Siemens SL45i), 446-447

# G

g.lock() method, 414

g.unlock() method, 414

gamasutra.com Web site, 17

Game class, 474

GameCanvas class, 315-316, 459, 461-462

gamedev.net Web site, 17

GameThread loop, 322-323

GarageClient MIDlet, 473-474

GarageServlet servlet, 382, 388

Garbage Collector, code optimization, 217

Gauge class, 481

methods, 490-491

Gauge(String label, boolean interactive, int maxValue, int initialValue) method, 490

gdse.com Web site, 17

General Packet Radio Services. *See* GPRS

genres, 9-12

Geographic Information System. *See* GIS

Get Nessie!, 64

get(int itemNum) method, 187

getAltText() method, 255

getAppProperty(String key) method, 197

getBlueComponent() method, 265

getCaretPosition(), 248

getChars(char[ ] data) method, 248

getClipHeight() method, 266

getClipWidth() method, 265

getClipX() method, 265

getClipY() method, 265

getColor() method, 265

getConstraints(), 248

getCurrent() method, 183

getDate method, 353

getDate(), 250

getDefaultTimeout() method, 193

getExpiration method, 353

getFile method, 353

getFont() method, 265

getGameAction(int keyCode) method, 260

getGraphics() method, 273

getGrayScale() method, 265

getGreenComponent() method, 265

getHeight() method, 260, 273

getHost method, 353

getImage() method, 193, 255

getImage(int elementNum) method, 244

getInputMode() method, 251

getKeyCode(int gameAction) method, 260

getKeyName(int keyCode) method, 260

getLabel(), 249

getLastModified() method (RecordStore class), 332

getLayout() method, 255

getLength method, 353

getMaxSize() method, 248

getMaxValue() method, 252

getMelody() method, 444-446

getNextRecordID() method (RecordStore class), 333

getNumRecords() method (RecordStore class), 333

getPort method, 353

getPriority() method (Thread class), 227

getProtocol method, 353

getRecord() method (RecordStore class), 332

getRedComponent() method, 265

getRequestMethod method, 353

getRequestProperty method, 353

getSelectedFlags(boolean[ ] selectedArray) method, 245

getSelectedIndex() method, 245

getSize() method (RecordStore class), 333

getSizeAvailable() method (RecordStore class), 333

getSprite(int index) method, 301

getSpritePosition(Sprite sprite) method, 301

getString() method, 193, 248

getString(int elementNum) method, 244

getStrokeStyle() method, 265

getText() method, 254

getTicker() method, 185

getTimeout() method, 193

getTitle() method, 185

getTranslateX() method, 265

getTranslateY() method, 265

getType method, 353

getType() method, 193

getURL method, 353

getValue() method, 252

getWidth() method, 260, 273

GIF formats, 143

Gif2Wbmp Web site, 104

GIS (Geographic Information System), 150

Gladiator, 55

GliderAction, 79

global data, 204

Global Positioning System. See GPS

Global System for Mobile Communications. See GSM

global variables, listing effects of, 16

Globtel Web site, 127

GO action type, 118

<go> tag, 94

Gobang, 77

golf

Miracle Golf, 81

On The Green, 57

Wentworth Golf, 54

Gomoku Narabe, 80

Gosling, James, 170

GOSUB action type, 118

GoZing Web site, 125

GPRS (General Packet Radio Services), 87

GPS (Global Positioning System), 153

Graphical User Interface. See GUIs

GraphicObject class (Siemens game), 432-435, 500

GraphicObjectManager class (Siemens game), 432, 501

graphics

reduced size, 215-216

sprites. See sprites

Graphics class, 481

clipRect(int x, int y, int width, int height) method, 266

drawArc(int x, int y, int width, int height, int startAngle, int arcAngle) method, 266

drawChar(char character, int x, int y, int anchor) method, 266

drawChars(char[ ] data, int offset, int length, int x, int y, int anchor) method, 266

drawImage(Image img, int x, int y, int anchor) method, 266

drawLine(int x1, int y1, int x2, int y2) method, 266

drawRect(int x, int y, int width, int height) method, 266

drawRoundRect(int x, int y, int width, int height, int arcWidth, int arcHeight) method, 266

drawString(String str, int x, int y, int anchor) method, 266

drawSubstring(String str, int offset, int len, int x, int y, int anchor) method, 266

fillArc(int x, int y, int width, int height, int startAngle, int arcAngle) method, 266

fillRect(int x, int y, int width, int height) method, 266

fillRoundRect(int x, int y, int width, int height, int arcWidth, int arcHeight) method, 266

getBlueComponent() method, 265

getClipHeight() method, 266

getClipWidth() method, 265

getClipX() method, 265

getClipY() method, 265

getColor() method, 265

getFont() method, 265

getGrayScale() method, 265

getGreenComponent() method, 265

getRedComponent() method, 265

getStrokeStyle() method, 265

getTranslateX() method, 265

getTranslateY() method, 265

methods, 488-489

methods, list of, 414-415

MIDP UI, 264-266

arcs, 269

colors, 267

draw strings, 271

fonts, 269-270

Images, 271-275

lines, 267-268

rectangles, 268-269

rounded rectangles, 269

stroke type, 267

setClip(int x, int y, int width, int height) method, 266

setColor(int red, int green, int blue) method, 265

setColor(int RGB) method, 265

setGrayScale(int value) method, 265

setStrokeStyle(int style) method, 265

translate(int x, int y) method, 265

**graphics engines, 18**

**Graphics GetGraphics() method, 413, 489**

**Graphics drawImage() method, 271**

**Graphics.drawline(), 267**

**GSM (Global System for Mobile Communications), 87, 446**

calls, 446

Missed Dialing Numbers (MDN), 447

SMS messages, 447

**GSM Location Positioning, 154**

**GUIs (Graphical User Interface), Screen class, 241-242**

Alert, 242

Form, 242

Item, 248-257

List, 242-247

Text Box, 247-248

Ticker, 257

# H

**half-duplex protocols, HTTP, 356**

**Handheld Device Markup Language.** *See* HDML

**handheld devices**

programming advantages, 454-455

programming disadvantages, 453-454

**handset-based solution (positioning technology), 152**

**Handspring Visor Edge, 32**

**Handy Games, 57-58**

**Hangman, 53**

**Hashtables, memory usage, 221-222**

**hasPointerEvents() method, 260**

**hasPointerMotionEvents() method, 260**

**hasRepeatEvents() method, 260**

**HCENTER constant, 272**

**HDML (Handheld Device Markup Language)**

<ACTION> tag, 117-118

activities, 116

<DISPLAY> tab, 116

hyperlinks, 118

images, 118

overview, 115

syntax, 116

WML versus, 115-116

**Header PNG file, 284**

**heap memory, 210**

**height attribute, 143**

**Height property (sprites), 278**

**HELP action type, 117**

**Help alert, 192**

**HELP command, 189**

**help command type, <do> tag, 102**

**help screens, 194-195**

**hidden fields, 140**

**hideNotify() method, 261**

**high-end devices, 28**

JavaPhone, 30

JavaTV, 30

PersonalJava 3.0, 28-30

PingTel, 30

Sharp NC-10 IP, 31

**high-level UI, 415**

**Hikkoshi Meijin, 80**

**Hitachi CdmaOne C451H, 39**

**Holy Moley Web site, 66**

**home appliances, 25**

**Home Run Derby, 55**

**Hornell, Karl, 66**

**HP chaiVM for Pocket PC, 38**

**<HR> tag, 139**

**href attribute, 94, 412**

**hspace attribute, 143**

**HTTP (Hyper Text Transport Protocol), 352**

connections, 353-354, 423-424

limitations, 356

multiple connections, 356-357

proxies, 357

racing car game, 363

connections, 364-365

polling, 364

session tracking, 365

reading in data, 355-356

response code, 354-355

setup mode, 352-353

**Hudson Soft games, 81**

**Hunters & Collectors, 63**

**Hyper Text Transfer Protocol.**
*See* HTTP

**hyperlinks, creating, 118**


# I

**i monde Web site, 145**

**<i> tag, 96**

**i-JADE Web site, 144, 426**

**i-Mimic Web site, 145**

**i-mode games, 62**

**i-mode networks**

character sets, 137

cost of using, 136

development tools, 144

emoji, 137

associations, 138

creating, 137

handset color screens, 136

overview, 135

page size, 136

partner sites, 135

testing, 144-146

**i-Skiing, 68**

**i-Tool Web site, 145**

**iAppli profile, 172**

**IApplication class, 509**

**IApplication GetCurrentApp()**
method, 413

**iApplis, 74**

ADF (Application Descriptor
File), 409-410

architecture, 408-409

Bandai networks, 79

basic program example, 412

Capcom, 79

Challenge! The Hard Boiled
Way, 76-77

developing, 425-428

Hudson Soft games, 81

Mini Game Tengoku services,
79-80

overview, 407

packages, 505

com.nttdocomo.io, 505

com.nttdocomo.lang, 506

com.nttdocomo.net, 506

com.nttdocomo.ui, 506-
508

com.nttdocomo.util, 508-
509

programs

activating, 411

dropping within i-mode
cHTML page, 411

provisioning, 409-411

resume() method, 412

Samurai Romanesque, 75-76

Sega, 78

Squiral, 75

**IBM J9 VM, 36**

**IceBlox, 73**

**id attribute, 93**

**iDEN (Integrated Digital
Enhanced Network), 87, 156**

**IDEs, 177**

**IEmulator Web site, 426**

**IJavaEngine i503 Web site, 426**

**Image class, 272-273, 335, 481,
489**

**Image getImage() method, 485,
491**

**Image getImage(int index)**
method, 486, 490

**Image Item, 254-255**

**Image property (sprites), 278**

**image/vnd.wap.wbmp, 108**

**ImageItem class, 481**

**ImageItem(String label, Image
img, int layout, String altText)
method, 491**

**images, 104, 295**

alt attribute, 104

converting, 104

displaying, 421

downloading, 296-297

formats, 143

HDML and, 118

loading, 420-421

Siemens SL45i, 432-433

blitting, 433-434

GraphicObject class
methods, 434-435

sprites, 278

loading, 283-284

size reduction, 284-285

transparency, 289-293

src attribute, 104

unpacking (RecordStore
class), 337-338

**Images class (Graphics class),
271-273**

BASELINE constant, 272

BOTTOM constant, 272

clipping, 273

double buffering, 274-275

HCENTER constant, 272

LEFT constant, 272

RIGHT constant, 272

TOP constant, 272

translating, 274

VCENTER constant, 272

<img> tag, 104

IMPLICIT lists, 243

IMPLICIT-CHOICE, 244

IMT 2000 (International Mobile Telecommunications 2000), 88

iname attribute, <select> tag, 100

incremental parsers, 360

INFO alert, 193

Information alerts, 326

initEnemies() method, 320, 463

initialization, sprite movement, 314-316

initPowerups() method, 466

input fields

attributes, list of, 98-99

option groups, 99

input methods, 399

<INPUT> tag, 140-141

input/output classes (Siemens game), 503-504

InputConnection interface, 350

inputs, listing effects, 15

insert(char[ ] data, int offset, int length, int position) method, 248

insert(int elementNum, String stringPart, Image imagePart) method, 245

insert(int itemNum, Item item) method, 187

insert(String src, int position) method, 248

insertSprite(Sprite sprite, int position) method, 301

installing PersonalJava applet, 402-403

instant wireless messaging

EMS (Enhanced Messaging Service), 133

gaming and, 122

MMS (Multimedia Messaging Service)

MMSC (Multimedia Message Service Center), 131

overview, 130

SMIL (Synchronized Multimedia Integration Language), 131-132

overview, 121

SMS (Short Message Service)

character lengths of, 123

Flash SMS, 124

Kuulalaakeri, 128

overview, 122

PDU mode, 123

popularity of, 122

rates, 123

receiving messages, 129

sending messages, 127-130

services, list of, 125-127

Smart Messaging, 124

SMS Gateway, 128

SMS-JDK, 128

SMSC (Short Message Service Center), 125

Text mode, 123

Unicode messages, 124

int append(Image image) method, 485

int append(Item item) method, 485

int append(String str) method, 485

int append(String stringElement, Image imageElement) method, 490

int charsWidth(char[ ] ch, int offset, int length) method, 487

int charWidth(char ch) method, 487

int getBaselinePosition() method, 487

int getBlueComponent() method, 488

int getCaretPosition() method, 486, 491

int getChars(char[ ] data) method, 486, 491

int getClipHeight() method, 488

int getClipWidth() method, 488

int getClipX() method, 488

int getClipY() method, 488

int getColor() method, 488

int getCommandType() method, 483

int getConstraints() method, 487, 491

int getDefaultTimeout() method, 485

int getFace() method, 487

int getGameAction(int keyCode) method, 484

int getGrayScale() method, 488

int getGreenComponent() method, 488

int getHeight() method, 413, 484, 487, 489

int getInputMode() method, 490

int getKeyCode(int gameAction) method, 484

int GetKeypadState() method, 413

int getLayout() method, 491

int getMaxSize() method, 487, 491

int getMaxValue() method, 491

int getPriority() method, 483

int getRedComponent() method, 488

int getSelectedFlags(boolean[ ] selectedArray_return) method, 486, 490

int getSelectedIndex() method, 486, 490

int getSize() method, 487

int getStrokeStyle() method, 489

int getStyle() method, 487

int getTimeout() method, 485

int getTranslateX() method, 489

int getTranslateY() method, 489

int getValue() method, 491

int getWidth() method, 413, 484, 489

int numColors() method, 483

int setMaxSize(int maxSize) method, 487, 492

int size() method, 486-487, 490, 492

int stringWidth(String str) method, 487

int substringWidth(String str, int offset, int len) method, 487

Integrated Digital Enhanced Network. *See* iDEN

interfaces

Choice, 482

com.nttdocomo.io, 505

com.nttdocomo.ui, 508

com.nttdocomo.util, 509

CommandListener, 482

Connection, 350-351

CrashCarEffect, 476

DummyCrash, 476

extension APIs, 476-478

ItemStateListener, 482

java.io package, 494

java.lang package, 495

java.util package, 496

javax.microedition.io package, 496

javax.microedition.lcdui package, 497

javax.microedition.rms package, 498

listing effects of, 16

SiemensCrash, 476-477

International Mobile Telecommuncations 2000. *See* IMT 2000

Internet Protocols. *See* IPs

InvalidRecordIDException, 334

IPs (Internet Protocols), 88

isAlive() method (Thread class), 227, 231

isColor() method, 183

isDoubleBuffered() method, 260

isInteractive() method, 252

isMutable() method, 273

isometric engines, 308

isSelected(int elementNum) method, 245

Item class, 248-249, 482

Choices, 249

Date, 250-251

Image Item, 254-255

Listener, 249

methods, 489

Progress Meters, 251-253

String Items, 254

Text Field, 255-257

Ticker, 257

ITEM command, 189

Item get(int index) method, 486

ItemStateListener interface, 482

ivalue attribute (<select> tag), 100

## J

J2EE (Java 2 Platform, Enterprise Edition), 164-165

J2ME(Java 2 Micro Edition), 3-5, 25, 164-165

advantages, 165-166

configurations, 166-167

Connected Device Configuration. *See* CDC

Connected, Limited Device Configuration. *See* CLDC

Devices, 206-207

Kilobyte virtual machine. *See* KVM

layers, 166-167

networking, 349

Connection interface, 350-351

DataInputStream class, 361

DataOutputStream class, 361

extensions, 5-6

game packets, 358-359

game server setup, 357-358

MIDP specification,
352-357

XML, 360-361

Palm games, 72-73

profiles, 166-167

CLDC, 168

Mobile Information
Device Profile. *See* MIDP

**J2ME Foundation Profile, 397**

**J2ME Multimedia Profile, 406**

**J2ME Wireless Toolkit, 178-180**

**J2SE (Java 2 Platform, Standard
Edition),
164-165**

**JAM (Java Application
Manager), 169, 409**

**Jamdat games, 55**

Gladiator, 55

Home Run Derby, 55

Krazy Konondrum, 55

Rock-Paper-Scissors, 56

**JAR files**

command-line development,
177

reduced size, 211

graphics, 215-216

obfuscators, 212-213

object-oriented program-
ming, 213-215

**Java.** *See also* Micro Java

Bluetooth and, 149

history, 163-165

**Java 2 Micro Edition.** *See* J2ME

**Java 2 Platform, Enterprise
Edition, 164-165**

**Java 2 Platform, Standard
Edition, 164-165**

**Java Application Manager
(JAM), 169, 409**

**Java Database Connector, 30**

**Java Dynamic Management, 30**

**Java Game Profile, 404-405**

**Java Management Extensions
(JMX), 30**

**Java Naming and Directory
Interface (JNDI), 30**

**Java Native Interface (JNI), 29,
454**

**Java Virtual Machine Debugging
Interface (JVMDI), 29**

**Java Virtual Machine Profiler
Interface (JVMPI), 29**

**Java virtual machines.** *See* JVMs

**java.awt.Panel, 242**

**java.io package, 170, 493-494**

**java.lang package, 170, 494-495**

**java.lang.Thread object, 227**

**java.util package, 170, 495-496**

**java.util.Timer class, 233**

**JavaCard, 48**

**JavaCheck program, 401**

**JavaPhone, 30**

**JavaServer Pages.** *See* JSPs

**Javasoft KVM for the Palm, 36**

**Javasoft MIDP for The PalmOS,
36**

**Javasoft PersonalJava for
Windows CE, 36**

**JavaTV, 30**

**javax.microdeition.lcdui.Canvas,
259-264**

**javax.microdeition.lcdui.Form,
242**

**javax.microdeition.lcdui.Graphic
s, 264-266**

arcs, 269

colors, 267

draw strings, 271

fonts, 269-270

Images, 271-275

lines, 267-268

rectangles, 268-269

rounded rectangles, 269

stroke type, 267

**javax.microdeition.lcdui.Screen,
241-242**

**javax.microedition.io package,
170, 496**

**javax.microedition.lcdui pack-
age, 497**

**javax.microedition.lcdui.Choice,
244-247**

**javax.microedition.lcdui.Choice
Group, 249**

**javax.microedition.lcdui.DateFiel
d, 250-251**

**javax.microedition.lcdui.Font,
269**

**javax.microedition.lcdui.Gauge,
251-253**

**javax.microedition.lcdui.Image,
272-273**

**javax.microedition.lcdui.ImageIt
em, 254-255**

**javax.microedition.lcdui.Item,
242, 248-249, 251-257**

**javax.microedition.lcdui.List,
242-247**

**javax.microedition.lcdui.StringIt
em, 254**

**javax.microedition.lcdui.TextBox
, 247-248**

**javax.microedition.lcdui.TextFiel
d, 255-257**

**javax.microedition.lcdui.Ticker,
257**

**javax.microedition.midlet pack-
age, 497**

javax.microedition.rms package, 497-498

JBuilder, 177

JDBC (Java Database Connector), 30

JDMK (Java Dynamic Management), 30

Jeode EVM (Jeode Embedded Virtual Machine ), 37

Jerry the Cat, 68-69

JMX (Java Management Extensions), 30

JNDI (Java Naming and Directory Interface), 30

JNI (Java Native Interface), 29, 454

join() method (Thread class), 227

Jornada, 33

JPG formats, 143

Jshape games, 70-71

JSPs (JavaServer Pages), 109
    chat application example, 110-112
    game lobby example, 109-111

Jump, 165

JVM layer, 166-167

JVMDI (Java Virtual Machine Debugging Interface), 29

JVMPI (Java Virtual Machine Profiler Interface), 29

JVMs (Java virtual machines), 35
    CLDC specifications, 170
    Esmertec Jbed Micro Edition CDLC, 36
    HP chaiVM for Pocket PC, 38
    IBM J9 VM, 36
    Javasoft KVM for the Palm, 36

Javasoft MIDP for The PalmOS, 36

Javasoft PersonalJava for Windows CE, 36

Jeode EVM, 37

Kadasystems Kada VM, 37

kAWT Extended KVM (xKVM), 36-37

MicroJBlend, 37

NSIcom CrEme, 37

SAVAJE XE Operating System, 38

Transvirtual Kaffe, 38

**K**

Kadasystems Kada VM, 37

kAWT Extended KVM (xKVM), 36-37

KEY PRESSED EVENT, 418

KEY RELEASED EVENT, 418

KeyboardInputPreferred method, 399

KeyListener, 419

keypad presses, 419

keyPressed(int keyCode) method, 260

keyReleased(int keyCode) method, 260

keyRepeated(int keyCode) method, 260

Kilobyte virtual machine. See KVM, 169, 453

Kittyhawk profile, 172

Krazy Konondrum, 55

Ktoolbar (J2ME Wireless Toolkit), 179-180

Kuulalaakeri tool (SMS gateway), 128

KVM (Kilobyte virtual machine), 169, 453

KvmVer parameter, 410

kXML, 360

**L**

label attribute (<do> tag), 101

lables, creating, 415

<large> tag, 96

LastModified parameter, 410

LaunchAt parameter, 410

layers, J2ME, 166-167

LAYOUT values (ImageItem object), 254

LBS (Location Based Services), 150-151

LEFT constant, 272

length() method, 444

Let Me Alone, 73

levels, 296, 298-299

LG Telecom p510 (i-Book), 39

LG Telecom phones, 40

LIF (Location Interoperability Forum), 151

lifecycles ((MIDlets), 181-183

Lifestylers, 56-57

Light class (Siemens game), 432, 442, 499

lines (Graphics class), 267-268

Linux, handheld PDAs, 35

List class, 242-247, 482, 486

List(String title, int listType) method, 486

List(String title, int listType, String[ ] stringElements, Image[ ] int append(String stringElement, Image imageElement) method, 486

ListBox element, 416

Listener Item class, 249

listeners

    KeyListener, 419

    SoftKeyListener class, 420

listings

    about screens, 194-195

    adding collision detection, 305

    adding collision detection to sprites, 287

    adding paint() method, 285

    adding to Sprite class, 280-283

    Cache class, 199

    CarItemFilter class, 344, 347

    CarStore class, 340-343

    checkCollision() and checkFinishLine() methods, 327

    choosing tracks, 245-246

    command listener, 190-191

    CrashCarEffect interface, 476

    creating a car using primitives, 291

    creating and calling forms, 185-186

    creating car stores, 470-472

    creating collision areas, 300-301

    creating collision levels, 299

    creating game threads, 317-318

    DummyCrash interface, 476

    Final Game Loop, 322-323

    Form object splash screen, 196-197

    GameCanvas class, 459-462

    help screens, 194-195

    improved painting, 303

    initializing sprites, 315-316

    loading an image resource, 283

    loading images from afar, 296-297

    MIDlet implementation, 182

    moving sprites, 318

    painting sprites, 319

    player sprite child class, 288

    ProgressForm, 252-253

    SiemensCrash interface, 476-477

    SpriteManager class, 301-304

    StartForm class, 186-188

    using clipping rectangles, 292-293

    Weapon class, 456-461, 471, 477-478

LMA Football Quiz, 54

loadImage() method, 297

loading

    data, Siemens SL45i, 448-449

    images, 420-421

    sound, 420-421

    sprite images, 283-284

local data, 204

Location Based Services, 150-151

Location Ineroperability Forum, 151

Location Management, 151

lock() method, 415

logical classes, 207

login parameter, 365

logout parameter, 365

loop attribute, 144

loops, GameThread, 322-323

## M

M format input field, 99

m-commerce (mobile commerce), 155-157

M-Type, 70

MADK Web site, 113

Mah Jong, 79

Managers (sprite), 301-305

<MARQUEE> tag, 144

masks (sprites), 436-437

mathematical classes, 218

Matsushita/Panasonic FOMA P2101V, 40

Matsushita/Panasonic P503i phones, 40

Matsushita/Panasonic P503iS phones, 40

MAX PRIORITY, 231

maxlength attribute (input fields), 98

maxLength() method, 444

MDN (Missed Dialing Numbers), GSM functions, 447

media, downloading, 297

melodies, Siemens SL45i, 443-446

Melody class (Siemens game), 432, 443-445, 502

MelodyComposer class (Siemens game), 432, 443-445, 499

memory

    heap, 210

    management, 217

    MIDP devices, 203, 205

        application, 203

        fragmentation, 204-205

        limitations, 203-204

Siemens SL45i

storage, 203, 205

working, 203-204

optimization, 210-211

usage, 220

arrays, 221-222

Hashtables, 221-222

String, 220-221

StringBuffer, 220-221

Vectors, 221-222

<MENU> tag, 139

menus, MIDP, 188-191

Mermaid, 59

messaging

EMS (Enhanced Messaging Service)

features supported by, 133

overview, 133

gaming, 122

MMS (Multimedia Messaging Service)

MMSC (Multimedia Message Service Center), 131

overview, 130

SMIL (Synchronized Multimedia Integration Language), 131-132

overview, 121

SMS (Short Message Service)

character lengths of, 123

Flash SMS, 124

Kuulalaakeri, 128

overview, 122

popularity of, 122

rates, 123

receiving messages, 129

sending messages, 127-130

services, list of, 125-127

Smart Messaging, 124

SMS Gateway, 128

SMS-JDK, 128

SMSC (Short Message Service Center), 125

Text mode, 123

Unicode messages, 124

UM (unified messaging), 158-159

<META> tag, 139

methods

abstract void paint(), 413

abstract void start(), 413

activeCount() (Thread class), 227

Alert class, 193, 485

AlertType, 483

cancel() (Timer class), 233-234

Canvas class, 260-261, 484

checkCollision(), 327

checkFinishLine(), 327

ChoiceGroup class, 490

Command class, 483

Connector class, 350

currentThread() (Thread class), 227

DateField class, 490

Display class, 183-184, 483

Displayable class, 484

dispose(), 422

drawPolyline, 414

File class, 448-449

fillPolygon(), 414

Font class, 487

Form class, 187-188, 485-486

g.lock(), 414

g.unlock(), 414

Gauge class, 490-491

getMelody(), 445-446

getPriority() (Thread class), 227

GraphicObject class, 434-435

Graphics class, 265-266, 488-489

Graphics GetGraphics(), 413

HTTP connections, 353-354

HTTP setup mode, 353

IApplicaton GetCurrentApp, 413

Image class, 335, 489

Images class, 273

initEnemies(), 320

int getHeight(), 413

int GetKeypadState(), 413

int getWidth(), 413

isAlive(), 227, 231

Item class, 489

javax.microedition.lcdui.Choice, 244-245

javax.microedition.lcdui.DateFiel, 251

javax.microedition.lcdui.Gauge, 252

javax.microedition.lcdui.ImageItem, 255

javax.microedition.lcdui.Item, 249

javax.microedition.lcdui.StringItem, 254

javax.microedition.lcdui.TextBox, 248

join() (Thread class), 227

List class, 486

lock(), 415

MelodyComposer class, 444-445

MIDlet class, 181-183

moveSprite(), 318

notify, 232-233

notifyAll(), 232-233

notifyListeners, 400

paint(), 229, 285, 399, 414

play(), 445-446

processEvent(), 413, 418

resume(), 412

run(), 231

   Thread class, 227, 229

   Timer class, 234

schedule() (Timer class), 233-234

scheduleatFixedRate() (Timer class), 234

Screen class, 185, 485

setColor(), 415

setEnabled(), 415

setOrigin(), 415

setPriority() (Thread class), 227

setVisible(), 415

sleep(), 227, 231

SoftKeyPressed(), 420

SoftKeyReleased(), 420

Sprite class, 435-436

SpriteManager class, 301

start(), 226, 231, 412

static, 218

stop() (Thread class), 226

String GetSourceUrl(), 413

StringItem class, 491

System.currentTimeMillis(), 237

terminate(), 413

TextBox class, 486-487

TextField class, 491

Ticker class, 492

unlock(), 415

unuse(), 422

update(), 399

URLEncoder.encode(), 130

Vibrator class, 442-443

void repaint(), 413

void setCurrent(), 413

void terminat(), 413

void resume(), 413

wait(), 231-233

yield() (Thread class), 227

**Metrowerks Code Warrior, 177**

**micro devices, 4-5, 25-26**

   advantages of J2ME, 26-27

      Asia, 27-28

      Europe, 28

      North America, 28

      support, 27

   future of, 3

   history of, 3

**Micro Java, supported devices, 395**

**Micro Racer game, 455-456**

   adding weapons, 456

      Cache class, 459

      GameCanvas class, 459, 461-462

      Weapon class, 456-461, 471, 477-478

   artificial intelligence, 463-464

   control, 464, 466

   future considerations, 475

online garage, 472-473

   adding garage to game menu, 474

   Game class, 474

   GarageClient, 473-474

persistent data, 469-472

power-ups, 466-469

sprites, 287

**microedition.encoding property, 198**

**microedition.locale property, 198**

**microedition.platform property, 198**

**microedition.profiles property, 198**

**MicroJBlend, 37**

**Microsoft Money for PocketPC, 33**

**MIDlet class, 181-183, 197**

**MIDlets**

   Alert class, 192-197

   Cache class, 198-199

   creating, 175

      command-line development, 175-177

      development environments, 177-180

      pre-verification, 175

   Display class, 183-184

   Form class, 185-188

   GarageClient, 473-474

   life cycles, 181-183

   properties, 197-198

   RecordStore class, 339-340

   Screen class, 184-185

**MIDP (Mobile Information Device Profile), 4, 168, 171-172**

advantages, 454-455

Alert class, 325

AlertType class, 326

Canvas class, 259-261

custom commands, 262

events, 261-262

game key, 262-263

pointer handler, 262-263

touch screens, 263-264

classes, 172

commands, 188-191

devices

limitations, 201-206

Motorola Accompli A008, 205

disadvantages, 453-454

games, 65

BlockBuster, 66

Cocoasoft games, 67-69

Cube, 70

Dope Wars, 71-72

DrawPoker, 67

Holy Moley, 66

Jshape, 70-71

MIDP-Man, 66

RomeBlack Mobile Internet Maze Game, 69

Spruce Team games, 71

Graphics class, 264-266

arcs, 269

colors, 267

draw strings, 271

fonts, 269-270

Images, 271-275

lines, 267-268

rectangles, 268-269

rounded rectangles, 269

stoke type, 267

limitations, 209

menus, 188-191

networking, 352-357

non-standard profiles, 172

packages, 493

java.io, 493-494

java.lang, 494-495

java.util, 495-496

javax.microedition.io, 496

javax.microedition.lcdui, 497

javax.microedition.midlet, 497

javax.microedition.rms, 497-498

plug-in for PersonalJava, 403

sound effects, 325-327

**MIDP-Man, 66**

**Military Checkers, 77**

**MIME (Multipurpose Internet Mail Extension), 108**

**MIN PRIORITY, 231**

**Mines, 52**

**Mini Game Tengoku services, 79-80**

**Miracle Detective, 81**

**Miracle Golf, 81**

**Miracle GP, 81**

**Miracle Quest, 81**

**Missed Dialing Numbers (MDN), 447**

**mission statements, 14-15**

**missions, 296**

**Missile Command, 10**

**Mitsubishi D503i and D503iS, 41**

**Mitsubishi J-D05, 41**

**MMS (Multimedia Messaging Service)**

MMSC (Multimedia Message Service Center), 131

overview, 130

SMIL (Synchronized Multimedia Integration Language), 131-132

**MMSC (Multimedia Message Service Center), 131**

**mobile commerce.** *See* m-commerce

**Mobile Information Device Profile.** *See* MIDP

**mobile phones, 25, 38**

advantages of J2ME, 26-27

Asia, 27-28

Europe, 28

North America, 28

support, 27

Casio CdmaOne C452CA, 38

Ericsson R380, 39

Fujitsu F503i, 39

Hitachi CdmaOne C451H, 39

JavaPhone, 30

LG Telecom p510 (i-Book), 39

LG Telecom phones, 40

Matsushita/Panasonic FOMA P2101V, 40

Matsushita/Panasonic P503i phones, 40

Matsushita/Panasonic P503iS phones, 40

Mitsubishi D503i and D503iS, 41

Mitsubishi J-D05, 41

Motorola Accompli 008/6288, 43-44

Motorola Accompli 009 PIC, 42-43

Motorola i50sx, 42

Motorola i85s, 41-42

NEC FOMA N2001, 44

NEC N503i, 44

Nokia 9210, 44-45

Nokia 9290 Communicator, 44-45

PingTel, 30

RIM/iPaq Blackberry, 45

Samsung, 46

Sharp J-SH07, 46

Sharp NC-10 IP, 31

Siemens SL45i, 46-47, 442-443

Sony SO503i, 47

Toshiba J-T06, 47

mobile positioning, 150

LBS (Location Based Services), 150

billing category, 151

emergency category, 151

GIS (Geographic Information System), 150

location based information category, 151

Location Management, 151

tracking category, 151

LIF (Location Interoperability Forum), 151

MPS (Mobile Positioning System), 152

positioning technologies, 152

A-GPS (Assisted GPS), 154

AOA (Angle Of Arrival), 155

DGPS (differential GPS), 154

E-OTD (Enhanced Observed Time Differential), 155

GPS (Global Positioning System), 153

GSM Location Positioning, 154

network-based solutions, 152

RF (radio frequency), 155

TDOA (Time Difference Of Arrival), 154

terminal and handset based solutions, 152

security/privacy layers, 152

WLIA (Wireless Location Industry Association), 151

MobImage Web site, 104

Mortal Kombat, 10

Motorola Accompli 008/6288, 43-44

Motorola Accompli 009 PIC, 42-43

Motorola Accompli A008, 205

Motorola i50sx, 42

Motorola i85s, 41-42

movement, sprites

collision detection, 319-320

creating game threads, 317-318

enemy player, 316-317

finishing games, 320-323

floating-point, 307-314

initialization, 314-316

moveSprite() method, 318, 464

MPS (Mobile Positioning System), 152

MTNSMS Web site, 125

Multimedia Message Service Center. See MMSC

Multimedia Messaging Service. See MMS

multiplayer engines, 19

multiplayer games, 2, 361-362

design, 362-363, 365-366

client side, 366, 380

HTTP considerations, 363-365

parameters, 365

server side, 380-382, 388

playing, 388, 390, 392

turn-based, 362

multiple areas, 298, 300-301

multiple levels, 298-299

MULTIPLE lists, 243

MULTIPLE-CHOICE, 244

Multipurpose Internet Mail Extension. See MIME

multithreading. See also threads

music, 422

Mystic Grapple, 79

## N

N format input field, 99

Namco, 78

name attribute

<A> tag, 142

<DISPLAY> tag, 116

<do> tag, 101

<INPUT> tag, 140

<select> tag, 100

Name variable, 459

NanoXML, 360

NEC FOMA N2001, 44

NEC N503i, 44

network-based solutions (positioning technology), 152

networking, J2ME, 349

Connection interface, 350-351

DataInputStream class, 361

DataOutputStream class, 361

game packets, 358-359

game server setup, 357-358

MIDP specification, 352-357

XML, 360-361

networks (wireless networks), 85

1G (first generation), 86

2.5G (second and a half generation), 87

2G (second generation), 86-87

3G (third generation), 87-88

loading sprite images, 283-284

new state, threads, 231

Nextel Web site, 126

nGame games, 60

Alien Fish Exchange, 60

Carrier Force, 61

Chop Suey Kung Fu, 61

Data Clash, 61-62

nGame Web site, 60

NoClassDefFoundError method, 399

NoInputPreferred method, 399

Nokia 9201 Communicator, 401

Nokia 9210, 44-45

Nokia 9290 Communicator, 44-45

Nokia Web site, 113

non-validating parsers, 360

NOOP action type, 118

NORM PRIORITY, 231

North America, 28

notify() method, 232-233

notifyAll() method, 232-233

notifyListeners() method, 400

NSIcom CrEme, 37

NTT DoCoMo Web site, 136

numbered lists, 416

numColors() method, 183

NUMERIC Text Field, 256

# O

OBEX protocol, 149

obfuscators

execution code, 212-213

JAR files, 212-213

<OBJECT> tag, 140, 411

object-oriented programming, 213-215

objects

java.lang.Thread, 227

SpriteManager, 466

Ohajiki Daisenso, 80

OK command, 189

<OL> tag, 140

On The Green, 57

online garage (Micro Racer), 472-473

adding garage to game menu, 474

Game class, 474

GarageClient, 473-474

onpick attribute, 99

open() method (Connector class), 350

openDataInputStream method, 353

openDataOutputStream method, 353

openInputStream method, 353

openOutputStream method, 353

Openwave SDK Web site, 113

opponents (sprites), 289

optimization

code, 209-210

class size, 210

clock speed, 210

constructors, 217-218

Garbage Collector, 217

memory, 210-211

size reduction, 211-216

speed, 216

sprite movement, 219-220

static methods, 218

drawing, 303-304

FPS (frames per second), 216-217

memory usage, 220-222

power consumption, 222

<option> tag, 99

options command type, <do> tag, 102

OTA (over the air), 431-432

OutputConnection interface, 350

outputs, listing effects of, 15

over the air (OTA), Siemens SL45i, 431-432

# P

<p> tag, 96, 140

Pac-Man, 10

packages
- CLDC, 170
- iAppli API, 505-509
- MIDP 1.1, 493-498

PackageURL parameter, 410

packets (data format), 358-359

pagers, 25, 38

paint() method, 229, 285, 303-304, 399, 414

paint(Graphics g) method, 261, 301

painting
- SpriteManager class, 303-304
- sprites, 319

Palm games, 72-73

PalmOS, 32

PalmWarp, 73

parsers, 359-361

password fields, 140, 256

PDA profile, 404

PDAs (Personal Digital Assistants), 25, 31, 395
- Ericsson R380, 39
- J2ME profile, 31
- Java virtual machines (JVMs), 35
  - Esmertec Jbed Micro Edition CDLC, 36
  - HP chaiVM for Pocket PC, 38
  - IBM J9 VM, 36
  - Javasoft KVM for the Palm, 36
  - Javasoft MIDP for the PalmOS, 36

Javasoft PersonalJava for Windows CE, 36

Jeode EVM, 37

Kadasystems Kada VM, 37

kAWT Extended KVM (xKVM), 36-37

MicroJBlend, 37

NSIcom CrEme, 37

SAVAJE XE Operating System, 38

Transvirtual Kaffe, 38

Linux, 35

PalmOS, 32

Sharp Zaurus SL-5000, 35

Siemens SX45, 34

Siemens SIMpad SL4, 33-34

Symbian EPOC, 34-35

Windows CE, 33

PDC (Personal Digital Cellular), 87

PDU (Protocol Description Unit) mode (SMS), 123

peer-to-peer networking, game server setup, 357-358

persistent data, adding to Micro Racer, 469-472

Personal Digital Assistants. See PDAs

Personal Digital Cellular. See PDC

Personal Profile, 397

Personal Trusted Device. See PTD

PersonalJava, 28-30, 395-396
- APIs, list of, 398
- applet, installing, 402-403
- design considerations, 403-404
- developer tools, 400-402

double buffering, 398-399

input methods, 399

MIDP plug-in, 403

NoClassDefFoundError method, 399

overview, 397-398

PJAE (PersonalJava Application Environment), 397

timer events, 400

unsupported features, 399

phone book, GSM functions, 447

PhoneBook class (Siemens game), 502

PHONENUMBER Text Field, 256

phones
- mobile phones, 25, 38
  - advantages of J2ME, 26-27
  - Asia, 27-28
  - Casio CdmaOne C452CA, 38
  - Ericsson R380, 39
  - Europe, 28
  - Fujitsu F503i, 39
  - Hitachi CdmaOne C451H, 39
  - JavaPhone, 30
  - LG Telecom p510 (i-Book), 39
  - LG Telecom phones, 40
  - Matsushita/Panasonic FOMA P2101V, 40
  - Matsushita/Panasonic P503i phones, 40
  - Matsushita/Panasonic P503iS phones, 40
  - Mitsubishi D503i and D503iS, 41

Mitsubishi J-D05, 41

Motorola Accompli 008/6288, 43-44

Motorola Accompli 009 PIC, 42-43

Motorola i50sx, 42

Motorola i85s, 41-42

NEC FOMA N2001, 44

NEC N503i, 44

Nokia 9210, 44-45

Nokia 9290 Communicator, 44-45

North America, 28

PingTel, 30

RIM/iPaq Blackberry, 45

Samsung SCH-X130, SCH-X230, SCH-X350, and SCH-X350, 46

Sharp J-SH07, 46

Sharp NC-10 IP, 31

Siemens SL45i, 46-47

Sony SO503i, 47

support, 27

Toshiba J-T06, 47

smartphones, 34

**physics engines, 19**

**PicoFun games, 56-57**

**PicoFun Web site, 56**

**Pincer Checkers, 77**

**PingTel, 30**

**pixels, drawing sprites, 289-291**

**Pixo Web site, 145**

**PJAE (PersonalJava Application Environment), 397**

**<PLAINTEXT> tag, 140**

**platforms.** *See* **J2SE; J2EE; J2ME**

**play() method, 445-446**

**player sprites, 287-288**

**playtesting (game design process), 19-20**

**playing**

audio files, 422

racing car game, 388, 390, 392

**PNG file**

data part, 284

header, 284

**Pocket Internet Explorer, 33**

**Pocket Outlook 2000, 33**

**pointer handler (Canvas class), 262-263**

**pointerDragged(int x, int y) method, 260**

**pointerPressed(int x, int y) method, 260**

**pointerReleased(int x, int y) method, 260**

**polling, car racing game, 364**

**Pong action game example, 10**

**PositionalInputPreferred method, 399**

**positioning.** *See* **mobile positioning**

**postpaid phone plans, 155**

**power batteries, 222**

**power-ups, adding to Micro Racer, 466-469**

**<PRE> tag, 140**

**pre-verification, 175**

CLDC, 171

**predefined movement, 316**

**prepaid phone plans, 155**

**preproduction (game design process), 8**

artificial intelligence, 16

background art, 15

background music, 15

documentation, 16

game levels, 15

genre, selecting, 9

action games, 10

adventure games, 11

card games, 12

cloning, 9-10

combat games, 10

games of chance, 12

puzzle games, 11

role playing games, 11

simulation games, 11-12

sports games, 12

strategy games, 11

toy games, 13

trivia games, 12

word games, 12

global variables, 16

graphical elements, 15

inputs, listing effects of, 15

interfaces, 16

mission statements, 14-15

outputs, listing effects of, 15

questions about, answering, 9

restrictions

designing around, 13-14

designing within, 13

rules, defining, 16-17

sound effects, 15

Web site resources, 17

**PREV action type, 117-118**

**prev command type (<do> tag), 102**

**priorities, threads, 231**

**privacy, mobile positioning, 152**

**process() function, 106**

**processEvent() method, 418**

processors, MIDP devices, 202-203

Profile layer (J2ME), 166

profiles, J2ME, 31, 166-167

    CLDC, 168

    Mobile Information Device. *See* MIDP

profit sharing programs, mobile carriers, 156-157

programming

    game design process, 18-19

    handheld devivces

        advantages, 454-455

        disadvantages, 453-454

Progress Meters Item class, 251-253

properties

    MIDlets, 197-198

    sprites, 278-279

protected abstract void paint(Graphics g) method, 484

protected boolean removeImageStore() method, 335

protected void hideNotify() method, 484

protected void keyPressed(int keyCode) method, 484

protected void keyReleased(int keyCode) method, 484

protected void keyRepeated(int keyCode) method, 484

protected void pointerDragged(int x, int y) method, 484

protected void pointerPressed(int x, int y) method, 484

protected void pointerReleased(int x, int y) method, 484

protected void showNotify() method, 484

Protocol Description Unit mode. *See* PDU mode

protocol stack (WAP), 89

protocols

    full-duplex, 356

    half-duplex, 356

    Hyper Text Transfer Protocol. *See* HTTP

prototyping (game design process), 17-18

provisioning, 409-410

proxies, HTTP, 357

Psion netBook, 34

Psion RevoPlus, 35

PTD (Personal Trusted Device), 148

public byte[ ][ ] getImageDataFromStore() method, 335

public void destroyApp(boolean unconditional) method, 182

public void pauseApp() method, 181

public void startApp() method, 181

public void storeImageData(byte[ ][ ] imageData) method, 335

puzzle games, 11

PyWeb Web site, 113

## Q-R

Quake, 10

Qualcomm pdQ, 32

Quizcall, 54

radio buttons, 100, 140

radio frequency (RF), 155

Rags 2 Riches, 60

receiving

    data, Siemens SL45i, 447-448

    SMS messages, 129

RecordEnumerator handling, 340-344, 347

recordId number, 330

RecordStore class, 329-331, 339-340

    code, 335-339

    exceptions, 334-335

    methods, 336-338

        addRecord(), 331

        deleteRecord(), 332

        deleteRecordStore(), 333, 336

        EnumerateRecords(), 333

        getLastModified(), 332

        getNextRecordID(), 333

        getNumRecords(), 333

        getRecord(), 332

        getSize(), 333

        getSizeAvailable(), 333

        setRecord(), 332

    MIDlet code, 339-340

    RecordEnumerator handling, 340-344, 347

    recordId number, 330

RecordStoreExeption, 334

RecordStoreFullException, 334

RecordStoreNotFoundException, 334

RecordStoreNotOpenException, 334

rectangles, Graphics class, 268-269

Remote Method Invocation. *See* RMI

removeCommand(Command cmd) method, 188

removeImageRecord(), 338

repaint() method, 260

repaint(int x, int y, int width, int height) method, 260

Research In Motion, 45

reset command type, Do tag, 102

resetMelody() method, 444

response code, HTTP, 354-355

restrictions

designing around, 13-14

designing within, 13

resume() method, 412

Retrologic Web site, 213

RETURN action type, 118

RF (radio frequency), 155

RFCOMM protocol, 149

RIGHT constant, 272

RIM Blackberry IDE, 177

RIM/iPaq Blackberry, 45

RMI (Remote Method Invocation), 30

Rock-Paper-Scissors, 56

Role Playing Games (RPG), 11

RombBlack Mobile Internet Maze Game, 69

root level, 298-299

rounded rectangles, Graphics class, 269

rules, 16-17

run() method, 231

Thread class, 227, 229

Timer class, 234

Runnable interface, 229

implementing threads using, 229-230

run() method, 229

runnable state, threads, 231

running flag, Thread class, 229-230

## S

Samsung SCH-X130, SCH-X230, SCH-X350, and SCH-X350, 46

Samurai Romanesque, 75-76

SAVAJE XE Operating System, 38

schedule() method (Timer class), 233-234

scheduleAtFixedRate() method (Timer class), 234

SciFiQuiz, 64

ScratchPad, 424-425

Screen class, 184, 241-242, 482

Alert, 242

Form, 242

Item, 248-257

List, 242-247

methods, 185, 485

Text Box, 247-248

Ticker, 257

SCREEN command, 189

screens

about, 194-195

help, 194-195

splash, 195-197

SDK (Software Development Kit), 402

second and a half generation (2.5G) wireless networks, 87

second generation (2G) wireless networks, 86-87

security

CDLC, 170-171

mobile positioning, 152

security layer (WAP protocol stack), 89

Seed no Bohken, 79

Seed no Meikyu Tanken, 79

Sega, 78

<select> tag, 100, 141

sell parameter, 365

SEND action type, 117

sending

data, Siemens SL45i, 447-448

SMS messages, 127-129

Kuulaaakeri tool, 128

sample server code, 129-130

SMS Gateway tool, 128

SMS-JDK tool, 128

server-side WAP, 108

development environments, 113

JSPs (JavaServer Pages), 109

chat application example, 110-112

game lobby example, 109-111

server configuration, 108-109

servers

Garage servlet, 380-382, 388

peer-to-peer networking, 357-358

servlets, GarageServlet, 382, 388

session layer (WAP protocol stack), 89

session tracking, 363, 365

set(int elementNum, String stringPart, Image imagePart) method, 245

set(int itemNum, Item item) method, 187

set-top boxes, 25

setAltText(String text) method, 255

setBPM(int bpm) method, 444

setChars(char[ ] data, int offset, int length) method, 248

setClip(int x, int y, int width, int height) method, 266

setColor() method, 415

setColor(int red, int green, int blue) method, 265

setColor(int RGB) method, 265

setCommandListener() method, 191

setCommandListener(Command Listener listener) method, 188

setConstraints(int constraints), 248

setCurrent() method, 195

setCurrent(Alert alert, Displayable nextDisplayable) method, 184

setCurrent(Displayable nextDisplayable) method, 183

setDate(Date date), 250

setEnabled() method, 415

setGrayScale(int value) method, 265

setImage(Image img) method, 193, 255

setInputMode(int mode) method, 251

setItemStateListener(ItemStateL istener listener) method, 187

setLabel(String label) method, 249-252, 254-255

setLayout(int layout) method, 255

setMaxSize(int maxSize), 248

setMaxValue(int maxValue) method, 252

setOrigin() method, 415

setPriority() method (Thread class), 227

setRecord() method (RecordStore class), 332

setRepeat method, 400

setSelectedFlags (boolean[ ] selectedArray) method, 245

setSelectedIndex(int elementNum, boolean selected) method, 245

setString(String str) method, 193

setString(String text) method, 248

setStrokeStyle(int style) method, 265

setText(String text) method, 254

setTicker(Ticker ticker) method, 185

setTime method, 400

setTimeout(Alert.FOREVER) method, 192

setTimeout(int time) method, 193

Settings dialog (Wireless Toolkit), 180

setTitle(String title) method, 185

setType(AlertType type) method, 193

setValue(int value), 252

setVisible() method, 415

Shapez, 59

Sharp J-SH07, 46

Sharp NC-10 IP, 31

Sharp Zaurus SL-5000, 35

Short Message Service Center. See SMSC

Short Message Service. See SMS

showNotify() method, 260

Siemens game classes, 499
    Call, 502
    Connection, 503
    ConnectionListener, 504
    ExtendedImage, 500
    File, 503
    GraphicObject, 500
    GraphicObjectManager, 501
    Light, 499
    Melody, 502
    MelodyComposer, 499
    PhoneBook, 502
    SMS, 503
    Sound, 502
    Sprite, 500
    TiledBackground, 501
    Vibrator, 502

Siemens SL45i, 46-47, 205, 296, 429
    com.siemens.mp.game package, 432
    com.siemens.mp.gsm package, 446
        calls, 446
        loading files, 448-449
        Missed Dialing Numbers (MDN), 447
        receiving data, 447-448
        saving files, 448-449
        sending data, 447-448
        SMS messages, 447
    compiling, 430

DataExchange software, 431

emulator, 430-431

images, 432-433

   blitting, 433-434

   GraphicObject class methods, 434-435

MMC (multimedia memory card), 205

mobile phone vibrations, 442-443

over the air (OTA), 431-432

setup, 429-430

sounds, 443-446

sprites, 432-433, 435-436

   creating, 436-437

   flashes, 442

   masks, 436-437

   sample code, 437

   TiledBackground class, 438-441

tiles, 438-441

Web site, 430

Siemens SX45, 34

SiemensCrash interface, 476-477

Siemens SIMpad SL4, 33-34

Simple Messaging System. See SMS

simulation games, 11-12

single-step document parsers, 360

size, sprites, 284-285

size attribute

   input fields and, 98

   <select> tag, 141

size() method, 187, 244, 248, 301

Sky Arts Web site, 70

sleep() method (Thread class), 227, 231

slots, 52

<small> tag, 96

smart cards, 47-48

Smart Messaging, 124

smart movement, 316

smartphones, 34

SMIL (Synchronized Multimedia Integration Language), 131

   sample file, 132

   supported formats, 132

SMS (Short Message Service)

   character lengths of, 123

   Flash SMS, 124

   Kuulalaakeri, 128

   overview, 122

   PDU mode, 123

   popularity of, 122

   rates, 123

   receiving messages, 129

   sending messages, 127-130

   services, list of, 125-127

   Smart Messaging, 124

   SMS Gateway, 128

   SMS-JDK, 128

   SMSC (Short Message Service Center), 125

   Text mode, 123

   Unicode messages, 124

SMS (Simple Messaging System) games, 5, 63

   Blue Factory, 63-64

   BotFighters, 64

   Fisupeli, 63

   GSM functions, 447

   Vizzavi, 65

SMS class (Siemens game), 503

SMSC (Short Message Service Center), 125

Snake, 80

SOFT1 action type, 117

SOFT2 action type, 117

SoftKeyListener class, 420

softKeyPressed() method, 420

SoftKeyReleased() method, 420

Software Development Kit (SDK), 402

Sony SO503i, 47

Sorcery, 51

sound, 295

   effects

      creating with MIDP, 325-327

      listing effects of, 15

   loading, 420-421

   Siemens SL45i, 443-446

Sound class (Siemens game), 432, 502

spam, 125

specifications, CLDC JVM, 170

speed, MIDP devices, 206

splash screens, 195-197

sponsorships, 20-21

sports games, 12

Sprint PCS Web site, 126

Sprite class, 279-283, 432, 500

   methods, 435-436

SpriteManager class, 301-304

   drawing optimizations, 303-304

   methods, 301

   sprite collision, 304-305

SpriteManager object, 466

sprites, 277-278

collision, 304-305

collision detection, 286-287, 320

drawing, 285

  chunks, 292

  pixels, 289-291

frames, 278-279

images, 278

  loading, 283-284

  size reduction, 284-285

  transparency, 289-293

managers, 301-305

movement, 219-220

  collision detection, 319-320

  creating game threads, 317-318

  enemy player, 316-317

  finishing games, 320-323

  floating-point, 307-314

  initialization, 314-316

opponents, 289

painting, 319

player sprites, 287-288

properties, 278-279

Siemens SL45i, 432-436

  creating, 436-437

  masks, 436-437

  sample code, 437

  TiledBackground class, 438-441

**Spruce Team games, 71**

**SPsize parameter, 410**

**Squiral, 75**

**src attribute, 104**

**src directory (Siemens Toolkit), 441**

**Standard Messaging System.** *See* **SMS**

**start() method (Thread class), 226, 231, 412**

**StartForm class, 186-188, 474**

**startVibrator() method, 442**

**static data, 204**

**static Display getDisplay(MIDlet c) method, 483**

**static Font getDefaultFont() method, 487**

**static Font getFont(int face, int style, int size) method, 487**

**static Image createImage(byte[ ] imageData, int imageOffset, int imageLength) method, 489**

**static Image createImage(byte[ ] imageData, int offset, int imageLength) method, 489**

**static Image createImage(Image image) method, 489**

**static Image createImage(int width, int height) method, 489**

**static Image createImage(String name) method, 489**

**static methods, 218, 483, 487, 489**

**stealing.** *See* **cloning**

**STOP command, 189**

**stop() method (Thread class), 226, 445**

**stopVibrator() method, 442**

**storage, 329**

  J2ME device memory, 205

  memory, MIDP devices, 203

**storage:Image class, 334-335**

**storage:RecordStore class, 329, 331, 336, 339-340**

  addRecord() method, 331

  clearing, 336

  code, 335-339

  deleteRecord() method, 332

  deleteRecordStore() method, 333, 336

  EnumerateRecords() method, 333

  exceptions, 334-335

  getLastModified() method, 332

  getNextRecordID() method, 333

  getNumRecords() method, 333

  getRecord() method, 332

  getSize() method, 333

  getSizeAvailable() method, 333

  MIDlet code, 339-340

  RecordEnumerator handling, 340-344, 347

  setRecord() method, 332

  unpacking images, 337-338

**storyboarding, 8**

**strategy games, 11**

**StreamConnection interface, 350**

**Street Fighter**

  action game example, 10

  rules of, 71

**String getAltText() method, 491**

**String getKeyName(int keyCode) method, 484**

**String getLabel() method, 483, 489**

**String GetSourceUrl() method, 413**

**String getString() method, 485, 487, 491-492**

**String getString(int index) method, 486, 490**

String getText() method, 491

String getTitle() method, 485

String Items Item class, 254

String to String() method, 483

StringBuffers, memory usage, 220-221

StringItem class, 482, 491

StringItem(String label, String text) method, 491

strings, memory usage, 220-221

stroke types, Graphics class, 267

<strong> tag, 96

Submit button, creating, 140

subscriptions, charging players for, 22

Sun
   Forte, 178
   J2ME Wireless Toolkit. *See* J2ME Wireless Toolkit

support, mobile telephones, 27

Symbian EPOC, 34-35

synchronizations, threads, 232

Synchronized Multimedia Integration Language. *See* SMIL

System.currentTimeMillis() method, 237

**T**

table tags, 97-98

tags
   <A>, 142
   <ACTION>, 117-118
   anchor, 94-95
   <b>, 96
   <BLINK>, 139

<BLOCKQUOTE>, 139

<BR>, 96, 139

case sensitivity, 92

<CENTER>, 139

<DD>, 139

<DIR>, 139

<DISPLAY>, 116

<DL>, 139

<do>, 101-102

<DT>, 139

<em>, 96

<FORM>, 140

<go>, 94

<HR>, 139

<I>, 96

<img>, 104

<INPUT>, 140-141

<large>, 96

<MARQUEE>, 144

<MENU>, 139

<META>, 139

<OBJECT>, 140, 411

<OL>, 140

option, 99

<O>, 96, 140

<PLAINTEXT>, 140

<PRE>, 140

<SELECT>, 141

<select>, 100

<small>, 96

<strong>, 96

<table>, 97-98

<td>, 97

text formatting, 96-97

<TEXTAREA>, 141

<tr>, 97

<U>, 96

<UL>, 140

user input, 98
   checkboxes, 100
   <do> tag, 101, 103
   field sets, 101
   form example, 101
   input fields, 98-99
   option groups, 99
   radio buttons, 100
   variables, 103

Takoyaki King, 80

Tanks, 52

TargetDevice parameter, 410

Tciker class, 482

<td> tag, 97

TDMA (Time Division Multiple Access), 86

TDOA (Time Difference Of Arrival), 154

Tekken Command Battle, 78

telephones. *See* phones

televisions, set-top boxes, 25

terminal-based solution (positioning technology), 152

terminate() method, 413

testing. *See also* playtesting

Text Box class, 247-248

text boxes, creating, 415-416

Text Field instance
   ANY, 256
   CONSTRAINT MASK, 256
   EMAILADDR, 256
   NUMERIC, 256
   PASSWORD, 256
   PHONENUMBER, 256
   Text class, 255-257
   URL, 256

text fields, 140

text formatting

EMS (Enhanced Messaging Service), 133

tags, 96-97

Text mode (SMS), 123

text/vnd.wap.wml, 108

text/vnd.wap.wmlscript, 108

<TEXTAREA> tag, 141

TextBox class, 482, 486-487

TextBox(String title, String text, int maxSize, int constraints) method, 486

TextField class, 482, 491

TextField(String label, String text, int maxSize, int constraints) method, 491

third generation (3G) wireless networks, 87-88

threads

animation threads, 226

blocked state, 231

considerations, 226

creating, 317-318

deadlocks, 231-232

defined, 225

implementing, using Timer class, 234-235

MAX PRIORITY, 231

MIN PRIORITY, 231

new state, 231

NORM PRIORITY, 231

runnable state, 231

start() method, 226

stop() method, 226

synchronizations and, 232

Thread class

activeCount() method, 227

currentThread() method, 227

getPriority() method, 227

implementing threads using, listing of, 228

isAlive() method, 227

join() method, 227

run() method, 227

Runnable interface, 229

Runnable interface, implementing threads using, 229-230

running flag, 229-230

setPriority() method, 227

sleep() method, 227

timer example, 236-237

yield() method, 227

wait() method, 232-233

Tic Tac Toe, 53

Ticker class, 257, 492

Ticker getTicker() method, 485

Ticker(String str) method, 492

tickers, creating, 417

TiledBackground class (Siemens game), 432, 438-441, 501

tiles, Siemens SL45i, 438-441

Time Difference of Arrival. See TDOA

Time Division Multiple Access. See TDMA

Time variable, 459

Timer class, 233

cancel() method, 233-234

implementing threads using, listing of, 234-235

run() method, 234

schedule() method, 233-234

scheduleAtFixedRate() method, 234

timers, 104-105, 400

title attribute, 93, 98

TOP constant, 272

Top Trumps, 54

Torunda!, 72

Toshiba J-T06, 47

touch screens, Canvas class, 263-264

toy games, 13

<tr> tag, 97

tracking category (Location Based Services), 151

tracks, 296

transaction layer (WAP protocol stack), 89

translate(int x, int y) method, 265

translating, Graphics class, 274

transparency, sprite images, 289-293

Transvirtual Kaffe, 38

Trantor Web site, 257

treads, dead state, 231

triggerVibrator(int duration) method, 442

trivia games

Blue Factory games, 64

examples of, 12

Truffle Graphical Toolkit, 29

Turibaka Kibun, 62

turn-based games, 362

type attribute

<do> tag, 102

input fields and, 99

Type variable, 459

TypeCannon, 80

# U

&lt;U&gt; tag, 96

&lt;UL&gt; tag, 140

UM (unified messaging), 158-159

UMTS (Universal Mobile Telecoms Network), 88

Uname parameter, 365

Unicode messages, 124

Unicode Web site, 124

unified messaging. *See* UM

Uniform Resource Locators. URLs, 88

Universal Mobile Telecoms Network. *See* UMTS

unknown command type, 102

unlock() method, 415

Unplugged Games Web site, 59

unuse() method, 422

update() method, 399

URL Text Field, 256

URLEncoder.encode() method, 130

URLs (Uniform Resource Locators), 88

UseNetwork parameter, 410

user agents, 89

user input tags, 98

    check boxes, 100

    &lt;do&gt; tag, 101, 103

    field sets, 101

    form example, 101

    input fields, 98-99

    option groups, 99

    radio buttons, 100

    variables, 103

user interface methods, 413

# V

validating parsers, 359

value attribute, 99

    input fields and, 99

    select tag, 100

variables, 103

VCENTER constant, 272

vectors, memory usage, 221-222

velocity Vx (sprite property), 278

velocity Vy (sprite property), 278

vending machines, wireless messages and, 150

vibrations, Siemens SL45i mobile phones, 442-443

Vibrator class (Siemens game), 432, 502

    methods, 442-443

videos, MIDP devices, 203, 206

Virtua Fighter, 10

Visibility property (sprites), 278

VisorPhone, 32

visual classes, 207

VisualPresenter component, 417

Vizzavi Web site, 65

voice activation, 157

    VoiceXML, 157-158

    WTAI (Wireless Telephony Application Interface), 158

Voice Genie software, 158

VoiceClient software, 158

VoiceXML, 157-158

void addCommand(Command cmd) method, 484-485

void callSerially(Runnable obj) method, 483

void clipRect(int x, int y, int width, int height) method, 488

void delete(int index) method, 486, 490

void delete(int offset, int length) method, 486, 491

void drawArc(int x, int y, int width, int height, int startAngle, int arcAngle) method, 488

void drawChar(char character, int x, int y, int anchor) method, 488

void drawChars(char[ ] data, int offset, int length, int x, int y, int anchor) method, 488

void drawImage(Image img, int x, int y, int anchor) method, 488

void drawLine(int x1, int y1, int x2, int y2) method, 488

void drawRect(int x, int y, int width, int height) method, 488

void drawRoundRect(int x, int y, int width, int height, int arcWidth, int arcHeight) method, 488

void drawString(String str, int x, int y, int anchor) method, 488

void drawSubstring(String str, int offset, int len, int x, int y, int anchor) method, 488

void fillArc(int x, int y, int width, int height, int startAngle, int arcAngle) method, 488

void fillRect(int x, int y, int width, int height) method, 488 void fillRoundRect(int x, int y, int width, int height, int arcWidth, int arcHeight) method, 488

void insert(char[ ] data, int offset, int length, int position) method, 487, 492

void insert(int index, Item item) method, 486

void insert(int index, String stringElement, Image imageElement) method, 486, 490

void insert(String src, int position) method, 487, 492

void processEvent() method, 413

Void Raider, 59

void removeCommand(Command cmd) method, 484

void repaint() method, 413, 484

void repaint(int x, int y, int width, int height) method, 484

void resume() method, 413

void serviceRepaints() method, 484

void set(int index, Item item) method, 486

void set(int index, String stringElement, Image imageElement) method, 486, 490

void setAltText(String text) method, 491

void setChars(char[ ] data, int offset, int length) method, 487, 492

void setClip(int x, int y, int width, int height) method, 489

void setColor(int red, int green, int blue) method, 489

void setColor(int RGB) method, 489

void setCommandListener(CommandListener l) method, 484-485

void setConstraints(int constraints) method, 487, 492

void setCurrent() method, 413

void setCurrent(Alert alert, Displayable next) method, 483

void setCurrent(Displayable next) method, 483

void setDate(Date date) method, 490

void setFont(Font font) method, 489

void setGrayScale(int value) method, 489

void setImage(Image img) method, 485, 491

void setInputMode(int mode) method, 490

void setItemStateListener(ItemStateListener iListener) method, 486

void setLabel(String label) method, 489

void setLayout(int layout) method, 491

void setMaxValue(int maxValue) method, 491

void setSelectedFlags(boolean[ ] selectedArray) method, 486, 490

void setSelectedIndex(int index, boolean selected) method, 486, 490

void setString(String str) method, 485, 492

void setString(String text) method, 487, 492

void setStrokeStyle(int style) method, 489

void setText(String text) method, 491

void setTicker(Ticker newTicker) method, 485

void setTimeout(int time) method, 485

void setType(AlertType type) method, 485

void setValue(int value) method, 491

void terninate() method, 413

void translate(int x, int y) method, 489

vspace attribute, 143

# W

W-CDMA (Wideband Code Division Multiple Access), 88

Waba, 165

WAE (Wireless Application Environment), 89

wait() method, 231-233

Wall Street Wizard, 57

WAP (Wireless Application Protocol), 5, 88

Alien Fish Exchange, 60

architecture, 89-91

Carrier Force, 61

Chop Suey Kung Fu, 61

content of, 88

Data Clash, 61-62

Funcaster.com, 59

Handy Games, 57-58

Jamdat games, 55-56

limitations, 51

nGame, 60

PicoFun, 56-57

protocol stack, 89

Rags 2 Riches, 60

server-side, 108

  development environ-
    ments, 113

  JSPs (JavaServer Pages),
    109-112

  server configuration, 108-
    109

Unplugged Games, 59

version 2.0, 118-119

Void Raider, 59

WAP Forum, 88

WAP gateway, 89

wireless games, 51

  Anagram, 53

  casino games, 52

  Code Breaker, 52

  Fight KO, 52

  Fours, 53

  Hangman, 53

  LMA Football Quiz, 54

  Mines, 52

  Quizcall, 54

  Sorcery, 51

  Tanks, 52

  Tic Tac Toe, 53

  Top Trumps, 54

  Wentworth Golf, 54

  Wireless Pets, 53

WML (Wireless Markup
Language), 88, 91-92

  anchor tag, 94-95

  cards, 92-93, 95

  decks, 93, 95

document definition tag
  example, 92

example code, 93

header example, 92

images, 104

table tags, 97-98

text formatting tags, 96-
  97

timers, 104-105

user input tags, 98-101,
  103

WMLScript, 105-108

Word Trader, 60

**WAP Crates, 58**

**WAP Girlfriends, 58**

**WAP Knights, 57**

**WAP Massacre, 58**

**WAP Tanks, 58**

**WapProfit i-mode Editor Web
site, 144**

**WARNING alert, 193**

**Warning alerts, 326**

**Wbmp Butterfly Web site, 104**

**WbmpCreator Web site, 104**

**WDP (Wireless Datagram
Protocol), 89**

**Weapon class, 456-461, 471,
477-478**

**weapons, adding to Micro
Racer, 456**

  Cache class, 459

  GameCanvas class, 459,
    461-462

  variables, 459

  Weapon class, 456-461, 471,
    477-478

**Web sites**

  Airtouch (Verizon), 126

  Alphaworks, 213

Anfy Team, 454

AT&T, 126

Block Buster, 66

Blue Factory, 63

BotFighters, 64

C. media Compact NetFront,
  145

Cingular, 126

Cocoasoft, 67

Condensity, 213

Digital Bridges, 51

Dwango, 62

Eastridge Technology, 213

Ericsson WapIDE, 113

Eurotel, 127

Ezos, 145

Fisupeli, 63

Funcaster.com, 59

gamasutra.com, 17

gamedev.net, 17

gdse.com, 17

Gif2Wbmp, 104

Globtel, 127

GoZing, 125

Handy Games, 57

Holey Moley, 66

i monde, 145

i-JADE, 144, 426

i-Mimic, 145

i-Tool, 145

iDEN Update, 156

IEmulator, 426

IjavaEngine i503, 426

JBuilder, 177

Jump, 165

MADK, 113

MIDP-Man, 66

MobImage, 104

MTNSMS, 125

Nextel, 126

nGame, 60

Nokia, 113

NTT DoCoMo, 136

OpenWave SDK, 113

PicoFun, 56

Pixe, 145

PyWeb, 113

Retrologic, 213

RIM Blackberry IDE, 177

Siemens, 430

Sky Arts, 70

Sprint PCS, 126

Trantor, 257

Unicode, 124

Unplugged Games, 59

Vizzavi, 65

Waba, 165

WapProfit i-mode Editor, 144

Wbmp Butterfly, 104

WBmpCreator, 104

Yospace, 113

Zucotto WHITEboard, 177

**Wentworth Golf, 54**

**Wideband Code Division Multiple Access.** *See* **W-CDMA**

**width attribute, 143**

**Width property (sprites), 278**

**Windows CE, 33**

**Wireless Application Environment.** *See* **WAE**

**Wireless Application Protocol.** *See* **WAP**

**Wireless Datagram Protocol.** *See* **WDP**

**wireless devices, 455**

**Wireless Location Industry Association.** *See* **WLIA**

**Wireless Markup Language.** *See* **WML**

**wireless messaging, UM (unified messaging), 158-159**

**wireless networks, 85**

1G (first generation), 86

2.5G (second and a half generation), 87

2G (second generation), 86-87

3G (third generation), 88

J2ME, 349

Connection Interface, 350-351

DataInputStream class, 361

DataOutputStream class, 361

game packets, 358-359

game server setup, 357-358

MIDP specification, 352-357

XML, 360-361

**Wireless Pets, 53**

**Wireless Session Protocol.** *See* **WSP**

**Wireless Telephony Application Interface.** *See* **WTAI**

**Wireless Transaction Protocol.** *See* **WTP**

**Wireless Transport Layer Security.** *See* **WTLS**

**WLIA (Wireless Location Industry Association), 151**

**WML (Wireless Markup Language), 88, 91-92**

anchor tag, 94-95

cards, 92

id attribute, 93

switching to new, 95

title attribute, 93

code example, 93

decks, 93, 95

document definition tag example, 92

header example, 92

images, 104

table tags, 97-98

text formatting tags, 96-97

timers, 104-105

user input tags, 98

checkboxes, 100

<do> tag, 101, 103

field sets, 101

form example, 101

input fields, 98-99

option groups, 99

radio buttons, 100

variables, 103

versus HDML, 115-116

**WMLScript, 106**

accessing, 106

GuessNumber.wml example, 106-107

RandomGuess.wml example, 107-108

**word games, examples of, 12**

**Word Trader, rules of, 60**

**working memory, MIDP devices, 203-204**

**WSP (Wireless Session Protocol), 89**

WTAI (Wireless Telephony Application Interface), 158

WTLS (Wireless Transport Layer Security), 89

WTP (Wireless Transaction Protocol), 89

# X

x format input field, 99

x position (sprite property), 278

xHTML, 118-119

XML (eXtensible Markup Language), 88, 359-361

xpress Window Toolkit. *See* xWT

xWT (xpress Window Toolkit), 30

# W-Z

y position (sprite property), 278

yield() method (Thread class), 227

Yospace Web site, 113

Zucotto WHITEboard, 177

—download and play games

—built-in digital camera

# Mobile Device Update

A joint venture between Ericsson and Sony has created several phones with beautiful color screens. These devices have been designed from the ground up to download and play games. The T68i is being released in Europe and Asia, with the Z700 to follow. The P800 will have a large screen, a built-in digital camera, and a personal organizer. Three similar devices with mono-chrome displays are planned for the American market.

URL: http://www.sonyericsson.com/

—a personal organizer

## Sony/Ericsson T68i, P800, and Z700

http://www.sonyericsson.com